Model Nonprofit Corporation Act

Third Edition

Official Text with Official Comments
and Statutory Cross-references
Adopted August 2008

Committee on Nonprofit Organizations

ABA Section of
BUSINESS LAW

Defending Liberty
Pursuing Justice

Commitment to Quality: ABA Section of Business Law is committed to quality in our publications. Our authors are experienced practitioners in their fields. Prior to publication, the contents of all our books are rigorously reviewed by experts to ensure the highest quality product and presentation. Because we are committed to serving our readers' needs, we welcome your feedback on how we can improve future editions of this book.

13 12 11 10 09 5 4 3 2 1

Printed in the United States of America.

Library of Congress Cataloging-in-Publication Data

Model nonprofit corporation act / edited by William H. Clark, Jr. — 3rd ed.
p. cm.
Includes index.
ISBN 978-1-60442-059-3
1. Nonprofit organizations—Law and legislation—United States. I. Clark, William H., 1951– II. American Bar Association.

KF1388.M627 2008
346.73'064—dc22

2008051218

Contents

CHAPTER 1
GENERAL PROVISIONS

[Subchapter] E
REVIEW OF CONTESTED CORPORATE ACTION

[Subchapter] F
RELIGIOUS CORPORATIONS

[Subchapter] G *[Optional]*
ATTORNEY GENERAL

CHAPTER 2
INCORPORATION

CHAPTER 3
PURPOSES AND POWERS

CHAPTER 4
NAME

CHAPTER 5
REGISTERED OFFICE AND AGENT

CHAPTER 6
MEMBERSHIPS AND FINANCIAL PROVISIONS

[Subchapter] A
ADMISSION OF MEMBERS

[Subchapter] B
RIGHTS AND OBLIGATIONS OF MEMBERS

[Subchapter] B
VOTING

[Subchapter] C
VOTING AGREEMENTS

CHAPTER 8
DIRECTORS AND OFFICERS

[Subchapter] A
BOARD OF DIRECTORS

[Subchapter] B
MEETINGS AND ACTION OF THE BOARD

[Subchapter] C
DIRECTORS

[Subchapter] D
OFFICERS

[Subchapter] E
INDEMNIFICATION AND ADVANCE FOR EXPENSES

CHAPTER 9
DOMESTICATION AND CONVERSION

[Subchapter] D
FOREIGN FOR-PROFIT DOMESTICATION AND CONVERSION

[Subchapter] E
ENTITY CONVERSION

CHAPTER 10
AMENDMENT OF ARTICLES OF INCORPORATION AND BYLAWS

[Subchapter] A
AMENDMENT OF ARTICLES OF INCORPORATION

[Subchapter] B
AMENDMENT OF BYLAWS

[Subchapter] C
SPECIAL RIGHTS

CHAPTER 11
MERGERS AND MEMBERSHIP EXCHANGES

CHAPTER 12
DISPOSITION OF ASSETS

CHAPTER 13
DERIVATIVE PROCEEDINGS

CHAPTER 14
DISSOLUTION

[Subchapter] A
VOLUNTARY DISSOLUTION

[Subchapter] B
ADMINISTRATIVE DISSOLUTION

[Subchapter] C
JUDICIAL DISSOLUTION

[Subchapter] D
MISCELLANEOUS

CHAPTER 15
FOREIGN CORPORATIONS

[Subchapter] A
CERTIFICATE OF AUTHORITY

[Subchapter] B
WITHDRAWAL OR TRANSFER OF AUTHORITY

Task Force to Revise the Model Nonprofit Corporation Act

Lizabeth A. Moody, Chair	St. Petersburg, Florida
William H. Clark, Jr., Reporter	Philadelphia, Pennsylvania
R. Franklin Balotti	Wilmington, Delaware
Lawrence J. Beaser	Philadelphia, Pennsylvania
Willard L. Boyd, III	Des Moines, Iowa
David P. Burke	Tampa, Florida
Louise P. Dempsey	Cleveland, Ohio
Jeannie Carmedelle Frey	Chicago, Illinois
Frances R. Hill	Coral Gables, Florida
Lynn A. Howell	Houston, Texas
Robert R. Keatinge	Denver, Colorado
Jesse Margolin	New York, New York
Jan E. Murray	Cleveland, Ohio
Cynthia R. Rowland	San Francisco, California
Lisa A. Runquist	Northridge, California

Foreword

By Lizabeth A. Moody

The Third Edition of The Model Nonprofit Corporation Act marks a significant development in the evolution of The Model Nonprofit Corporation Act ("the MNCA") in that the Business Law Section of the American Bar Association (the "BLS") becomes the publisher of the MNCA, the previous edition having been published by a private company under the direction of the Committee on Nonprofit Organizations of the Section on Business Law.

The original MNCA was prepared by the Committee on Corporate Laws of the Section of Corporation, Banking, and Business Law (now the Section on Business Law) of the American Bar Association in 1952. Until promulgated with the 1952 Act, most "non business" organizations, if they chose to incorporate, used devices such as "nonstock" provisions found within the state's general corporation law, or, as was the case with most churches, petitioned the state legislature for a charter. Amendments to the original MNCA by the Committee on Corporate Laws took place in 1957 and 1964.

In the Foreword to the 1952 Act, the Committee stated: "It [the Model Nonprofit Corporation Act] is a companion to the Model Business Corporation Act prepared by the Committee. In organization, style and procedures, the Model Nonprofit Corporation Act follows the Model Business Corporation Act as closely as the subject matter permits."

In 1979, the Committee on Nonprofit Corporations (as it was then called) of the BLS accepted a charge to revise the MNCA. A drafting committee was appointed and met regularly over the next eight years. The completed revision was approved in 1987 and published in 1988 by Prentiss Hall Law and Business as the Revised Model Nonprofit Corporation Act.

The fundamental policy decisions for the Revised MNCA were as follows: The Revised MNCA was to supersede the earlier versions of the MNCA and would be a single integrated statute covering all nonprofit corporations. Further, "[t]the Revised Act was to attempt to provide a framework in which an organization could be structured by its creators to implement their goals and allow them flexibility in operation and design." As with the first act, the Revised Model Act was to follow the Model Business Corporation Act, "as closely as the subject matter permits." The Drafting Committee met for the next eight years on a regular basis as a free standing committee.

The Revised MNCA adopted a scheme of classifying nonprofit corporations into public benefit corporations, mutual benefit corporations, and religious corporations as a result of legislative developments in two states. New York had adopted a nonprofit corporation statute totally different from the MNCA that divided nonprofit corporations into four distinct classifications: Type A (mutual corporations), Type B (charitable organizations), Type C (business-like organizations), and Type D (miscellaneous). Each classification had differing rules and a different regulatory pattern. In the late 1970s, California, after passing a revolutionary business corporation statute, passed an equally revolutionary nonprofit statute in 1980. The California statute was unrelated to the new California business corporation statute. Somewhat following New York's lead, California adopted a classification system where nonprofit corporations were divided into three parts: Public Benefit, Mutual Benefit, and Religious. The California statute essentially was to become the pattern for the Revised MNCA.

Following the adoption of the Revised MNCA in 1987, there was no further action with respect to the MNCA until 2000. In the meantime, the Model Business Corporation Act (MBCA) was continually reviewed and amended by the BLS Committee on Corporate Laws. Although between 1988 and 2000, many states adopted new nonprofit corporation legislation, relatively few used the Revised MNCA in its entirety. Very few adopted the classification system for nonprofit corporations that had been built into the Revised MNCA. The BLS Committee on Nonprofit Corporations (chaired at the time by Lynn Havell) decided to undertake a general revision of the Revised MNCA.

The MNCA Third Edition is the work of volunteers who dedicated many hours of time to the project. The Drafting Committee members represented many areas of nonprofit law. They included academics teaching and writing in the field, a general counsel for three nonprofits, a former CEO and president of a large nonprofit organization, and practitioners associated with both large and small firms (representing a range of clients including churches, hospitals, schools, country clubs, and philanthropic organizations). All of them had served as officers or directors of nonprofit organizations.

A program describing the changes to be made in the MNCA as they had been developed to that date was presented at the Spring Meeting of the BLS in Tampa, Florida, in 2006. Drafts were also reviewed by members of the Committee on Corporate Laws. The chair of the drafting committee also appeared as a panelist on the subject of the new revision at the meetings of the ABA Section of Taxation and the Association of American Law Schools. In the summer of 2006, a version of the black letter provisions was widely distributed to interested parties and all comments were recorded at subsequent meetings of the committee. A completed version of black letter laws along with official comments was put on the Section of Business Law's website in February 2008. Comments of interested parties to the exposure draft were reviewed at meetings during the spring and summer. The final version was approved at the Annual Meeting of the American Bar Association in August 2008.

SIGNIFICANT ASPECTS OF THE THIRD EDITION

Initial decisions made by the drafting committee at the beginning of its deliberations on preparing the Third Edition were to: (1) follow the Model Business Corporation Act provisions to the extent possible, considering certain differences that distinguish nonprofit corporations from for profit corporations; (2) eliminate the classification scheme included in the Revised MNCA; and (3) make the provisions pertaining to the role of the attorney general optional, if desired, with a suggestion to adopting states that provisions regarding the supervision of nonprofit organizations would be better located in a different place in a state's statutory scheme. Other significant changes involve fundamental transactions, the use of alternative governance arrangements, and the elimination of cumulative voting.

1. Classification of Nonprofit Corporations.

In the earlier versions of the MNCA, prior to adoption of the Revised MNCA in 1987, all types of nonprofit corporations were defined as "a corporation no part of the income or profit of which is distributable to its member directors or officer," with special provisions where needed. The major differences between the three categories of corporations introduced in the Revised MNCA related to distributions; the repurchase of memberships from members or controlling persons; the standards for conflict of interest transactions; indemnification; and the powers of supervision vested in the attorney general of the state of incorporation. Except in those areas, all nonprofit organizations were treated alike under the statute.

Despite the insistence on the inclusion of the classification system when the Revised MNCA was adopted, the classification system became the most disputed part of the Revised MNCA after its adoption. Many of the states that adopted the Revised MNCA did not incorporate the classification provisions. Often for those that did, problems arose out of incorrect selection. The fact that the classifications did not mirror those of the Internal Revenue Service with respect to tax-exempt organizations turned the choice into a trap for the unwary.

Although the Third Edition has eliminated the classification system, it still recognizes the special position of certain nonprofit corporations; for example, it includes two important restrictions that apply to charities. One of those restrictions provides that a fundamental transaction property held in trust or otherwise dedicated to a charitable purpose may not be diverted from that purpose without an appropriate order. The other restriction prohibits private inurement in transactions such as mergers.

2. Role of the Attorney General

The decision of the drafting committee to mark as optional the provisions relating to the role of the attorney general was based on the fact that charitable organizations may not necessarily be structured as a corporation, with the result that supervisory provisions for them might be inadvertently omitted from a state's statutory scheme. Charities may be organized as unincorporated nonprofit associations or, under the law of some states, as limited liability companies, and to cover some other forms of entities requires a statute with broader scope. Critics have also characterized powers granted to the attorney generals as ineffective, and perhaps unconstitutional, under the U.S. Constitution, with respect to certain religious organizations.

3. Fundamental Transactions

Following the pattern of the MBCA, a series of transactions derived from the Model Entity Transactions Act (META) have been included in the Third Edition, including domestications, conversations to another form of entity, and cross-entity mergers.

4. Alternative Governance Arrangements

The Third Edition contains a series of provisions dealing with the concept of a "designated body." That concept was included in the Revised MNCA, but in a way that was relatively opaque and not well understood. The Third Edition defines a "designated body" as "a person or group, other than a committee of the board of directors, that has been vested by the articles of incorporation or bylaws with powers that, if not vested by the articles or bylaws in that person or group, would be required by this [act] to be exercised by the board or the members." Its effect is to allow "some, but less than all" the powers of the board of directors to be exercised by a designated body, in which case the rules applicable to the board of directors apply to the designated body and the actual directors are relieved from their duties and liabilities to the extent they have been replaced by the designated body.

5. Elimination of Cumulative Voting

Although the Revised MNCA provided that a corporation could hold elections of directors by cumulative voting if the articles of incorporation so provided, the Third Edition has eliminated cumulative voting (subject to a transitional provision applicable to corporations with cumulative voting at the time the Third Edition is enacted) as inappropriate for nonprofit corporations because the voting power of members should not be tied to their economic investment and because a nonprofit director is often chosen for reasons other than the betterment of the economic results of the corporation.

THE FUTURE OF NONPROFIT CORPORATION LAW

The Third Edition of the MNCA undoubtedly will not be the last word on what has become a dynamic area of law. The BLS has committed to a continual review of the MNCA and a procedure to effect amendments appropriate to the time and society.

CHAPTER 1

General Provisions

Subchapter

A. Short Title and Savings Provisions
B. Filing Documents
C. Secretary of State
D. Definitions
E. Review of Contested Corporate Action
F. Religious Corporations
G. Attorney General [*Optional*]

[Subchapter] A
SHORT TITLE AND SAVINGS PROVISIONS

§ 1.01. SHORT TITLE

This [act] shall be known and may be cited as the "[*name of state*] Nonprofit Corporation Act."

> *Source Note:* Patterned after Model Business Corporation Act, 3d Ed. (2002) § 1.01. Reenactment of Revised Model Nonprofit Corporation Act (1987) § 1.01.

CROSS-REFERENCES

Application of act to existing domestic nonprofit corporation, see § 17.01.

Application of act to existing qualified foreign nonprofit corporation, see § 17.02.

Effective date of act, see § 17.06.

Saving provisions, see § 17.03.

OFFICIAL COMMENT

The short title provided by Section 1.01 creates a convenient name for the enacting state's nonprofit corporation act.

See the Introduction for a general description of the development of this act, the purposes it is intended to serve, the principles under which it was prepared, and the roles of the Cross-References and Official Comments.

§ 1.02. RESERVATION OF POWER TO AMEND OR REPEAL

The [*name of state legislature*] has power to amend or repeal all or part of this [act] at any time and all domestic and foreign nonprofit corporations subject to this [act] are governed by the amendment or repeal.

> *Source Note:* Patterned after Model Business Corporation Act, 3d Ed. (2002) § 1.02. Reenactment of Revised Model Nonprofit Corporation Act (1987) § 1.02.

CROSS-REFERENCES

Application of act to existing domestic nonprofit corporation, see § 17.01.

Application of act to existing qualified foreign nonprofit corporation, see § 17.02.

Effective date of act, see § 17.06.

Saving provisions, see § 17.03.

OFFICIAL COMMENT

Provisions similar to Section 1.02 have their genesis in *Trustees of Dartmouth College v. Woodward*, 17 U.S. (4 Wheat) 518 (1819), which held that the United States Constitution prohibited the application of newly enacted statutes to existing corporations while suggesting the efficacy of a reservation of power similar to Section 1.02. The purpose of Section 1.02 is to avoid any possible argument that a nonprofit corporation or a member, beneficiary, or any other person has contractual or vested rights in any specific statutory provision and to ensure that the state may in the future modify its corporation statutes as it deems appropriate and require existing corporations to comply with the statutes as modified.

All articles of incorporation or certificates of authority granted under this act are subject to the reservation of power set forth in Section 1.02. Further, corporations "governed" by this act—which includes all corporations formed or qualified under earlier, general incorporation statutes that contain a reservation of power—are also subject to the reservation of power of Section 1.02 and bound by subsequent amendments to this act.

Many states have constitutional provisions mandating the reservation of power to amend or modify corporate statutes and charters. In those states, Section 1.02 is also supported by specific constitutional authorization.

§ 1.03. RELATIONSHIP OF [ACT] TO OTHER LAWS

(a) Unless displaced by particular provisions of this [act], the principles of law and equity supplement this [act].

(b) This [act] does not authorize an act prohibited by, and does not affect the application or requirements of, law other than this [act].

Source Note: Patterned after Model Entity Transactions Act § 103.

OFFICIAL COMMENT

Section 103(a) is a standard provision in uniform and model acts and has been included to make clear that unless a particular provision of this act displaces "other law," the principles of law and equity continue to apply, including with respect to the rights of creditors, transferees, assignees, or other similar parties.

Subsection (b) preserves regulatory jurisdiction over actions and fundamental transactions under the act, such as amendments of the articles, mergers, sales of assets, and dissolution. The provisions of the act must be read together with any applicable regulatory law and, to the extent they are irreconcilable, the provisions of the regulatory law will control.

This section does not create an independent power of a court or regulatory agency to enjoin or reverse an action or fundamental transaction. The appropriate remedy for violation of a regulatory law will be determined under the regulatory law itself.

Charitable corporations also must comply with applicable provisions of the Internal Revenue Code.

[Subchapter] B
FILING DOCUMENTS

§ 1.20. FILING REQUIREMENTS

(a) To be entitled to filing by the secretary of state under this [act], a record must satisfy the following requirements and the requirements of any other provision of this [act] that adds to or varies these requirements:

(1) This [act] requires or permits filing the record in the office of the secretary of state.

(2) The record contains the information required by this [act] and may contain other information.

(3) The record is in the English language, but the name of an entity need not be in English if written in English letters or Arabic or Roman numerals. The certificate of existence required of foreign nonprofit corporations need not be in English if accompanied by a reasonably authenticated English translation.

(4) The record is signed on behalf of the domestic or foreign entity as follows:

(i) if the entity is a domestic or foreign nonprofit corporation, by the chair of the board of directors, a member of a designated body, or an officer;

(ii) if directors or members of a designated body have not been selected or the corporation has not been formed, by an incorporator;

(iii) if the entity is not a domestic or foreign nonprofit corporation, by a person with authority to sign for the entity; or

(iv) if the entity is in the hands of a custodian, receiver, trustee, or other court-appointed fiduciary, by that fiduciary.

(5) The record states the name and capacity of the person signing it. The record may, but need not, contain a corporate seal, attestation, acknowledgment, or verification.

(6) The record is delivered to the office of the secretary of state for filing. Delivery may be made by electronic transmission if and to the extent permitted by the secretary of state. If the record is filed in typewritten or printed form and not transmitted electronically, the secretary of state may require one exact or conformed copy to be delivered with the record.

(b) When the record is delivered to the office of the secretary of state for filing, the correct filing fee, and any franchise tax, license fee, or penalty required to be paid therewith by this [act] or other law is paid or provision for payment is made in a manner permitted by the secretary of state.

(c) Whenever a provision of this [act] permits any of the terms of a plan or a filed record to be dependent on facts objectively ascertainable outside the plan or filed record, the following provisions apply:

(1) The manner in which the facts will operate upon the terms of the plan or filed record shall be set forth in the plan or filed record.

(2) The facts may include:

(i) any of the following that is available in a nationally recognized news or information medium either in print or electronically: statistical or market indices, market prices of any security or group of securities, interest rates, currency exchange rates, or similar economic or financial data;

(ii) a determination or action by any person or body, including the nonprofit corporation or any other party to a plan or filed record; or

(iii) the terms of, or actions taken under, an agreement to which the corporation is a party, or any other agreement or record.

(3) As used in this subsection:

(i) "filed record" means a record filed with the secretary of state under any provision of this [act] except [Chapter] 15 or Section 16.21; and

(ii) "plan" means a plan of domestication, business conversion, entity conversion, merger, or membership exchange.

Source Note: Patterned after Model Entity Transactions Act § A1-1. Derived from Revised Model Nonprofit Corporation Act (1987) § 1.20.

CROSS-REFERENCES

Corporate name, see Ch. 4 and § 15.06.

Correcting filed record, see § 1.24.

Date of filing, see § 1.25(b).

"Deliver" defined, see § 1.40.

"Designated body" defined, see § 1.40.

Effective time and date of filing, see § 1.23.

Filing fees, see § 1.22.

Forms, see § 1.21.

Penalty for signing false record, see § 1.29.

"Record" defined, see § 1.40.

"Secretary" of corporation defined, see § 1.40.

Secretary of state's filing duty, see § 1.25.

"Sign" defined, see § 1.40.

OFFICIAL COMMENT

1. In General

Subchapters 1B and C provide the general procedures for filings under the act with the secretary of state. Similar procedures are also needed to govern filings with the secretary of state under other entity laws. States should consider whether to expand the scope of Subchapters 1B and C so that they also apply to filings under other entity laws and place the subchapters in a different location in their state code or, alternatively, to make filings under the act subject to other provisions of law instead of Subchapters 1B and C.

Section 1.20 standardizes the filing requirements for all records required or permitted by this act to be filed with the secretary of state. In a few instances, other sections of the act impose additional requirements that must also be complied with if the record in question is to be filed. Section 1.20 relates only to records that the act expressly requires or permits to be filed with the secretary of state; it does not authorize or direct the secretary of state to accept or reject for filing other records relating to nonprofit corporations and does not treat records required or permitted to be filed under other statutes.

The purposes of the filing requirements of Chapter 1 are: (1) to simplify the filing requirements by the elimination of formal or technical requirements that serve little purpose; (2) to minimize the number of items to be processed by the secretary of state; and (3) to eliminate all possible disputes between persons seeking to make filings and the secretary of state as to the legal efficacy of the filings.

The requirements of Section 1.20 are summarized in the following comments.

2. Form

This act permits a filing to be made in typewritten or printed form through physical delivery to the secretary of state or, alternatively, by electronic transmission. Electronic transmission is intended to include the evolving methods of electronic delivery, including facsimile transmissions and e-mail, as may be permitted by the secretary of state. See Official Comment 7 to Section 1.40. The filing must also be in the English language (except to the limited extent permitted by Section 1.20(a)(3)). The secretary of state is permitted to prescribe forms but Section 1.21 provides that their use is not mandatory. As a result the secretary of state may not reject documents on the basis of form if they contain the information called for by the specific statutory requirement and meet the minimal formal requirements of this section.

3. Signature

To be filed a record must simply be signed by a corporate officer. No specific corporate officer is designated as the appropriate officer to sign although the record must state the office or capacity in which the officer signs the record. Among the officers who are expressly authorized to sign a record is the chair of the board of directors or a member of a designated body, a choice that may be appropriate if the corporation has a board of directors or designated body but has not appointed officers. If a corporation has not been formed or has neither officers nor a board of directors or designated body, an incorporator may sign the record. See Section 1.40 for a description of the manner in which a document may be "signed." See also the definition of "officer" in Section 1.40.

The requirement in some state statutes that records must be acknowledged or verified as a condition for filing has not been included. These requirements serve little purpose in connection with records filed under corporation statutes. (See in this connection Section 1.29, which makes it a criminal offense for any person to sign a record for filing with knowledge that it contains materially false information.) On the other hand, many organizations, like lenders or title companies, may desire that specific records include acknowledgments, verifications, or seals; Section 1.20(a)(5) therefore provides that the addition of these forms of additional authentication does not affect the eligibility of the record for filing.

4. Contents

A record must be filed by the secretary of state if it contains the information required by the act. The record may contain additional information or statements and their presence is not grounds for the secretary of state to reject the record for filing. These records must be accepted for filing even though the secretary of state believes that the language is irrelevant or not authorized by the act or by general legal principles. In view of the very limited discretion granted to secretaries of state under this section, Section 1.25(d) defines the secretary of state's role as "ministerial" and provides that no inference or presumption arises from the fact that the secretary of state accepted a record for filing. See the Official Comments to Sections 1.25 and 1.30.

5. Number of Copies

The act permits the secretary of state to require an exact or conformed copy of a document that is being filed in typewritten or printed form, thus providing the secretary of state flexibility to determine whether or not such copies serve any purpose. There is no such requirement with respect to records transmitted electronically.

Under Section 1.20(a)(6) an "exact" copy is a reproduction of the executed original document, while a "conformed" copy is a copy on which the existence of signatures is entered or noted on the copy. A person submitting "duplicate originals" meets any requirement for an exact or conformed copy since the secretary of state may treat the duplicate original as a "conformed copy."

6. Reference to Extrinsic Facts

Section 1.20(c) permits any of the terms of a filed record or a plan to be made dependent on facts outside the record or plan. Terms of a filed record or plan may be made dependent on a fact outside the control of the corporation. A common example is a reference to an interest rate such as the federal funds rate. Section 1.20(c)(2) also provides that the facts on which a filed record or plan may be made dependent include facts within the control of the corporation in order to make clear that those facts do not need to occur independently. In addition to a determination or action by the corporation, references to extrinsic facts may also include references to determinations or actions by the board of directors, a designated body, a committee of the board or a designated body, an officer, employee or agent of the corporation, or any other person.

The only limitations on referring to extrinsic facts in a filed record or plan are that the facts must be objectively ascertainable and that the filed record or plan must state the manner in which the facts will operate. The purpose of these requirements is to avoid disputes over whether an extrinsic fact has occurred or its effect.

If the terms of a filed record or plan are made dependent on an agreement or other record as authorized by Section 1.20(c)(2)(iii), care should be taken to identify the agreement or record appropriately. The agreement or record must be identified in a manner that satisfies the objectively ascertainable standard, and the manner in which the terms or events under it are to operate must be specified. Consideration should also be given to the intended effects of an amendment to the agreement or record. A simple reference to an agreement will presumably include subsequent amendments, while a reference to the same agreement as in effect on a specified date presumably will not.

Chapters 9 and 11 generally require the board of directors to adopt a plan. If the terms of such a plan are determined by reference to extrinsic facts, the board should take care to establish appropriately defined parameters for such terms in order to discharge its statutory duties.

§ 1.21. FORMS

The secretary of state may prescribe and furnish on request forms for filings required or permitted under this [act], but their use is not mandatory.

Source Note: Patterned after Model Entity Transactions Act § A1-2. Derived from Revised Model Nonprofit Corporation Act (1987) § 1.21.

CROSS-REFERENCES

Annual report, see § 16.21.

Application for certificate of authority, see § 15.03.

Application for certificate of withdrawal, see § 15.20.

Certificate of existence, see § 1.28.

Effective time and date of filing, see § 1.23.

Filing fees, see § 1.22.

Filing requirements, see § 1.20.

OFFICIAL COMMENT

As described in the Official Comment to Section 1.20, records are entitled to filing under the act if they meet the substantive and formal requirements of the act; they may also contain additional information if the person submitting the record so elects. See the Official Comments to Sections 1.20 and 1.25. In these circumstances it is not appropriate to vest the secretary of state with general authority to establish mandatory forms for use under the act.

§ 1.22. FILING, SERVICE, AND COPYING FEES

Alternative A

(a) The secretary of state shall collect the following fees when the records described in this subsection are delivered to the secretary of state for filing:

	Document	Fee
(1)	Articles of incorporation	$____.
(2)	Application for use of indistinguishable name	$____.
(3)	Application for reserved name	$____.

(4)	Notice of transfer of reserved name	$___.
(5)	Application for registered name	$___.
(6)	Application for renewal of registered name	$___.
(7)	Corporation's statement of change of registered agent or registered office or both	$___.
(8)	Agent's statement of change of registered office for each affected corporation, not to exceed a total of $_____	$___.
(9)	Agent's statement of resignation	No fee.
(10)	Articles of domestication	$___.
(11)	Articles of charter surrender	$___.
(12)	Articles of business conversion	$___.
(13)	Articles of domestication and conversion	$___.
(14)	Articles of entity conversion	$___.
(15)	Amendment of articles of incorporation	$___.
(16)	Restatement of articles of incorporation with amendment of articles	$___.
(17)	Articles of merger or membership exchange	$___.
(18)	Articles of dissolution	$___.
(19)	Articles of revocation of dissolution	$___.
(20)	Certificate of administrative dissolution	No fee.
(21)	Application for reinstatement following administrative dissolution	$___.
(22)	Certificate of reinstatement	No fee.
(23)	Certificate of judicial dissolution	No fee.
(24)	Application for certificate of authority	$___.
(25)	Application for amended certificate of authority	$___.
(26)	Application for certificate of withdrawal	$___.
(27)	Application for transfer of authority	$___.
(28)	Certificate of revocation of authority to conduct activities	No fee.
(29)	Annual report	$___.
(30)	Articles of correction	$___.
(31)	Application for certificate of existence or authorization	$___.

(32) Any other document required or permitted to be filed by this [act] $___.

(b) The secretary of state shall collect a fee of $ ______ each time process is served on the secretary of state under this [act]. The party to a proceeding causing service of process may recover this fee as costs if that party prevails in the proceeding.

(c) The secretary of state shall collect the following fees for copying and certifying the copy of any record filed under this [act]:

(1) $______ a page for copying; and

(2) $ ______ for the certificate.

Source Note: Patterned after Model Business Corporation Act, 3d Ed. (2002) § 1.22. Substantially a reenactment of Revised Model Nonprofit Corporation Act (1987) § 1.22, except subsection (a)(10)–(14) and (27) which are new.

Alternative B

The secretary of state shall promulgate rules, in accordance with the [state's administrative procedure act], setting fees for filings and services by the secretary of state under this [act].

CROSS-REFERENCES

Agent's change of registered office, see § 5.02.

Agent's resignation, see § 5.03.

Amended certificate of authority, see § 15.04.

Amendment of articles of incorporation, see §§ 10.06 and 10.08.

Annual report, see § 16.21.

Certificate of authority, see § 15.03.

Certificate of withdrawal, see § 15.20.

Corporation's change of registered agent or office, see § 5.02.

Correction, see § 1.24.

Dissolution:

administrative, see § 14.21.

judicial, see § 14.31.
reinstatement, see § 14.22.
revocation, see § 14.04.
voluntary, see §§ 14.01 and 14.03.

Evidentiary effect of certified copy, see § 1.27.

Existence, see § 1.28.

Incorporation, see § 2.01.

Membership exchange, see § 11.03.

Merger, see § 11.02.

Registered name, see § 4.03.

Renewal of registered name, see § 4.03.

Reserved name, see § 4.02.

Restatement of articles of incorporation, see § 10.07.

Revocation of certificate of authority, see § 15.31.

Service on secretary of state, see §§ 15.20 and 15.31.

Transfer of registered name, see § 4.03.

OFFICIAL COMMENT

Section 1.22 establishes in a single section the filing fees for all records that may be filed under the act. The dollar amounts for each record should be inserted by each state as it adopts the act.

The list of filings in Section 1.22 includes all records that are authorized to be filed with the secretary of state under the act. The catchall in paragraph (a)(32) will apply to any filing for which a state does not establish a specific filing fee plus any filing that later amendments to the statute may authorize or direct be filed with the secretary of state without establishing a specific filing fee.

Paragraph (a)(8) contains a maximum fee for filing a change of address of a registered agent. Since corporation service companies serve as registered agents for thousands of corporations in many jurisdictions, their change of address may require a very large number of filings. Hence, the fee is broadly based on the number of corporations affected but a maximum fee is specified to reflect that as the number of changes increases the cost per change should decrease.

Paragraph (a)(9) states that no fee is applicable to filing the resignation of a registered agent. This provision permits a person who is named as a registered agent without the person's consent, or who agrees to serve as registered agent for a fee and the fee is not paid, to eliminate any reference to the person as a registered agent in the records of the secretary of state without expense.

Sections 11.07, 15.20, and 15.31 require the secretary of state to serve process on foreign corporations under the circumstances there specified. The fee for this service is set forth in Section 1.22(b).

Section 1.22(c) establishes standard fees for copying filed records and certifying that copies are true copies under Section 1.27.

§ 1.23. EFFECTIVE TIME AND DATE OF FILING

(a) Except as provided in subsection (b) and Section 1.24(b), a record accepted for filing is effective:
  (1) at the date and time of filing, as evidenced by such means as the secretary of state may use for the purpose of recording the date and time of filing; or
  (2) at the time specified in the record as its effective time on the date it is filed.

(b) A record may specify a delayed effective time and date, and if it does so the record becomes effective at the time and date specified. If a delayed effective date but no time is specified, the record is effective at the close of business on that date. A delayed effective date for a record may not be later than the 90th day after the date it is filed.

Source Note: Patterned after Model Business Corporation Act, 3d Ed. (2002) § 1.23. Substantially a reenactment of Revised Model Nonprofit Corporation Act (1987) § 1.23.

CROSS-REFERENCES

Effective date:

domestication, see § 9.22.

entity conversion, see § 9.53.
for-profit conversion, see § 9.32.
foreign for-profit domestication and conversion, see § 9.41.
merger or membership exchange, see § 11.06.
voluntary dissolution, see § 14.03.

Filing duty of secretary of state, see § 1.25.

Filing fees, see § 1.22.

Filing requirements, see § 1.20.

OFFICIAL COMMENT

Section 1.23(a) provides that records accepted for filing become effective at the date and time of filing, or at another specified time on that date, unless a delayed effective date is selected under Section 1.23(b). This section gives express statutory authority to the common practice of most secretaries of state of ignoring processing time and treating a record as effective as of the date it is submitted for filing even though it may not be reviewed and accepted for filing until several days later.

Section 1.23(a) requires secretaries of state to maintain some means of recording the date and time of filing of records and provides that records become effective at the recorded time on the date of filing. This provision should eliminate any doubt about situations involving same-day transactions in which a filing—for example, articles of merger—is made on the morning of the date the merger is to become effective. Section 1.23(a) contemplates that the time of filing, as well as the date, will be routinely recorded.

Section 1.23(b) provides an alternative method of establishing the effective date of a filing. The record itself may fix as its effective date any date within 90 days after the date it is filed; it may also fix the time it becomes effective on that date. If no time is specified, the filing becomes effective as of the close of business on the specified date. The act also allows the effective date fixed in a filing to be corrected to a limited extent. See the Official Comment to Section 1.24.

Section 1.23(b) does not authorize or contemplate the establishment of a retroactive effective date that is prior to the date of filing.

§ 1.24. CORRECTING A FILED RECORD

(a) A domestic or foreign entity may correct a record filed by the secretary of state by filing with the secretary of state articles of correction, signed by the corporation or other party in interest, that:
  (1) describe the record (including its filing date) or attach a copy of it to the articles, and
  (2) specify the correction being made.

(b) Articles of correction are effective on the effective date of the filing they correct except as to persons relying on the uncorrected filing and adversely affected by the correction. As to those persons, articles of correction are effective when filed.

Source Note: Derived from Revised Model Nonprofit Corporation Act (1987) § 1.24.

CROSS-REFERENCES

"Deliver" defined, see § 1.40.

Effective time and date of filing, see § 1.23.

Filing fees, see § 1.22.

Filing requirements, see § 1.20.

OFFICIAL COMMENT

Section 1.24 permits making corrections in filed records without refiling the entire record or submitting formal articles of amendment. This correction procedure has two advantages: (1) filing articles of correction may be less expensive than refiling the record or filing articles of amendment, and (2) articles of correction do not alter the effective date of the underlying filing being corrected. Indeed, under Section 1.24(b), even the correction relates back to the original effective date of the filing except as to persons relying on the original filing and adversely affected by the correction. As to these persons, the effective date of articles of correction is the date the articles are filed.

Unlike many organic laws, the act does not contain a list of the types of problems that may be corrected under this section. The rule in Section 1.24(b) on how a correction will operate was considered a sufficient safeguard against abuse of the correction procedure and thus the list in the prior version of the act of what could be corrected has been omitted. Any problem that could be corrected under the prior version of the act, of course, may also be corrected under the broader correction procedure of current Section 1.24.

A provision in a filing setting an effective date (Section 1.23) may be corrected under this section, but the corrected effective date must comply with Section 1.23 measured from the date of the original filing being corrected, *i.e.*, it cannot be before the date of the original filing or more than 90 days thereafter.

§ 1.25. FILING DUTY OF SECRETARY OF STATE

(a) A record delivered to the office of the secretary of state for filing that satisfies the requirements of Section 1.20 must be filed by the secretary of state.

(b) The secretary of state files a record by recording it as filed on the date and time of receipt. After filing a record, the secretary of state shall deliver to the person making the filing or the person's representative a copy of the record with an acknowledgement of the date and time of filing.

(c) If the secretary of state refuses to file a record, the secretary of state shall return it to the person making the filing or the person's representative within five days after the record was delivered, together with a brief explanation in the form of a record of the reason for the refusal to file it.

(d) The duty of the secretary of state to file records under this section is ministerial. Except as provided in Section 2.03(b), the filing or refusal to file a record does not create a presumption that the record is valid or invalid or that information contained in the record is correct or incorrect.

(e) If a law other than this [act] prohibits the disclosure by the secretary of state of information contained in a record delivered for filing, the secretary of state shall file the record if it otherwise complies with this act but may redact such information so that it is not available to the public.

Source Note: Patterned after Model Entity Transactions Act § A1-6. Derived from Revised Model Nonprofit Corporation Act (1987) § 1.25.

CROSS-REFERENCES

Appeal from rejection of filing, see § 1.26.

"Deliver" defined, see § 1.40.

Effective time and date of filing, see § 1.23.

Filing requirements:
- fees, see § 1.22.
- generally, see § 1.20.

Powers of secretary of state, see § 1.30.

Resignation of registered agent, see §§ 5.03 and 15.09.

Service on foreign nonprofit corporation, see § 15.10.

OFFICIAL COMMENT

1. *Filing Duty in General*

Under Section 1.25 the secretary of state is required to file a record if it "satisfies the requirements of Section 1.20." This language should be contrasted with those state statutes that require the secretary of state to ascertain whether a record "conforms with law" before filing it. The purpose of the formulation used in this act is to limit the discretion of the secretary of state to a ministerial role in reviewing the contents of records. If the record satisfies the requirements of Section 1.20 and contains the information required by the applicable provision of the act, the secretary of state under Section 1.25 must file it even though it contains additional provisions the secretary of state may feel are irrelevant or not authorized by the act or by general legal principles. Consistent with this approach, Section 1.25(d) states that the filing duty of the secretary of state is ministerial and provides that filing a record with the secretary of state does not affect the validity or invalidity of any provision contained in the record and does not create any presumption with respect to any provision. Persons adversely affected by provisions in a filing may test their validity in a proceeding appropriate for that purpose. Similarly, the attorney general of the state may also question the validity of provisions of records filed with the secretary of state in an independent suit brought for that purpose; in neither case should any presumption or inference be drawn about the validity of the provision from the fact that the secretary of state accepted the record for filing.

2. Mechanics of Filing

Section 1.25(b) provides that when the secretary of state files a record, the secretary of state records it as filed on the date and time of receipt, retains the original filing for the state's records, and delivers a copy of the filing to the corporation or its representative with an acknowledgement of the date and time of filing. The acknowledgement may be endorsed on the record or be provided separate from the filed record. In the case of a filing transmitted electronically, delivery of the acknowledgement may be made by electronic transmission.

The copy returned by the secretary of state will be the exact or conformed copy if one has been required by the secretary of state, or will be a copy made by the secretary of state if an exact or conformed copy was not required. Consideration was given to dispensing with a copy of the filing and providing only for the return of an acknowledgement of filing. Several states currently follow this practice with respect to articles of incorporation and other documents. It was felt to be important, however, to continue a practice by which each corporation receives back from the secretary of state a record that on its face shows that it is a copy of the record that was filed with the secretary of state. This copy is usually placed in the minute book and is available for informal inspection without requiring a person to examine the records of the secretary of state. Of course, a person desiring a certified copy of any filed record may obtain it from the office of the secretary of state by paying the fee prescribed in Section 1.22(c). Sections 5.03 and 15.09 also require the secretary of state to send a copy of a statement of resignation filed by a registered agent to the corporation previously represented by the agent.

3. Rejection of Filing by Secretary of State

Because of the simplification of formal filing requirements and the limited discretion granted to the secretary of state by the act, rejection of filings should occur only rarely. Section 1.25(c) provides that if the secretary of state does reject a record for filing, the secretary of state must return it to the person making the filing or the person's representative within five days together with a brief written explanation of the reason for rejection. In the case of a record transmitted electronically, rejection of the record may be made electronically by the secretary of state or by a mailing to the corporation at its registered office. A rejection may be the basis of judicial review under Section 1.26.

§ 1.26. REFUSAL OF SECRETARY OF STATE TO FILE RECORD

(a) If the secretary of state refuses to file a record delivered for filing because it does not satisfy the requirements of Section 1.20, the record may be resubmitted accompanied by an opinion in the form of a record from a lawyer admitted to practice in this state stating why the record does satisfy those requirements and the authorities upon which the opinion is based. The secretary of state may rely with respect to any disputed point of law upon the opinion in determining whether the record conforms to law.

(b) If the secretary of state refuses to file a record delivered for filing, and as an alternative to resubmitting the record under subsection (a), or following a refusal to file the record after it is resubmitted under subsection (a), the person that submitted the record may appeal the refusal to the [*name or describe*] court [*of the county where the entity's principal office (or, if none in this state, its registered office) is or will be located*] [*of county*] under the following procedures:

(1) The appeal is commenced by petitioning the court to compel filing the record and by attaching to the petition the record and the explanation of the secretary of state for the refusal to file.

(2) The court may summarily order the secretary of state to file the record or take other action the court considers appropriate.

(3) The final decision of the court may be appealed as in other civil proceedings.

Source Note: Subsection (a) is patterned after CA Corp. Code § 5008. Subsection (b) is derived from Revised Model Nonprofit Corporation Act (1987) § 1.26.

CROSS-REFERENCES

"Deliver" defined, see § 1.40.

Filing fees, see § 1.22.

Filing requirements, see § 1.20.

"Principal office":
- defined, see § 1.40.
- designated in annual report, see § 16.21.

Registered office:
- designated in annual report, see § 16.21.
- requirement, see §§ 2.02, 5.01, and 15.07.

Secretary of state's filing duty, see § 1.25.

OFFICIAL COMMENT

1. The Court with Jurisdiction to Hear Appeals from the Secretary of State

The identity of the specific court with jurisdiction to hear appeals from the secretary of state under Section 1.26(b) must be supplied by each state when enacting this section. It is intended that this should be a court of general civil jurisdiction. It may be either the court located in the capital of the state or the court in the county where the corporation's principal business office is located in the state or, if the corporation does not have a principal office in the state, the court located in the county in which its registered office is located. The annual report of the corporation must state where the principal office of the corporation (which need not be within the state) is located. See Section 16.21. Other sections of the act also contemplate that the court with jurisdiction over substantive corporate matters will be designated in the statute. See, for example, Section 7.03, relating to the ordering of a members' meeting after the corporation fails to hold such a meeting. It is expected that jurisdiction over litigation with respect to substantive matters will normally be vested in the court in the county of the corporation's principal or registered office. See the Official Comment to Section 7.03.

2. "Summary" Orders

In view of the limited discretion of the secretary of state under the act, a "summary" order appears to be appropriate in Section 1.26(b). Throughout the act the term "summarily order" or similar language is used where courts are authorized to order action taken and the person charged with taking the original action has little or no discretion. The words "summarily order" are not used in a technical sense but to refer to a class of cases where the court might appropriately order that action be taken on the face of the pleadings or after an oral hearing but without any need to resolve disputed factual issues.

3. Burden of Proof and Review Standard

The act does not address either the burden of proof or the standard for review in judicial proceedings challenging action of the secretary of state. It is contemplated that these matters will be governed by general principles of judicial review of agency action in each adopting state.

§ 1.27. EVIDENTIARY EFFECT OF COPY OF FILED RECORD

A certificate from the secretary of state delivered with a copy of a record filed by the secretary of state conclusively establishes that the original record is on file with the secretary of state.

Source Note: Patterned after Model Entity Transactions Act § A1-8. Derived from Revised Model Nonprofit Corporation Act (1987) § 1.27.

CROSS-REFERENCES

Certifying fee, see § 1.22.

Forms, see § 1.21.

Secretary of state's filing duty, see § 1.25.

OFFICIAL COMMENT

The secretary of state may be requested to certify that a specific record has been filed with the secretary of state upon payment of the fees specified in Section 1.22(c). Section 1.27 provides that the certificate conclusively establishes that the record is on file. The limited effect of the certificate is consistent with the ministerial filing obligation imposed on the secretary of state under the act. The certificate from the secretary of state, as well as the copy of the record, may be delivered by electronic transmission.

§ 1.28. CERTIFICATE OF EXISTENCE

(a) Anyone may apply to the secretary of state to furnish a certificate of existence for a domestic nonprofit corporation or a certificate of authorization for a qualified foreign nonprofit corporation.

(b) A certificate of existence or authorization sets forth:

   (1) the name of the domestic nonprofit corporation or the name used by the foreign nonprofit corporation in this state;

   (2) that:

 (i) the domestic corporation is duly incorporated under the law of this state, along with the date of its incorporation and the period of its duration if less than perpetual; or
 (ii) the foreign corporation is authorized to conduct activities in this state;
 (3) that all fees, taxes, and penalties owed to this state have been paid, if:
 (i) payment is reflected in the records of the secretary of state, and
 (ii) nonpayment affects the existence or authorization of the domestic or foreign corporation;
 (4) that its most recent annual report required by Section 16.21 has been filed with the secretary of state;
 (5) that articles of dissolution have not been filed; and
 (6) other facts of record in the office of the secretary of state that may be requested by the applicant.

(c) Subject to any qualification stated in the certificate, a certificate of existence or authorization issued by the secretary of state may be relied upon as conclusive evidence that the domestic or foreign nonprofit corporation is in existence or is authorized to conduct activities in this state.

Source Note: Patterned after Model Business Corporation Act, 3d Ed. (2002) § 1.28. Substantially a reenactment of Revised Model Nonprofit Corporation Act (1987) § 1.28.

CROSS-REFERENCES

Filing fees, see § 1.22.

Filing requirements, see § 1.20.

Forms, see § 1.21.

"Principal office":
 defined, see § 1.40.
 designated in annual report, see § 16.21.

Registered office
 designated in annual report, see § 16.21.
 requirement, see §§ 2.02, 5.01, and 15.07.

OFFICIAL COMMENT

Section 1.28 establishes a procedure by which anyone may obtain a conclusive certificate from the secretary of state that a particular domestic or foreign nonprofit corporation is in existence or is authorized to conduct activities in the state. The certificate will probably be a standardized form. The secretary of state is to make the judgment whether or not the corporation is in existence or is authorized to conduct activities from public records only and is not expected to make a more extensive investigation. In appropriate cases, the secretary of state may issue a certificate subject to specified qualifications.

Section 1.28(b)(3) refers only to fees, taxes, or penalties the payment of which is reflected in the records of the secretary of state. Those fees, taxes, and penalties include those collected by the secretary of state or collected by other agencies and reported to the secretary of state. In some states the secretary of state may ascertain from other agencies that other fees, taxes, or penalties have been paid and include this information in the certificate. In states where this procedure does not unduly delay the issuance of certificates, Section 1.28 may be revised appropriately. Section 1.28(b)(3) relates only to fees, taxes, or penalties to the extent their nonpayment affects the existence or authorization to conduct activities of the corporation.

A certificate of existence or authorization that may be relied on as binding and conclusive is of material assistance to attorneys who may be required to give formal legal opinions in connection with corporate transactions.

§ 1.29. PENALTY FOR SIGNING FALSE RECORD

A person commits a [______] misdemeanor [*punishable by a fine not to exceed $ ______*] if the person signs a record knowing it is false in any material respect and the record is delivered to the secretary of state for filing.

Source Note: Patterned after Model Entity Transactions Act § A1-9. Derived from Revised Model Nonprofit Corporation Act (1987) § 1.29.

CROSS-REFERENCES

"Deliver" defined, see § 1.40.

"Sign" defined, see § 1.40.

OFFICIAL COMMENT

Section 1.29 makes it a criminal offense for any person to sign a record that the person knows is false in any material respect with intent that the record be submitted for filing to the secretary of state. As provided in Section 1.40, "sign" includes actions to authenticate or adopt a record beyond just a manual signature.

Section 1.29 is keyed to the classification of offenses provided by the Model Penal Code. If a state has not adopted this classification, the dollar amount of the fine should be substituted for the misdemeanor classification.

[Subchapter] C
SECRETARY OF STATE

§ 1.30. POWERS

The secretary of state has the powers reasonably necessary to perform the duties required of the secretary of state by this [act].

Source Note: Patterned after Model Business Corporation Act, 3d Ed. (2002) § 1.30. Reenactment of Revised Model Nonprofit Corporation Act (1987) § 1.30.

CROSS-REFERENCES

Administrative dissolution, see § 14.20.

Revocation of certificate of authority of foreign nonprofit corporation, see Subch. 15C.

Secretary of state's filing duty, see § 1.25.

OFFICIAL COMMENT

Section 1.30 is intended to grant the secretary of state the authority necessary for the efficient performance of the filing and other duties imposed by the act but is not intended to give the secretary of state general authority to establish public policy. The most important aspects of a modern corporation statute relate to the creation and maintenance of relationships among persons interested in or involved with a corporation. These relationships basically should be a matter of concern to the parties involved and not subject to regulation or interpretation by the secretary of state. Further, even in situations where it is claimed that the corporation has been formed or is being operated for purposes that may violate the public policies of the state, the secretary of state generally should not be the governmental official who determines the scope of public policy through administration of the filing responsibilities under the act. Rather, the attorney general may seek to enjoin the illegal conduct or to dissolve involuntarily the offending corporation.

[Subchapter] D DEFINITIONS

§ 1.40. [ACT] DEFINITIONS

In this [act], unless the context clearly indicates otherwise:

(1) "Articles" or "articles of incorporation" means the original articles of incorporation, all amendments thereof, and any other records filed with the secretary of state with respect to a domestic nonprofit corporation under any provision of this [act] except Section 16.21. If any record filed under this [act] restates the articles in their entirety, thenceforth the articles shall not include any prior filings.

Source Note: Patterned after Model Business Corporation Act, 3d Ed. (2002) § 1.40(1). Compare Revised Model Nonprofit Corporation Act (1987) § 1.40.

(2) "Board" or "board of directors" means the group of individuals responsible for the management of the activities and affairs of the nonprofit corporation, regardless of the name used to refer to the group. The term includes a designated body to the extent:

(i) the authority, powers, or functions of the board have been vested in, or are exercised by, the designated body; and

(ii) the provision of this [act] in which the term appears is relevant to the discharge by the designated body of its authority, powers, or functions.

Source Note: Patterned in part after first two sentences of 15 Pa. Cons. Stat. § 5103 (2008) ("board of directors"). Compare Revised Model Nonprofit Corporation Act (1987) § 1.40(3).

(3) "Business corporation" or "domestic business corporation" means a corporation incorporated under the laws

of this state and subject to the provisions of the [*Model Business Corporation Act*].

Source Note: Patterned after Model Business Corporation Act, 3d Ed. (2002) § 1.40(4).

(4) "Bylaws" means the code or codes of rules (other than the articles of incorporation) adopted for the regulation and governance of the internal affairs of the nonprofit corporation, regardless of the name or names used to refer to those rules.

Source Note: Derived from Revised Model Nonprofit Corporation Act (1987) § 1.40(4).

(5) "Charitable corporation" means a domestic nonprofit corporation that is operated primarily or exclusively for one or more charitable purposes.

Source Note: New.

(6) "Charitable purpose" means a purpose that:
   (i) would make a corporation operated exclusively for that purpose eligible to be exempt from taxation under Section 501(c)(3) or (4) of the Internal Revenue Code, or
   (ii) is considered charitable under law other than this [act] or the Internal Revenue Code.

Source Note: New.

(7) "Conspicuous" means so written, displayed, or presented that a reasonable person against whom the record is to operate should have noticed it. For example, text in italics, boldface, contrasting color, or capitals, or that is underlined, is conspicuous.

Source Note: Patterned after Model Business Corporation Act, 3d Ed. (2002) § 1.40(3).

(8) "Corporation," "domestic corporation," "domestic nonprofit corporation," or "nonprofit corporation" means a corporation incorporated under or subject to the provisions of this [act] that is not a foreign corporation.

Source Note: Patterned after Model Business Corporation Act, 3d Ed. (2002) § 1.40(4). Compare Revised Model Nonprofit Corporation Act (1987) § 1.40(6) and (11).

(9) "Delegate" means a person elected or appointed to vote in a representative assembly for the election of directors or on other matters.

Source Note: Substantially a reenactment of Revised Model Nonprofit Corporation Act (1987) § 1.40(7).

(10) "Deliver" or "delivery" means any method of delivery used in conventional commercial practice, including delivery by hand, mail, commercial delivery, and electronic transmission, except that delivery to the secretary of state means actual receipt by the secretary of state.

Source Note: Patterned after Model Business Corporation Act, 3d Ed. (2002) § 1.40(5). Compare Revised Model Nonprofit Corporation Act (1987) § 1.40(8).

(11) "Designated body" means a person or group, other than a committee of the board of directors, that has been vested by the articles of incorporation or bylaws with powers that, if not vested by the articles or bylaws in that person or group, would be required by this [act] to be exercised by the board or the members.

Source Note: Patterned in part after 15 PA. CONS. STAT. § 5103 (2008) ("other body").

(12) "Director" means an individual designated, elected, or appointed, by that or any other name or title, to act as a member of the board of directors, while the individual is holding that position. The term does not include a member of a designated body, as such.

Source Note: Patterned in part after 15 PA. CONS. STAT. § 5103 (2008) ("directors"). Compare Revised Model Nonprofit Corporation Act (1987) § 1.40(9).

(13) "Domestic unincorporated entity" means an unincorporated entity whose internal affairs are governed by the laws of this state.

Source Note: Patterned after Model Business Corporation Act, 3d Ed. (2002) § 1.40(6A).

(14) "Effective date of notice" is provided for in Section 1.41.

Source Note: Patterned after Model Business Corporation Act, 3d Ed. (2002) § 1.40(7). Reenactment of Revised Model Nonprofit Corporation Act (1987) § 1.40(12).

(15) "Electronic" means relating to technology having electrical, digital, magnetic, wireless, optical, electromagnetic, or similar capabilities.

Source Note: Patterned after Uniform Electronic Transactions Act § 2(5).

(16) "Eligible entity" means a domestic or foreign unincorporated entity or a domestic or foreign business corporation.

Source Note: Patterned after Model Business Corporation Act, 3d Ed. (2002) § 1.40(7B).

(17) "Eligible interests" means interests or shares.

Source Note: Patterned after Model Business Corporation Act, 3d Ed. (2002) § 1.40(7C).

(18) "Employee" does not include an individual serving as an officer or director who is not otherwise employed by the corporation.

Source Note: Substantially a reenactment of Revised Model Nonprofit Corporation Act (1987) § 1.40(13).

(19) "Entitled to vote" means entitled to vote on the matter under consideration pursuant to the articles of incorporation or bylaws of the nonprofit corporation or any applicable controlling provision of law.

Source Note: Patterned after 15 PA. CONS. STAT. § 5103 (2008) ("entitled to vote").

(20) "Entity" includes a domestic or foreign business corporation, domestic or foreign nonprofit corporation,

domestic or foreign unincorporated entity, estate, trust, state, the United States, foreign government, or governmental subdivision.

Source Note: Patterned in part after Model Business Corporation Act, 3d Ed. (2002) § 1.40(9). Derived from Revised Model Nonprofit Corporation Act (1987) § 1.40(14).

(21) "Filing entity" means an unincorporated entity that is created by filing a public organic record.

Source Note: Patterned after Model Business Corporation Act, 3d Ed. (2002) § 1.40(9B).

(22) "Foreign business corporation" means a corporation for profit incorporated under a law other than the law of this state that would be a business corporation if incorporated under the law of this state.

Source Note: Patterned after Model Business Corporation Act, 3d Ed. (2002) § 1.40(10).

(23) "Foreign corporation" or "foreign nonprofit corporation" means a corporation incorporated under a law other than the law of this state that would be a nonprofit corporation if incorporated under the law of this state.

Source Note: Patterned after Model Business Corporation Act, 3d Ed. (2002) § 1.40(10A). Substantially a reenactment of Revised Model Nonprofit Corporation Act (1987) § 1.40(16).

(24) "Foreign unincorporated entity" means an unincorporated entity whose internal affairs are governed by an organic law of a jurisdiction other than this state.

Source Note: Patterned after Model Business Corporation Act, 3d Ed. (2002) § 1.40(10B).

(25) "Fundamental transaction" means an amendment of the articles of incorporation or bylaws, merger, membership exchange, sale of all or substantially all of the assets, domestication, conversion, or dissolution of a nonprofit corporation.

Source Note: New.

(26) "Governmental subdivision" includes an authority, county, district, and municipality.

Source Note: Patterned after Model Business Corporation Act, 3d Ed. (2002) § 1.40(11). Reenactment of Revised Model Nonprofit Corporation Act (1987) § 1.40(17).

(27) "Governor" means a person by or under whose authority the powers of an unincorporated entity are exercised and under whose direction the business, activities, or affairs of the entity are managed pursuant to the organic law and organic records of the entity.

Source Note: Patterned after Model Entity Transactions Act § 102(16).

(28) "Includes" denotes a partial definition.

Source Note: Patterned after Model Business Corporation Act, 3d Ed. (2002) § 1.40(12). Reenactment of Revised Model Nonprofit Corporation Act (1987) § 1.40(18).

(29) "Individual" means a natural person.

Source Note: Patterned after Model Business Corporation Act, 3d Ed. (2002) § 1.40(13). Compare Revised Model Nonprofit Corporation Act (1987) § 1.40(19).

(30) "Interest" means either or both of the following rights under the organic law of an unincorporated entity:

(i) the right to receive distributions from the entity either in the ordinary course or upon liquidation; or

(ii) the right to receive notice or vote on issues involving its internal affairs, other than as an agent, assignee, proxy, or person responsible for managing its business, activities, or affairs.

Source Note: Patterned after Model Business Corporation Act, 3d Ed. (2002) § 1.40(13A).

(31) "Interest holder" means a person who holds of record an interest.

Source Note: Patterned after Model Business Corporation Act, 3d Ed. (2002) § 1.40(13B).

(32) "Interest holder liability" means personal liability for a debt, obligation, or liability of a domestic or foreign business or nonprofit corporation or unincorporated entity that is imposed on a person:

(i) solely by reason of the person's status as a shareholder, interest holder, or member; or

(ii) by the articles of incorporation, bylaws, or an organic record pursuant to a provision of the organic law authorizing the articles, bylaws, or an organic record to make one or more specified shareholders, interest holders, or members liable in their capacity as shareholders, interest holders, or members for all or specified debts, obligations, or liabilities of the entity.

Source Note: Patterned after Model Business Corporation Act, 3d Ed. (2002) § 1.40(15C).

(33) "Internal Revenue Code" means the Internal Revenue Code of 1986 (Public Law 99-514, 26 U.S.C. § 1 et seq.), as amended.

Source Note: New.

(34) "Material interest" means an actual or potential benefit or detriment, other than one that would devolve on the nonprofit corporation or the members generally, that would reasonably be expected to impair the objectivity of an individual's judgment when participating in the action to be taken.

Source Note: Patterned after Model Business Corporation Act, 3d Ed. (2005) § 1.43(b)(2).

(35) "Material relationship" means a familial, financial, professional, employment, or other relationship that would reasonably be expected to impair the objectivity of an individual's judgment when participating in the action to be taken.

Source Note: Patterned after Model Business Corporation Act, 3d Ed. (2005) § 1.43(b)(1).

(36) "Means" denotes an exhaustive definition.

Source Note: Patterned after Model Business Corporation Act, 3d Ed. (2002) § 1.40(14). Substantially a reenactment of Revised Model Nonprofit Corporation Act (1987) § 1.40(20).

(37) "Member" means:

(i) A person who has the right, in accordance with the articles of incorporation or bylaws and not as a delegate, to select or vote for the election of directors or delegates or to vote on any type of fundamental transaction. See Section 6.02(d) (admission).

(ii) A designated body to the extent:

(A) the authority, powers, or functions of the members have been vested in, or are exercised by, the designated body; and

(B) the provision of this [act] in which the term appears is relevant to the discharge by the designated body of its authority, powers, or functions.

Source Note: Compare Revised Model Nonprofit Corporation Act (1987) § 1.40(21).

(38) "Membership" means the rights and any obligations of a member in a nonprofit corporation.

Source Note: Patterned in part after Revised Model Nonprofit Corporation Act (1987) § 1.40(22). Compare Model Business Corporation Act, 3d Ed. (2002) § 1.40(14A).

(39) "Membership corporation" means a nonprofit corporation whose articles of incorporation or bylaws provide that it shall have members.

Source Note: New.

(40) "Nonfiling entity" means an unincorporated entity that is not created by filing a public organic record.

Source Note: Patterned after proposed Model Business Corporation Act, 3d Ed. (2002) § 1.40(14B).

(41) "Nonmembership corporation" means a nonprofit corporation whose articles of incorporation or bylaws do not provide that it shall have members.

Source Note: New.

(42) "Nonqualified foreign corporation" means a foreign corporation that is not authorized to conduct activities in this state.

Source Note: New.

(43) "Notice" is provided for in Section 1.41.

Source Note: Patterned after Model Business Corporation Act, 3d Ed. (2002) § 1.40(15). Reenactment of Revised Model Nonprofit Corporation Act (1987) § 1.40(24).

(44) "Officer" includes:

(i) a person who is an officer as provided in Section 8.40; and

(ii) if a nonprofit corporation is in the hands of a custodian, receiver, trustee or other court-appointed fiduciary, that fiduciary or any person appointed by that fiduciary to act as an officer for any purpose under this [act].

Source Note: Patterned after 15 PA. CONS. STAT. § 5103 (2008) ("officer").

(45) "Organic law" means the statute principally governing the internal affairs of a domestic or foreign business or nonprofit corporation or unincorporated entity.

Source Note: Patterned after Model Business Corporation Act, 3d Ed. (2002) § 1.40(15B).

(46) "Organic record" means a public organic record or the private organic rules.

Source Note: Patterned after Model Business Corporation Act, 3d Ed. (2002) § 1.40(15A).

(47) "Person" includes an individual or an entity.

Source Note: Patterned after Model Business Corporation Act, 3d Ed. (2002) § 1.40(16). Substantially a reenactment of Revised Model Nonprofit Corporation Act (1987) § 1.40(25).

(48) "Principal office" means the office (in or out of this state) designated in the annual report as the location of the principal executive office of a domestic or foreign nonprofit corporation.

Source Note: Patterned after Model Business Corporation Act, 3d Ed. (2002) § 1.40(17). Substantially a reenactment of Revised Model Nonprofit Corporation Act (1987) § 1.40(26).

(49) "Private organic rules" means any record (other than the public organic record, if any) that determines the internal governance of an unincorporated entity. Where the private organic rules have been amended or restated, the term means the private organic rules as last amended or restated.

Source Note: Patterned after Model Business Corporation Act, 3d Ed. (2002) § 1.40(17A).

(50) "Proceeding" includes civil suit and criminal, administrative, and investigatory action.

Source Note: Patterned after Model Business Corporation Act, 3d Ed. (2002) § 1.40(18). Reenactment of Revised Model Nonprofit Corporation Act (1987) § 1.40(27).

(51) "Public organic record" means the record, if any, that is filed of public record to create an unincorporated entity. Where a public organic record has been amended or restated, the term means the public organic record as last amended or restated.

Source Note: Patterned after Model Business Corporation Act, 3d Ed. (2002) § 1.40(17B).

(52) "Qualified foreign corporation" means a foreign corporation authorized to conduct activities in this state.

Source Note: New.

(53) "Record" means information that is inscribed on a tangible medium or that is stored in an electronic or other medium and is retrievable in perceivable form.

Source Note: Patterned after Uniform Electronic Transactions Act § 2(13), Uniform Limited Partnership Act (2001) § 102(17), and Uniform Limited Liability Company Act (2006) § 102(17).

(54) "Record date" means the date established under Section 7.07 on which a nonprofit corporation determines the identity of its members and the membership interests they hold for purposes of this [act]. The determinations shall be made as of the close of business on the record date unless another time for doing so is specified when the record date is fixed.

Source Note: Patterned after Model Business Corporation Act, 3d Ed. (2002) § 1.40(19). First sentence is substantially a reenactment of Revised Model Nonprofit Corporation Act (1987) § 1.40(29).

(55) "Secretary" means the corporate officer to whom the articles of incorporation, bylaws, or board of directors has delegated responsibility under Section 8.40(b) for custody of the minutes of the meetings of the board of directors, any designated body, committees, and the members, and for authenticating records of the nonprofit corporation.

Source Note: Patterned after Model Business Corporation Act, 3d Ed. (2002) § 1.40(20). Substantially a reenactment of Revised Model Nonprofit Corporation Act (1987) § 1.40(31).

(56) "Shareholder" means the person in whose name shares are registered in the records of a domestic or foreign business corporation or the beneficial owner of shares to the extent of the rights granted by a nominee certificate on file with such a corporation.

Source Note: Patterned after Model Business Corporation Act, 3d Ed. (2002) § 1.40(21).

(57) "Shares" means the units into which the proprietary interests in a domestic or foreign business corporation are divided.

Source Note: Patterned after Model Business Corporation Act, 3d Ed. (2002) § 1.40(22).

(58) "Sign" means, with present intent to authenticate or adopt a record:

(i) to execute or adopt a tangible symbol; or

(ii) to attach to or logically associate with the record an electronic sound, symbol, or process.

Source Note: Patterned after Uniform Electronic Transactions Act § 2(8) ("electronic signature"), Uniform Limited Partnership Act (2001) § 102(19), and Uniform Limited Liability Company Act (2006) § 101(18).

(59) "State," when referring to a part of the United States, includes a state or commonwealth, the District of Columbia, the Commonwealth of Puerto Rico, a territory or insular possession of the United States, and any agency or governmental subdivision of any of the foregoing.

Source Note: Patterned after Model Business Corporation Act, 3d Ed. (2002) § 1.40(23). Reenactment of Revised Model Nonprofit Corporation Act (1987) § 1.40(32).

(60) "Unincorporated entity" means an organization or artificial legal person that either has a separate legal existence or has the power to acquire an estate in real property in its own name and that is not any of the following: a domestic or foreign business or nonprofit corporation, an estate, a trust, a governmental subdivision, a state, the United States, or a foreign government. The term includes a general partnership, limited liability company, limited partnership, business or statutory trust,

joint stock association, and unincorporated nonprofit association.

Source Note: Patterned after Model Business Corporation Act, 3d Ed. (2002) § 1.40(24A).

(61) "United States" includes a district, authority, bureau, commission, department, and any other agency of the United States.

Source Note: Patterned after Model Business Corporation Act, 3d Ed. (2002) § 1.40(25). Reenactment of Revised Model Nonprofit Corporation Act (1987) § 1.40(33).

(62) "Vote," "voting," or "casting a vote" includes the giving of consent in the form of a record without a meeting. The term does not include either recording the fact of abstention or failing to vote for a candidate or for approval or disapproval of a matter, whether or not the person entitled to vote characterizes such conduct as voting or casting a vote.

Source Note: Patterned after 15 PA. CONS. STAT. § 1103 (2008) ("voting").

(63) "Voting group" means one or more classes of members that under the articles of incorporation, bylaws, or this [act] are entitled to vote and be counted together collectively on a matter at a meeting of members. All members entitled by the articles of incorporation, bylaws, or this [act] to vote generally on the matter are for that purpose a single voting group.

Source Note: Patterned after Model Business Corporation Act, 3d Ed. (2002) § 1.40(26).

(64) "Voting power" means the current power to vote in the election of directors or delegates, or to vote on approval of any type of fundamental transaction.

Source Note: Patterned after Model Business Corporation Act, 3d Ed. (2002) § 1.40(27). Compare Revised Model Nonprofit Corporation Act (1987) § 1.40(35).

CROSS-REFERENCES

Special definitions:

"corporate action," see § 1.50.
"corporation," see § 8.50.
"court," see § 1.50.
"derivative proceeding," see § 13.01.
"director," see § 8.50.
"disinterested director;" see § 8.50.
"exchanging entity," see § 11.01.
"expenses," see § 8.50.
"liability," see § 8.50.
"membership exchange," see § 11.01.
"merger," see § 11.01.
"officer," see § 8.50.
"official capacity," see § 8.50.
"outstanding shares," see § 6.03.
"party," see § 8.50.
"party to a merger," see § 11.01.
"party to a membership exchange," see § 11.01.
"proceeding," see § 8.50.
"survivor," see § 11.01.

OFFICIAL COMMENT

1. Board of Directors and Designated Body

The term "designated body" was not found in the prior version of the act, although the prior act did contain a rudimentary version of the concept in former Section 8.01(c). More detail has been provided in this version of the act to give nonprofit corporations greater certainty when using the flexibility inherent in the concept of a designated body when organizing their affairs. The concept of a designated body recognizes that it is sometimes desirable for a nonprofit corporation to depart from the traditional governance structure based on a board of directors and, in appropriate circumstances, members.

There is no limitation in the act on the number of designated bodies that a nonprofit corporation may create.

When a designated body is exercising a power that would otherwise be exercised by the board of directors, the members of the designated body have the duties and liabilities of directors. See Section 8.12. However, when a designated body is exercising a power that would otherwise be exercised by the members, the members of the designated body should be subject only to the duties and liabilities of members or delegates.

2. Bylaws

The "bylaws" are those rules that are intended to have the status of bylaws under this act regardless of how the corporation chooses to refer to them. Some corporations, for example, adopt a "constitution" that serves as bylaws.

Many nonprofit corporations adopt codes of conduct and other policies that have an important place in the conduct of the corporation's activities but are not intended to have the status of bylaws under the act. A code of conduct that is not intended to be part of the bylaws, for example, will not be subject to the provisions of the act governing the adoption and amendment of bylaws in Chapters 2 and 10B. On the other hand, a corporation could choose to include a code of conduct in its bylaws, in which case the code of conduct would be subject to the provisions of the act in the same manner as the other provisions of the bylaws.

3. Charitable Corporation and Charitable Purposes

The prior version of the act classified nonprofit corporations into three types: mutual benefit corporations, public benefit corporations, and religious corporations. See Revised Model Nonprofit Corporation Act (1987) § 1.40(23), (28), and (30). Separate rules on a variety of subjects were then provided for those differing types of corporations. *See, e.g.*, Revised Model Nonprofit Corporation Act (1987) §§ 6.11 (transfers of membership), 8.31 (director conflicts of interest), and 11.01 (plans of merger). That classification scheme was not widely embraced and led to the prior act being seen as unduly complicated and restrictive.

There are, nonetheless, certain areas in which public policy concerns are more sensitive with respect to some nonprofit corporations than others. The act accordingly provides different rules for charitable corporations with respect to certain subjects.

The prior act included a definition of "charitable purposes" that listed those purposes that were considered to be charitable purposes. Specifying what constitutes a charitable purpose provides certainty as to the scope of the term, and thus which nonprofit corporations will be subject to the rules in the act regarding charitable corporations. But providing a definition of charitable purposes also means that the act's definition may diverge from the meaning of charitable purposes under Section 501(c)(3) or (4) of the Internal Revenue Code and similar provisions of state law. Instead of providing a specific list of purposes that are considered charitable for purposes of the act, Section 1.40(6) looks to what constitutes a charitable purpose under Section 501(c)(3) or (4) or other law.

4. *Conspicuous*

"Conspicuous" is defined in Section 1.40(7) similarly to the way it is defined in Section 1-201(10) of the Uniform Commercial Code. Even though the definition indicates some of the methods by which a provision may be made attention-calling, the test is whether attention can reasonably be expected to be called to it.

5. *Corporation, Domestic Corporation, Domestic Nonprofit Corporation, Foreign Corporation, Foreign Nonprofit Corporation, and Nonprofit Corporation*

"Corporation," "domestic corporation," "domestic nonprofit corporation," "foreign corporation," "foreign nonprofit corporation," and "nonprofit corporation" are defined in Sections 1.40(8) and (23). The word "corporation" refers only to domestic nonprofit corporations and is only used where a more complete term has already been used in the same subsection. In a few instances, the phrase "domestic corporation" has been used in order to contrast it with a foreign corporation. The phrase "domestic nonprofit corporation" has been used on occasion to contrast it with a domestic business corporation.

6. Delegate

Professional associations, churches, political parties, and numerous other organizations hold representative assemblies from time to time at which major corporate and policy decisions are made. These representative assemblies may be called conventions, annual meetings, or some other name. The people elected or appointed to vote at these representative assemblies are "delegates" for purposes of the act even if they are called by some other name.

7. Electronic

The definition of "electronic" is patterned after the definition of that term in Uniform Electronic Transactions Act § 2(5). While not all of the technologies listed are technically "electronic" in nature (*e.g.*, optical fiber technology), the term was chosen in the Uniform Electronic Transactions Act as the most descriptive term available to describe current technologies. The term should be construed broadly to include developing technologies arguably within any aspect of the definition. Because "delivery" is defined to include electronic transmission, the use of such means as e-mail, fax, and telephone are permissible ways of delivering notices under the act. But the use of electronic technology will not always involve a "record" as defined in this section. A telephone conversation between two people will involve electronic technology, but will not create a "record" because the conversation will not later be "retrievable" as required to create a record. Leaving a message on voicemail, however, results in a record because the voicemail message is retrievable and capable of reproduction in perceivable form.

8. Eligible Entity, Entity, and Unincorporated Entity

The term "entity," defined in Section 1.40(20), appears in the definition of "person" in Section 1.40(47) and is included to cover all types of artificial persons. Estates and trusts and general partnerships are included even though they may not, in some jurisdictions, be considered artificial persons. The usage of "trust" in Section 1.40(60) in contrast to "business or statutory trust" in that same provision indicates that "trust" by itself means a nonbusiness trust, such as a traditional testamentary trust, inter vivos trust, or charitable trust.

The term "entity" is significantly broader than the term "unincorporated entity" which is defined in Section 1.40(60) because the term "entity" includes all types of corporations, estates, and trusts, as well as public and quasi-public organizations. See also the definitions of "governmental subdivision" in Section 1.40(26), "state" in Section 1.40(59), and "United States" in Section 1.40(61).

A form of co-ownership of property or sharing of returns from property that is not a partnership under the Uniform Partnership Act (1997) will not be an "unincorporated entity." In that connection, Section 202(c) of the Uniform Partnership Act (1997) provides, among other things, that:

> In determining whether a partnership is formed, the following rules apply:
>
> (1) Joint tenancy, tenancy in common, tenancy by the entireties, joint property, common property, or part ownership does not by itself establish a partnership, even if the co-owners share profits made by the use of the property.
>
> (2) The sharing of gross returns does not by itself establish a partnership, even if the persons sharing them have a joint or common right or interest in property from which the returns are derived.

The term "eligible entity" is used in the act to refer to those types of entities that can engage in mergers and other types of fundamental transactions under the act with a nonprofit corporation. Because the term "eligible entity" includes business corporations, for example, the provisions of Chapter 11 permitting a nonprofit corporation to merge with an eligible entity will permit a merger between a nonprofit corporation and a business corporation. Similarly, a nonprofit corporation may merge under Chapter 11 with a limited liability company because a limited liability company is also an eligible entity.

9. Member and Membership

"Member" and "membership" are defined in Sections 1.40(37) and (38) for purposes of this act to refer only to the rights of a member in a nonprofit corporation. Although the owners of a limited liability company are generally referred to as "members," for purposes of this act they are referred to as "interest holders" and what they own in the limited liability company is referred to in this act as an "interest."

A nonprofit corporation will sometimes refer to contributors or other persons interested in the activities of the corporation as "members" even though those persons do not fit within the definition in Section 1.40(37). If a person does not have the right to vote for the election of directors or delegates or to vote on fundamental transactions, the person will not be a "member" for purposes of this act even though the person may be referred to informally by the corporation as a member. However, a person who is designated as a member pursuant to an applicable provision of the bylaws will have that status regardless of what rights may or may not be conferred by the bylaws.

A person who has the right to select or vote for the election of members of a designated body, but who does not have the right to vote for the election of directors or on approval of any type of fundamental transaction, is not within the definition of "member."

10. Organic Records, Public Organic Records, and Private Organic Rules

The term "organic records" as defined in Section 1.40(46) includes both public organic records and private organic rules. The term "public organic record" includes such filings as the certificate of limited partnership of a limited partnership, the articles of organization or certificate of formation of a limited liability company, the deed of trust of a business trust, and comparable documents, however denominated, that are publicly filed to create other forms of unincorporated entities. The term "private organic rules" includes a partnership agreement of a general or limited partnership, an operating agreement of a limited liability company, and comparable agreements, however denominated, of other forms of unincorporated entities.

11. Owner Liability

The term "owner liability" is used in the context of provisions in Chapters 9 and 11 that preserve the personal liability of shareholders, interest holders, and members when the entity in which they own shares or interests is the subject of a transaction under those chapters. The term includes only liabilities that are imposed by or pursuant to statute on shareholders, interest holders, or members. Liabilities that a shareholder, interest holder, or member incurs by contract are not included. Thus, for example, if a state's nonprofit corporation law were to make members personally liable for unpaid wages, that liability would be an "owner liability." If, on the other hand, a member were to guarantee payment of an obligation of a corporation, that liability would not be an "owner liability." The reason for excluding contractual liabilities from the definition of "owner liability" is that those liabilities are constitutionally protected from impairment and thus do not need to be separately protected in Chapters 9 and 11.

12. Person

The term "person" is defined in Section 1.40(47) to include an individual or an entity. In the case of an individual this act assumes that the person is competent to act in the matter under general state law independent of the corporation statute.

13. Principal Office

Section 1.40(48) defines the principal office of a corporation to be the office within or without the state where the principal executive office of the corporation is located. Many corporations maintain numerous offices, but there is usually one office, sometimes colloquially referred to as the home office, headquarters, or executive suite, where the principal corporate officers are located. The corporation must designate its principal office address in the annual report required by Section 16.21. In case of doubt as to which corporate office is the principal office, the designation by the corporation in its annual report should be accepted as establishing the principal office of the corporation.

14. Record

The definition of "record" is patterned after the definitions of that term in Uniform Electronic Transactions Act § 2(13), Uniform Limited Partnership Act (2001) § 102(17), and Uniform Limited Liability Company Act (2006) § 102(17). Those definitions, in turn, were based on the same definition in section 106(9) of the Electronic Signatures in Global and National Commerce Act, 15 U.S.C. § 7006(9). The term includes both communication systems that in the normal course produce paper, such as telegrams and facsimiles, as well as communication systems that transmit and permit the retention of data that is then subject to subsequent retrieval and reproduction in perceivable form. The term is intended to be broadly construed and include the evolving methods of electronic delivery, such as e-mail, the Internet, and electronic transmissions between computers. A voicemail message creates a record. See Comment 7 on the definition of "electronic."

15. Secretary

The term "secretary" is defined in Section 1.40(55) since this act does not require the corporation to maintain any specific or titled officers. See Section 8.40. However, some corporate officer, however titled, must perform the functions described in this definition, and that officer is referred to as the "secretary" in various sections of the act that impose a duty to perform those functions.

16. Sign

The definition of "sign" is patterned after the definitions of that term in Uniform Electronic Transactions Act § 2(8) ("electronic signature"), Uniform Limited Partnership Act (2001) § 102(19), and Uniform Limited Liability Company Act (2006) § 101(18). Those definitions, in turn, were based on the definition of "electronic signature" in section 106(5) of the Electronic Signatures in Global and National Commerce Act, 15 U.S.C.

§ 7006(5). The term includes manual, facsimile, conformed, or electronic signatures. In this regard, it is intended that any manifestation of an intention to execute or authenticate a record will be accepted. Electronic signatures are expected to encompass any methodology approved by the secretary of state for purposes of verification of the authenticity of the record. This could include a typewritten conformed signature or other electronic entry in the form of a computer data compilation of any characters or series of characters constituting a name intended to evidence authorization and execution of a record.

17. Unincorporated Entity

The term "unincorporated entity" is a subset of the broader term "entity."

There is some question as to whether a partnership subject to the Uniform Partnership Act (1914) is an entity or merely an aggregation of its partners. That question has been resolved by Section 201 of the Uniform Partnership Act (1997), which makes clear that a general partnership is an entity with its own separate legal existence. Section 8 of the Uniform Partnership Act (1914) gives partnerships subject to it the power to acquire estates in real property and thus such a partnership will be an "unincorporated entity." As a result, all general partnerships will be "unincorporated entities" regardless of whether the state in which they are organized has adopted the new Uniform Partnership Act (1997).

The term "unincorporated entity" includes limited liability partnerships and limited liability limited partnerships because those entities are forms of general partnerships and limited partnerships, respectively, that have made the additional required election claiming that status.

Section 4 of the Uniform Unincorporated Nonprofit Association Act gives an unincorporated nonprofit association the power to acquire an estate in real property and thus an unincorporated nonprofit association organized in a state that has adopted that act will be an "unincorporated entity." At common law, an unincorporated nonprofit association was not a legal entity and did not have the power to acquire real property. Most states that have not adopted the Uniform Act have nonetheless modified the common law rule, but states that have not adopted the Uniform Act should analyze whether they should modify the definition of "unincorporated entity" to add an express reference to unincorporated nonprofit associations.

"Business or statutory trust" includes any trust carrying on a business, such as a Massachusetts trust, real estate investment trust, or other common law or statutory business trust. The term "unincorporated entity" expressly excludes estates and trusts (*i.e.*, trusts that are not business trusts), whether or not they would be considered artificial persons under the governing jurisdiction's law, to make it clear that they are not eligible to participate in a conversion under Subchapter E of Chapter 9 or a merger or share exchange under Chapter 11. If a nonprofit corporation wishes to merge with a charitable trust it will be necessary to first incorporate the trust.

18. Voting Group

Section 1.40(63) defines "voting group" for purposes of this act as a matter of convenient reference. A "voting group" consists of all the members of one or more classes that under the articles of incorporation, bylaws, or the act are entitled to vote and be counted together collectively on a matter. Members entitled to vote "generally" on a matter under the articles of incorporation, bylaws, or the act are for that purpose a single voting group. The word "generally" signifies all members entitled to vote on the matter by the articles of incorporation, bylaws, or the act that do not expressly have the right to be counted or tabulated separately. "Voting groups" are thus the basic units of collective voting at a members' meeting, and voting by voting groups may provide essential protection to one or more classes of members against actions that are detrimental to the rights or interests of that class.

The determination of which members form part of a single voting group must be made from the provisions of the articles of incorporation, bylaws, and the act. In a few instances under the act, the board of directors or a designated body may establish the right to vote by voting groups. On most matters coming before members' meetings, only a single voting group, consisting of a class of voting members, will be involved, and action on such a matter is effective when approved by that voting group pursuant to Section 7.24. See Section 7.25(a). If a second class of members is also entitled to vote on the matter, then a further determination must be made as to whether that class is to vote as a separate voting group or whether it is to vote along with the other voting members as part of a single voting group.

Members of the board of directors are usually elected by the single voting group of members entitled to vote generally; in some circumstances, however, some members of the board may be selected by one voting group and other members by one or more different voting groups. See Section 8.04.

The definition of a voting group permits the establishment by statute of quorum and voting requirements for a variety of matters considered at members' meetings in corporations with multiple classes of members. See Sections 7.25 and 7.26. Depending on the circumstances, two classes of members may vote together collectively on a matter as a single voting group, they may be entitled to vote on the matter separately as two voting groups, or one or both of them may not be entitled to vote on the matter at all.

19. Voting Power

Under Section 1.40(64) the term "voting power" means the current power to vote in the election of directors or delegates, or on approval of a fundamental transaction. Application of this definition turns on whether the relevant members have the power to vote as of the time a vote is being conducted. If members have the power to vote in an election of directors only under a certain contingency, for example, those members would not have voting power within the meaning of Section 1.40(64) unless the contingency has occurred, and then only during the period when the voting rights are in effect. Members that have the power to vote for any directors as of the time a vote is conducted have the current power to vote in the election of directors within the meaning of Section 1.40(64) even if the members do not have the power to vote for all directors.

§ 1.41. NOTICE

(a) Notice under this [act] must be in the form of a record unless oral notice is authorized by this [act] or is reasonable under the circumstances.

(b) Notice may be communicated in person or by delivery. If these forms of communication are impracticable, notice may be communicated by a newspaper of general circulation in the area where published, or by radio, television, or other form of public broadcast communication.

(c) Notice in the form of a record by a membership corporation to a member is effective:

(1) upon deposit in the United States mail or with a commercial delivery service, if the postage or delivery charge is paid and the notice is correctly addressed to the member's address shown in the corporation's current record of members, or

(2) when given if the notice is delivered in any other manner that the member has authorized.

(d) Notice to a domestic or qualified foreign nonprofit corporation may be delivered to its registered agent at its registered office or to the corporation or its secretary at its principal office shown in its most recent annual report or, in the case of a foreign corporation that has not yet delivered an annual report, in its application for a certificate of authority.

(e) Except as provided in subsection (c), notice is effective at the earliest of the following:

(1) when received;

(2) when left at the recipient's residence or usual place of business;

(3) five days after its deposit in the United States mail or with a commercial delivery service, if the postage or delivery charge is paid and the notice is correctly addressed;

(4) on the date shown on the return receipt, if sent by registered or certified mail, return receipt requested, or by commercial delivery service.

(f) Oral notice is effective when communicated, if communicated in a comprehensible manner.

(g) If this [act] prescribes notice requirements for particular circumstances, those requirements govern. If bylaws prescribe notice requirements, not inconsistent with this section or other provisions of this [act], those requirements govern.

(h) With respect to electronic communications:

(1) Unless otherwise provided in the articles of incorporation or bylaws, or otherwise agreed between the sender and the recipient, an electronic communication is received when:

(i) it enters an information processing system that the recipient has designated or uses for the purpose of receiving electronic records or information of the type sent and from which the recipient is able to retrieve the electronic record; and

(ii) it is in a form capable of being processed by that system.

(2) An electronic communication is received under paragraph (h)(1) even if no individual is aware of its receipt.

(3) Receipt of an electronic acknowledgement from an information processing system described in paragraph (h)(1) establishes that a record was received but, by itself, does not establish that the content sent corresponds to the content received.

(i) An authorization by a member of delivery of notices or communications by e-mail or similar electronic means may be revoked by the member by notice to the nonprofit corporation in the form of a record. Such an authorization is deemed revoked if (i) the corporation is unable to deliver two consecutive notices or other communications to the member in the manner authorized; and (ii) the inability becomes known to the secretary or other person responsible for giving the notice or other communication; but the failure to treat the inability as a revocation does not invalidate any meeting or other action.

Source Note: Subsections (a)–(g) patterned in part after Model Business Corporation Act, 3d Ed. (2002) § 1.41, and derived from Revised Model Nonprofit Corporation Act (1987) § 1.41.

Subsection (h) patterned after Uniform Electronic Transactions Act § 15(b), (e), and (f). Subsection (i) patterned after 8 DEL. CODE § 232(a).

CROSS-REFERENCES

Annual report, see § 16.21.

Application for certificate of authority, see § 15.03.

"Deliver" defined, see § 1.40.

"Electronic" defined, see § 1.40.

Meetings:
- board of directors, see § 8.22.
- members, see § 7.05.

"Principal office":
- defined, see § 1.40.
- designated in annual report, see § 16.21.

"Record" defined, see § 1.40.

Record of members, see § 16.01.

Special notice requirements:
- attorney general, see §§ 1.53 and 1.70.
- derivative proceedings, see § 13.09.
- resignation of registered agent, see §§ 5.03 and 15.09.
- service on corporation, see §§ 5.04 and 15.10.

OFFICIAL COMMENT

Section 1.41 establishes rules for determining how notice may be given and when notice is effective for a variety of purposes under the act. Those rules permit many other sections of the act to be phrased simply in terms of delivering notice without repeating details with respect to how notice should be given and when it is effective in various circumstances.

1. Notice by a Corporation to Its Members

Section 1.41(c) provides that notice by a corporation to its members is effective when mailed if correctly addressed with sufficient postage. Similarly, notice is effective when deposited with a commercial delivery service if correctly addressed with the delivery charge prepaid. The correct address for this purpose is the address shown in the corporation's member records. Notice includes notice by electronic transmission, but notice may be provided through electronic transmission only if specifically authorized by the member. This allows corporations to provide notices by electronic means, but only when, and in the manner, authorized by the member. Absent such authorization, notice must be provided to the shareholder in the traditional manner consistent with the other provisions of Section 1.41.

Notice to members by persons other than the corporation is effective as provided in Section 1.41(e). Notice by the corporation to its members that is not addressed to the record address of a member is effective when received under Section 1.41(e).

2. *Notice to the Corporation*

Section 1.41(d) provides that notice to a corporation may be delivered to the registered agent of the corporation at its registered office or to the corporation or its secretary at the principal office of the corporation as shown in its most recent filing with the secretary of state. An officer, director, member of a designated body, or member of a corporation will normally give notice to the corporation by delivering or mailing a copy of the notice to the corporation or to the secretary of the corporation at its principal office. Such a notice is effective when it is received. Such notice may be given for a variety of purposes under the act, *e.g.*, notice of a demand to inspect books and records (Section 16.02), and notices of resignation (Sections 8.07 and 8.43). This method of giving notice to the corporation, however, is not exclusive, and an officer, director, member of a designated body, or member of the corporation may give notice in other ways as well.

Persons who have no prior relationship with the corporation may give notice either to the registered agent of the corporation or, if they wish, to the corporation or its secretary at its principal office.

3. Miscellaneous Provisions

Section 1.41 also contains a variety of general provisions dealing with notice. It recognizes, for example, that notice on some occasions may be given orally if that is reasonable under the circumstances, which could include oral notice through voicemail or other similar means. It also deals with situations where notice may be sought to be given to persons for whom no current address is available, or where personal notice is impractical. Notice delivered to the person's last known address is effective as described in Section 1.41(e) even though never actually received by the person. Section 1.41(b) also authorizes notice by publication in some circumstances, including radio, television, or other form of public broadcast communication.

Section 1.41(g) recognizes that other sections of the act prescribe specific notice requirements for particular situations—*e.g.*, service of process on a corporation's registered agent under Section 5.04—and that these specific requirements, rather than the general requirements of Section 1.41, control. Finally, the second sentence of Section 1.41(g) permits a corporation's articles of incorporation or bylaws to prescribe the corporation's own notice requirements, if they are not inconsistent with the general requirements of this section or specific requirements of other sections of the act.

Section 1.41(h)(2) makes clear that receipt of an electronic communication is not dependent on a person having notice that the record is in the person's system. Receipt occurs when the record reaches the designated system whether or not the recipient ever retrieves the record. The paper analog is the recipient who never reads a mail notice. Section 1.41(h)(3) provides legal certainty regarding the effect of an electronic acknowledgement. It only addresses the fact of receipt, not the quality of the content, nor whether the electronic record was read or "opened."

[Subchapter] E
REVIEW OF CONTESTED CORPORATE ACTION

§ 1.50. DEFINITIONS

(a) This [subchapter] applies to, and the term "corporate action" in this [subchapter] means, any of the following actions:
   (1) The election, appointment, designation, or other selection and the suspension, removal, or expulsion of members, delegates, directors, members of a designated body, or officers of a nonprofit corporation.
   (2) The taking of any action on any matter that is required under this [act] or under any other provision of law to be, or which under the articles of incorporation or bylaws may be, submitted for action to the members, delegates, directors, members of a designated body, or officers of a nonprofit corporation.

(b) The "court" referred to in this [subchapter] is the [*name or describe*] court [*of the county where the corporation's principal office (or, if none in this state, its registered office) is located*] [*of county*].

> *Source Note:* Subsection (a) patterned after 15 PA. CONS. STAT. § 5791 (2008). See also DEL. GCL §§ 211(c) and 225 (2008). Subsection (b) patterned after new § 1.26(b). Former Revised Model Nonprofit Corporation Act (1987), § 1.50 is now § 6.44.

CROSS-REFERENCES

"Delegates" defined, see § 1.40.

"Designated body" defined, see § 1.40.

"Members" defined, see § 1.40.

"Officers" defined, see § 1.40.

OFFICIAL COMMENT

The rights to seek judicial relief provided in this subchapter are available for all types of nonprofit corporations. It is expected, however, that the courts will use their discretion to avoid becoming overly entangled in the affairs of religious corporations.

§ 1.51. PROCEEDINGS PRIOR TO CORPORATE ACTION

(a) Where under applicable law or the articles of incorporation or bylaws of a nonprofit corporation there has been a failure to hold a meeting to take corporate action and the failure has continued for 30 days after the date designated or appropriate therefor, the court may summarily order a meeting to be held upon the application of [*the attorney general in the case of a charitable corporation or*] any person entitled, either alone or in conjunction with other persons similarly seeking relief under this section, to call a meeting to consider the corporate action in issue.

(b) The court may determine the right to vote at the meeting of persons claiming that right, may appoint an individual to hold the meeting under such orders and powers as the court may deem proper, and may take such action as may be required to give due notice of the meeting and convene and conduct the meeting in the interests of justice.

Source Note: Patterned after 15 PA. CONS. STAT. § 5792 (2008). See also DEL. GCL § 211(c) (2008). Compare Revised Model Nonprofit Corporation Act (1987) § 1.60.

CROSS-REFERENCES

"Corporate action" defined, see § 1.50.

OFFICIAL COMMENT

This section provides a way to conduct meetings or take corporate action when it is otherwise impractical or impossible to do so. For example, a corporation may have a quorum requirement that effectively prevents it from holding a meeting of members because of the difficulty of securing the required attendance of members. Or a corporation may have inaccurate records and be unable to identify its members or directors.

The power of the court to order a meeting under this section is discretionary. If the court decides to order a meeting, this section allows the court to order a meeting and frame the manner in which it is to be conducted even if it is necessary to dispense with otherwise applicable requirements of the articles of incorporation, bylaws, or the act.

§ 1.52. REVIEW OF CONTESTED CORPORATE ACTION

(a) Upon petition of a person whose status as, or whose rights or duties as, a member, delegate, director, member of a designated body, or officer of a corporation are or may be affected by any corporate action, the court may hear and determine the validity of the corporate action.

(b) The court may make such orders in any such case as may be just and proper, with power to enforce the production of any books, papers, and records of the corporation and other evidence that may relate to the issue. The court shall provide for notice of the pendency of the proceedings under this section to all persons affected thereby. If it is determined that no valid corporate action has been taken, the court may order a meeting to be held in accordance with Section 1.51.

(c) Subsection (a) shall not apply if a nonprofit corporation has provided in its articles of incorporation or bylaws for a means of resolving a challenge to a corporate action, but the court may enforce the articles or bylaws if appropriate.

Source Note: Subsections (a) and (b) patterned after 15 PA. CONS. STAT. § 5793 (2008). See also DEL. GCL § 225 (2008).

CROSS-REFERENCES

"Corporate action" defined, see § 1.50.

OFFICIAL COMMENT

This section provides an expeditious way to secure judicial review of corporate elections, the filling of corporate positions in other fashions, or the taking of action on matters such as fundamental transactions. The court has broad powers to fashion relief in the manner it considers appropriate.

§ 1.53. NOTICE TO ATTORNEY GENERAL [OPTIONAL]

The plaintiff in a proceeding under this [subchapter] must notify the attorney general within ten days after commencing the proceeding if it involves a charitable corporation.

Source Note: Patterned after Revised Model Nonprofit Corporation Act (1987) § 6.30(f).

CROSS-REFERENCES

"Charitable corporation" defined, see § 1.40.

OFFICIAL COMMENT

This section is marked optional for two reasons. As a general matter, an enacting state should consider whether the substance of the section would be better placed with the other provisions of its law relating to the powers and duties of the attorney general. See the Official Comment to Section 1.70. Even if an enacting state decides to retain a requirement of notice to the attorney general in this act, this section will not be needed if Section 1.70 is included in the state's version of the act.

Notice to the attorney general of a proceeding under this subchapter involving a charitable corporation gives the attorney general an opportunity to learn of and evaluate the dispute. This section does not require the attorney general to join an action under this subchapter and does not detract from the jurisdiction the attorney general may otherwise have in states adopting this act.

[Subchapter] F
RELIGIOUS CORPORATIONS

§ 1.60. SUBORDINATION TO CANON LAW

If religious doctrine or canon law governing the affairs of a nonprofit corporation is inconsistent with the provisions of this [act] on the same subject, the religious doctrine or canon law shall control to the extent required by the Constitution of the United States or the Constitution of [*name of state*] or both.

Source Note: Patterned after 15 PA. CONS. STAT. § 5107 (2008). Derived from Revised Model Nonprofit Corporation Act (1987) § 1.80.

CROSS-REFERENCES

"Nonprofit corporation" defined, see § 1.40.

OFFICIAL COMMENT

As a result of history, policy, and constitutional principles, religious corporations are entitled to protections not available to business or other nonprofit corporations. Courts have been reluctant to interfere with the internal affairs of religious organizations. They will not decide between conflicting religious doctrine or determine the "true" faith. However, courts have often decided internal property disputes by applying neutral principles of contract or corporate law to organizational documents of religious organizations. *See* Mansfield, *The Religious Clauses of the First Amendments and the Philosophy of the Constitution*, 72 CALIF. L. REV. 847 (1984); Ellman, "Driven from the Tribunal: Judicial Resolution of Internal Church Disputes, " 69 CAL. L. REV. 1378 (1981).

This reluctance is based in part on the First Amendment to the United States Constitution which provides: "Congress shall make no law respecting an establishment of religion, or prohibiting the free exercise thereof. . . ." The establishment clause applies to states, *Everson v. Board of Education*, 330 U.S. 1 (1947), as does the free exercise clause, *Cantwell v. Connecticut*, 310 U.S. 296 (1940). The act attempts to walk the thin line between the establishment clause and the free exercise clause. It allows religious corporations to be formed and gives them the same rights and privileges as other corporations. The act avoids interfering with the free exercise of religion by negating or allowing religious corporations to negate provisions of the act that might result in excessive entanglement in religious activities by the state. By limiting state intrusion, the act uses the least restrictive means to provide an orderly structure in which religious corporations can be formed and operate.

Section 1.60 is based on the recognition that some provisions of the act may conflict with religious doctrines or canon law protected by the United States Constitution or state constitutions. The exact scope of constitutional limitations is less than clear and is subject to debate. Section 1.60 overcomes this difficulty by providing that, to the extent canon law or religious doctrine applicable to a religious corporation sets forth provisions inconsistent with provisions of the act, the canon law or religious doctrine controls, but only to the extent required by the United States Constitution or applicable state constitutions.

While in one sense Section 1.60 simply states the obvious, it is helpful to remind those dealing with religious corporations that they must consider constitutional mandates. The approach of Section 1.60 also allows a case-by-case determination of difficult questions and automatically conforms the act to the opinions of the United States Supreme Court and applicable state courts.

[Subchapter] G [*Optional*]
ATTORNEY GENERAL

§ 1.70. NOTICE TO ATTORNEY GENERAL [OPTIONAL]

(a) The attorney general must be given notice of the commencement of any proceeding that this [act] authorizes the attorney general to bring but that has been commenced by another person.

(b) Whenever any provision of this [act] requires that notice be given to the attorney general before or after commencing a proceeding or permits the attorney general to commence a proceeding:

(1) if no proceeding has been commenced, the attorney general may take appropriate action including, but not limited to, seeking injunctive relief; and

(2) if a proceeding has been commenced by a person other than the attorney general, the attorney general, as of right, may intervene in such proceeding.

Source Note: Reenactment of Revised Model Nonprofit Corporation Act (1987) § 1.70.

CROSS-REFERENCES

Derivative actions, § 13.09.

Dissolution:

judicial, § 14.31.

voluntary, § 14.02.

Removal of directors, § 8.09.

Ultra-vires, § 3.04.

OFFICIAL COMMENT

This section is marked optional because an enacting state should consider whether the substance of the section would be better placed with the other provisions of its law relating to the powers and duties of the attorney general. If that approach is taken, the state should consider whether a cross-reference to that other statute should be added to this act.

Subsection (a) requires that the attorney general be given notice of any proceeding that could have been brought by the attorney general, but is commenced by another person. Subsection (b)(1) grants the attorney general independent authority to act when notice is required under subsection (a) or any other provision of this act. This carries out the policy implicit in such notice requirements by specifically empowering the attorney general to protect the public interest when it may be adversely affected. Subsection (b)(2) permits the attorney general to intervene in any proceeding that the attorney general could have commenced but that was brought by another person, such as a director or member. To protect the public interest, the attorney general may either commence a proceeding or intervene in a proceeding commenced by another person who is authorized to do so.

This section does not detract from the jurisdiction the attorney general may otherwise have in states adopting this act.

CHAPTER 2

Incorporation

§ 2.01. INCORPORATORS

One or more persons may act as the incorporators of a nonprofit corporation by delivering articles of incorporation to the secretary of state for filing.

> *Source Note:* Patterned after Model Business Corporation Act, 3d Ed. (2002), § 2.01. Reenactment of Revised Model Nonprofit Corporation Act (1987), § 2.01.

CROSS-REFERENCES

Articles of incorporation, see § 2.02.

"Deliver" defined, see § 1.40.

Effective time and date of filing, see § 1.23.

Filing and signature requirements, see § 1.20.

Filing fees, see § 1.22.

Organization of corporation by incorporators, see § 2.05.

"Person" defined, see § 1.40.

OFFICIAL COMMENT

The only functions of incorporators under the act are (1) to sign the articles of incorporation, (2) to deliver them for filing with the secretary of state, and (3) to complete the formation of the corporation to the extent set forth in Section 2.05. One or more "persons" may serve as incorporator; "person" is defined in Section 1.40 to include both individuals and entities; "entity" is also defined in that section to include corporations, unincorporated entities, trusts, estates, and governments.

The act also simplifies the formalities of signature and filing. The requirement in some state statutes that articles be acknowledged or verified has been eliminated. Also, the requirement that "duplicate originals" (each being executed as an original document) be submitted has been eliminated. The secretary of state may require under Section 1.20 that a filing made on paper include the signed original and an "exact or conformed" copy. Submission of copies of filings made electronically is not required.

§ 2.02. ARTICLES OF INCORPORATION

(a) The articles of incorporation must set forth:
- (1) a name for the nonprofit corporation that satisfies the requirements of Section 4.01;
- (2) the street address of the corporation's initial registered office and the name of its initial registered agent at that office;
- (3) that the corporation is incorporated under this [act]; and
- (4) the name of each incorporator.

(b) The articles of incorporation may set forth:
- (1) the names of the individuals who are to serve as the initial directors;
- (2) provisions creating one or more designated bodies;
- (3) the names of the initial members of a designated body;
- (4) whether the corporation will have members;
- (5) the names of the initial members, if any;
- (6) provisions not inconsistent with law regarding:
  - (i) the purpose or purposes for which the nonprofit corporation is organized;
  - (ii) managing the business and regulating the affairs of the corporation;
  - (iii) defining, limiting, and regulating the powers of the corporation, its board of directors, any designated body, and the members, if any;
  - (iv) the characteristics, qualifications, rights, limitations, and obligations attaching to each or any class of members; or
  - (v) the distribution of assets on dissolution;
- (7) any provision that this [act] requires or permits to be set forth in the articles or bylaws;
- (8) a provision permitting or making obligatory indemnification of a director for liability (as defined in Section 8.50(5)) to any person for any action taken, or any failure to take any action, as a director, except liability for:
  - (i) receipt of a financial benefit to which the director is not entitled;

(ii) an intentional infliction of harm;
(iii) a violation of Section 8.33; or
(iv) an intentional violation of criminal law; and

(9) provisions required if the corporation is to be exempt from taxation under federal, state, or local law.

(c) The liability of a director of a nonprofit corporation that is not a charitable corporation may be eliminated or limited by a provision of the articles of incorporation that a director shall not be liable to the corporation or its members for money damages for any action taken, or any failure to take any action, as a director, except liability for:

(1) the amount of a financial benefit received by the director to which the director is not entitled;
(2) an intentional infliction of harm;
(3) a violation of Section 8.33; or
(4) an intentional violation of criminal law.

(d) The articles of incorporation need not set forth any of the corporate powers enumerated in this [act].

(e) Provisions of the articles of incorporation may be made dependent upon facts objectively ascertainable outside the articles of incorporation in accordance with Section 1.20(c).

(f) See Sections 3.01(a) (purposes), 8.31(d) (standards of liability for directors) and 8.58(c) (variation of indemnification).

Source Note: Patterned after Model Business Corporation Act, 3d Ed. (2002), § 2.02. Derived from Revised Model Nonprofit Corporation Act (1987), § 2.02. Paragraphs (a)(3), (b)(2), (3), (5), (8)(v), (9), and (c)(5), and subsection (f) are new.

CROSS-REFERENCES

Amendment of articles, see Ch. 10A.

Bylaws, see § 2.06 and Ch. 10B.

Duration of corporate existence, see § 3.02.

Filing and signature requirements, see § 1.20.

Filing fees, see § 1.22.

Incorporators, see § 2.01.

Indemnification, see Subch. 8E.

Powers, see § 3.02.

Purposes, see § 3.01.

Restated articles, see § 10.07.

OFFICIAL COMMENT

1. Introduction

Section 2.02(a) sets forth the minimum mandatory requirements for all articles of incorporation, while Section 2.02(b) describes optional provisions that may be included. A nonprofit corporation that is formed solely pursuant to the mandatory requirements will generally have the broadest powers and least restrictions on activities permitted by the act.

No reference is made in Section 2.02(a) to the period of duration of the corporation. A corporation formed under these provisions will automatically have perpetual duration under Section 3.02 unless a special provision is included providing a shorter period.

2. Requirements

The only information required in the articles of incorporation to form a "standard" nonprofit corporation based on the default rules in the act is:

(1) The name, which must meet the requirements of Chapter 4.

(2) The street address of the corporation's initial registered office and the name of its initial registered agent. A mailing address consisting only of a post office box is not sufficient.

(3) A statement that the corporation is incorporated under the act.

(4) The name of each incorporator.

No reference need be made in these "standard" articles to a variety of other matters that are referred to in the statutes of some states. Generally, no substantive effect should be given to the absence of a specific reference to such matters in Section 2.02 since they are referred to in other sections of the act which usually provide an "opt in" privilege that permits a corporation to elect special treatment if so desired.

Charitable corporations must comply with additional requirements imposed by Section 501(c)(3) of the Internal Revenue Code, such as the requirement that the corporation be organized for one or more purposes listed in that section and the requirement that there be limitations on the distributions of assets upon dissolution.

3. *Optional Provisions*

Section 2.02(b) describes specific options that may be elected by a nonprofit corporation and contains general authorization to include other provisions relevant to the authority of the corporation, its officers and board of directors, or to the management of the corporation's internal affairs. These provisions include:

A. INITIAL BOARD OF DIRECTORS

Under Section 2.02(b)(1) an election may be made to have a nonprofit corporation organized by a person or persons other than the incorporators. See the Official Comment to Section 2.05. These persons, described as "initial directors," may either remain in office or be replaced after the corporation is organized.

B. PURPOSE CLAUSE

The articles of incorporation must include a statement that the nonprofit corporation is incorporated for a nonprofit purpose. No further detail regarding the purpose of the corporation is required and if only the required statement of a nonprofit purpose is included the corporation will automatically have the purpose of engaging in any lawful business under Section 3.01(a).

Under Section 2.02(b)(6)(i), a nonprofit corporation may elect a limited purpose clause or provide for specific purposes without limiting the broad purposes provided in Section 3.01. Specific purposes may be needed, among other reasons, for qualification in certain domestic and foreign jurisdictions, to obtain tax-exempt status, or to obtain licenses. The corporation may also wish to define its mission.

C. DURATION

Under current practice nearly every nonprofit corporation is formed with perpetual duration, but a corporation may elect a shorter duration under Section 2.02(b)(7).

D. CORPORATE POWERS

Section 2.02(d) makes it unnecessary to set forth any corporate powers in the articles. Section 3.02 grants every nonprofit corporation essentially the same power that an individual possesses with respect to his or her affairs. This grant of power, however, may be considered overbroad for certain corporations; if so, it may be qualified or narrowed by appropriate provisions in the articles.

E. MANAGEMENT OF THE CORPORATION GENERALLY

Under Section 2.02(b)(6)(ii) and (iii) a nonprofit corporation may include any provision not inconsistent with law for "managing the business and regulating the affairs of the corporation" and "defining, limiting, and regulating the powers of the corporation, its board of directors, any designated body, and the members." This language is designed to allow the corporation to place in the articles any number of miscellaneous provisions that it considers sufficiently important to be of public record or, in the case of a membership corporation, subject to amendment only by the processes applicable to amendments of articles of incorporation which generally require member approval.

The responsibility of the board of directors to manage the affairs of a nonprofit corporation includes both a decision-making function and an oversight function. See Section 8.01. In recent years the oversight function of the board of directors has become increasingly prominent. References throughout the act to the management of the affairs of a corporation, such as in Section 2.02(b)(6)(ii), include the oversight function of the board.

F. SELF-DEALING TRANSACTIONS

When subsidiaries or corporate joint ventures are being formed, special consideration should be given to the inclusion of provisions designed to limit or avoid the unexpected application of the doctrines of corporate opportunity and conflict of interest. While this type of clause will not provide total protection, it may be given limited effect, for example, by shifting the burden of proving unfairness or "exonerating" an arrangement from "adverse influences."

Charitable corporations must carefully review joint ventures and similar transactions for compliance with the provisions of laws applicable to charitable corporations, including the Internal Revenue Code.

G. DIRECTOR LIABILITY

Section 2.02(c) authorizes the inclusion in the articles of incorporation of a nonprofit corporation that is not a charitable corporation of a provision eliminating or limiting, with certain exceptions, the liability of the directors to the corporation or its members for money damages. This grant of authority to the members is consistent with the more general authorization of Section 2.02(b)(6)(ii) for the articles to include a wide range of provisions regulating various matters affecting the corporation, including allocating power between the directors and the members. Developments in the mid- and late 1980s highlighted the need to permit reasonable protection of directors from exposure to personal liability, in addition to indemnification, so that directors would not be discouraged from fully and freely carrying out their duties, including responsible entrepreneurial risk-taking. These developments included increased costs and reduced availability of director and officer liability insurance, the decision of the Delaware Supreme Court in *Smith v. Van Gorkom*, 488 A.2d 858 (1985), and the resulting reluctance of qualified individuals to serve as directors.

Section 2.02(c) only applies to nonprofit corporations that are not charitable corporations. Inclusion of the type of provision authorized by Section 2.02(c) in the articles of incorporation of a charitable corporation is not necessary because the same liability shield is provided for directors of a charitable corporation by Section 8.31(d). The prior act did not provide an automatic liability shield for directors of charitable corporations, and thus the articles of most charitable corporations incorporated under the prior act will have the type of provision authorized by Section 2.02(c). It is not necessary to delete such a provision. When this act takes effect in a state, the liability shield in Section 8.31(d) will become applicable to those charitable corporations incorporated under the prior act that did not include a liability shield in their articles. Encouraging individuals to serve as directors of charitable corporations by shielding them from liability for service in that capacity was considered appropriate as a matter of public policy, even if their corporation had not previously chosen to do so.

So long as any such liability-limitation provision does not extend to liability to third parties, members should be permitted—except when important societal values are at stake—to decide how to allocate the economic risk of the directors' conduct between the nonprofit corporation and the directors. Because members of a corporation that is not a charitable corporation may have a financial interest in the corporation, members of one corporation may view the issue substantially differently than members of another corporation. Accordingly, Section 2.02(c) is optional rather than self-executing. In addition, it follows the path of virtually all the states that have adopted charter option statutes and is applicable only to money damages and not to equitable relief. Likewise, nothing in Section 2.02(c) in any way affects the right of the members to remove directors under Section 8.08(a), with or without cause.

The language "any action taken, or any failure to take any action, as a director" parallels Section 8.31(d). The phrase "as a director" emphasizes that Section 2.02(c) applies to a director's actions or failures to take action in his or her capacity as a director and not in any other capacity, such as officer, employee, or controlling member. However, it is not intended to exclude coverage of conduct by individuals, even though they are officers, when they are acting in their capacity as directors.

Because adoption of a liability-limitation provision is left to the decision of the members, they are given considerable latitude in the extent to which they are permitted to limit directors' liability. Accordingly, the exceptions to the statute are few and narrow. As important as validating the members' right to determine for themselves the extent of the directors' liability is stating the limits of this right in terms promoting a clear understanding of the conduct which is and which is not included in the limitation of liability. Terms such as "duty of loyalty," "good faith," "bad faith," and "recklessness" seem no more precise than (and therefore as potentially expansive as) "gross negligence." All of these formulations are characterizations of conduct rather than definitions of it. Characterizations by nature tend to be more elastic than definitions.

Directors should be afforded reasonable predictability; they are entitled to know whether a contemplated course of action will result in personal liability for money damages. Limits on their exculpation from liability are appropriate but should be expressed in terms that minimize the opportunity for after-the-fact second-guessing.

The language of the exceptions to Section 2.02(c) is intended to express the parameters of the members' right to limit the directors' liability in terms that will promote predictability. First, some types of improper conduct are so clearly without any societal benefit that the law should not appear to endorse such conduct, especially in the case of a state-created entity such as a nonprofit corporation. Second, any liability limitation will be prospective and, therefore, by definition, the members will not be able to know in advance the exact nature or extent of any claims that they may be giving up. Third, the public has an interest in encouraging good corporate governance. While the exceptions to the members' right to limit liability are few and narrow, they validate important standards of conduct. Finally, in many cases, there will be members who do not vote in favor of the liability limitation. For these members, there should be an irreducible core of protection, especially in view of the fact that, in some cases, the votes of the directors themselves as members may be sufficient to approve adoption of the provision.

Financial Benefit

If Section 2.01(c) (and by analogy Section 8.31(d)) were to permit limitation of the liability of a director for receipt of a financial benefit to which the director is not entitled, that would validate conduct in which the director could realize a personal gain. Corporate law has long subjected transactions from which a director could benefit personally to special scrutiny. The exception is limited, however, to the amount of the benefit actually received. Thus, liability for punitive damages could be eliminated. However, punitive damages are not eliminated in either the exception for infliction of harm or for violation of criminal law and, thus, in a particular case (for example, theft), punitive damages may be available. The benefit must be financial rather than in less easily measurable and more conjectural forms, such as business goodwill, personal reputation, or social ingratiation. The phrase "received by a director" is not intended to be a "bright line." As a director's conduct moves toward the edge of what may be exculpated, the director should bear the risk of miscalculation. Depending upon the circumstances, a director may be deemed to have received a benefit that the director caused to be directed to another person, for example, a relative, friend, or affiliate. The conduct of directors of charitable corporations is subject to regulation under the Internal Revenue Code and, possibly, other state laws. Such regulation may vary from the standards and restrictions specified in this act.

Intentional Infliction of Harm

There may be situations in which a director intentionally causes harm to a nonprofit corporation or its members even though the director does not receive any improper benefit. The use of the word "intentional," rather than a less precise term such as "knowing," is meant to refer to the specific intent to perform, or fail to perform, the acts with actual knowledge that the director's action, or failure to act, will cause harm, rather than a general intent to perform the acts which cause the harm. No public policy should permit the members to eliminate or limit the liability of directors for conduct intended to cause harm to the corporation or its members.

Intentional Violation of Criminal Law

Historically, the criminal law has represented society's statement of the conduct that it most emphatically rejects. Accordingly, even though a director committing a crime may intend to benefit the nonprofit corporation, the members should not be permitted to exculpate the director for any harm caused by the director's crime, including, for example, fines and legal expenses of the corporation in defending a criminal prosecution. The use of the word "intentional," rather than a less precise term such as "knowing," is meant to refer to the specific intent to perform, or fail to perform, the acts with actual knowledge that the director's action, or failure to act, constitutes a violation of criminal law.

In order to recover for conduct included within any of the exceptions, the plaintiff will continue to be required to establish causation, damages, and other elements imposed by applicable law.

An amendment authorized by Section 2.02(c) will become effective in the manner provided by Section 1.23 generally for amendments to the articles of incorporation. In addition, in accordance with Section 10.09, an amendment under Section 2.02(c) will not affect a cause of action existing in favor of the nonprofit corporation against any directors at the effective time of the amendment.

H. INDEMNIFICATION

Section 2.02(b)(8) permits a nonprofit corporation to include in its articles of incorporation a provision authorizing permissible or mandatory indemnification of a director in accordance with Section 8.51(a)(2). Section 2.02(b)(8) specifically excepts liability arising out of improper financial benefit received by a director, an intentional infliction of harm on the corporation or the members, an unlawful distribution, or an intentional violation of criminal law. These excepted liabilities parallel those a corporation is not permitted to limit or eliminate under Section 2.02(c). See "Director liability," above. Officers are not included in the language of Section 2.02(b)(8) because, as provided in Section 8.56, mandatory indemnification of officers does not require a provision in the articles of incorporation.

Unlike the liability shield provided automatically for directors of a charitable corporation by Section 8.31(d), the act does not automatically provide for indemnification of directors of a charitable corporation. Thus, the option of taking advantage of Section 2.02(b)(8) should be evaluated by both charitable corporations and other nonprofit corporations.

4. *Provisions That May Be Elected Only in the Articles of Incorporation*

Unlike the prior act, which followed the pattern of many business corporation laws and provided that provisions on certain subjects could be placed in either the articles of incorporation or the bylaws while provisions on other subjects could be placed only in the articles, this act permits most subjects to be addressed in either the articles or the bylaws. The only subjects that may be addressed only in the articles and not in the bylaws are limitations on the purposes or powers of a nonprofit corporation. See Sections 3.01 and 3.02.

§ 2.03. INCORPORATION

(a) Unless a delayed effective date is specified, the corporate existence begins when the articles of incorporation are filed.

(b) The filing of the articles of incorporation by the secretary of state is conclusive proof that the incorporators satisfied all conditions precedent to incorporation except in a proceeding by the state to cancel or revoke the incorporation or involuntarily dissolve the nonprofit corporation.

Source Note: Patterned after Model Business Corporation Act, 3d Ed. (2002), § 2.03. Reenactment of Revised Model Nonprofit Corporation Act (1987), § 2.03.

CROSS-REFERENCES

Duration, see § 3.02.

Effective time and date of filing, see § 1.23.

Filing fees, see § 1.22.

Filing requirements, see § 1.20.

Secretary of state's filing duty, see § 1.25.

OFFICIAL COMMENT

Section 2.03(a) provides that the existence of a nonprofit corporation begins when the articles of incorporation are filed, unless a delayed effective date is specified under Section 1.23. Chapter 1 contains detailed rules for the processing and effective dates of filings, all of which are applicable to articles of incorporation and other filings. These filing rules simplify the process of creating a corporation in several respects.

Section 1.25 provides that the secretary of state files the articles by marking them "filed" and recording the date and time of receipt. The secretary of state does not issue a separate certificate of incorporation, as was the older practice still followed in some states.

Section 2.03(a) ties the precise time of incorporation to the effective date and time of the filed articles. Section 1.23 provides in turn that this is the date and time the articles are received by the secretary of state; in other words, consistent with the practice of many secretaries of state, processing time is ignored and the date and time of receipt of the articles are the date and time of incorporation. The creators of the nonprofit corporation may, however, specify that the corporation's existence will begin on a later date than the date of filing, and at a precise time on such a date, to the extent permitted by Section 1.23.

Under Section 2.03(b) the filing of the articles of incorporation is conclusive proof that all conditions precedent to incorporation have been met, except in proceedings brought by the state. Thus the filing of the articles of incorporation is conclusive as to the existence of limited liability for persons who enter into transactions on behalf of the nonprofit corporation. If articles of incorporation have not been filed, Section 2.04 generally imposes personal liability on all persons who prematurely act as or on behalf of a "corporation" knowing that articles have not been filed. Section 2.04 may protect some of these persons to a limited extent, however; see the Official Comment to that section.

§ 2.04. LIABILITY FOR PREINCORPORATION TRANSACTIONS

All persons purporting to act as or on behalf of a nonprofit corporation, knowing there was no incorporation under this [act], are jointly and severally liable for all liabilities created while so acting.

Source Note: Patterned after Model Business Corporation Act, 3d Ed. (2002), § 2.04. Reenactment of Revised Model Nonprofit Corporation Act (1987), § 2.04.

CROSS-REFERENCES

Incorporation, see § 2.03.

"Person" defined, see § 1.40.

OFFICIAL COMMENT

The statutes of some states provide that corporate existence begins only with the acceptance of articles of incorporation by the secretary of state. Some states also have statutes that provide expressly that those who prematurely act as or on behalf of a nonprofit corporation are personally liable on all transactions entered into or liabilities incurred before incorporation. A review of recent case law indicates, however, that even in states with such statutes courts have continued to rely on common law concepts of de facto corporations, de jure corporations, and corporations by estoppel that provide uncertain protection against liability for preincorporation transactions.

Incorporation under modern statutes is so simple and inexpensive that a strong argument may be made that nothing short of filing articles of incorporation should create the privilege of limited liability. A number of situations have arisen, however, in which the protection of limited liability arguably should be recognized even though the simple incorporation process established by modern statutes has not been completed.

(1) The strongest factual pattern for immunizing participants from personal liability occurs in cases in which the participant honestly and reasonably but erroneously believed the articles had been filed. In *Cranson v. International Business Machines Corp.*, 234 Md. 477, 200 A.2d 33 (1964), for example, the defendant had been shown executed articles of incorporation some months earlier before he invested in the corporation and became an officer and director. He was also told by the corporation's attorney that the articles had been filed, but in fact they had not been filed because of a mix-up in the attorney's office. The defendant was held not liable on the "corporate" obligation.

(2) Another class of cases, which is less compelling, but in which the participants sometimes have escaped personal liability, involves the defendant who mails in articles of incorporation and then enters into a transaction in the corporate name; either the letter is delayed or the secretary of state's office refuses to file the articles after receiving them or returns them for correction. *See, e.g.*, *Cantor v. Sunshine Greenery, Inc.*, 165 N.J. Super. 411, 398 A.2d 571 (1979). Many state filing agencies adopt the practice of treating the date of receipt as the date of filing even though the review process may result in the completion of the filing process sometime after original receipt of the filing. The finding of nonliability in cases of this second type can be considered an extension of this principle by treating the date of original receipt and filing as the date of incorporation.

(3) A third class of cases in which the participants sometimes have escaped personal liability involves situations where the third person has urged immediate execution

of the contract in the corporate name even though he knows that the other party has not taken any steps toward incorporating. *See, e.g., Quaker Hill, Inc. v. Parr*, 148 Colo. 45, 364 P.2d 1056 (1961).

(4) In another class of cases the defendant has represented that a corporation exists and entered into a contract in the corporate name knowing that no corporation has been formed, either because no attempt has been made to file articles of incorporation or because the defendant has already received rejected articles of incorporation from the filing agency. In these cases, the third person has dealt solely with the "corporation" and has not relied on the personal assets of the defendant. The imposition of personal liability in this class of case, it has sometimes been argued, gives the plaintiff more than originally bargained for. On the other hand, to recognize limited liability in this situation threatens to undermine the incorporation process, since one then may obtain limited liability by consistently conducting business in the corporate name. Most courts have imposed personal liability in this situation. *See, e.g., Robertson v. Levy*, 197 A.2d 443 (D.C. 1964).

After a review of these situations, it seemed appropriate to impose liability only on persons who act as or on behalf of corporations "knowing" that no corporation exists. Analogous protection has long been accorded under the uniform limited partnership acts to limited partners who contribute capital to a partnership in the erroneous belief that a limited partnership certificate has been filed.

While no special provision is made in Section 2.04, the section does not foreclose the possibility that persons who urge defendants to execute contracts in the corporate name knowing that no steps to incorporate have been taken may be estopped to impose personal liability on individual defendants. This estoppel may be based on the inequity perceived when persons, unwilling or reluctant to enter into a commitment under their own name, are persuaded to use the name of a nonexistent nonprofit corporation, and then are sought to be held personally liable under Section 2.04 by the party advocating that form of execution. By contrast, persons who knowingly participate in a business under a corporate name are jointly and severally liable on "corporate" obligations under Section 2.04 and may not argue that plaintiffs are "estopped" from holding them personally liable because all transactions were conducted on a corporate basis.

By its terms, this section only applies when persons purport to act as or on behalf of a nonprofit corporation. Thus, this section will not affect the personal liability of persons purporting to act as or on behalf of some other form of entity, such as an unincorporated nonprofit association or limited liability company. Personal liability in those situations will be determined under other law applicable to the type of entity involved.

§ 2.05. ORGANIZATION OF CORPORATION

(a) After incorporation:

(1) if initial directors or members of a designated body are named in the articles of incorporation, those persons must hold an organizational meeting, as appropriate, at the call of a majority of them, to complete the organization of the nonprofit corporation by electing directors (when the organization of the corporation is to be completed by a designated body), appointing officers, adopting bylaws, and carrying on any other business brought before the meeting;

(2) if initial directors or members of a designated body are not named in the articles, the incorporator or incorporators must hold an organizational meeting at the call of a majority of the incorporators:

(i) to elect directors and complete the organization of the nonprofit corporation; or

(ii) to elect a board of directors who shall complete the organization of the corporation.

(b) Action required or permitted by this [act] to be taken by incorporators at an organizational meeting may be taken without a meeting if the action taken is evidenced by one or more consents in the form of a record describing the action taken and signed by each incorporator.

(c) An organizational meeting may be held in or out of this state.

Source Note: Patterned after Model Business Corporation Act, 3d Ed. (2002), § 2.05. Reenactment of Revised Model Nonprofit Corporation Act (1987), § 2.05.

CROSS-REFERENCES

Articles of incorporation, see § 2.02.

Bylaws, see § 2.06.

Director action without meeting, see § 8.21.

Incorporators, see § 2.01.

OFFICIAL COMMENT

Following incorporation, the organization of a new nonprofit corporation must be completed so that it may engage in its activities. This usually requires adoption of bylaws, the appointment of officers and agents, and the election of a board of directors or designated body.

Earlier versions of the act required initial directors to be named in the articles and provided that they complete the organization of the nonprofit corporation. Many states followed this pattern, but others provided that the incorporators organize the corporation or meet to elect a board of directors to organize the corporation. The goal of all these provisions was usually to permit the completion of the organization of the corporation with minimum expense and formality, although in many cases it was felt necessary for substantive decisions to be made at an early stage by the persons with responsibility for operation of the corporation.

Section 2.05 simplifies the formation process by allowing alternative methods of completing the formation of the nonprofit corporation.

First, Section 2.05(a)(1) contemplates that if initial directors or members of a designated body are named in the articles of incorporation, the persons so named will organize the nonprofit corporation. It is expected that these persons will be named only if they will remain in office and there is no objection to the disclosure of their identity in the articles of incorporation.

Second, Section 2.05(a)(2) provides that the incorporators may themselves complete the organization, or they may simply meet to elect a board of directors who are then to complete the organization.

Sections 2.05(b) and (c) are limited to meetings of incorporators, since Sections 8.21 and 8.22 permit the same actions by the board of directors. If a meeting of members is necessary, Sections 7.01 and 7.04 give them the same flexibility that is given incorporators under Sections 2.05(b) and (c).

The provisions of Section 2.05(a)(2) also apply to a designated body under Section 8.12. Thus if neither directors nor members of a designated body are named in the articles of incorporation, Section 2.05(a)(2) will permit a designated body to hold an organizational meeting to complete whatever steps in the organization of the nonprofit corporation require action by the designated body.

An organizational action by the incorporators, the board of directors, or a designated body may be taken without a meeting, if the action taken is evidenced by one or more signed consents in the form of a record describing the action taken.

§ 2.06. BYLAWS

(a) The incorporators or the board of directors of a nonprofit corporation may adopt initial bylaws for the corporation.

(b) The bylaws of a nonprofit corporation may contain any provision for managing the activities and regulating the affairs of the corporation that is not inconsistent with law or the articles of incorporation.

Source Note: Patterned after Model Business Corporation Act, 3d Ed. (2002), § 2.06. Reenactment of Revised Model Nonprofit Corporation Act (1987), § 2.06. Revised Model Nonprofit Corporation Act (1987), § 2.07 regarding emergency bylaws omitted as unnecessary in light of § 3.03 and otherwise obsolete.

CROSS-REFERENCES

Amendment, see Subch. 10B.

Organizing corporation, see § 2.05.

OFFICIAL COMMENT

The responsibility for adopting the original bylaws is placed on the person or persons completing the organization of the nonprofit corporation. The powers of the board of directors under this section may be exercised by a designated body pursuant to Section 8.12.

The power to amend or repeal bylaws, or adopt new bylaws after the formation of the corporation is completed, is addressed in Subchapter 10B.

The responsibility of the board of directors to manage the affairs of a nonprofit corporation includes both a decision-making function and an oversight function. See Section 8.01. In recent years the oversight function of the board of directors has become increasingly prominent. References throughout the act to the management of the affairs of a corporation, such as in Section 2.06(b), include the oversight function of the board.

CHAPTER 3

Purposes and Powers

§ 3.01. PURPOSES

(a) Every nonprofit corporation has the purpose of engaging in any lawful activity unless a more limited purpose is set forth in the articles of incorporation.

(b) A corporation engaging in an activity that is subject to regulation under another statute of this state may incorporate under this [act] only if incorporating under this [act] is not prohibited by the other statute. The corporation shall be subject to all the limitations of the other statute.

Source Note: Patterned after Model Business Corporation Act, 3d Ed. (2002) § 3.01. Substantially a reenactment of Revised Model Nonprofit Corporation Act (1987) § 3.01.

CROSS-REFERENCES

"Articles of incorporation" defined, see § 1.40.

Foreign corporations, see § 15.05.

Statement of purpose in articles, see § 2.02.

OFFICIAL COMMENT

Section 3.01(a) provides that every nonprofit corporation automatically has the purpose of engaging in any lawful activity unless a narrower purpose is described in the articles of incorporation.

While Section 3.01 does not impose any limitations on the purposes of a nonprofit corporation or the use of its assets, those forming a nonprofit corporation may limit the corporate purposes in the articles of incorporation. Such limitations may be added to obtain tax-exempt status, to attract significant contributions, or to provide a limited purpose for the corporation.

The limited scope of the ultra vires concept in litigation between the nonprofit corporation and outsiders means that a third person entering into a transaction that violates the restrictions in the purpose clause may be able to enforce the transaction in accordance with its terms if the person was unaware of the narrow purpose clause when entering into the transaction. See the Official Comment to Section 3.04.

Section 3.01(b) is designed to tie in the limitless lawful purpose corporation permitted by Section 3.01(a) with the numerous state statutes that impose regulations or limitations on corporations engaging in certain activities. Many nonprofit corporations are subject to those types of regulations or limitations. Hospitals, colleges, secondary schools, and health maintenance organizations, for example, are subject to extensive regulation.

Charitable corporations must comply with additional requirements imposed by Section 501(c)(3) of the Internal Revenue Code such as the requirement that the charitable corporation be organized for one or more of the purposes listed in that section and the requirement that there be limitations on the distributions of assets upon dissolution.

§ 3.02. GENERAL POWERS

Unless its articles of incorporation provide otherwise, every nonprofit corporation has perpetual duration and succession in its corporate name and has the same powers as an individual to do all things necessary or convenient to carry out its affairs including, without limitation, power:

(1) to sue and be sued, complain and defend in its corporate name;
(2) to have a corporate seal, which may be altered at will, and to use it, or a facsimile of it, by impressing or affixing it or in any other manner reproducing it;
(3) to make and amend bylaws, not inconsistent with its articles of incorporation or with the laws of this state, for managing and regulating the affairs of the corporation;
(4) to purchase, receive, lease, or otherwise acquire, and own, hold, improve, use, and otherwise deal with, real or personal property, or any legal or equitable interest in property, wherever located;
(5) to sell, convey, mortgage, pledge, lease, exchange, and otherwise dispose of all or any part of its property;
(6) to purchase, receive, subscribe for, or otherwise acquire, own, hold, vote, use, sell, mortgage, lend, pledge, or other-

wise dispose of, and deal in and with shares or other interests in, or obligations of, any other entity;

(7) to make contracts and guarantees, incur liabilities, borrow money, issue notes, bonds, and other obligations, and secure any of its obligations by mortgage or pledge of any of its property or income;

(8) to lend money, invest and reinvest its funds, and receive and hold real and personal property as security for repayment[, *except as limited by Section 8.32*];

(9) to be a promoter, partner, member, associate, or manager of any partnership, joint venture, trust, or other entity;

(10) to conduct its activities, locate offices, and exercise the powers granted by this [act] within or without this state;

(11) to elect directors and appoint officers, employees, and agents of the corporation, define their duties, fix their compensation, and lend them money and credit[, *except as limited by Section 8.32*];

(12) to pay pensions and establish pension plans, pension trusts, and benefit or incentive plans for any or all of its current or former directors, officers, employees, and agents;

(13) to make donations for charitable purposes;

(14) to impose dues, assessments, admission, and transfer fees on its members;

(15) to establish conditions for admission of members, admit members, and issue memberships;

(16) to carry on a business; and

(17) to make payments or donations, or do any other act, not inconsistent with law, that furthers the purposes, activities, and affairs of the corporation.

Source Note: Patterned after Model Business Corporation Act, 3d Ed. (2002) § 3.02. Substantially a reenactment of Revised Model Nonprofit Corporation Act (1987) § 3.02.

CROSS-REFERENCES

Bylaws, see §§ 2.06, 10.20.

Compensation of directors, see § 8.11.

Debt and security interests, see § 6.43.

Disposition of assets, see Ch. 12.

"Employee" defined, see § 1.40.

"Entity" defined, see § 1.40.

Foreign corporations, see § 15.05.

Indemnification, see Subch. 8E.

"Members" defined, see § 1.40.

"Membership" defined, see § 1.40.

Ultra vires, see § 3.04.

OFFICIAL COMMENT

The law of corporations has always proceeded on the fundamental assumption that corporations are creations with limited power; such an assumption was articulated by the United States Supreme Court as early as 1804, *Head & Armory v. Providence Insurance Co.*, 6 U.S. (2 Cranch) 127, 169 (1804), and appears never to have been seriously questioned as a judicial matter.

It is clear that narrow and limited powers clauses are undesirable: they encourage litigation by bringing into question reasonable transactions that further the activities and interests of the corporation and to the extent transactions are unauthorized, may defeat valid and reasonable expectations. The history of many state statutes in this area is largely one ensuring that corporate powers are broad enough to cover all reasonable transactions. The issue of corporate powers must be distinguished from corporate purposes. A limitation on the purposes of a nonprofit corporation may be desirable, for example, to obtain tax-exempt status.

In developing Section 3.02, serious consideration was given to whether there was a continued need for a long list of corporate powers or whether a general provision granting every nonprofit corporation power to act to the same extent as an individual might be substituted. Because of the long history of these powers, it was feared that no matter how broadly phrased a general provision might be, a court might conclude that some power might not exist because no specific reference to it was made in the statute. It was also feared that cautious attorneys might begin to restore power clauses to articles of incorporation out of concern that a general clause of the type in question might not be interpreted literally. Hence, this section retains a general clause granting the corporation essentially the same powers as an individual, coupled with a nonexclusive listing of powers, including the traditional power clauses that appear in many state statutes.

The general philosophy of Section 3.02 is thus that nonprofit corporations formed under the act should be automatically authorized to engage in all acts and have all powers that an individual may have. Because broad grants of power of this nature may not be desired in some nonprofit corporations, Section 3.02 generally authorizes articles of incorporation to deny or limit specific powers to a specific corporation if that is felt desirable. Limitations may be imposed to obtain federal or state tax status, because a donor or grantor wishes to limit the activities of a corporation, or for some other reason. Illustrative of the powers that may be appropriate for limitation in specific corporations are the powers to make political contributions or to make expenditures to influence elections to the extent permitted by law.

The responsibility of the board of directors to manage the affairs of a nonprofit corporation includes both a decision-making function and an oversight function. See Section 8.01. In recent years the oversight function of the board of directors has become increasingly prominent. References throughout the act to the management of the affairs of a corporation, such as in Section 3.02(3), include the oversight function of the board.

The optional provisions of Section 3.02(8) and (11) should be used if loans to directors and officers are prohibited. The prior version of the act included as Section 8.32 an outright prohibition on loans to directors and officers. Section 8.32 has been made optional in the current version of the act because the approach to this issue varies among the states. Some states prohibit loans to directors and officers, while other states leave the wisdom and propriety of such loans to be evaluated on the basis of general fiduciary standards. A nonprofit corporation organized under the law of a state that does not prohibit loans to directors and officers should use particular care to ensure that any such loans serve a valid corporate purpose.

While Section 3.02(16) permits a nonprofit corporation to carry on any lawful business without restriction, nonprofit corporations need to be mindful that carrying on certain types of business can jeopardize their exempt status.

Section 3.02(17) permits payments or donations or other acts "that further the purposes, activities, and affairs of the corporation." This clause, which is in addition to and independent of the power to make charitable and similar donations under Section 3.02(13), permits contributions for purposes that may not be charitable, such as for political purposes or to influence elections. This power exists only to the extent consistent with law other than the act. For example, many states prohibit corporations of all types from making political contributions. It is the purpose of this section to authorize all corporate actions that are lawful or not against public policy.

The powers of a nonprofit corporation under the act exist independently of whether the corporation has a broad or narrow purpose clause. A corporation with a narrow purpose clause nevertheless has the same powers as an individual to do all things necessary or convenient to carry out its activities. Many actions are therefore intra vires even though they do not directly affect the limited purpose for which the corporation is formed. In some instances, however, a limited or narrow purpose clause may be considered to be a restriction on corporate powers as well as a restriction on purposes. Since the same ultra vires rule is applicable to corporations that exceed their purposes or powers (see the Official Comment to Section 3.04), it is not necessary to determine whether a narrow purpose clause also limits the powers of the corporation but simply whether the purpose of the transaction in question is consistent with the purpose clause. Of course, these issues cannot arise in corporations with an "any lawful activity" purpose clause.

§ 3.03. EMERGENCY POWERS

(a) In anticipation of or during an emergency, the board of directors of a nonprofit corporation may:
   (1) modify lines of succession to accommodate the incapacity of any director, officer, employee, or agent; and
   (2) relocate the principal office, designate alternative principal offices or regional offices, or authorize the officers to do so.

(b) During an emergency, unless the articles of incorporation or bylaws provide otherwise:
   (1) notice of a meeting of the board of directors need be given only to those directors it is practicable to reach and may be given in any practicable manner; and
   (2) one or more officers of the nonprofit corporation present at a meeting of the board of directors may be deemed to be directors for the meeting, in order of rank and within the same rank in order of seniority.

(c) Corporate action taken in good faith during an emergency to further the ordinary affairs of the nonprofit corporation:
   (1) binds the corporation; and
   (2) may not be used to impose liability on a director, officer, employee, or agent.

(d) An emergency exists for purposes of this section if a quorum of the directors cannot readily be assembled because of some catastrophic event.

Source Note: Patterned after Model Business Corporation Act, 3d Ed. (2002) § 3.03. Substantially a reenactment of Revised Model Nonprofit Corporation Act (1987) § 3.03.

CROSS-REFERENCES

Corporate powers, see § 3.02.

"Notice" defined, see § 1.41.

Notice of directors' meeting, see § 8.22.

"Principal office" defined, see § 1.40.

OFFICIAL COMMENT

Section 3.03 grants every corporation limited powers to act in an emergency.

An "emergency" for purposes of Section 3.03 is defined in subsection (d) as any catastrophic event that makes it difficult or impossible to assemble a quorum of directors. In this situation, Section 3.03(b) dispenses with or relaxes notice requirements and permits corporate officers to serve as directors in order to achieve a quorum. The section also authorizes the board of directors, either before or during an emergency, to modify lines of succession and relocate the principal business office of the corporation. These actions may be taken only by the board of directors at a meeting at which a quorum is present after giving effect, if necessary, to Section 3.03(b).

These minimal provisions, it is believed, should permit a corporation to continue to function in the face of an emergency.

What constitutes notice in a practicable manner, as required by Section 3.03(b)(1), will depend on the nature of the emergency. In appropriate circumstances, practicable notice may involve the use of radio or publication, while in other circumstances more direct notice may be practicable.

§ 3.04. ULTRA VIRES

(a) Except as provided in subsection (b), the validity of corporate action may not be challenged on the ground that the nonprofit corporation lacks or lacked power to act.

(b) The power of a nonprofit corporation to act may be challenged:

(1) in a derivative proceeding under [Chapter] 13 by a member, director, or member of a designated body against the corporation to enjoin the act;

(2) in a proceeding by the corporation, directly, derivatively, or through a receiver, trustee, or other legal representative, against an incumbent or former director or member of a designated body, officer, employee, or agent of the corporation; or

(3) in a proceeding by the attorney general under Section 14.30.

(c) In a proceeding by a member, director, or member of a designated body under subsection (b)(1) to enjoin an unauthorized corporate act, the court may enjoin or set aside the act, if equitable and if all affected persons are parties to the proceeding, and may award damages for loss (other than anticipated profits) suffered by the corporation or another party because of enjoining the unauthorized act.

Source Note: Patterned after Model Business Corporation Act, 3d Ed. (2002) § 3.04. Derived from Revised Model Nonprofit Corporation Act (1987) § 3.04.

CROSS-REFERENCES

Corporate powers, see § 3.02.

Corporate purposes, see § 3.01.

Derivative proceedings, see Ch. 13.

Dissolution, see Ch. 14.

"Employee" defined, see § 1.40.

"Proceeding" defined, see § 1.40.

OFFICIAL COMMENT

The basic purpose of Section 3.04—as has been the purpose of all similar statutes during the 20th century—is to eliminate any vestiges of the doctrine of inherent incapacity of corporations. See Campbell, *The Model Business Corporation Act*, 11 BUS. LAW. 98, 102 (1956). Under this section it is unnecessary for purposes of dealing with a nonprofit corporation to inquire into limitation on its purpose or powers that may appear in its articles of incorporation. A person who is unaware of these limitations when dealing with the corporation is not bound by them. The phrase in Section 3.04(a) that the "validity of corporate action may not be challenged on the ground that the corporation lacks or lacked power to act" applies equally to the use of the doctrine as a sword or as a shield: a third person may no more avoid an undesired contract with a corporation on the ground that the corporation was without authority to make the contract than a corporation may defend a suit on a contract on the ground that the contract is ultra vires.

The language of Section 3.04 extends beyond contracts and conveyances of property; "corporate action" of any kind cannot be challenged on the ground of ultra vires. For this reason it makes no difference whether a limitation in articles of incorporation is considered to be a limitation on a purpose or a limitation on a power; both are equally subject to Section 3.04. Corporate action also includes inaction or refusal to act. The common law of ultra vires distinguished between executory contracts, partially executed contracts, and fully executed ones; Section 3.04 treats all corporate action the same—except to the extent described in Section 3.04(b)—and the same rules apply to all contracts no matter at what stage of performance.

Section 3.04, however, does not validate corporate conduct that is made illegal or unlawful by statute or common law decision. This conduct is subject to whatever sanction, criminal or civil, is provided by the statute or decision. Whether or not illegal corporate conduct is voidable or rescindable depends on the applicable statute or substantive law and is not affected by Section 3.04.

Section 3.04 also does not address the validity of essentially intra vires conduct that is not approved by appropriate corporate action. It does not deal, for example, with the enforceability of an executory contract to sell substantially all the assets of a corporation not in the ordinary course of business that was not approved by the members as required by Section 12.02. This type of transaction is not beyond the purposes or powers of the corporation; it simply has not been approved by the corporate authorities as required by law. Similarly, Section 3.04 does not deal with whether a corporation is bound by the action of a corporate agent if the action requires, but has not received, approval by the board of directors. Whether or not the corporation is bound by this action depends on the law of agency, particularly the scope of apparent authority and whether the third party knew or should have known of the defect in the corporate approval process. These actions may be ultra vires with respect to the agent's authority but they are not ultra vires with respect to the corporation and are not controlled by Section 3.04.

Similarly, corporate action is not ultra vires under Section 3.04 merely because it constitutes a breach of fiduciary duty. For example, a misuse of corporate assets for personal purposes by an officer or director is a breach of fiduciary duty and may be enjoined. Similarly, in some circumstances a lien on corporate assets and a contract entered into by the corporation may be cancelled or enjoined if they constitute breaches of fiduciary duty and the third person is charged with knowledge that they were improper. These transactions, however, are not ultra vires with respect to the corporation, and cannot be attacked under Section 3.04. They may be enjoined because of the breach of fiduciary duty, not because the transaction exceeds the powers or purposes of the corporation.

Section 3.04(b) permits challenges to a lack of power by a nonprofit corporation in three limited classes of cases:

(1) In suits by the attorney general under Section 14.30. This provision does not answer the question whether or not a corporation may be dissolved or enjoined by the attorney general for committing an ultra vires act; it simply preserves the power of the state to assert that certain corporate action was ultra vires.

(2) In a suit by the corporation, either directly or through a legal representative, against incumbent or former directors, members of a designated body, or officers for authorizing or causing the corporation to engage in an ultra vires act. Again, this section does not address whether or not there is liability for causing the corporation to enter into an ultra vires act; it simply preserves the power of the corporation to assert that certain corporate action was ultra vires.

(3) In a derivative suit by a member, director, or member of a designated body against the corporation to enjoin an ultra vires act. This suit, however, is subject to the requirements of Section 3.04(c). Under this subsection an ultra vires act

> may be enjoined only if all "affected parties" are parties to the suit. The requirement that the action be "equitable" generally means that only third persons dealing with a corporation while specifically aware that the corporation's action was ultra vires will be enjoined. The general phrase "if equitable" was included because of the possibility that other circumstances may exist that make it equitable to refuse to enjoin an ultra vires contract. Further, if enforcement of the contract is enjoined, either the third person or the corporation may in the discretion of the court be awarded damages from the other for loss (excluding anticipated profits).

Section 3.04(c) thus authorizes a court to enjoin or set aside an ultra vires act or grant other relief that may be necessary to protect the interests of all affected persons, including the interests of third persons who deal with the nonprofit corporation.

CHAPTER 4

Name

§ 4.01. CORPORATE NAME

(a) The name of a nonprofit corporation may not contain language stating or implying that the corporation is organized for a purpose other than that permitted by Section 3.01 and its articles of incorporation.

(b) Except as authorized by subsection (c) or (d), the name of a nonprofit corporation must be distinguishable upon the records of the secretary of state from:

(1) the name of a nonprofit or business corporation incorporated or authorized to conduct activities or transact business in this state;

(2) the name of a filing entity organized under the law of this state or authorized to transact business in this state;

(3) a name reserved or registered under Section 4.02 or 4.03; [*and*]

(4) the fictitious name adopted by a foreign nonprofit or business corporation or filing entity authorized to transact business in this state because its real name is unavailable[.] [;]

[*(5) a name reserved or registered under [cite provisions of the state's business corporation and other entity laws corresponding to Sections 4.02 and 4.03]*;]

[*(6) the name of a limited liability company organized under the laws of this state or qualified to transact business in this state; and*]

[*(7) a fictitious name registered under [cite state's fictitious name law]*.]

(c) A nonprofit corporation may apply for authorization to use a name that is not distinguishable upon the records of the secretary of state from one or more of the names described in subsection (b). The secretary of state shall permit use of the name applied for if:

(1) the other entity consents to the use in writing and submits an undertaking in form satisfactory to the secretary of state to change its name to a name that is distinguishable upon the records of the secretary of state from the name of the applying corporation; or

(2) the applicant delivers to the secretary of state a certified copy of a final judgment of a court of competent jurisdiction establishing the applicant's right to use the name applied for in this state.

(d) A nonprofit corporation may use a name that is otherwise unavailable under subsection (b) if the nonprofit corporation wishing to use the name:

(1) has merged with the other entity;

(2) has been formed by reorganization of the other entity; or

(3) has acquired all or substantially all of the assets, including the name, of the other entity.

(e) A name is distinguishable upon the records of the secretary of state only if the name differs from every other name of record in a way other than:

(1) use of punctuation marks;

(2) use of a definite or indefinite article; and

(3) use of any of the following terms, or an abbreviation thereof, in any language to designate the status of an entity: corporation, company, incorporated, limited, association, fund, syndicate, limited partnership, limited liability company, limited liability partnership, limited liability limited partnership, trust, statutory trust, or business trust.

(f) This [act] does not control the use of fictitious names.

Source Note: Patterned in part after Model Business Corporation Act, 3d Ed. (2002) § 4.01. Derived from Revised Model Nonprofit Corporation Act (1987) § 4.01. Subsection (e) is patterned after 15 PA. CONS. STAT. § 135(e).

CROSS-REFERENCES

Appeal from refusal of secretary of state to file a document, see § 1.26.

"Deliver" defined, see § 1.40.

Effective time and date of filing, see § 1.23.

Filing fees, see § 1.22.

Filing requirements, see § 1.20.

Foreign corporations, see Ch. 15.

Registered name, see § 4.03.

Reserved name, see § 4.02.

Statement of name in articles, see § 2.02.

OFFICIAL COMMENT

1. No Required Indication of Corporate Status

While the Model Business Corporation Act requires business corporations to include in their names an indication that they are corporations, the Model Nonprofit Corporation Act has never included such a requirement. Imposition of such a requirement for nonprofit corporations would be contrary to the practice of nonprofit corporations, would not materially protect the public, and would entail considerable effort and cost. Hospitals, colleges, museums, trade associations, and other nonprofit institutions typically do not include in their names an indication of corporate status.

2. Names That Are "Distinguishable upon the Records of the Secretary of State"

The provisions of Chapter 4 are based on the fundamental premise that the name provisions in the act should only ensure that each nonprofit corporation has a sufficiently distinctive name so that it may be distinguished from other entities upon the records of the secretary of state. A nonprofit corporation statute should not be a partial substitute for a general assumed name, unfair competition, or antifraud statute. As a result, the act does not restrict the power of a corporation to adopt or use an assumed or fictitious name with the same freedom as an individual. Principles of unfair competition, not entity organic laws, provide the limits on the competitive use of similar names.

The phrase "distinguishable upon the records of the secretary of state" has become the generally accepted standard used in entity organic laws for name availability. The principal justifications for requiring a distinguishable official name are (1) to prevent confusion within the secretary of state's office and the tax office, and (2) to permit accuracy in naming and serving corporate defendants in litigation. Thus, confusion in an absolute or linguistic sense is the appropriate test under the act, not the competitive relationship between the entities, which is the test for fraud or unfair competition. Subsection (e) provides guidance for the secretary of state in applying the standard of "distinguishable upon the records."

Rejection of the "deceptively similar" requirement that was used at one time in many state statutes and the specific recognition appearing in Section 4.01(f), that corporations may use artificial or fictitious names to the same extent an individual can, are based on the fact that the secretary of state does not generally police the unfair competitive use of names and, indeed, usually does not have resources to do so.

3. *Classes of Unavailable Names*

Section 4.01(b) lists classes of "official names" that are not available. Where a foreign corporation or filing entity plans to qualify in a state and discovers that its name is not available in that state, it must adopt an assumed or fictitious name as its "official name" in the state, see Section 15.06. Such a fictitious or assumed name is thereafter an "official" name and is unavailable to the same extent as any other "official name" in use is unavailable.

Under the laws of some states, registering as a limited liability partnership blocks the use of the partnership's name by other entities. In states where that is the case, optional Section 4.01(b)(6) should be used. Similarly, in some states registering a fictitious name blocks its use by other entities and in states where that is the case, optional Section 4.01(b)(7) should be used.

4. *Consent to Use*

Section 4.01(c)(1) authorizes the secretary of state to accept a name that is indistinguishable from the name of another entity if that entity files an undertaking in a form satisfactory to the secretary of state that it will thereafter change its name to a name that is distinguishable upon the records of the secretary of state. This privilege may be important in acquisition transactions where a nonprofit corporation is to take over the business of an existing entity without a change in name. The secretary of state may require the undertaking to specify the new name that the corporation will adopt and the time period within which the change will be made. The requirements imposed on the undertaking should be consistent with the limited role of the secretary of state in the administration of Section 4.01.

§ 4.02. RESERVED NAME

(a) A person may reserve the exclusive use of a name including a fictitious name for a foreign nonprofit corporation whose name is not available, by delivering an application to the secretary of state for filing. The application must set forth the name and address of the applicant and the name proposed to be reserved. Upon finding that the name applied for is available, the secretary of state shall reserve the name for the exclusive use of the applicant for 120 days.

(b) The owner of a reserved name may transfer the reservation to another person by delivering to the secretary of state a signed notice of the transfer that states the name and address of the transferee.

Source Note: Patterned after Model Business Corporation Act, 3d Ed. (2002) § 4.02. Derived from Revised Model Nonprofit Corporation Act (1987) § 4.02.

CROSS-REFERENCES

Appeal from refusal of secretary of state to file a document, see § 1.26.

Availability of names, see § 4.01.

Consent to use corporate name, see § 4.01.

"Deliver" defined, see § 1.40.

Effective time and date of filing, see § 1.23.

Filing fees, see § 1.22.

Filing requirements, see § 1.20.

Foreign corporation, see Ch. 15.

"Person" defined, see § 1.40.

Registered name, see § 4.03.

OFFICIAL COMMENT

The "reservation" of a corporate name is basically a device to simplify the formation of a new nonprofit corporation or the qualification of a foreign nonprofit corporation. By reserving a name, the persons considering the formation or qualification of the corporation can order stationery, prepare documents, etc., on the assumption that the reserved name will be available. Reference to a specific intent to form a new corporation is not required by the statute, however, since a secretary of state is not equipped and should not be asked to determine whether the requisite intent actually exists. For the same reason, "any person" is permitted to reserve a corporate name without reference to specific classes of persons who might wish to reserve a name for various purposes.

Under Section 4.02, an available name may be reserved, for example:

(1) By persons considering the formation of a new domestic corporation.
(2) By persons considering the formation of a corporation in another state and the immediate qualification of that new corporation in this state.
(3) By a foreign corporation planning or considering qualification in this state. The name reserved may be the foreign corporation's "official name" (if that name is available) or another name. The foreign corporation may thereafter use the reserved name as the name of a domestic subsidiary or, if its real name is unavailable, as a fictitious "official name" for its qualification under Section 15.06.

The foregoing examples are designed to suggest the scope and flexibility of Section 4.02, and not to exhaust the possible uses to which a reserved name may be put.

Consideration was given to whether reservation of a corporate name should be made renewable. The modern requirements for incorporation of a domestic nonprofit corporation or the qualification of a foreign nonprofit corporation are so simple that it is unlikely that more than 120 days could ever be realistically required to form or qualify a corporation. Also, it was believed to be undesirable to allow the reservation procedure to be used for other purposes, such as permanently setting aside a name by successive renewals. At the same time, it was recognized that circumstances might arise where a reservation period longer than 120 days might be useful. To balance those concerns, this section authorizes reserving a name for 120 days. A name reservation is not renewable, but a new reservation may be filed upon the expiration of a reservation. When a reservation lapses, another party may file a reservation of the same name unless the party initially reserving the name is careful to file a new reservation immediately upon the lapse of the initial reservation. Nothing prevents the formation of an inactive corporation specifically to hold the desired name if a longer period of reservation is desired than the 120-day period specified by Section 4.02 and the reserving party does not wish to run the risk of another party reserving the name upon the lapse of a reservation.

§ 4.03. REGISTERED NAME

(a) A nonqualified foreign corporation may register its name, or its name with any addition required by Section 15.06, if the name is distinguishable upon the records of the secretary of state from the names that are not available under Section 4.01(b).

(b) A nonqualified foreign corporation registers its name, or its name with any addition required by Section 15.06, by delivering to the secretary of state for filing an application:

(1) setting forth:
  (i) its name, or its name with any addition required by Section 15.06;
  (ii) the date and state or other jurisdiction of its incorporation; and
  (iii) a brief description of the nature of the activities in which it is engaged; and

(2) accompanied by a certificate of existence (or a document of similar import) from its state or other jurisdiction of incorporation.

(c) The name is registered for the exclusive use of the applicant upon the effective date of the application. The registration is effective through December 31 of the following year.

(d) A nonqualified foreign corporation whose registration is effective may renew it for successive years by delivering to the secretary of state for filing a renewal application, which complies with the requirements of subsection (b), between October 1 and December 31 of the preceding year. The renewal application when filed renews the registration for the following calendar year.

(e) A nonqualified foreign corporation whose registration is effective may thereafter become a qualified foreign corporation under the registered name or consent in a record to the use of that name by a corporation thereafter incorporated under this [act] or by another foreign corporation thereafter authorized to conduct activities in this state. The registration terminates when the domestic corporation is incorporated or the foreign corporation qualifies or consents to the qualification of another foreign corporation under the registered name.

Source Note: Patterned in part after Model Business Corporation Act, 3d Ed. (2002) § 4.03. Derived from Revised Model Nonprofit Corporation Act (1987) § 4.03.

CROSS-REFERENCES

Appeal from refusal of secretary of state to file a document, see § 1.26.

Certificate of existence, see § 1.28.

Consent to use corporate name, see § 4.01.

"Deliver" defined, see § 1.40.

Effective time and date of filing, see § 1.23.

Filing and signature requirements, see § 1.20.

Filing fees, see § 1.22.

Foreign corporations, see Ch. 15.

Reserved name, see § 4.02.

"State" defined, see § 1.40.

OFFICIAL COMMENT

The "registration" of a corporate name is basically a device by which a foreign nonprofit corporation, not qualified to conduct activities in the state, can preserve the right to use its unique "real" name if it decides later to qualify in the state. In effect, registration ensures "real" name availability in areas of potential future expansion.

It is believed desirable to limit Section 4.03 to this purpose and not allow it to become an indirect device for the preservation of trademarks, trade names, or possible assumed names. For this reason, generally only "real" names of foreign nonprofit corporations may be registered (with exceptions described below). A broader approach would create issues better resolved under a trademark or similar statute, or by litigation under unfair competition principles, and might impose duties on secretaries of state that they are generally not equipped to handle, or could handle only at increased cost.

Confusion sometimes exists between "reservation" of names under Section 4.02 and registration of names under Section 4.03. A foreign nonprofit corporation that is planning to qualify as a foreign corporation and finds that its name is available in the state may either register or reserve the name. Often a foreign corporation will have to decide whether to qualify or to create a domestic subsidiary; this well may be decided after the exclusive right to use the name in the state is obtained either by reservation or by registration. If the corporation registers its name, it will be kept indefinitely; if it reserves, it will be kept for 120 days and then become available again. That is the foreign corporation's choice. If a foreign corporation registers its name and then elects to form a domestic or foreign subsidiary, the written consent procedure of Section 4.03(e) allows the secretary of state to ascertain that the domestic subsidiary is related to the foreign corporation and that use of the registered name by that subsidiary is acceptable to the foreign parent.

If a foreign corporation's "real" name is unavailable, a foreign corporation may *reserve* any name—including one that is assumed or fictitious when compared with the corporation's "real" name—for 120 days, but it may not *register* this type of name in light of the policy against allowing the name provisions of the act to be used for purposes broader than the "unique name" issue. Nevertheless, a foreign corporation that wishes to be certain that a particular fictitious or assumed name will be available in the future may create an inactive domestic subsidiary with the desired name to preserve its future availability. See also the Official Comment to Section 15.06.

Section 4.03(e) provides that the protection of the name provided by this section terminates when the name is used pursuant to this section by the foreign corporation or its domestic or foreign subsidiary.

CHAPTER 5

Registered Office and Agent

§ 5.01. REQUIREMENT OF REGISTERED OFFICE AND REGISTERED AGENT

Each nonprofit corporation must continuously maintain in this state:

(1) a registered office, which may be the same as any of its places of business; and
(2) a registered agent, which may be:
  (i) an individual who resides in this state and whose business office is identical with the registered office;
  (ii) a domestic nonprofit or business corporation or filing entity whose business office is identical with the registered office; or
  (iii) a foreign nonprofit or business corporation or filing entity authorized to transact business in this state whose business office is identical with the registered office.

Source Note: Patterned after Model Business Corporation Act, 3d Ed. (2002) § 5.01. Substantially a reenactment of Model Nonprofit Corporation Act (1987) § 5.01.

CROSS-REFERENCES

Annual report disclosure, see § 16.21.

Changing registered office or agent, see § 5.02.

Effect of dissolution of corporation, see § 14.05.

"Filing entity" defined, see § 1.40.

Foreign corporations, see Ch. 15.

Involuntary dissolution for failure to appoint and maintain registered agent and office, see § 14.20.

Naming registered agent and office in articles of incorporation, see § 2.02.

"Principal office":

defined, see §1.40.

designated in annual report, see § 16.21.

Resignation of registered agent, see § 5.03.

Service on corporation, see § 5.04.

OFFICIAL COMMENT

The requirements that a nonprofit corporation continuously maintain a registered office and a registered agent at that office are based on the premises that at all times a corporation should have an office where it may be found and a person at that office on whom any notice or process required or permitted by law may be served. This covers not only service of process in connection with litigation but also tax notices and communications from the secretary of state and other governmental offices. The street address of the registered office must appear in the public records maintained by the secretary of state. A mailing address, such as a post office box, is not sufficient since the registered office is the designated location for service of process.

The act assumes that formal communications to a nonprofit corporation will normally be addressed to the registered agent at the registered office. If the communication itself deals with the registered office or registered agent, however, copies must be sent to the principal office of the corporation. Moreover, the act authorizes corporations to retain records at, or to provide information to members through, offices other than the registered office. The act consistently recognizes that the registered office may be a "legal" rather than a "business" office.

Many nonprofit corporations designate their registered office to be a business office of the corporation and a corporate officer at that office to be the registered agent. Since most of the communications to the registered agent at the registered office deal with legal matters, however, corporations often designate their regular legal counsel or his nominee as their registered agent and the counsel's office as the registered office of the corporation. This practice may also encourage regular communication between the corporation and its legal counsel.

The registered agent need not be an individual. Corporation service companies often provide, as a commercial service, registered offices and registered agents at the office of the corporation service company.

The voluntary dissolution of the corporation does not of itself terminate the authority of the registered agent to accept service of process or other communications on behalf of the dissolved corporation. See Section 14.05.

§ 5.02. CHANGE OF REGISTERED OFFICE OR REGISTERED AGENT

(a) A nonprofit corporation may change its registered office or registered agent by delivering to the secretary of state for filing a statement of change that sets forth:
   (1) the name of the corporation;
   (2) the street address of its current registered office;
   (3) if the current registered office is to be changed, the street address of the new registered office;
   (4) the name of its current registered agent;
   (5) if the current registered agent is to be changed, the name of the new registered agent and the new agent's signed consent in the form of a record (either as part of the statement or accompanying it) to the appointment; and
   (6) that after the change or changes are made, the street addresses of its registered office and the business office of its registered agent will be identical.

(b) If the street address of a registered agent's business office is changed, the agent may change the street address of the registered office of any corporation for which the agent is the registered agent by notifying the corporation in the form of a record of the change and signing and delivering to the secretary of state for filing a statement that complies with the requirements of subsection (a) and recites that the corporation has been notified of the change.

Source Note: Patterned after Model Business Corporation Act, 3d Ed. (2002) § 5.02. Substantially a reenactment of Model Nonprofit Corporation Act (1987) § 5.02.

CROSS-REFERENCES

Deletion of initial agent and office from articles of incorporation, see § 10.05.

"Deliver" defined, see § 1.40.

Effect of dissolution of corporation, see § 14.05.

Effective time and date of filing, see § 1.23.

Filing fees, see § 1.22.

Filing requirements, see § 1.20.

Involuntary dissolution for failure to file notice of change of registered agent or office, see § 14.20.

Notice, see § 1.41.

Resignation of registered agent, see § 5.03.

OFFICIAL COMMENT

Changes of registered office or registered agent are usually routine matters that do not affect the rights of members. The purpose of this section is to permit these changes without a formal amendment of the articles of incorporation, without approval of the members, and, indeed, even without formal approval of the board of directors.

Changes of registered office or registered agent are often of particular concern to corporation service companies that routinely serve as registered agent and routinely provide a registered office for literally thousands of corporations within many states.

Prior experience with the change of registered agent and registered office provisions in the statutes of many states revealed several minor problems with these largely formal provisions that are addressed in the act:

(1) Changes of registered office or registered agent need not be authorized by the board of directors. Many changes (such as the name of a specific registered agent at a registered office) are so routine that they should not require action by the board of directors.

(2) In the case of a change of registered agent, the written consent of the new registered agent is required. This is designed to prevent naming persons as registered agents without their knowledge.

(3) The procedure by which a registered agent may change the street address of the registered office applies to any location

within the state and the agent is expressly required to notify the nonprofit corporation of the change. But a notice in a record from the agent is acceptable since a corporation service company changing its street address may be required to file a form for each of the thousands of corporations for which it serves as registered agent and to notify each corporation of the change.

Resignation of the registered agent is separately treated in Section 5.03.

§ 5.03. RESIGNATION OF REGISTERED AGENT

(a) A registered agent may resign as registered agent by signing and delivering to the secretary of state for filing a statement of resignation. The statement may include a statement that the registered office is also discontinued.
(b) After filing the statement, the secretary of state shall deliver notice of the filing of the statement to the registered office (if not discontinued) and to the nonprofit corporation at its principal office.
(c) The agency appointment is terminated, and the registered office discontinued if so provided, on the 31st day after the date on which the statement was filed.

Source Note: Patterned after Model Business Corporation Act, 3d Ed. (2002) § 5.03. Substantially a reenactment of Model Nonprofit Corporation Act (1987) § 5.03.

CROSS-REFERENCES

Annual report, see § 16.21.

Change of registered agent, see § 5.02.

"Deliver" defined, see § 1.40.

Effect of dissolution of corporation, see § 14.05.

Effective time and date of filing, see § 1.23.

Filing fees, see § 1.22.

Filing requirements, see § 1.20.

"Principal office":
defined, see § 1.40.
designated in annual report, see § 16.21.

OFFICIAL COMMENT

The resignation of registered agents under some state statutes has created special problems. Most of these problems arose in connection with corporation service companies that serve as registered agent for an annual fee. If the fee was not paid, the corporation service company obviously desired to terminate the representation promptly. Often the agent did not have a current business address for the nonprofit corporation and was uncertain whether the corporation was still actively engaged in business. Some statutes required the agent to submit the statement of resignation in duplicate and the secretary of state was directed to mail one copy "forthwith . . . to the corporation at its registered office." This resulted in a circularity in notice: the duplicate was mailed back to the registered agent who originally filed the copy. The probability that the corporation would receive a copy of the resignation under these circumstances was obviously low.

Section 5.03 resolves the circularity problem by requiring the secretary of state to deliver a notice of the filing to the nonprofit corporation at its registered office and the other to the corporation "at its principal office." Delivery to this second address appears to be the only option regularly available to "break the circle" of the corporation "receiving" the notice through an agent whose resignation is being communicated.

This section also permits the discontinuance of the registered office as well as the resignation of the agent. Corporation service companies desiring to resign their agency for nonpayment of fees will normally wish to discontinue the registered office as well as their service as the registered agent.

§ 5.04. SERVICE ON CORPORATION

(a) The registered agent of a nonprofit corporation is the corporation's agent for service of process, notice, or demand required or permitted by law to be served on the corporation.

(b) If a nonprofit corporation has no registered agent, or the agent cannot with reasonable diligence be served, the corporation may be served by delivery of the process in record form to the secretary of the corporation at its principal office. Service is effective under this subsection as provided in Section 1.41(e).

(c) This section does not prescribe the only means, or necessarily the required means, of serving a nonprofit corporation.

Source Note: Patterned in part after Model Business Corporation Act, 3d Ed. (2002) § 5.04. Derived from Model Nonprofit Corporation Act (1987) § 5.04.

CROSS-REFERENCES

Foreign corporations, see Ch. 15.

Notice, see § 1.41.

"Principal office":
- defined, see § 1.40.
- designated in annual report, see § 16.21.

Registered office and agent:
- designated in annual report, see § 16.21.
- required, see §§ 2.02, 5.01, and 15.07.

"Secretary" defined, see § 1.40.

OFFICIAL COMMENT

Somewhat the same circularity problem that arose in connection with the resignation of registered agents (see the Official Comment to Section 5.03) also sometimes arose in connection with service of process under some state statutes. If service could not be made on the registered agent at its registered office, a duplicate of the process was forwarded to the secretary of state, who served it at the registered office (where the agent previously could not be found). It is unlikely that this arrangement resulted in the copy being forwarded routinely to the nonprofit corporation. Instead of providing for service on the secretary of state if service cannot be perfected on the registered agent, therefore, Section 5.04 provides for service on the secretary of the corporation at its principal office shown in its most recent annual report.

Section 5.04(c) provides that this section does not prescribe the only, or necessarily the required, means of serving a nonprofit corporation. Service may also be perfected under civil practice statutes, under rules of civil procedure, or under statutes that provide special service requirements applicable to certain types of corporations.

Section 5.04 simplifies the recordkeeping requirements of the secretary of state, who is no longer required to keep records of service of process on domestic corporations.

CHAPTER 6

Memberships and Financial Provisions

Subchapter
A. Admission of Members
B. Rights and Obligations of Members
C. Resignation and Termination
D. Delegates
E. Financial Provisions

[Subchapter] A
ADMISSION OF MEMBERS

§ 6.01. NO REQUIREMENT OF MEMBERS

(a) A nonprofit corporation is not required to have members.

(b) Where the articles of incorporation or bylaws of a nonprofit corporation do not provide that it shall have members, or where a corporation has in fact no members entitled to vote on a matter, any provision of this [act] or any other provision of law requiring notice to, the presence of, or the vote, consent, or other action by members of the corporation in connection with the matter shall be satisfied by notice to, the presence of, or the vote, consent, or other action by the board of directors or a designated body of the corporation.

Source Note: Subsection (a) is a reenactment of Model Nonprofit Corporation Act (1987) § 6.03. Subsection (b) is patterned after 15 Pa. Cons. Stat. § 5751(b).

CROSS-REFERENCES

"Board of directors" defined, see § 1.40.

"Designated body" defined, see § 1.40.

"Member" defined, see § 1.40.

"Membership corporation" defined, see § 1.40.

"Nonmembership corporation" defined, see § 1.40.

Self-perpetuating board, see § 8.04(b).

OFFICIAL COMMENT

Nonprofit corporations are not required to have members. They may operate with designated or appointed directors, or a self-perpetuating board or designated body. See Section 8.04(b). They may also operate with a system of delegates who are entitled to vote in a representative assembly for the election of directors or on other matters. The delegates may or may not themselves be members of the corporation, and may or may not be selected by persons that are members of the corporation. See Section 6.30.

§ 6.02. ADMISSION

(a) The articles of incorporation or bylaws of a membership corporation may establish criteria or procedures for admission of members.
(b) A person may not be admitted as a member without the person's consent.
(c) If a membership corporation provides certificates of membership to the members, the certificates shall not be registered or transferable except as provided in the articles of incorporation or bylaws.
(d) A person is not a member of a nonprofit corporation unless the person meets the definition of a "member" in Section 1.40, regardless of whether the corporation designates or refers to the person as a member.

> *Source Note:* Subsections (a) and (b) are substantially a reenactment of Model Nonprofit Corporation Act (1987) § 6.01. As to subsection (c), compare 15 Pa. Cons. Stat. 5753. Subsection (d) is patterned in part after Cal. Corp. Code § 5332.

CROSS-REFERENCES

Consideration for admission, see § 6.03.

"Membership corporation" defined, see § 1.40.

Resignation and termination of members, see Subch. 6C.

Rights and obligations of members, see Subch. 6B.

OFFICIAL COMMENT

Section 3.02(15) allows corporations to "establish conditions for admission of members" and "admit members." The requirements for admission are normally set forth in the articles, the bylaws, or a resolution adopted by the board. These requirements will be upheld unless they conflict with federal or state law.

Any person may be admitted as a member. See Section 1.40(36) ("member"). As the definition of "person" contained in Section 1.40(46) is all-encompassing, minors, corporations, partnerships, governmental subdivisions, and any other person without limitation may be admitted to membership. See New York Not-for-Profit Corporation Law § 601.

Subdivision (b) prevents nonprofit corporations from admitting people as members unless they consent to becoming members. Consent may be express or implied, and thus the consent does not have to be in the form of a record. For example, consent may be implied by acceptance of membership benefits knowing that the benefits are only offered to members.

Nonprofit corporations sometimes name people as members without knowing or having the ability to identify individual members. For example, a corporation's bylaws may provide that "all poor people within one mile of city hall are members entitled to vote for directors." In many instances there is no way to prepare a list of these "members" or meet the notice or other requirements of the act as to them, unless they identify themselves to the corporation. As a result of Section 6.02(a), the above bylaw provision simply authorizes poor people in the area to become members. Before they became members they would have to apply for membership or consent to join by attending a meeting, voting, or otherwise evidencing consent. Until they had manifested this consent they would not be "members" as that term is defined in Section 1.40(36).

A membership corporation may provide certificates to its members that indicate their membership in the corporation. Subsection (c) makes those certificates nontransferable, with the result that the only way a membership may be transferred is in compliance with Section 6.11.

§ 6.03. CONSIDERATION

Except as provided in its articles of incorporation or bylaws, a membership corporation may admit members for no consideration or for such consideration as is determined by the board of directors. The consideration may take any form, including promissory notes, intangible property, or past or future services. Payment of the consideration may be made at such times and upon such terms as are set forth in or authorized by the articles of incorporation, the bylaws, or a resolution of the board.

> *Source Note:* The first sentence is substantially a reenactment of Model Nonprofit Corporation Act (1987) § 6.02. The second sentence is derived from the Official Comment to Model Nonprofit Corporation Act (1987) § 6.02.

CROSS-REFERENCES

Admission of members, see § 6.02.

"Board of directors" defined, see § 1.40.

"Member" defined, see § 1.40.

"Membership corporation" defined, see § 1.40.

OFFICIAL COMMENT

Issuance of a membership, unlike the sale of stock, does not necessarily confer something of value. Nonprofit corporations need the ability to issue memberships for no consideration or such consideration as is set forth in or determined by their articles, bylaws, or board. Section 6.03 provides this flexibility.

If memberships are to be issued for consideration, the board of directors has wide discretion to fix the consideration. It may be a stated amount or based on a formula. For example, in some trade associations the cost of joining is based on the sales, net worth, or other characteristics of the applicant.

Provisions regarding the amount, nature, and time of payment may be set forth in the articles of incorporation, the bylaws, or a resolution adopted by the board. To the extent the articles or bylaws do not deal with those subjects, the board has the authority to act as it considers appropriate. When determining the nature, timing, and amount, if any, of payments, board members must act consistently with their duties of care and loyalty. The obligation of members to make payments to their corporation is dealt with in Section 6.13.

The provisions of this section also apply to a designated body under Section 8.12. Thus a designated body may determine the consideration for memberships and how the consideration is to be paid.

[Subchapter] B
RIGHTS AND OBLIGATIONS OF MEMBERS

§ 6.10. DIFFERENCES IN RIGHTS AND OBLIGATIONS OF MEMBERS

(a) Except as otherwise provided in the articles of incorporation or bylaws, each member of a membership corporation has the same rights and obligations as every other member with respect to voting, dissolution, membership transfer, and other matters.

(b) See Section 10.22(a) (bylaw amendments requiring member approval).

Source Note: Subsection (a) is derived from Model Nonprofit Corporation Act (1987) § 6.10. Subsection (b) is new.

CROSS-REFERENCES

Admission of members, see § 6.02.

Consideration for memberships, see § 6.03.

Member meetings and voting, see Ch. 7.

"Membership corporation" defined, see § 1.40.

OFFICIAL COMMENT

Section 6.10 allows great flexibility and diversity in membership rights. In the absence of an applicable provision in the articles of incorporation or bylaws, all members have the same rights and obligations with respect to voting, dissolution, transfer of their memberships, and other matters.

The differences among members may relate to dues, assessments, transfers of memberships, use of facilities, termination or suspension of members, voting, distributions on dissolution, and other factors. Distinctions may be made between individual, corporate, and other entities that are members of the corporation. These distinctions among members may be based on size, net worth, number of employees, activity, and other factors. These distinctions do not necessarily result in classes having the right to vote separately on matters requiring a member vote. See Sections 10.04 and 10.22.

Once members have been admitted, a vote of the members may be required to change membership rights and obligations. See Sections 10.03, 10.04, 10.21, and 10.22. The obligations of members to their corporation are dealt with in Section 6.13.

§ 6.11. TRANSFERS

(a) Except as provided in the articles of incorporation or bylaws, a member of a membership corporation may not transfer a membership or any right arising therefrom.

(b) Where the right to transfer a membership has been provided, a restriction on that right shall not be binding with respect to a member holding a membership issued prior to the adoption of the restriction unless the restriction is approved by the affected member.

Source Note: Derived from Model Nonprofit Corporation Act (1987) § 6.11.

CROSS-REFERENCES

Differences in rights and obligations of members, see § 6.10.

"Membership" defined, see § 1.40.

"Membership corporation" defined, see § 1.40.

OFFICIAL COMMENT

Subdivision (a) provides that a membership in a membership corporation cannot be transferred unless the articles or bylaws provide for transfers. A corporation's articles or bylaws may provide for transfers if the members want transferable memberships.

The articles or bylaws may impose limitations, conditions, and fees as a condition to transferring memberships. For example, the articles or bylaws could provide that transfers may be made only with the approval of the board of directors.

Subdivision (b) is particularly important to members of mutual benefit corporations if their memberships represent a valuable asset. It provides that no restriction on transfer can be imposed after the fact without approval of the affected member.

As subsection (a) makes clear, the membership transfers to which this section applies are actions taken by the member. A new member may also be substituted for an existing member identified in the articles of incorporation or bylaws by an appropriate amendment of the articles or bylaws, but that type of action is not a transfer subject to this section.

§ 6.12. MEMBER'S LIABILITY TO THIRD PARTIES

A member of a membership corporation is not, as such, personally liable for the acts, debts, liabilities, or obligations of the corporation.

Source Note: Substantially a reenactment of Model Nonprofit Corporation Act (1987) § 6.12.

CROSS-REFERENCES

Liability for preincorporation transactions, see § 2.04.

"Member" defined, see § 1.40.

"Membership corporation" defined, see § 1.40.

OFFICIAL COMMENT

Section 6.12 sets forth the general rule that members have no personal liability to third parties for the acts, debts, liabilities, or obligations of their corporation. Following incorporation, members have limited liability in the absence of: (i) facts allowing a court to pierce the corporate veil; or (ii) a legally enforceable obligation of a member to the corporation. See Section 2.04 as to the liability of persons purporting to act as or on behalf of a corporation that has not been formed.

§ 6.13. MEMBER'S LIABILITY FOR DUES, ASSESSMENTS, AND FEES

(a) A membership corporation may levy dues, assessments, and fees on its members to the extent authorized in the articles of incorporation or bylaws. Dues, assessments, and fees may be imposed on members of the same class either alike or in different amounts or proportions, and may be imposed on a different basis on different classes of members. Members of a class may be made exempt from dues, assessments, and fees to the extent provided in the articles or bylaws.

(b) The amount and method of collection of dues, assessments, and fees may be fixed in the articles of incorporation or bylaws, or the articles or bylaws may authorize the board of directors or members to fix the amount and method of collection.

(c) The articles of incorporation or bylaws may provide reasonable means, such as termination and reinstatement of membership, to enforce the collection of dues, assessments, and fees.

(d) See Section 10.22(a) (bylaw amendments requiring member approval).

Source Note: Subsections (a)–(c) are patterned after 15 PA. CONS. STAT. § 5544. Compare Model Nonprofit Corporation Act (1987) § 6.13. Subsection (d) is new.

CROSS-REFERENCES

Creditor's action against member, see § 6.14.

Liability to third parties, see § 6.12.

"Member" defined, see § 1.40.

"Membership corporation" defined, see § 1.40.

Obligations of members, see § 6.10.

OFFICIAL COMMENT

Shareholders rarely obligate themselves to make payments to business corporations in addition to the amounts they pay to acquire their shares. Members, on the other hand, particularly members of professional associations or other mutual benefit corporations, often agree to pay dues to support the purposes of their corporation and may make yearly or other payments for benefits or services provided by membership corporations.

Persons who become members in a corporation whose bylaws authorize dues, assessments, or fees agree to the imposition of those items by virtue of accepting their membership in the corporation.

The term "fees" includes initiation fees.

The provisions of this section also apply to a designated body under Section 8.12. Thus Section 6.13(c) will permit the bylaws to authorize a designated body to fix the amount and method of collection of fees, assessments, and dues.

§ 6.14. CREDITOR'S ACTION AGAINST MEMBER

(a) A proceeding may not be brought by a creditor of a membership corporation to reach the liability, if any, of a member to the corporation unless final judgment has been rendered in favor of the creditor against the corporation and execution has been returned unsatisfied in whole or in part or unless the proceeding would be useless.

(b) All creditors of a membership corporation, with or without reducing their claims to judgment, may intervene in any creditor's proceeding brought under subsection (a) to reach and apply unpaid amounts due the corporation. Any or all members who owe amounts to the corporation may be joined in the proceeding.

Source Note: Substantially a reenactment of Model Nonprofit Corporation Act (1987) § 6.14.

CROSS-REFERENCES

Liability for fees, etc., see § 6.13.

Liability to third parties, see § 6.12.

"Membership corporation" defined, see § 1.40.

OFFICIAL COMMENT

Section 6.14 requires a creditor to obtain a final judgment against a membership corporation before suing its members unless a proceeding against the corporation would be useless. A proceeding usually would be useless if a corporation were bankrupt or it was obvious that it did not have sufficient assets to meet the obligation. Section 6.14 is not intended to preclude the availability of other remedies to a creditor, as, for example, under the Uniform Fraudulent Transfer Act.

[Subchapter] C
RESIGNATION AND TERMINATION

§ 6.20. RESIGNATION

(a) A member of a membership corporation may resign at any time.

(b) The resignation of a member does not relieve the member from any obligations incurred or commitments made prior to resignation.

Source Note: Substantially a reenactment of Model Nonprofit Corporation Act (1987) § 6.20.

CROSS-REFERENCES

Liability for fees, etc., see § 6.13.

Liability to third parties, see § 6.12.

"Membership corporation" defined, see § 1.40.

OFFICIAL COMMENT

Section 6.20(a) sets forth the basic right of a member to resign from a membership corporation at any time. A nonprofit organization generally cannot force a person to belong to it, except in limited instances where membership is required by law, such as certain homeowners associations or bar associations in states that have an integrated bar. See Section 1.03, which preserves the application of such other laws.

Although a membership corporation generally may not force a person to be a member, a person may be liable to the corporation for wrongfully withdrawing in violation of contractual or other obligations to remain as a member. Under Section 6.20(b) a person may be liable for obligations incurred or commitments made prior to the resignation. These commitments may extend beyond the time the member resigns.

Resignation from membership will not allow a person to avoid liability for goods or services already provided or for ongoing obligations to which the member agreed prior to resignation. Section 6.20(b). This provision is particularly important to membership corporations that provide benefits or services to members' businesses. The member in joining the organization may promise to use its facilities or services for a specified period of time. While Section 6.20(a) allows a member to resign at any time, Section 6.20(b) allows the corporation to enforce or obtain damages for violation of a member's agreement.

§ 6.21. TERMINATION AND SUSPENSION

(a) A membership in a membership corporation may be terminated or suspended for the reasons and in the manner provided in the articles of incorporation or bylaws.

(b) A proceeding challenging a termination or suspension for any reason must be commenced within one year after the effective date of the termination or suspension.

(c) The termination or suspension of a member does not relieve the member from any obligations incurred or commitments made prior to the termination or suspension.

(d) See Section 10.22(a) (bylaw amendments requiring member approval).

Source Note: Derived from Model Nonprofit Corporation Act (1987) § 6.21. Subsection (c) is patterned after Model Nonprofit Corporation Act (1987) § 6.20(b). Subsection (d) is new.

CROSS-REFERENCES

"Member" defined, see § 1.40.

"Membership" defined, see § 1.40.

"Membership corporation" defined, see § 1.40.

OFFICIAL COMMENT

Section 6.21 does not deal with the question of the substantive grounds for termination. It also does not specify any requirements that the procedures for termination or suspension must satisfy, but leaves the determination of those procedures to the members. The procedures will require due process for the member being terminated or suspended, but the nature of the process to be provided will depend on the reason for the termination or suspension. Suspension for failure to comply with administrative requirements such as paying dues, for example, do not require the type of due process required when a member is to be terminated for misconduct.

The prior version of the act differentiated between termination and expulsion, using the term "termination" when speaking of memberships and the term "expulsion" when speaking of members. That distinction has been eliminated from the current act in favor of the single term "termination."

If the membership in a membership corporation is limited to persons who are members in good standing in a lodge, church, club, society, or other entity, the articles of incorporation or bylaws may provide that failure on the part of a person to remain in good standing in the other entity will be sufficient cause to terminate the membership of the person in the corporation.

To provide finality subsection (b) requires that a proceeding challenging a termination or suspension be commenced within one year after the date of the termination or suspension.

A person who has been terminated or suspended is liable for dues, assessments, and fees based on commitments made or obligations incurred prior to the termination or suspension. If the person has contracted or agreed to make payments to the nonprofit corporation regardless of his or her status as a member, that obligation continues even though the person is suspended or is no longer a member.

§ 6.22. PURCHASE OF MEMBERSHIPS

(a) Except as provided in the articles of incorporation or bylaws, a membership corporation that is not a charitable corporation may not purchase any of its memberships or any right arising therefrom.

(b) See Sections 1.03(b) (application of other laws) and 10.22(a) (bylaw amendments requiring member approval).

Source Note: Derived from Model Nonprofit Corporation Act (1987) § 6.22.

CROSS-REFERENCES

"Membership corporation" defined, see § 1.40.

Rights and obligations of members, see § 6.10.

When repurchases may not be made, see § 6.41.

OFFICIAL COMMENT

Assets of membership corporations that are held for a public, charitable, or religious purpose are not available for distribution to members either upon dissolution or while the corporation is operating. Corporations that hold such assets are prohibited by other laws from purchasing their memberships because such a purpose can have the effect of impermissibly distributing restricted assets to the members. As provided in Section 1.03(b), those other laws control over this section. Members in mutual benefit corporations, on the other hand, may have an economic interest in the corporation and their memberships may represent a valuable asset. Upon dissolution, any surplus may be distributed to members in the absence of some other distribution provision.

Certain protections must be provided to the creditors of the corporation to ensure that the assets are not improperly diverted to members thereby rendering the corporation unable to meet its liabilities. Consequently, the repurchase of a membership is made subject to the restrictions on distributions in Section 6.41(b).

A bylaw provision authorizing purchase of memberships must be approved by the members. See Section 10.22.

The repurchase of a membership under this section is different from a termination of membership under Section 6.21 because a termination usually does not involve the payment of any consideration to the member being terminated.

[Subchapter] D
DELEGATES

§ 6.30. DELEGATES

(a) A membership corporation may provide in its articles of incorporation or bylaws for delegates.

(b) The articles of incorporation or bylaws may set forth provisions relating to:

  (1) the characteristics, qualifications, rights, limitations, and obligations of delegates including their selection and removal;

  (2) calling, noticing, holding, and conducting meetings of delegates; and

  (3) carrying on corporate activities during and between meetings of delegates.

(c) An assembly or other organized group of delegates constitutes a designated body.

Source Note: Subsections (a) and (b) are substantially a reenactment of Model Nonprofit Corporation Act (1987) § 6.40, except that a reference in subsection (a) to delegates having the authority of members has been omitted.

CROSS-REFERENCES

"Designated body," see § 8.12.

Notice, see § 1.41.

OFFICIAL COMMENT

Section 6.30 authorizes nonprofit corporations to operate with delegates rather than or in addition to members or a board of directors. Section 6.30 authorizes the articles of incorporation or bylaws to set forth rules in regard to delegates, meetings of delegates, and carrying on corporate activities during and between meetings of delegates.

The prior version of the act provided in subsection (a) that delegates could have "some or all of the authority of members." That restriction has been omitted because delegates may be given not just some or all of the authority of members, but also some of the authority of the board of directors to act on those matters specified in the articles of incorporation or bylaws.

Insofar as the delegates have been given the powers of members, they have analogous rights, duties, and obligations. Similarly, when delegates are exercising powers of the board of directors they will have the duties and liabilities of directors. See Section 8.12.

[Subchapter] E
FINANCIAL PROVISIONS

§ 6.40. DISTRIBUTIONS PROHIBITED

(a) Except as permitted under Section 6.22 or 6.41, a nonprofit corporation shall not pay dividends or make distributions of any part of its assets, income, or profits to its members, directors, members of a designated body, or officers.

(b) This section does not apply to a contract or transaction authorized pursuant to Section 8.60.

Source Note: Derived from Model Nonprofit Corporation Act (1987) §§ 1.40(10) ("distribution") and 13.01.

CROSS-REFERENCES

Compensation and other permitted payments, see § 6.41.

"Designated body" defined, see § 1.40.

"Director" defined, see § 1.40.

"Member" defined, see § 1.40.

"Officer" defined, see § 1.40.

Purchase of memberships, see § 6.22.

OFFICIAL COMMENT

Section 6.40 sets forth the basic rule that a nonprofit corporation is prohibited from paying dividends or making other types of distributions. If a transfer is a direct payment to a member as a result of the member's interest in the nonprofit corporation, it is prohibited except to the extent provided in Section 6.41. Cash dividends from whatever source are the clearest example of prohibited dividends. *See Kubik v. American Composers Alliance, Inc.*, 54 N.Y.S.2d 764 (1945).

The question arises as to what a nonprofit corporation can do with profits it generates as it cannot use the profits to pay dividends. Corporations that are exempt from federal income tax under Section 501(c)(3) of the Internal Revenue Code typically use profits to further their public, charitable, or religious purposes. Other nonprofit corporations may use profits to improve their facilities and services. In *Burton Potter Post No. 185, American Legion v. Epstein*, 219 N.Y.S.2d 224 (1961), a nonprofit club generated profits from its activities which were used to improve the club facilities. The court found that the corporation was "not organized for pecuniary profit as long as it devotes its income to club purposes." *Id.* at 227.

While the members benefit from the use of funds for club purposes, that benefit is not a dividend and is not considered a distribution because the nonprofit corporation is conferring benefits upon its members in conformity with its purposes.

A payment by a nonprofit corporation that is not derived from "any part of its income or profit" is not a distribution. Thus the return of an overcharge or the provision of services for which members have paid is not a distribution, nor is the payment of reasonable compensation for services.

A payment by a nonprofit corporation pursuant to a contract or transaction authorized under Section 8.60 is not a distribution.

§ 6.41. COMPENSATION AND OTHER PERMITTED PAYMENTS

(a) A nonprofit corporation may pay reasonable compensation or reimburse reasonable expenses to members, directors, members of a designated body, or officers for services rendered.

(b) A nonprofit corporation may confer benefits upon or make contributions to members or nonmembers in conformity with its purposes, repurchase its memberships only to the extent provided in Section 6.22, or repay capital contributions, except when:

(1) the corporation is currently insolvent or would thereby be made insolvent or rendered unable to carry on its purposes; or

(2) the fair value of the assets of the corporation remaining after the conferring of benefits, contribution, repurchase, or repayment would be insufficient to meet its liabilities.

(c) A nonprofit corporation may make distributions of cash or property to members upon dissolution or final liquidation only as permitted by this [act].

Source Note: Subsections (a) and (b) are patterned after 15 PA. CONS. STAT. § 5551(b) and (c). Subsection (c) is derived from Model Nonprofit Corporation Act (1987) § 13.02(b).

CROSS-REFERENCES

Corporate purposes, see § 3.01.

"Designated body" defined, see § 1.40.

"Director" defined, see § 1.40.

Dissolution, see Ch. 14.

"Member" defined, see § 1.40.

"Officer" defined, see § 1.40.

Purchase of memberships, see § 6.22.

OFFICIAL COMMENT

Distributions upon dissolution or final liquidation are governed by Chapter 14. Normally, the members of a nonprofit corporation that is not a charitable corporation will receive its net worth upon dissolution. Members of a charitable corporation, in contrast, normally will not share in its net worth upon dissolution since they do not have any economic interest in its assets. Under limited circumstances, however, a charitable corporation may distribute its assets to its members, if those members are themselves charitable corporations or otherwise recognized as exempt under Section 501(c)(3) of the Internal Revenue Code.

§ 6.42. CAPITAL CONTRIBUTIONS OF MEMBERS

(a) A membership corporation that is not a charitable corporation may provide in its articles of incorporation or bylaws that members, upon or subsequent to admission, must make capital contributions. Except as provided in the articles or bylaws, the amount shall be fixed by the board of directors. The requirement of a capital contribution may apply to all members, or to the members of a single class, or to members of different classes in different amounts or proportions.

(b) The adoption or amendment of a capital contribution requirement, whether or not approved by the members, shall not apply to a member who did not vote in favor of the adoption or amendment until 30 days after the member has been given notice of the adoption or amendment.

Source Note: Subsection (a) is patterned in part after 15 PA. CONS. STAT. § 5541(a). Subsection (b) is new.

CROSS-REFERENCES

Dues, assessments, and fees, see § 6.13.

"Membership corporation" defined, see § 1.40.

When capital contributions may not be repaid, § 6.41.

OFFICIAL COMMENT

Mutual benefit corporations may find it desirable to require the members to make capital contributions at certain times, for example, to fund improvements to a clubhouse or other facilities of the corporation. Capital contributions are typically different from membership obligations like dues in that capital contributions are larger in amount and sporadic or nonrecurring. They also differ in that capital contribution requirements must be set forth in the articles of incorporation or bylaws. As a result, Section 6.42(b) provides that adoption or amendment of a capital contribution will not apply to a member who does not vote in favor of the change until 30 days after notice to the member. This will permit the member to resign if the member does not wish to satisfy the capital contribution requirement. A similar delay does not apply to changes in dues, assessments, or fees.

The provisions of this section also apply to a designated body under Section 8.12. Thus a designated body may perform any of the functions of the board of directors described in this section.

§ 6.43. DEBT AND SECURITY INTERESTS

(a) A nonprofit corporation shall not issue bonds or other evidences of indebtedness except for money or other property, tangible or intangible, or labor or services actually received by or performed for the corporation or for its benefit or in its formation or reorganization, or a combination thereof. In the absence of fraud, the judgment of the board of directors as to the value of the consideration received by the corporation is conclusive.

(b) The board of directors may authorize a mortgage or pledge of, or the creation of a security interest in, all or any part of the property of the nonprofit corporation, or any interest therein. Unless otherwise restricted in the articles of incorporation or bylaws, the vote or consent of the members shall not be required to make effective such action by the board.

Source Note: Patterned after 15 PA. CONS. STAT. § 5543.

CROSS-REFERENCES

When debt instruments may not be repaid, § 6.41.

OFFICIAL COMMENT

Issuance of bonds or debt instruments must be done in compliance with applicable federal and state securities laws, subject to any applicable exemptions from registration under those laws. The application of such laws is preserved by Section 1.03.

The provisions of this section also apply to a designated body under Section 8.12. Thus the functions of the board of directors under this section with respect to debts and security interests may be assigned to a designated body instead.

§ 6.44. PRIVATE FOUNDATIONS

(a) Except as provided in subsection (b), a nonprofit corporation that is a private foundation as defined in Section 509(a) of the Internal Revenue Code shall:
   (1) distribute such amounts for each taxable year at such time and in such manner as not to subject the corporation to tax under Section 4942 of the Internal Revenue Code;
   (2) not engage in any act of self-dealing as defined in Section 4941(d) of the Internal Revenue Code;
   (3) not retain any excess business holdings as defined in Section 4943(c) of the Internal Revenue Code;
   (4) not make any investments in such manner as to subject the corporation to tax under Section 4944 of the Internal Revenue Code; and
   (5) not make any taxable expenditures as defined in Section 4945(d) of the Internal Revenue Code.

(b) Subsection (a) does not apply to a nonprofit corporation incorporated before January 1, 1970 that has been properly relieved from the requirements of Section 508(e)(1) of the Internal Revenue Code by a timely judicial proceeding.

Source Note: Derived from Model Nonprofit Corporation Act (1987) § 1.50.

CROSS-REFERENCES

Powers, see § 3.02.

Purposes, see § 3.01.

OFFICIAL COMMENT

Under Section 508(e)(1) of the Internal Revenue Code, a private foundation (as defined in Section 509(a)) is not exempt from federal income tax under Section 501(a) unless its governing instrument includes provisions the effects of which are:

(1) to require its income for each taxable year to be distributed at such time and in such manner as not to subject the foundation to tax under Section 4942; and
(2) to prohibit the foundation from engaging in any act of self-dealing (as defined in Section 4941(d)), from retaining any excess business holdings (as defined in Section 4943(c)), from making any investments in such manner as to subject the foundation to tax under Section 4944, and from making any taxable expenditures (as defined in Section 4945(d)).

Section 1.508-3(d) of the Income Tax Regulations provides that a private foundation's governing instrument is deemed to conform with the requirements of Section 508(e) of the Internal Revenue Code if valid provisions of state law have been enacted which either require the foundation to comply with the provisions of Section 508(e)(1), or treat the required provisions as contained in the foundation's governing instrument.

Section 508(e)(2) of the Internal Revenue Code provides that the requirements of paragraph 1 of the section do not apply to a private foundation organized before January 1, 1970 which has been excused from complying with the requirements of paragraph 1 by a court order secured in a proceeding begun before January 1, 1972. That exception is preserved by Section 6.44(b).

Under the applicable Income Tax Regulation (Section 1.508(3)(d)), this section satisfies the requirement that a private foundation's governing instrument include such provisions. The section applies only to foundations that are corporations, and does not satisfy the requirements of Section 508(e) in the case of trusts or other entities that qualify as private foundations under Section 509(a) of the Code.

CHAPTER 7

Member Meetings

[Subchapter] A
PROCEDURES

§ 7.01. ANNUAL AND REGULAR MEETINGS

(a) A membership corporation shall hold a meeting of members annually at a time stated in or fixed in accordance with the articles of incorporation or bylaws.

(b) A membership corporation may hold regular meetings on a regional or other basis at times stated in or fixed in accordance with the articles of incorporation or bylaws.

(c) Except as provided in subsection (e), annual and regular meetings of the members may be held in or out of this state at the place stated in or fixed in accordance with the articles of incorporation or bylaws. If no place is stated in or fixed in accordance with the articles or bylaws, annual and regular meetings shall be held at the nonprofit corporation's principal office.

(d) The failure to hold an annual or regular meeting at the time stated in or fixed in accordance with the articles of incorporation or bylaws does not affect the validity of any corporate action.

(e) The articles of incorporation or bylaws may provide that an annual or regular meeting of members does not need to be held at a geographic location if the meeting is held by means of the Internet or other electronic communications technology in a fashion pursuant to which the members have the opportunity to read or hear the proceedings substantially concurrently with their occurrence, vote on matters submitted to the members, pose questions, and make comments.

Source Note: Subsections (a), (c), and (d) are patterned after Model Business Corporation Act, 3d Ed. (2002) § 7.01. Subsections (a)–(d) are derived from Revised Model Nonprofit Corporation Act (1987) § 7.01(a)–(c) and (f). Subsection (e) is patterned after 15 Pa. Cons. Stat. § 1704(a) (last sentence).

CROSS-REFERENCES

Action by ballot, see § 7.09.

Action without meeting, see § 7.04.

Court-ordered meeting, see § 7.03.

List of members at meeting, see § 7.20.

"Membership corporation" defined, see § 1.40.

Notice of meeting, see § 7.05.

"Principal office":
  defined, see § 1.40.
  designated in annual report, see § 16.21.

Proxies, see § 7.22.

Quorum and voting requirements, see §§ 7.24–7.26.

Special meeting, see § 7.02.

OFFICIAL COMMENT

Section 7.01(a) requires every membership corporation to hold an annual meeting of members each year. The principal action to be taken at the annual meeting is the election of directors pursuant to Section 8.04, but the purposes of an annual meeting are not limited and any matters appropriate for member action may also be considered at that meeting. An annual meeting is also an appropriate forum for a member to raise any relevant question about the corporation's operations.

Rather than holding an annual meeting, the members may elect directors and take other appropriate action by consent under Section 7.04. If the members fail to elect directors, the directors currently in office continue in office under Section 8.05 beyond the expiration of their terms.

Some membership corporations hold regular meetings of members in addition to holding an annual meeting of members. Section 7.01(b) recognizes this practice and allows corporations to hold regular meetings at times stated in or fixed in accordance with their articles of incorporation or bylaws. The act does not specify any particular business that must be considered at regular meetings.

The time and place of the annual meeting may be "stated in or fixed in accordance with the articles of incorporation or bylaws." If the articles or bylaws do not themselves fix a time and place for the annual meeting, authority to fix them may be delegated to the board of directors or to a specified corporate officer. This section thus gives nonprofit corporations the flexibility to hold annual meetings in varying places at varying times as convenience may dictate.

The annual meeting may be held either inside or outside the state or in a foreign country, but if the bylaws do not fix, or state the method of fixing, the place of the meeting, the meeting must be held at the "principal office" of the membership corporation. The principal office is defined in Section 1.40 as the location of the principal executive office of the corporation and may or may not be its registered or official office under Section 5.01. Section 16.21 requires that the address of the principal office be specified in the corporation's annual report. An annual meeting may also be held electronically if the requirements of Section 7.01(e) are satisfied.

If the annual meeting is not held either within 6 months of the close of the nonprofit corporation's fiscal year or within 15 months of the last annual meeting, a member may compel an annual meeting to be held under Section 7.03. In the absence of a demand for a meeting, a corporation can operate indefinitely without actually holding an annual meeting.

§ 7.02. SPECIAL MEETING

(a) A membership corporation shall hold a special meeting of members:

  (1) at the call of its board of directors or the persons authorized to do so by the articles of incorporation or bylaws; or

  (2) if the holders of at least 10%, or such other amount up to 25% as the articles of incorporation or bylaws shall specify, of all the votes entitled to be cast on an issue proposed to be considered at the proposed special meeting sign, date, and deliver to the corporation one or more demands in the form of a record for the meeting describing the purpose for which it is to be held.

(b) Unless otherwise provided in the articles of incorporation or bylaws, a demand for a special meeting may be revoked by notice to that effect received by the membership corporation from the members calling the meeting prior to the receipt by the corporation of demands sufficient in number to require the holding of a special meeting.

(c) If not otherwise fixed under Section 7.03 or 7.07, the record date for determining members entitled to demand a special meeting is the date the first member signs a demand.

(d) Except as provided in subsection (f), special meetings of the members may be held in or out of this state at the place stated in or fixed in accordance with the articles of incorporation or bylaws. If no place is stated or fixed in accordance with the articles or bylaws, special meetings shall be held at the corporation's principal office.

(e) Only business within the purpose or purposes described in the meeting notice required by Section 7.05(c) may be conducted at a special meeting of the members.

(f) The articles of incorporation or bylaws may provide that a special meeting of members does not need to be held at a geographic location if the meeting is held by means of the Internet or other electronic communications technology in a fashion pursuant to which the members have the opportunity to read or hear the proceedings substantially concurrently with their occurrence, vote on matters submitted to the members, pose questions, and make comments.

Source Note: Subsections (a)–(e) are patterned after Model Business Corporation Act, 3d Ed. (2002) § 7.02, and derived from Revised Model Nonprofit Corporation Act (1987) § 7.02. Subsection (f) is patterned after 15 PA. CONS. STAT. § 1704(a) (last sentence).

CROSS-REFERENCES

Action by ballot, see § 7.09.

Action without meeting, see § 7.04.

Annual meeting, see § 7.01.

Court-ordered meeting, see § 7.03.

List of members at meeting, see § 7.20.

"Membership corporation" defined, see § 1.40.

Notice of meeting, see § 7.05.

"Principal office":
- defined, see § 1.40.
- designated in annual report, see § 16.21.

Quorum and voting requirements, see §§ 7.24–7.26.

Regular meeting, see § 7.01.

Waiver of notice, see § 7.06.

OFFICIAL COMMENT

Any meeting other than an annual or regular meeting is a special meeting under Section 7.02. A special meeting must be called for specific purposes and may only consider matters within those purposes.

1. Who May Call a Special Meeting

A special meeting may be called under Section 7.02(a) by the board of directors or the persons authorized to do so by the articles of incorporation or bylaws. Typically, the persons holding certain designated offices within the corporation, *e.g.*, the president, chair of the board of directors, or chief executive officer, are given authority to call special meetings of the members. In addition, the holders of at least 10% of the votes entitled to be cast on a proposed issue at the special meeting may require the membership corporation to hold a special meeting by signing, dating, and delivering one or more demands for a special meeting that set forth the purpose of the desired meeting. That percentage may be decreased or increased (but to not more than 25%) by a provision in the articles of incorporation or bylaws fixing a different percentage.

Members demanding a special meeting do not all need to sign a single demand, but the demands must all describe essentially the same purpose. Revocations of demands will be effective if notice is delivered to the corporation in the manner contemplated by Section 1.41 and received before the corporation receives the requisite number of demands requiring that a special meeting be called. However, revocations received after that time will be a nullity and will have no effect. Upon receipt of demands by members with the requisite number of votes, the corporation (through an appropriate officer) must call the special meeting at a reasonable time and place. The members' demand may suggest a time and place but the final decision on such matters belongs to the corporation. If no meeting is held within the time periods specified in Section 7.03, the members may obtain a summary court order under that section requiring that the meeting be held.

Section 7.02(c) fixes a record date for determining the members entitled to sign a demand for a special meeting of members. Unless a record date is otherwise fixed for this purpose, the record date is the date the first member signs the demand. If a member initially signs a demand but later seeks to withdraw the demand, the corporation may permit the member to do so.

2. Discretion as to Call of Special Meeting

Under Section 7.02(a)(2) it is possible that more than one faction of members may demand meetings at roughly the same time or that a single (or changing) faction of members may request consecutive, overlapping, or repetitive meetings. The responsible corporate officers should have some discretion as to the call and purposes of a meeting, and where demands are repetitious or overlapping, they should have the right to refuse to call a meeting for a purpose identical or similar to a purpose for which a previous special meeting was held in the recent past. Similarly, they should have some discretion to decline to call a special meeting when an annual or regular meeting will be held in the near future. This limited discretion of the corporation to deny repetitive or overlapping demands may ultimately be tested under Section 7.03, which itself gives the court discretion whether or not to compel the holding of a special meeting under these circumstances. See the Official Comment to Section 7.03.

3. Business That May Be Conducted at a Special Meeting

Section 7.05(c) provides that a notice of a special meeting must include a "description of the purpose for which the meeting is called." Section 7.02(e) states that only business that is within that purpose may be conducted at the special meeting. The word "within" was chosen, rather than a broader phrase like "reasonably related to," to describe the relationship between the notice and the authorized business to assure a member who does not attend a special meeting that new or unexpected matters will not be considered in the member's absence.

4. Location

A special meeting may be held either inside or outside the state or in a foreign country, but if the bylaws do not fix, or state the method of fixing, the place of the meeting, the meeting must be held at the "principal office" of the membership corporation. The principal office is defined in Section 1.40 as the location of the principal executive office of the corporation and may or may not be its registered or official office under Section 5.01. Section 16.21 requires that the address of the principal office be specified in the corporation's annual report. A special meeting may also be held electronically if the requirements of Section 7.02(f) are satisfied.

5. Designated Body

The provisions of this section relating to the board of directors also apply to a designated body under Section 8.12. Thus a designated body may be given the authority to call and otherwise act with respect to a special meeting.

§ 7.03. COURT-ORDERED MEETING

(a) The [*name or describe*] court of the county where the principal office of a membership corporation (or, if not in this state, its registered office) is located may summarily order a meeting to be held:
  (1) on application of any member entitled to participate in an annual or regular meeting if an annual meeting was not held within the earlier of 6 months after the end of the corporation's fiscal year or 15 months after its last annual meeting; or
  (2) on application of a member who signed a demand for a special meeting under Section 7.02, if:
    (i) notice of the special meeting was not given within 30 days after the date the demand was delivered to the corporation's secretary; or
    (ii) the special meeting was not held in accordance with the notice.

(b) The court may fix the time and place of the meeting, determine the members entitled to participate in the meeting, specify a record date for determining members entitled to notice of and to vote at the meeting, prescribe the form and content of the meeting notice, fix the quorum required for specific matters to be considered at the meeting (or direct that the votes represented at the meeting constitute a quorum for action on those matters), and enter other orders necessary to accomplish the purpose or purposes of the meeting.

Source Note: Patterned after Model Business Corporation Act, 3d Ed. (2002) § 7.03. Derived from Revised Model Nonprofit Corporation Act (1987) § 7.03.

CROSS-REFERENCES

Annual meeting, see § 7.01.

Effective date of notice, see § 1.41.

Member list for voting at meeting, see § 7.20.

"Membership corporation" defined, see § 1.40.

Notice of meeting, see § 7.05.

"Principal office":
- defined, see § 1.40.
- designated in annual report, see § 16.21.

Quorum and voting requirements, see §§ 7.24–7.26.

Registered office:
- designated in annual report, see § 16.21.
- required, see §§ 2.02, 5.01, and 15.07.

Regular meeting, see § 7.01.

Voting entitlement generally, see § 7.21.

OFFICIAL COMMENT

Section 7.03 provides the remedy for members if the membership corporation refuses or fails to hold a meeting of members as required by Section 7.01 or 7.02. A member entitled to participate in a meeting may apply for a summary court order to command the holding of a meeting if (1) an annual meeting is not held within 6 months after the end of the corporation's fiscal year or 15 months after its last annual meeting, or (2) a special meeting is not properly noticed within 30 days after a valid demand is delivered to the secretary of the corporation or, if properly noticed, is not held in accordance with the notice. Since a meeting must be held within 60 days of the notice date under Section 7.05, the maximum delay between the demand for a special meeting and the right to petition a court for a summary order is 90 days.

1. The Court with Jurisdiction to Administer Section 7.03

The identity of the specific court with jurisdiction to order a meeting of members under Section 7.03(a) must be supplied by each state when enacting this section. It is intended that this should be a court of general civil jurisdiction. Generally, all matters relating to a nonprofit corporation should be addressed to the court in the county where the corporation's principal office is located in the state or, if the corporation does not have its principal office in the state, to the court in the county in which its registered office is located.

2. Discretion of the Court

The court has discretion under Section 7.03 since the language of the statute is that the court "may summarily order" that a meeting be held. A court, for example, may refuse to order a special meeting if the specified purpose is repetitive of the purpose of a special meeting held in the recent past. See the Official Comment to Section 7.02. Alternatively, the court may view the demand as a good faith request for reconsideration of an action taken in the recent past and may order a meeting to be held. Similarly, even though a demand for an annual meeting is not a formal prerequisite for an application for an order under this section, the court may withhold setting a time and date for the annual meeting for a reasonably short period in order to permit the corporation to do so.

3. Burden of Proof

A member applying for an order to hold a meeting has the burden of showing that the member is entitled to the order. In the case of a special meeting, the member has the burden of showing that the demand was executed by the holders of at least 10% of the votes entitled to be cast on the record date and that the demand was duly delivered to the corporation's secretary.

4. Notice, Time, Place, and Quorum Requirements

If the court orders that a meeting be held, it may fix the time and place of the meeting, determine the voting groups entitled to participate in the meeting, set the record date, order notice to be given as required by Section 7.05, and enter such other orders as may be appropriate for the holding of the meeting. The court may also establish the quorum requirements for specific matters to be considered at the meeting or direct that the votes represented at the meeting automatically constitute a quorum for the taking of any action without regard to Section 7.24 or any provision to the contrary in the nonprofit corporation's articles of incorporation or bylaws. In order to prevent misunderstanding about a special quorum requirement, if one is imposed, it is appropriate for the court to order that the notice of the meeting state specifically and conspicuously that a special quorum requirement is applicable to the court-ordered meeting.

5. Status as Annual Meeting

The court may provide that a meeting it has ordered is to be the annual meeting. If so provided, the meeting should be viewed as compliance with Section 7.01, precluding all other member requests for an annual meeting for that year.

§ 7.04. ACTION WITHOUT MEETING

(a) Except as provided in the articles of incorporation or bylaws, action required or permitted by this [act] to be taken at a meeting of the members may be taken without a meeting if the action is taken by all the members entitled to vote on the action. The action must be evidenced by one or more consents in the form of a record bearing the date of signature and describing the action taken, signed by all the members entitled to vote on the action, and delivered to the membership corporation for inclusion in the minutes or filing with the corporate records.

(b) If not otherwise fixed under Section 7.03 or 7.07, the record date for determining members entitled to take action without a meeting is the date the first member signs the consent under subsection (a). A consent shall not be effective to take the corporate action referred to therein unless, within 60 days after the earliest date appearing on a consent delivered to the membership corporation in the manner required by this section, consents signed by members entitled to cast the required number of votes on the action are received by the corporation. A consent may be revoked by a signed notice in the form of a record to that effect received by the corporation prior to receipt by the corporation of unrevoked consents sufficient in number to take corporate action.

(c) A consent signed under this section has the effect of a meeting vote and may be described as such.

(d) If this [act], the articles of incorporation, or the bylaws require that notice of proposed action be given to members not entitled to vote on the action and the action is to be taken by consent of the members entitled to vote, the membership corporation must deliver to the members not entitled to vote notice of the proposed action at least 10 days before the action is taken. The notice must contain or be accompanied by the same material that would have been required to be delivered to members not entitled to vote in a notice of meeting at which the proposed action would have been submitted to the members for action.

Source Note: Patterned after Model Business Corporation Act, 3d Ed. (2002) § 7.04. Derived from Revised Model Nonprofit Corporation Act (1987) § 7.04.

CROSS-REFERENCES

Acceptance of consents, see § 7.23.

"Deliver" defined, see § 1.40.

"Membership corporation" defined, see § 1.40.

Notice, see § 1.41.

"Secretary" defined, see § 1.40.

"Sign" defined, see § 1.40.

Voting entitlement generally, see § 7.21.

OFFICIAL COMMENT

Section 7.04 provides as a default rule that all the members entitled to vote on an issue may validly act by unanimous consent without a meeting. Unanimous consent is obtainable, as a practical matter, only on matters on which there are only a relatively few members entitled to vote. The default rule is based on the fundamental premise that if all the voting members desire some action to be taken, no purpose is served by requiring the formality of holding a meeting of members. Although Section 7.04 only authorizes unanimous consent, it permits the articles of incorporation or bylaws to vary that rule. Thus, the articles or bylaws could provide for consent by less than all the members (typically a majority) or prohibit action by consent and require a meeting whenever the members are to act on an issue.

Action by consent has the same effect as a meeting vote and may be described as such, including in filings with the secretary of state. Unless the articles of incorporation or bylaws expressly limit the use of action by consent, Section 7.04 is applicable to any action taken by the members, including, without limitation, election of directors, approval of mergers or sales of substantially all the corporate property not in the ordinary course of business, amendments of articles of incorporation, and dissolution.

1. Form of Consent

To be effective, consents must be in the form of a record, dated, signed by all the members entitled to vote, and delivered to the membership corporation in the manner contemplated by Section 1.41(d). The phrase "one or more consents" is included in Section 7.04(a) to make it clear that all members do not need to sign the same piece of paper or electronic record. The record date for determining who is entitled to vote, if not otherwise fixed by or in accordance with the articles of incorporation or bylaws, is the date the first member signs a consent. To minimize the possibility that action by consent will be authorized by action of persons who may no longer be members at the time the action is taken, Section 7.04(b) requires that all consents be signed within 60 days after the earliest signature date appearing on the consents delivered to the corporation.

2. Revocation of Consent

Action by consent is effective only when the last member has signed and all consents have been delivered to the membership corporation in the manner contemplated by Section 1.41(d). Before that time, any member may withdraw a consent simply by advising the corporation of that fact. *Cf. Calumet Industries, Inc. v. McClure*, 464 F. Supp. 19 (N.D. Ill. 1978). If consents must be unanimous in a particular case, the withdrawal of a single consent will prohibit action by consent. Withdrawal of a consent in cases where less than unanimity is required may or may not make action by consent impossible. If a member seeks to withdraw a consent after the requisite number of members have signed consents and filed them with the corporation, the withdrawal will be a nullity and will not be given effect.

3. Consent to Fundamental Corporate Changes

Section 7.04 is applicable to all member actions, including the approval of fundamental corporate changes described in Chapters 9, 10, 11, 12, and 14. If these actions were taken at an annual, regular, or special meeting, members who were not entitled to vote on the matter would nevertheless be entitled to receive notice of the meeting, including a description of the transaction proposed to be considered at the meeting. See, *e.g.*, Sections 10.03 (notice of proposed amendment) and 12.02 (notice of sale of assets). In order to ensure that members who are not entitled to vote have essentially the same rights if action is taken by consent rather than at a meeting, Section 7.04(d) provides that members who are not entitled to vote must be given at least 10 days' notice of the fundamental corporate changes that are proposed for approval by consent.

§ 7.05. NOTICE OF MEETING

(a) A membership corporation must give notice to the members of the date, time, and place of each annual, regular, or special meeting of the members. Except as provided in the articles of incorporation or the bylaws, the notice must be given no fewer than 10 nor more than 60 days before the meeting date. Except as provided in this [act], the articles, or the bylaws, the corporation must give notice only to members entitled to vote at the meeting.

(b) Unless this [act], the articles of incorporation, or the bylaws require otherwise, notice of an annual meeting need not include a description of the purpose for which the meeting is called.

(c) Notice of a special meeting must include a description of the purpose for which the meeting is called.

(d) If not otherwise fixed under Section 7.03 or 7.07, the record date for determining members entitled to notice of and to vote at an annual or special meeting of the members is the day before the first notice is given to members.

(e) Unless the articles of incorporation or bylaws require otherwise, if an annual, regular, or special meeting of the members is adjourned to a different date, time, or place, notice need not be given of the new date, time, or place if the new date, time, or place is announced at the meeting before adjournment. If a new record date for the adjourned meeting is or must be fixed under Section 7.07, notice of the adjourned meeting must be given under this section to the members entitled to vote on the new record date.

Source Note: Patterned after Model Business Corporation Act, 3d Ed. (2002) § 7.05. Derived from Revised Model Nonprofit Corporation Act (1987) § 7.05.

CROSS-REFERENCES

Annual meeting, see § 7.01.

"Deliver" defined, see § 1.40.

"Membership corporation" defined, see § 1.40.

Notice, see § 1.41.

Notice otherwise required:
- amendment, see § 10.03.
- conversion, see § 9.52.
- disposition of assets, see § 12.02.
- dissolution, see § 14.02.

domestication, see § 9.21.
merger and membership exchange, see § 11.04.

Regular meeting, see § 7.01.

Special meeting, see § 7.02.

Waiver of notice, see § 7.06.

OFFICIAL COMMENT

Members entitled to notice must be given notice of annual, regular, and special meetings pursuant to Section 7.05 unless the notice is waived pursuant to Section 7.06. Notice must be given at least 10 but not more than 60 days before the meeting date.

1. Members Entitled to Notice

Generally, only members who are entitled to vote at a meeting are entitled to notice. Thus, notice usually needs to be sent only to members entitled to vote for an election of directors or generally on other matters (in the case of an annual or regular meeting), and on matters within the specified purposes set forth in the notice (in the case of a special meeting), and only to such members on the record date. The last sentence of Section 7.05(a), however, recognizes that other sections of the act require that notice of meetings at which certain types of fundamental corporate changes are to be considered must be sent to all members, including members who are not entitled to vote on any matter at the meeting. See, *e.g.*, Sections 12.02 and 14.02. In addition, the articles of incorporation or bylaws may require that notice of meeting be given to all or specified voting groups of members who are not entitled to vote on the matters considered at those meetings.

2. Statement of Matters to Be Considered at an Annual Meeting

Notice of all special meetings must include a description of the purpose or purposes for which the meeting is called and the matters acted upon at the meeting are limited to those within the notice of meeting. By contrast, the act does not require that the notice of an annual or regular meeting refer to any specific purpose or purposes, and any matter appropriate for member action may be considered. As recognized in subsection (b), however, other provisions of the act provide that certain types of fundamental corporate changes may be considered at an annual or regular meeting only if specific reference to the proposed action appears in the notice of meeting. See, *e.g.*, Sections 10.03, 11.04, 12.02, and 14.02. If the board of directors chooses, a notice of an annual or regular meeting may contain references to purposes or proposals not required by statute. In the event that management intends to present nonroutine proposals for a member vote and members have not otherwise been informed of such proposals, good corporate practice suggests that references to such proposals be made in the notice. In any event, if a notice of an annual or regular meeting refers specifically to one or more purposes, the meeting is not limited to those purposes.

3. Record Date

Section 7.05(d) is a catchall record date provision for annual, regular, and special meetings. If the record date for notice and for voting entitlement is not otherwise fixed pursuant to Sections 7.03 or 7.07, the record date for purposes of determining who is entitled to notice and to vote at the meeting is the day before the notice is given to the first members.

The selection of the day before the notice is given as the catchall record date is intended to permit the corporation to deliver notices to members on a given day without regard to any changes in membership during that day. For this reason, this section is not inconsistent with the general principle set forth in the last sentence of Section 7.07(a) that the board of directors may not fix a retroactive record date.

4. Notice of Adjourned Meetings

Section 7.05(e) provides rules for adjourned meetings and determines whether new notice must be given to members. Under this subsection a meeting may be adjourned to a different date, time, or place without additional notice to the members (unless the bylaws require otherwise) if the new date, time, or place is announced before adjournment. But new notice is required if a new record date is or must be fixed under Section 7.07(c). If a new record date is or must be fixed, all of the requirements of Section 7.05 must be complied with as notice is given to the persons who are members as of the new record date. A new quorum for the adjourned meeting must also be established. See Section 7.24.

Section 7.24 provides that if a quorum exists for a meeting, it is deemed to continue to exist automatically for an adjourned meeting unless a new record date is or must be set for the adjourned meeting.

5. Alternative Forms of Notice

The manner in which notice may be delivered to the members is governed by Section 1.41. A church or similar religious body may decide to provide for notice of meetings by announcement at church or religious services, in which case it should specify the frequency and timing of notice (*e.g.*, "announcement at any two services held during different weeks within 30 days before the time at which the meeting of members will be held"). Other nonprofit corporations may choose to deliver notice in a manner similar to the way business corporations deliver notice to their shareholders.

§ 7.06. WAIVER OF NOTICE

(a) A member may waive any notice required by this [act], the articles of incorporation, or the bylaws before or after the date and time stated in the notice of the meeting or action. The waiver must be in the form of a record, be signed by the member entitled to the notice, and be delivered to the membership corporation for inclusion in the minutes or filing with the corporate records.

(b) The attendance of a member at a meeting:

(1) waives objection to lack of notice or defective notice of the meeting, unless the member at the beginning of the

meeting objects to holding the meeting or transacting business at the meeting;

(2) waives objection to consideration of a particular matter at the meeting that is not within the purpose described in the meeting notice, unless the member objects at the meeting to considering the matter.

Source Note: Patterned after Model Business Corporation Act, 3d Ed. (2002) § 7.06. Derived from Revised Model Nonprofit Corporation Act (1987) § 7.06.

CROSS-REFERENCES

Acceptance of waiver, see § 7.23.

Action without meeting, see § 7.04.

Meeting notice, see § 7.05.

"Membership corporation" defined, see § 1.40.

Notice, see § 1.41.

Proxies, see § 7.22.

OFFICIAL COMMENT

Section 7.06(a) permits any member to waive any notice required by Section 7.05 by a waiver in the form of a record, signed by the member and delivered to the membership corporation. A waiver is effective even though it is signed at or after the time set for the meeting.

A notice of member meetings serves two principal purposes: (1) it advises members of the date, time, and place of the annual, regular, or special meeting, and (2) in the case of a special meeting (or an annual or regular meeting at which fundamental changes may be made), it advises members of the purposes of the meeting. If a member attends a meeting, the member has probably received some form of notice of the date, time, and place of the meeting, whether from the membership corporation or from another source. As a result, Section 7.06(b)(1) provides that attendance at a meeting constitutes waiver of any failure to receive the notice or defects in the statement of the date, time, and place of any meeting. Defects waived by attendance for this purpose include a failure to send the notice altogether, delivery to the wrong address, a misstatement of the date, time, or place of the meeting, and a failure to notice the meeting within the time periods specified in Section 7.05(a). If a member believes that the defect in or failure of notice was in some way prejudicial, the member must object and state at the beginning of the meeting that the member objects to holding the meeting or transacting any business. If this objection is made, the corporation may correct the defect by sending proper notice to the members for a subsequent meeting or by obtaining waivers of notice from all members who did not receive the notice required by Section 7.05.

For purposes of this section, "attendance" at a meeting involves the presence of the member in person or by proxy. A member who attends a meeting solely for the purpose of objecting to the notice may be counted as present for purposes of determining whether a quorum is present. See the Official Comment to Section 7.24.

In the case of special meetings, or annual or regular meetings at which fundamental corporate changes are considered, a second purpose of the notice is to tell members what is to be considered at the meeting. An objection that a particular matter is not within the stated purposes of the meeting obviously cannot be raised until the matter is presented. Thus Section 7.06(b)(2) provides that a member waives this kind of objection if the member fails to object promptly after the matter is first presented. If this objection is made, the membership corporation may correct the defect by sending proper notice to the members for a subsequent meeting or obtaining waivers of notice from all members. Of course, whether or not a specific matter is within a stated purpose of a meeting is ultimately a matter for judicial determination, typically in a suit to invalidate action taken at the meeting brought by a member who was not present at the meeting or who was present at the meeting and preserved an objection under Section 7.06(b).

The purpose of both waiver rules in Section 7.06(b) is to require members with technical objections to holding the meeting or considering a specific matter to raise them at the outset and not reserve them to be raised only if they are unhappy with the outcome of the meeting. The rules set forth in this section differ in some respects from the waiver rules for directors set forth in Section 8.23 where a waiver is inferred if the director acquiesces in the action taken at a meeting even if the director raised a technical objection to the notice of a meeting at the outset.

§ 7.07. RECORD DATE

(a) The articles of incorporation or bylaws may fix or provide the manner of fixing the record date to determine the members entitled to notice of a meeting of the members, to demand a special meeting, to vote, or to take any other action. If the articles or bylaws do not fix or provide for fixing a record date, the board of directors of the membership corporation may fix a future date as the record date.

(b) A record date fixed under this section may not be more than 70 days before the meeting or action requiring a determination of members.

(c) A determination of members entitled to notice of or to vote at a meeting of the members is effective for any adjournment of the meeting unless the board of directors fixes a new record date, which it must do if the meeting is adjourned to a date more than 120 days after the date fixed for the original meeting.

(d) If a court orders a meeting adjourned to a date more than 120 days after the date fixed for the original meeting, it may provide that the original record date continues in effect or it may fix a new record date.

Source Note: Patterned after Model Business Corporation Act, 3d Ed. (2002) § 7.07. Derived from Revised Model Nonprofit Corporation Act (1987) § 7.07.

CROSS-REFERENCES

Annual meeting, see § 7.01.

Court-ordered meeting, see § 7.03.

"Membership corporation" defined, see § 1.40.

Other record date provisions:
- action without meeting, see § 7.04.
- notice of meeting, see § 7.05.
- special meeting, see § 7.02.

OFFICIAL COMMENT

Section 7.07 authorizes the board of directors to fix record dates for any action unless the articles of incorporation or bylaws themselves fix or provide for the fixing of a record date. A separate record date may be established for each voting group entitled to vote separately on a matter at a meeting, or a single record date may be established for all voting groups entitled to participate in the meeting. If a record date for a specific action is not fixed by the articles, the bylaws, or the board, the section of this act that deals with that action itself fixes the record date. For example, Section 7.05(d), relating to giving notice of a meeting, provides that the record date for determining who is entitled to notice of a meeting (if not otherwise fixed) is the close of business on the day before the date the corporation first gives notice to members of the meeting.

A record date may not be fixed more than 70 days before the meeting or action in question and may not be fixed retroactively. Once set, the same record date may be utilized for an adjournment of the meeting that reconvenes within 120 days after the date fixed for the original meeting or the board of directors may fix a new record date. If the adjourned meeting takes place more than 120 days after the date fixed for the original meeting, Section 7.07(c) requires that a new record date be fixed. But if an adjournment is ordered by a court, Section 7.07(d) allows the court to provide that the original record date continues to be applicable or to fix a different date. In any event, if a different record date is or must be fixed under this section, Section 7.05 requires that new notice be given to the persons who are members as of the new record date, and Section 7.24 requires that a quorum be reestablished for that meeting.

§ 7.08. CONDUCT OF MEETING

(a) At each meeting of members, an individual must preside as chair. The chair shall be appointed:
   (1) as provided in the articles of incorporation or bylaws;
   (2) in the absence of a provision in the articles or bylaws, by the board of directors; or
   (3) in the absence of both a provision in the articles or bylaws and an appointment by the board, by the members at the meeting.

(b) Except as provided in the articles of incorporation or bylaws, the chair shall determine the order of business and shall have the authority to establish rules for the conduct of the meeting.

(c) Any rules adopted for, and the conduct of, the meeting shall be fair to the members.

(d) The chair of the meeting shall announce at the meeting when the polls close for each matter voted upon. If no announcement is made, the polls shall be deemed to have closed upon the final adjournment of the meeting. After the polls close, no ballots, proxies, or votes, nor any otherwise permissible revocations or changes thereto, may be accepted.

Source Note: Patterned after Model Business Corporation Act, 3d Ed. (2002) § 7.08.

CROSS-REFERENCES

Annual meeting, see § 7.01.

Court-ordered meeting, see § 7.03.

Regular meeting, see § 7.01.

Special meeting, see § 7.02.

OFFICIAL COMMENT

Section 7.08 provides that, at any meeting of the members, there shall be a chair who shall preside over the meeting. The chair is appointed in accordance with the articles of incorporation or bylaws. Generally, the chair of the board of directors presides over the meeting. However, the articles of incorporation or bylaws could provide that the chief executive officer, if different than the chair of the board, preside over the meeting and they should provide a means of designating an alternate if that individual is for any reason unable to preside.

Section 7.08(b) gives the chair, unless the articles of incorporation or bylaws provide otherwise, the authority to determine in what order items of business should be discussed and decided. Inherent in the chair's power to establish rules for the conduct of the meeting is the authority to require that the order of business be observed and that any discussion or comments from members or their proxies be confined to the business item under discussion. However, it is also expected that the chair will not misuse the power to determine the order of business and to establish rules for the conduct of the meeting so as to unfairly foreclose the right of members—subject to the act, the articles of incorporation, and the bylaws—to raise items which are properly a subject for member discussion or action at some point in the meeting prior to adjournment.

The act provides that only business within the purpose or purposes described in the meeting notice may be conducted at a special meeting of members. See Sections 7.02(e) and 7.05(c).

Section 7.08(b) also provides that the chair shall have the authority to establish rules for the conduct of the meeting. Complicated parliamentary rules ordinarily are not appropriate for meetings of the members. The rules may cover such subjects as the proper means for obtaining the floor, who shall have the right to address the meeting, the manner in which members will be recognized to speak, time limits per speaker, the number of times a member may address the meeting, and the person to whom questions should be addressed. The substance of the rules should be communicated to members prior to or at the beginning of the meeting. The chair is entitled to wide latitude in conducting the meeting and, unless inconsistent with a previously prescribed rule, may set requirements, observe practices, and follow customs that facilitate a fair and orderly meeting. Since, absent a modifying provision in the articles or bylaws, the chair has exclusive authority with respect to the rules for and the conduct of the meeting, rulings by the chair may not be overruled by members. On the other hand, any rule for or conduct of the meeting which does not satisfy the fairness mandate of Section 7.08(c) would be subject to a judicial remedy.

Section 7.08(d) requires that an announcement be made at the meeting of members specifying when the polls will close for each matter voted upon. It also provides that, once the polls close, no ballots, proxies, or votes and no changes thereto may be accepted. This statutory provision eliminates an area of uncertainty that had developed in the relatively sparse case law dealing with the effect of closing the polls, some of which suggested that, notwithstanding the closing of the polls, votes could be changed up until the time that the inspectors of election announced the results. *Young v. Jebbett*, 213 A.D. 774, 211 N.Y.S. 61 (N.Y. App. Div. 1925); *State ex rel. David v. Dailey*, 158 P.2d 330 (Wash. 1945). Any abusive use of the poll-closing power would be subject to judicial review under subsection (c) as well as under that line of cases requiring that meetings of members be conducted fairly and proscribing inequitable manipulations of the voting machinery. *See, e.g., Duffy v. Loft, Inc.*, 151 A. 223 (Del. Ch. 1930); *Schnell v. Chris-Craft Industries, Inc.*, 285 A.2d 437 (Del. 1971).

§ 7.09. ACTION BY BALLOT

(a) Except as otherwise restricted by the articles of incorporation or bylaws, any action that may be taken at any annual, regular, or special meeting of members may be taken without a meeting if the membership corporation delivers a ballot to every member entitled to vote on the matter.

(b) A ballot must:

 (1) be in the form of a record;

(2) set forth each proposed action;
(3) provide an opportunity to vote for, or withhold a vote for, each candidate for election as a director; and
(4) provide an opportunity to vote for or against each other proposed action.

(c) Approval by ballot pursuant to this section of action other than election of directors is valid only when the number of votes cast by ballot equals or exceeds the quorum required to be present at a meeting authorizing the action, and the number of approvals equals or exceeds the number of votes that would be required to approve the matter at a meeting at which the total number of votes cast was the same as the number of votes cast by ballot.

(d) All solicitations for votes by ballot must:
(1) indicate the number of responses needed to meet the quorum requirements;
(2) state the percentage of approvals necessary to approve each matter other than election of directors; and
(3) specify the time by which a ballot must be received by the membership corporation in order to be counted.

(e) Except as otherwise provided in the articles of incorporation or bylaws, a ballot may not be revoked.

Source Note: Substantially a reenactment of Revised Model Nonprofit Corporation Act (1987) § 7.08.

CROSS-REFERENCES

Acceptance of ballot, see § 7.23.

Action by members by consent, see § 7.04.

Election of directors, see § 7.27.

"Members" defined, see § 1.40.

"Membership corporation" defined, see § 1.40.

OFFICIAL COMMENT

If ballots are used in the manner authorized by this section, the membership corporation does not need to convene a meeting of its members. Thus the use of ballots under this section is different from the distribution of ballots at a meeting to facilitate voting at the meeting.

Voting by ballot under this section is an alternative to acting by consent under Section 7.04. In effect, the use of ballots is a way to conduct a vote of members remotely instead of at a meeting. Thus Section 7.09(d) provides rules which are substantively similar to the rules on quorums and required vote applicable to member meetings, but which differ from the rules in Section 7.04 on action by consent.

[Subchapter] B VOTING

§ 7.20. MEMBERS LIST FOR MEETING

(a) After fixing a record date for a meeting, a membership corporation shall prepare an alphabetical list of the names of all its members who are entitled to notice of that meeting of the members. The list must show the address of and the number of votes each member is entitled to cast at the meeting.

(b) The list of members must be available for inspection by any member, beginning two business days after notice of the meeting is given for which the list was prepared and continuing through the meeting, at the membership corporation's principal office or at a place identified in the meeting notice in the city where the meeting will be held. A member or the member's agent is entitled on demand in the form of a record to inspect and, subject to the requirements of Section 16.02(c), to copy the list, during regular business hours and at the member's expense, during the period it is available for inspection.

(c) The membership corporation must make the list of members available at the meeting, and a member or the member's agent is entitled to inspect the list at any time during the meeting or any adjournment.

(d) If a membership corporation refuses to allow a member or the member's agent to inspect the list of members before or at the meeting (or copy the list as permitted by subsection (b)), the [*name or describe*] court of the county where the corporation's principal office (or, if none in this state, its registered office) is located, on application of the member, may:

(1) summarily order the inspection or copying at the corporation's expense;

(2) postpone the meeting for which the list was prepared until the inspection or copying is complete;

(3) order the corporation to pay the member's costs (including reasonable counsel fees) incurred to obtain the order; and

(4) order other appropriate relief.

(e) Refusal or failure to prepare or make available the list of members does not affect the validity of action taken at the meeting.

(f) Instead of making the list of members available as provided in subsection (b), a membership corporation may state in a notice of meeting that the corporation has elected to proceed under this subsection. A member of a corporation that has elected to proceed under this subsection must state in the member's demand for inspection a proper purpose for which inspection is demanded. Within 10 business days after receiving a demand under this subsection, the corporation must deliver to the member making the demand an offer of a reasonable alternative method of achieving the purpose identified in the demand without providing access to or a copy of the list of members. An alternative method that reasonably and in a timely manner accomplishes the proper purpose set forth in the demand relieves the corporation from making the list of members available under subsection (b), unless within a reasonable time after acceptance of the offer the corporation fails to do the things it offered to do. Any rejection of the corporation's offer must be in the form of a record and must indicate the reasons the alternative proposed by the corporation does not meet the proper purpose of the demand.

Source Note: Patterned after Model Business Corporation Act, 3d Ed. (2002) § 7.20. Subsections (a)–(e) are substantially a reenactment of Revised Model Nonprofit Corporation Act (1987) § 7.20(a)–(e). Subsection (f) is patterned after CAL. CORP. CODE § 6330.

CROSS-REFERENCES

Annual meeting, see § 7.01.

Charge for providing copy, see § 16.03.

Inspection of corporate records generally, see Ch. 16A.

"Membership corporation" defined, see § 1.40.

Notice, see § 1.41.

Notice of meeting, see § 7.05.

"Principal office":
  defined, see § 1.40.
  designated in annual report, see § 16.21.

Proper purpose for copying, see § 16.02.

Record date, see § 7.07.

Record of members, see § 16.01.

Registered office:
  designated in annual report, see § 16.21.
  required, see §§ 2.02, 5.01, and 15.07.

Regular meeting, see § 7.01.

Special meeting, see § 7.02.

Voting entitlement generally, see § 7.21.

"Voting group" defined, see § 1.40.

OFFICIAL COMMENT

Section 7.20 requires the preparation of a list of members entitled to notice of a meeting and requires that this list be made available on request to members within two business days after the meeting notice is given.

The list of members is often referred to as the "voting list" and usually the list will include only the names of those members entitled to vote at the meeting. The list, however, must also include the names of nonvoting members if they are entitled to notice of the meeting by reason of the nature of the actions proposed to be taken at the meeting. See Section 7.05 and its Official Comment.

1. When the List Must Be Available

The list must generally be available for inspection two business days after notice of the meeting is given and continuously thereafter until the meeting occurs. If, however, notice of the meeting is waived by all the members, the list need be available only at the meeting itself under Section 7.20(c) unless one or more waivers are conditioned upon receipt of the list.

2. Where the List Must Be Maintained

Section 7.20(b) permits the list to be maintained either at the membership corporation's principal office or at another location in the city in which the meeting is to be held, the precise location to be designated in the notice of the meeting. If the corporation changes the location of its annual meeting, it thus may correspondingly change the location of the list of members pursuant to this subsection.

Section 7.20(c) also requires a copy of the list of members to be available at the meeting itself for inspection. This list may be used to determine attendance, the presence or absence of a quorum, and the right to vote.

3. Form in Which the List Is Maintained

Section 7.20 does not require the list of members to be in any particular form. If the list is maintained in other than written form, however, suitable equipment must be provided so that a comprehensible list may be inspected by a member as permitted by this section.

4. Consequences of Failing to Prepare the List or Refusal to Make It Available

Section 7.20 creates a corporate obligation rather than an obligation imposed upon a corporate officer. If the membership corporation fails to prepare the list or refuses to permit a member to inspect it, either before the meeting as required by Section 7.20(b) or at the meeting itself as required by Section 7.20(c), a member may apply to the appropriate court under Section 7.20(d) for a summary order permitting inspection of the list; the court may further order the meeting to be postponed for a reasonable time. If the court orders a copy of the list to be provided to the members, the copying is at the corporation's expense; if the corporation produces the list voluntarily pursuant to Section 7.20(b) or (c), any inspection and copying are the member's expense.

This judicial remedy is the only sanction for violation of Section 7.20 since Section 7.20(e) provides that the failure to prepare, maintain, or produce the list does not affect the validity of any action taken at the meeting.

5. *Right to Obtain a Copy of the List*

Section 7.20(b) permits members to "inspect" the list without limitation, but permits the member to "copy" the list only if the member complies with the requirement of Section 16.02(c), that the demand be "made in good faith and for a proper purpose." The right to copy the list includes, if reasonable, the right to receive a copy of the list upon payment of a reasonable charge. See Sections 16.03(b) and (c). The distinction between "inspection" and "copying" set forth in Section 7.20(b) reflects an accommodation between competing considerations of permitting members access to the list before a meeting and possible misuse of the list.

6. *Relationship to Right to Inspect Corporate Records Generally*

The rights of members under Section 7.20 are independent of the rights of members to inspect corporate records under Subchapter 16A. A member may obtain the right to inspect the list of members as provided in Subchapter 16A without regard to the provisions relating to the pendency of a meeting in Section 7.20, and similarly the limitations of Subchapter 16A are not applicable to the right of inspection created by Section 7.20

except to the extent the member seeks to copy the list in advance of the meeting.

The right to inspect under Subchapter 16A is also broader in the sense that in some circumstances the member may be entitled to receive copies of the documents he or she may inspect. See Section 16.03.

§ 7.21. VOTING ENTITLEMENT OF MEMBERS

Except as provided in the articles of incorporation or bylaws, each member is entitled to one vote on each matter voted on by the members.

Source Note: Patterned after Model Business Corporation Act, 3d Ed. (2002) § 7.21(a). Substantially a reenactment of Revised Model Nonprofit Corporation Act (1987) § 7.21(a). Revised Model Nonprofit Corporation Act (1987) § 7.21(b) omitted as supplied by Section 7.23.

CROSS-REFERENCES

Acceptance of votes, see § 7.23.

Meetings of members, see §§ 7.01–7.03.

Proxy voting, see § 7.22.

Voting by nominees, see § 7.23.

Voting by voting groups, see §§ 1.40, 7.24, 7.25.

OFFICIAL COMMENT

Section 7.21 deals with the entitlement of members to vote, while Section 7.22 deals with voting by proxy and Section 7.23 establishes rules for a membership corporation's acceptance or rejection of votes.

Section 7.21 provides that each member, regardless of class, is entitled to one vote unless otherwise provided in the articles of incorporation or bylaws. See Section 6.01 and its Official Comment. The articles or bylaws may provide for multiple or fractional votes, and may provide that some classes of members are nonvoting on some or all matters, or that some classes of members have a single vote per member or different multiple or fractional votes per member, or that some classes constitute one or more separate voting groups and are entitled to vote separately on the matter.

In order to reflect the possibility that members may have multiple or fractional votes, all provisions relating to quorums, voting, and similar matters in the act are phrased in terms of "votes" rather than "members."

§ 7.22. PROXIES

(a) Except as otherwise provided in the articles of incorporation or bylaws, a member may vote in person or by proxy.

(b) A member or the member's agent or attorney-in-fact may appoint a proxy to vote or otherwise act for the member by signing an appointment form in the form of a record. An appointment form must contain or be accompanied by information from which it can be determined that the member or the member's agent or attorney-in-fact authorized the appointment of the proxy.

(c) An appointment of a proxy is effective when a signed appointment in the form of a record is received by the inspectors of election, the officer or agent of the membership corporation authorized to tabulate votes, or the secretary. An appointment is valid for 11 months unless a longer period, which may not exceed three years, is expressly provided in the appointment form.

(d) The death or incapacity of the member appointing a proxy does not affect the right of the membership corporation to accept the proxy's authority unless notice of the death or incapacity is received by the inspectors of election, the officer or agent authorized to tabulate votes, or the secretary before the proxy exercises his authority under the appointment.

(e) Subject to Section 7.23 and to any express limitation on the proxy's authority stated in the appointment form, a membership corporation is entitled to accept the proxy's vote or other action as that of the member making the appointment.

Source Note: Patterned after Model Business Corporation Act, 3d Ed. (2002) § 7.22(a)–(c), (e), and (h). Substantially a reenactment of Revised Model Nonprofit Corporation Act (1987) § 7.24.

CROSS-REFERENCES

Acceptance of proxy votes, see § 7.23.

"Membership corporation" defined, see § 1.40.

Notice, see § 1.41.

"Secretary" defined, see § 1.40.

OFFICIAL COMMENT

Section 7.22 provides that members may vote in person or by proxy and establishes the basic rules for appointing a proxy.

1. Nomenclature

The word "proxy" is often used ambiguously, sometimes referring to the grant of authority to vote, sometimes to the document granting the authority, and sometimes to the person to whom the authority is granted. In the act the word "proxy" is used only in the last sense; the term "appointment form" is used to describe the document or communication appointing the proxy; and the word "appointment" is used to describe the grant of authority to vote.

2. Appointment of Proxy

A member may appoint a proxy to vote by signing an appointment form, either personally or by his agent or attorney-in-fact. Section 7.22(b) is intended to sanction the practice whereby members who have been provided in proxy materials with a personal identification number may call in their vote and identifying number to a person who, acting as the member's agent, causes that information to be transmitted, directly or indirectly, to the inspector of election.

The appointment is effective when a written appointment form or an electronic transmission (or documentary evidence thereof, including verification information) is received by the inspectors of election, the officer or agent of the corporation authorized to receive and tabulate votes, or the secretary. The proxy has the same power to vote as that possessed by the member, unless the appointment form contains an express limitation on the power to vote or direction as to how to vote the membership on a particular matter, in which event the corporation must tabulate the votes in a manner consistent with that limitation or direction. See Section 7.22(e).

3. Duration of Proxy

Section 7.22(c) limits the validity of an appointment form that contains no expiration date to 11 months. See Section 7.22(c). This ensures that in the normal course a new appointment will be solicited at least once every 12 months. But an appointment form may validly specify a longer period if the parties agree.

While death or incapacity of the appointing member revokes an agency appointment under common law principles, Section 7.22(d) modifies the common law rule to provide that the corporation may accept the vote of the proxy until the appropriate person receives notice of the member's death or incapacity. Section 7.22(d) does not affect the validity of the proxy appointment or its manner of exercise as between the proxy and the personal representatives of the decedent or incompetent. That relationship is governed by the law of agency independent of the act.

§ 7.23. ACCEPTANCE OF VOTES

(a) If the name signed on a ballot, consent, waiver, or proxy appointment corresponds to the name of a member, the membership corporation if acting in good faith is entitled to accept the ballot, consent, waiver, or proxy appointment and give it effect as the act of the member.

(b) If the name signed on a ballot, consent, waiver, or proxy appointment does not correspond to the name of its member, the membership corporation if acting in good faith is nevertheless entitled to accept the ballot, consent, waiver, or proxy appointment and give it effect as the act of the member if:

(1) the member is an entity and the name signed purports to be that of an officer or agent of the entity;

(2) the name signed purports to be that of an administrator, executor, guardian, or conservator representing the member and, if the corporation requests, evidence of fiduciary status acceptable to the corporation has been presented with respect to the ballot, consent, waiver, or proxy appointment;

(3) the name signed purports to be that of a receiver or trustee in bankruptcy of the member and, if the corporation requests, evidence of this status acceptable to the corporation has been presented with respect to the ballot, consent, waiver, or proxy appointment;

(4) the name signed purports to be that of a beneficial owner or attorney-in-fact of the member and, if the corporation requests, evidence acceptable to the corporation of the signatory's authority to sign for the member has been presented with respect to the ballot, consent, waiver, or proxy appointment;

(5) two or more persons are the member as cotenants or fiduciaries and the name signed purports to be the name of at least one of the co-owners and the person signing appears to be acting on behalf of all the co-owners.

(c) The membership corporation is entitled to reject a ballot, consent, waiver, or proxy appointment if the secretary or other officer or agent authorized to tabulate votes, acting in good faith, has reasonable basis for doubt about the validity of the signature on it or about the signatory's authority to sign for the member.

(d) The membership corporation and its officer or agent who accepts or rejects a ballot, consent, waiver, or proxy appointment in good faith and in accordance with the standards of this section or Section 7.22(b) are not liable in damages to the member for the consequences of the acceptance or rejection.

(e) Corporate action based on the acceptance or rejection of a ballot, consent, waiver, or proxy appointment under this section is valid unless a court of competent jurisdiction determines otherwise.

Source Note: Patterned after Model Business Corporation Act, 3d Ed. (2002) § 7.24. Derived from Revised Model Nonprofit Corporation Act (1987) § 7.27. As to subsection (b)(5), see Revised Model Nonprofit Corporation Act (1987) § 7.21(b).

CROSS-REFERENCES

Action by ballot, see § 7.09.

Consents, see § 7.04.

"Entity" defined, see § 1.40.

Inspectors of election, see § 7.28.

"Membership corporation" defined, see § 1.40.

Officers, see § 8.40.

Proxies, see § 7.22.

"Secretary" defined, see § 1.40.

"Sign" defined, see § 1.40.

Waiver of notice, see § 7.06.

OFFICIAL COMMENT

Membership corporations are often asked to accept a written instrument as evidence of action by a member. These instruments usually involve appointment forms for a proxy to vote on behalf of a member, but may also include waivers of notice, consents to action without a meeting, requests for a special meeting of members, and similar instruments involving action by the members. Included within the scope of this section are both ballots used as provided in Section 7.09 as a substitute for a vote at a meeting and ballots distributed at a meeting for the use of the members and proxies in attendance at the meeting. Usually the corporation or its officers will have no personal knowledge of the circumstances under which the instrument was executed and no way of verifying whether the signature on the instrument is in fact the signature of the member or other appropriate person.

Section 7.23 establishes general rules permitting the membership corporation and its officers or agents to accept these instruments if they appear to be executed by the member or by a person who has authority to execute the instrument for the member and they are accompanied by whatever authenticating evidence the corporation reasonably requests. The rules set forth in this section are not exclusive and may be supplemented by additional rules appropriately established by the corporation. Section 7.23(a) authorizes acceptance of an instrument if the name appearing on the instrument "corresponds" to the name of the member, while Section 7.23(b) permits the acceptance of an instrument executed by a person other than the member if there is a designation or evidence of the capacity of the person executing the instrument that indicates the act of the person is the act of the member. On the other hand, Section 7.23(c) permits rejection of an instrument if the officer or agent tabulating votes has a "reasonable basis for doubt" about the validity of the signature or about the authority of the person acting on behalf of the member.

Section 7.23(b)(2) does not validate the transfer of a membership to an administrator, executor, or guardian, but if there has been a valid transfer to such a person the corporation will be required to accept their vote.

The purpose of Section 7.23 is to protect the membership corporation and its officers or agents from liability for damages to the member if action is taken in accordance with the section. Thus Section 7.23(d) provides that there is no liability to the member if the corporation's officer or agent, acting in good faith, accepts an instrument that meets the requirements of Section 7.23(a) or (b) or accepts an electronic transmission authorized by Section 7.22(b), even if it turns out that the execution was invalid or unauthorized; similarly, no liability exists if the officer or agent, again acting in good faith, rejects an instrument because of a "reasonable basis for doubt," even though it turns out that the instrument was properly executed by the member. But Section 7.23 does not address the question whether an action was properly or improperly taken or approved, and Section 7.23(e) makes clear that the validity or invalidity of corporate action is ultimately a matter for judicial resolution through review of the results of an election in a suit to enjoin or compel corporate action. It is contemplated that any such suit will be brought promptly, typically before the corporate action is consummated or the corporation's position otherwise changes in reliance on the vote, and that any suit that is not brought promptly under the circumstances would normally be barred because of laches.

Similarly, Section 7.23 does not address the liability of the proxy to the member for exercising authority beyond that granted or for disobeying instructions. These matters are governed by the law of agency and not by Section 7.23.

As indicated in the Official Comment to Section 7.22, a proxy is simply an agent of the member, and appointment as a proxy therefore involves primarily the law of agency. The law of agency determines the rights and duties of the member and the proxy, and it is important to recognize that Section 7.23 is not intended to affect these rights and duties. Rather, it recognizes that the great bulk of instruments signed by or on behalf of a member are in fact authorized and the corporation and its officers should be encouraged to accept them rather than to adopt unduly narrow requirements.

§ 7.24. QUORUM AND VOTING REQUIREMENTS FOR VOTING GROUPS

(a) Members entitled to vote as a separate voting group may take action on a matter at a meeting only if a quorum of those members exists with respect to that matter. Except as provided in the articles of incorporation or bylaws, a majority of the votes entitled to be cast on the matter by the voting group constitutes a quorum of that voting group for action on that matter.

(b) Once a member is represented for any purpose at a meeting, the member is deemed present for quorum purposes for the remainder of the meeting and for any adjournment of that meeting unless a new record date is or must be set for that adjourned meeting.

(c) If a quorum exists, action on a matter (other than the election of directors) by a voting group is approved if the votes cast within the voting group favoring the action exceed the votes cast opposing the action, unless the articles of incorporation or bylaws require a greater number of affirmative votes.

(d) An amendment of the articles of incorporation or bylaws adding, changing, or deleting a quorum or voting requirement for a voting group greater than specified in subsection (a) or (c) is governed by Section 7.26.

(e) If a meeting cannot be organized because a quorum is not present, those members present may adjourn the meeting to such time and place as they may determine. Except as provided in the articles of incorporation or bylaws, when a meeting that has been adjourned for lack of a quorum is reconvened, those members present, although less than a quorum as fixed in this section, the articles, or the bylaws, nonetheless constitute a quorum.

(f) The election of directors is governed by Section 7.27.

Source Note: Patterned after Model Business Corporation Act, 3d Ed. (2002) § 7.25. Derived from Revised Model Nonprofit Corporation Act (1987) §§ 7.22 and 7.23.

CROSS-REFERENCES

Adjourned meeting record date, see § 7.07.

Amendment of articles of incorporation, see Subch. 10A.

Amendment of bylaws, see Subch. 10B.

Multiple voting groups, see § 7.25.

Proxy voting, see § 7.22.

Record date, see § 7.07.

Supermajority requirements, see § 7.26.

"Voting group" defined, see § 1.40.

OFFICIAL COMMENT

Section 7.24 establishes general quorum and voting requirements for voting groups for purposes of the act. As defined in Section 1.40, a "voting group" consists of all members of a class that under the articles of incorporation, the bylaws, or the act are entitled to vote and be counted together collectively on a matter. Members entitled to vote "generally" on a matter (that is, all members entitled to vote on the matter by the articles, the bylaws, or the act that do not expressly have the right to be counted or tabulated separately) are a single voting group. The determination of which members form part of a single voting group must be made from the provisions of the articles, the bylaws, and the act. On most matters coming before meetings of the members, only a single voting group, consisting of a class of members, will be involved, and action on such a matter is effective when approved by that voting group pursuant to Section 7.24. See Section 7.25(a).

The voting group concept permits a single section of the act to deal with quorum and voting rules applicable to a variety of single and multiple voting group situations.

1. Determination of Voting Groups

Under the act, classes of members are generally not entitled to vote separately by voting group except to the extent specifically authorized by the articles of incorporation or bylaws. But Sections 10.04 and 11.04 of the act grant classes of members the right to vote separately when fundamental changes are proposed that may adversely affect that class.

In addition to the provisions of the act, separate voting by voting group may be authorized by the articles of incorporation or bylaws in such instances and on such terms as may be desired (except that the statutory privilege of voting by separate voting groups cannot be diluted or reduced). Finally, on some matters the board of directors may condition its submission of matters to members on their approval by specific voting groups designated by the board of directors. Sections 7.24 and 7.25 establish the mechanics by which all voting by single or multiple voting groups is carried out.

In some situations, members of a single class may be entitled to vote in two different voting groups. See the Official Comment to Section 7.25.

2. Quorum and Voting Requirements in General

Implicit in Section 7.24 is the concept that the determination of the voting groups entitled to vote, and the quorum and voting requirements applicable thereto, must be determined separately for each "matter" coming before a meeting. As a result, different quorum and voting requirements may be applicable to different portions of a meeting, depending on the matter being considered. In the normal case where only a single voting group is entitled to vote on all matters coming before a meeting of members, a single quorum and voting requirement will usually be applicable to the entire meeting.

3. Quorum Requirements for Action by Voting Group

Sections 7.24(a) and (b) provide standard rules for the determination of a quorum for each voting group required to act at a meeting of the members on a matter. In the absence of a provision in the articles of incorporation or bylaws, Section 7.24(a) provides that a quorum consists of a majority of the votes entitled to be cast on the matter at the meeting.

Section 7.24(b) retains the common law view that once a member is present at a meeting, the member is deemed present for quorum purposes throughout the meeting. Thus, a voting group may continue to act despite the withdrawal of members in an effort "to break the quorum." In this respect, a meeting of members is governed by a different rule than a meeting of directors, where a sufficient number of directors must be present to constitute a quorum at the time action is taken. See Section 8.24 and its Official Comment.

Once a member is present at a meeting the member is also deemed to be present at any adjourned meeting unless a new record date is or must be set for that adjourned meeting. See Section 7.07. If a new record date is set, new notice must be given to members of a voting group and a quorum must be established from within the members of that voting group on the new record date.

A member who comes to a meeting to object on grounds of lack of notice may be counted toward the presence of a quorum. Similarly, a member who attends a meeting solely for purposes of raising the objection that a quorum is not present is counted toward the presence of a quorum. Attendance at a meeting, however, does not constitute a waiver of other objections to the meeting such as the lack of notice. Such waivers are governed by Section 7.06(b).

As used in Sections 7.24 and 7.25, "represented at the meeting" means the physical presence of the member (whether in person or by proxy) in the meeting room after the meeting has been called to order or the presiding officer has commenced consideration of the business of the meeting, and before the final adjournment of the meeting.

4. Voting Requirements for Approval by Voting Group

Section 7.24(c) provides that an action (other than the election of directors, which is governed by Section 7.27) is approved by a voting group at a meeting at which a quorum is present if the votes cast in favor of the action exceed the votes cast opposing the action. This section changes the traditional rule that an action is approved at a meeting at which a quorum is present if it receives the affirmative vote "of a majority of the members represented at that meeting." The traditional rule in effect treated abstentions as negative votes; the act treats them truly as abstentions. The rule set forth in Section 7.24(c) is considered desirable in part because it permits action to be taken by the members when considered appropriate by a majority of those with views on the matter in question.

In the absence of a specific provision in the articles of incorporation or bylaws, members of a class that is entitled by statute to vote as a separate voting group are entitled to one vote per share. See Section 7.21.

5. *Modification of Standard Requirements*

The articles of incorporation or bylaws may modify the quorum and voting requirements of Section 7.24 for a single voting group or for all voting groups entitled to vote on any matter. The articles or bylaws may increase the quorum and voting requirements to any extent desired up to and including unanimity upon compliance with Section 7.26; they may also require that members of different classes are entitled to vote separately or together on specific issues or provide that actions are approved only if they receive the favorable vote of a majority of the members of a voting group present at a meeting at which a quorum is present. The articles or bylaws may also decrease the quorum requirement as desired.

Section 7.24(d) provides that Section 7.26 governs the adoption or amendment of provisions in the articles of incorporation or bylaws that impose greater quorum or voting requirements than provided for in this section.

§ 7.25. ACTION BY SINGLE AND MULTIPLE VOTING GROUPS

(a) If this [act], the articles of incorporation, or the bylaws provide for voting by a single voting group on a matter, action on that matter is taken when voted upon by that voting group as provided in Section 7.24.

(b) If this [act], the articles of incorporation, or the bylaws provide for voting by two or more voting groups on a matter, action on that matter is taken only when voted upon by each of those voting groups counted separately as provided in Section 7.24.

Source Note: Patterned after Model Business Corporation Act, 3d Ed. (2002) § 7.26.

CROSS-REFERENCES

Change of voting group requirements, see § 7.26.

Number of votes per member, see § 7.21.

Quorum and voting requirements, see § 7.24.

Supermajority requirements, see § 7.26.

Voting by voting groups on amendments of articles of incorporation, see § 10.04.

"Voting group" defined, see § 1.40.

OFFICIAL COMMENT

Section 7.25(a) provides that when a matter is to be voted upon by a single voting group, action is taken when the voting group votes upon the action as provided in Section 7.24. In most instances the single voting group will consist of all the members of the class or classes entitled to vote by the articles of incorporation or bylaws; voting by two or more voting groups as contemplated by Section 7.25(b) is the exceptional case.

Section 7.25(b) basically requires that if more than one voting group is entitled to vote on a matter, favorable action on a matter is taken only when it is voted upon favorably by each voting group, counted separately. Implicit in this section are the concepts that (1) different quorum and voting requirements may be applicable to different matters considered at a single meeting, and (2) different quorum and voting requirements may be applicable to different voting groups voting on the same matter. See the Official Comment to Section 7.24. Thus, each group entitled to vote must independently meet the quorum and voting requirements established by Section 7.24. But if a quorum is present for one or more voting groups but not for all voting groups, Section 7.25(b) provides that the voting groups for which a quorum is present may vote upon the matter.

A single meeting, furthermore, may consider matters on which action by several voting groups is required and also matters on which only a single voting group may act. Action may be taken on the matters on which the single voting group may act even though no quorum is present to take action on other matters.

1. Voting Requirements of Multiple Voting Group Matters

In many multiple voting group situations under the act, proposals are adopted only if a majority of all the votes entitled to be cast by each voting group approve the proposal. This percentage of votes is higher than that required by Section 7.24, and is required, for example, under Sections 10.03(7) for certain amendments to articles of incorporation.

2. Participation of Members in Multiple Voting Groups

As described in Section 7.25(b), if voting by multiple voting groups is required, the votes of members of each voting group must be separately tabulated. Normally, each class of members will participate in only a single voting group. But since members entitled by the articles of incorporation or bylaws to vote generally on a matter are always entitled to vote in the voting group consisting of the general voting members, in some instances classes of members may be entitled to be counted simultaneously in two voting groups. This will occur whenever a class of members entitled to vote generally on a matter under the articles or bylaws is affected by the matter in a way that gives rise to the right to have its vote counted separately as an independent voting group under the act.

§ 7.26. DIFFERENT QUORUM OR VOTING REQUIREMENTS

(a) The articles of incorporation or bylaws may provide for a higher or lower quorum or voting requirement for members (or voting groups of members) than is provided for by this [act].

(b) An amendment to the articles of incorporation or bylaws that adds, changes, or deletes a greater quorum or voting requirement must meet the same quorum requirement and be adopted by the same vote and voting groups required to take action under the quorum and voting requirements then in effect.

Source Note: Patterned after Model Business Corporation Act, 3d Ed. (2002) § 7.27.

CROSS-REFERENCES

Amendment of articles of incorporation, see Ch. 10A.

Amendment of bylaws, see Ch. 10B.

Quorum and voting requirements in general, see § 7.25.

Voting by voting group, see § 7.25.

"Voting group" defined, see § 1.40.

OFFICIAL COMMENT

Section 7.26(a) permits the articles of incorporation or bylaws to increase or decrease the quorum or voting requirements for approval of an action by members to any desired level, including, in the case of an increase, unanimity. These provisions may relate to ordinary or routine actions by the general voting group (which otherwise may be acted upon under Section 7.24 if the number of affirmative votes exceeds the number of negative votes at a meeting at which a quorum of that voting group is present) or to one or more other voting groups or to actions for which the act provides a greater voting requirement—for example, changes of a fundamental nature in the corporation like certain amendments to articles of incorporation (Section 10.03), mergers (Section 11.04), sales of all or substantially all the property of a corporation not in the ordinary course of business (Section 12.02), and dissolution (Section 14.02). Generally, the act requires these fundamental changes to receive the affirmative vote of a majority of the votes entitled to be cast on the proposal by each voting group entitled to vote thereon rather than by a majority of the members voting affirmatively or negatively at a meeting at which a quorum is present.

A provision that increases the requirement for approval of an ordinary matter or a fundamental change is usually referred to as a "supermajority" provision. Section 7.26(b) requires any amendment of the articles of incorporation or bylaws that adds, modifies, or repeals any supermajority provision to be approved by the quorum and vote required by the articles or bylaws before their amendment. Thus, a supermajority provision in the articles that requires an 80% affirmative vote of all eligible votes of a voting group present at the meeting may not be removed from the articles or reduced in any way except by an 80% affirmative vote. If the 80% requirement is coupled with a quorum requirement for a voting group that members entitled to cast 2/3 of the total votes must be present in person or by proxy, both the 80% voting requirement and the 2/3 quorum requirement are immune from reduction except at a meeting of the voting group at which the 2/3 quorum requirement is met and the reduction is approved by an 80% affirmative vote.

§ 7.27. VOTING FOR DIRECTORS

(a) Except as provided in the articles of incorporation or bylaws, directors of a membership corporation are elected by a plurality of the votes cast by the members entitled to vote in the election at a meeting at which a quorum is present.

(b) Members do not have a right to cumulate their votes for directors.

Source Note: Patterned after Model Business Corporation Act, 3d Ed. (2002) § 7.28(a) and (b), except that the ability to provide for cumulative voting by appropriate provision in the articles of incorporation has been omitted. Derived from Revised Model Nonprofit Corporation Act (1987) § 7.26. Revised Model Nonprofit Corporation Act (1987) § 7.25 specifying the mechanics of cumulative voting is omitted.

CROSS-REFERENCES

“Membership corporation” defined, see § 1.40.

Proxies, see § 7.22.

Quorum of members, see § 7.24.

“Voting group” defined, see § 1.40.

OFFICIAL COMMENT

Section 7.27(a) provides that directors are elected by a plurality of the votes cast in an election of directors at a meeting at which a quorum is present of the voting group entitled to participate in the election. A "plurality" means that the individuals with the largest number of votes are elected as directors up to the maximum number of directors to be chosen at the election. In elections in which several factors are competing within a voting group, the individuals elected may have fewer than a majority of all the votes cast in the election. The articles of incorporation or bylaws of a membership corporation may, however, provide a different manner of election of directors.

The entire board of directors may be elected by a single voting group or the articles of incorporation may provide that different voting groups are entitled to elect a designated number or fraction of the board of directors. See Section 8.04. Elections are contested only within specific voting groups.

The prior version of the act permitted a nonprofit corporation to provide for cumulative voting. The purpose of cumulative voting in for-profit corporations is to increase the ability of minority shareholders to secure representation on the board of directors. The rights of minority members in a nonprofit corporation are less sensitive and Section 7.27(b) eliminates cumulative voting in nonprofit corporations as unnecessary and potentially disruptive. Existing cumulative voting rights are preserved, however, by Section 17.03(c).

§ 7.28. INSPECTORS OF ELECTION

(a) A membership corporation may appoint one or more inspectors to act at a meeting of members and make a report in the form of a record of the inspectors' determinations. Each inspector shall execute the duties of inspector impartially and according to the best of his or her ability.

(b) The inspectors shall:

  (1) ascertain the number of members and their voting power;

(2) determine the members present at a meeting;
(3) determine the validity of proxies and ballots;
(4) count all votes; and
(5) determine the result.

(c) An inspector may, but need not, be a director, member of a designated body, member, officer, or employee of the membership corporation. A person who is a candidate for office to be filled at the meeting may not be an inspector.

Source Note: Patterned after Model Business Corporation Act, 3d Ed. (2002) § 7.29.

CROSS-REFERENCES

"Membership corporation" defined, see § 1.40.

Officers of the corporation, see § 8.40.

Proxies, see § 7.22.

OFFICIAL COMMENT

Section 7.28(a) permits a membership corporation to appoint inspectors of election. It is contemplated that the selection of inspectors would be made by responsible officers or by the directors, as authorized either generally or specifically in the corporation's bylaws. Alternate inspectors could also be designated to replace any inspector who fails to act. The requirement of a report is to facilitate judicial review of determinations made by inspectors.

Section 7.28(b) specifies the duties of inspectors of election. If no challenge of a determination by the inspectors within the authority given them under this section is timely made, such determination shall be conclusive. In the event of a challenge of any determination by the inspectors in a court of competent jurisdiction, the court should give such weight to determinations of fact by the inspectors, as it shall deem appropriate, taking into account the relationship of the inspectors, if any, to the management of the company and other persons interested in the outcome of the vote, the evidence available to inspectors, whether their determinations appear to be reasonable, and such other circumstances as the court shall regard as relevant. The court should review de novo all determinations of law made implicitly or explicitly by the inspectors.

Normally, in making the determinations contemplated by Section 7.28(b), the only facts before the inspectors should be appointment forms and electronic transmissions (or written evidence thereof), envelopes submitted with appointment forms, ballots, and the regular books and records of the corporation. However, inspectors may consider other reliable information for the limited purpose of reconciling appointment forms, electronic transmissions, and ballots. If the inspectors do consider such other information, it should be specifically referred to in their report, including the person or persons from whom they obtained the information, when the information was obtained, the means by which the information was obtained, and the basis for the inspectors' belief that such information is accurate and reliable.

Section 7.28(c) permits an inspector to be a director, member of a designated body, member, officer, or employee of the nonprofit corporation, so long as the person is not a candidate for office at the meeting. However, good corporate practice suggests that such inspectors should be independent persons who are neither employees nor officers if there is a contested matter or a member proposal to be considered. Not only will the issue of independent inspectors enhance the members' perception as to the fairness of the voting process, but also the report of independent inspectors can be expected to be given greater evidentiary weight by any court reviewing a contested vote.

[Subchapter] C
VOTING AGREEMENTS

§ 7.30. VOTING AGREEMENTS

(a) Two or more members may provide for the manner in which they will vote by signing an agreement in the form of a record for that purpose. A voting agreement may be valid for a period of up to 10 years.

(b) A voting agreement created under this section is specifically enforceable, except that a voting agreement is not enforceable to the extent that enforcement of the agreement would violate the purposes of the membership corporation.

Source Note: Patterned in part after Model Business Corporation Act, 3d Ed. (2002) § 7.31. Substantially a reenactment of Revised Model Nonprofit Corporation Act (1987) § 7.30, except the last sentence of subsection (a) has been made the last clause of subsection (b).

CROSS-REFERENCES

Corporate purposes, see § 3.01.

"Member" defined, see § 1.40.

"Membership corporation" defined, see § 1.40.

OFFICIAL COMMENT

Section 7.30(a) explicitly recognizes agreements among two or more members as to voting. The only formal requirements are that they be in the form of a record and signed by all the participating members; in other respects their validity is to be judged as any other contract.

Section 7.30(b) provides that voting agreements may be specifically enforceable. This section recognizes that damages are not likely to be an appropriate remedy for breach of a voting agreement, and also avoids the result reached in *Ringling Bros. Barnum & Bailey Combined Shows v. Ringling,* 53 A.2d 441 (Del. 1947), where the court held that the appropriate remedy to enforce a vote pooling agreement was to refuse to permit any voting by the breaching party. A voting agreement is not enforceable, however, to the extent that its enforcement would violate the nonprofit corporation's purposes.

CHAPTER 8

Directors and Officers

Subchapter

A. Board of Directors
B. Meetings and Action of the Board
C. Directors
D. Officers
E. Indemnification and Advance for Expenses
F. Conflicting Interest Transactions
G. Business Opportunities

[Subchapter] A
BOARD OF DIRECTORS

§ 8.01. REQUIREMENT FOR AND FUNCTIONS OF BOARD OF DIRECTORS

(a) A nonprofit corporation must have a board of directors.

(b) Except as provided in Section 8.12, all corporate powers must be exercised by or under the authority of the board of directors of the nonprofit corporation, and the activities and affairs of the corporation must be managed by or under the direction, and subject to the oversight, of its board of directors.

Source Note: Patterned after Model Business Corporation Act, 3d Ed. (2002) § 8.01. Derived from Model Nonprofit Corporation Act (1987) § 8.01(a) and (b).

CROSS-REFERENCES

Designated body, see § 8.12.

Director standards of conduct, see § 8.30.

Indemnification, see §§ 8.50–8.58.

Officers, see §§ 8.40 and 8.41.

OFFICIAL COMMENT

Section 8.01(a) requires that every nonprofit corporation have a "board of directors." That term is defined in Section 1.40 to include a designated body to the extent the powers, authority, or functions of the board have been vested in the designated body. The ability to create one or more designated bodies permits wide flexibility when designing the governance structure of a particular corporation.

The definition of "board of directors" in Section 1.40 provides that the term refers to "the group of individuals responsible for the management of the activities and affairs of the nonprofit corporation, regardless of the name used to refer to the group." Thus the board of directors may be referred to as the "board of trustees" or by some other name. Regardless of the name by which it is known, if a group satisfies the definition of "board of directors" it will have that status.

Section 8.01(b) states that "the activities and affairs of the corporation must be managed by or under the direction, and subject to the oversight, of its board of directors." The phrase "by or under the direction, and subject to the oversight, of" encompasses the varying functions of boards of directors of different nonprofit corporations. In some corporations, the board of directors may be involved in the day-to-day activities and affairs and it may be reasonable to describe management as being "by" the board of directors. But in many other corporations, the activities and affairs are managed "under the direction, and subject to the oversight, of" the board of directors, since operational management is delegated to officers and other professional managers.

While Section 8.01(b), in providing for corporate powers to be exercised under the authority of the board of directors, allows the board of directors to delegate to appropriate officers, employees, or agents of the nonprofit corporation authority to exercise powers and perform functions not required by law to be exercised or performed by the board of directors itself, responsibility to oversee the exercise of that delegated authority nonetheless remains with the board of directors. The scope of that oversight responsibility will vary depending on the nature of the corporation's activities.

Although delegation does not relieve the board of directors of its responsibilities of oversight, directors should not be held personally responsible for actions or omissions of officers, employees, or agents of the nonprofit corporation, so long as the directors have relied reasonably and in good faith upon those officers, employees, or agents. See Sections 8.30 and 8.31 and their Official Comments. Directors generally have the power to probe into day-to-day management to any depth they choose, but they have the obligation to do so only to the extent that the directors' oversight responsibilities may require, or, for example, when they become aware of matters that make reliance on management or other persons unwarranted.

§ 8.02. QUALIFICATIONS OF DIRECTORS

A director of a nonprofit corporation must be an individual. The articles of incorporation or bylaws may prescribe other qualifications for directors. A director need not be a resident of this state or a member of the corporation unless the articles or bylaws so prescribe.

> *Source Note:* Patterned after Model Business Corporation Act, 3d Ed. (2002) § 8.02. Derived from Model Nonprofit Corporation Act (1987) § 8.02.

CROSS-REFERENCES

Articles of incorporation, see § 2.02 and Ch. 10A.

Bylaws, see § 2.06 and Ch. 10B.

OFFICIAL COMMENT

The elimination of mandatory special qualifications for directors is now nearly universal, but the articles of incorporation or bylaws may prescribe special qualifications where a nonprofit corporation considers that appropriate. Although this section requires that directors be individuals, there is no such requirement with respect to members of a designated body or delegates and the definitions in Section 1.40 refer simply to the "persons" who compose those groups.

This section does not apply to a designated body. The qualifications of members of a designated body are dealt with in Section 8.12(c).

§ 8.03. NUMBER OF DIRECTORS

(a) A board of directors must consist of three or more directors, with the number specified in or fixed in accordance with the articles of incorporation or bylaws.
(b) The number of directors may be increased or decreased (but to no fewer than three) from time to time by amendment to, or in the manner provided in, the articles of incorporation or bylaws.

Source Note: Patterned after Model Business Corporation Act, 3d Ed. (2002) § 8.03(a) and (b). Substantially a reenactment of Model Nonprofit Corporation Act (1987) § 8.03.

CROSS-REFERENCES

Annual meeting of members, see § 7.01.

Classification of board of directors, see § 8.06.

Deadlocked board of directors as ground for dissolution, see § 14.30.

Terms generally, see § 8.05.

Voting for directors, see § 7.27.

OFFICIAL COMMENT

Section 8.03 prescribes rules for (i) determining the size of the board of directors and (ii) changing the number of directors once the board's size has been established.

1. Minimum Number of Directors

Section 8.03(a) requires a nonprofit corporation to have a minimum of three directors. So long as that limitation is satisfied, the size of the board of directors may be "specified in or fixed in accordance with" the articles of incorporation or bylaws. The size of the board of directors thus may be fixed initially in one or more of the fundamental corporate documents, or the decision as to the size of the initial board of directors may be made thereafter in the manner authorized in those documents.

2. Changes in the Size of the Board of Directors

Section 8.03(b) provides a nonprofit corporation with the freedom to design the provisions of its articles of incorporation and bylaws relating to the size of the board with a view to achieving the combination of flexibility for the board of directors and protection for members that it deems appropriate. The articles or bylaws could provide for a specified number of directors or a variable-range board, thereby requiring member action to change the fixed size of the board, to change the limits established for the size of the variable-range board, or to change from a variable-range board to a fixed board or vice versa. The articles or bylaws could permit amendment by the board of directors, or the articles or bylaws could require that any amendment, in whole or in part, be made only by the members. Typically, the board of directors would be permitted to change the board size within the established variable range. If a corporation wishes to ensure that any change in the number of directors be approved by members, then an appropriate restriction would need to be included in the articles or bylaws.

The board's power to change the number of directors, like all other board powers, is subject to compliance with applicable standards governing director conduct. In particular, it may be inappropriate to change the size of the board for the primary purpose of maintaining control or defeating particular candidates for the board. *See Blasius Industries, Inc. v. Atlas Corp.*, 564 A.2D 651 (Del. Ch. 1988).

§ 8.04. SELECTION OF DIRECTORS

(a) The directors of a membership corporation (other than any initial directors named in the articles of incorporation or elected by the incorporators) shall be elected at the first annual meeting of members, and at each annual meeting thereafter, unless the articles or bylaws provide some other time or method of election, or provide that some or all of the directors are appointed by some other person or designated in some other manner.

(b) The directors of a nonmembership corporation (other than any initial directors named in the articles of incorporation or elected by the incorporators) shall be elected, appointed, or designated as provided in the articles or bylaws. If no method of designation or appointment is set forth in the articles or bylaws, the directors (other than any initial directors) shall be elected by the board.

Source Note: Substantially a reenactment of Model Nonprofit Corporation Act (1987) § 8.04.

CROSS-REFERENCES

Initial directors:

appointed by incorporators, see § 2.05.

named in articles, see § 2.02.

"Membership corporation" defined, see § 1.40.

"Nonmembership corporation" defined, see § 1.40.

Number of directors, see § 8.03.

Staggered terms for directors, see § 8.06.

Terms of directors generally, see § 8.05.

OFFICIAL COMMENT

1. Membership Corporations

If a nonprofit corporation has members, the members are entitled to elect all the directors in the absence of a contrary provision in the articles of incorporation or bylaws. The articles or bylaws may set forth a simple one-vote-per-member structure or may provide for election by voting groups of members, chapters, or other organizational units or by region or other geographic groupings. See Sections 2.02 and 2.05 as to appointment of initial directors. See Sections 7.04, 7.09, 7.21, 7.25, and 7.27 as to the ways in which members may vote.

Section 8.04 should be applied in a manner consistent with the concept that an election procedure must be reasonable. *See Dozier v. Automobile Club of Michigan*, 69 MICH. APP. 114, 244 N.W.2D 376 (1976); *Braude v. Havenner*, 38 CAL. APP. 3D 526, 113 CAL. RPTR. 386 (1974); *Valle v. North Jersey Automobile Club*, 125 N.J. SUPER. 302, 310 A.2D 518 (1973). The act does not specify detailed procedures, but leaves the matter to developing case law.

Even if a nonprofit corporation has members, the members need not elect some or all of the directors. Directors may hold office as a result of designation in the articles of incorporation or bylaws or as a result of being appointed by some person or entity.

Designation occurs when the articles of incorporation or bylaws name an individual as a director or designate the holder of some office or position as a director. For example, the President of Harvard, the Bishop of New York, or the head of a union may become a director of a nonprofit corporation pursuant to an article or bylaw provision designating the holder of his or her position as a director of the corporation. The individual would cease to be a director upon ceasing to hold the designated position.

2. Nonmembership Corporations

Section 8.04 authorizes self-perpetuating boards of directors. If a nonprofit corporation does not have members, the board elects directors in the absence of a provision in the articles of incorporation or bylaws setting forth some other approach.

3. "Ex Officio" Directors

An individual may serve as a director of a nonprofit corporation "ex officio," which means that the individual is a director because of some other office or position that the individual holds. Although an ex officio director is sometimes not entitled to vote as a director, the term "ex officio" does not include the concept that the position is nonvoting. If an ex officio director is to be nonvoting, that must be provided for expressly.

§ 8.05. TERMS OF DIRECTORS GENERALLY

(a) The articles of incorporation or bylaws may specify the terms of directors. If a term is not specified in the articles or bylaws, the term of a director is one year. Except for directors who are appointed by persons who are not members or who are designated in a manner other than by election or appointment, the term of a director may not exceed five years.

(b) A decrease in the number of directors or term of office does not shorten an incumbent director's term.

(c) Except as provided in the articles of incorporation or bylaws, the term of a director elected to fill a vacancy expires at the end of the unexpired term that the director is filling.

(d) Despite the expiration of a director's term, the director continues to serve until the director's successor is elected, appointed, or designated and until the director's successor takes office unless otherwise provided in the articles of incorporation or bylaws.

Source Note: Patterned in part after Model Business Corporation Act, 3d Ed. (2002) § 8.05. Derived from Model Nonprofit Corporation Act (1987) § 8.05.

CROSS-REFERENCES

Annual members meeting, see § 7.01.

Court-ordered members meeting, see § 7.03.

Removal, see §§ 8.08 and 8.09.

Resignation, see § 8.07.

Size of board, see § 8.03.

Staggered terms, see § 8.06.

Vacancies, see § 8.10.

OFFICIAL COMMENT

The usual term of directors is one year, but Section 8.05(a) permits the articles of incorporation or bylaws to provide for longer terms. In the case of directors elected by the members, the permissible longer term is limited to five years. However, Section 8.05(a) permits directors who are not elected to serve for terms longer than five years. Directors who serve "ex officio" are "designated" for purposes of Section 8.05(a) and thus are not limited to a term of five years. The act does not provide for term limits and thus a director may be elected to more than one term, regardless of the length of a term, unless the articles of incorporation or bylaws limit the number of terms a director may serve.

Section 8.05(b) provides that a decrease in the number of directors does not shorten the term of an incumbent director or divest any director of his or her office. Rather, the incumbent director's term expires at the meeting of members at which the incumbent's successor would otherwise be elected.

Section 8.05(d) provides for "holdover" directors so that directorships do not automatically become vacant at the expiration of their terms but the same persons continue in office until successors qualify for office, unless otherwise provided in the articles of incorporation or bylaws. Thus the power of the board of directors to act continues uninterrupted even though an annual meeting of the members is not held or the members are deadlocked and unable to elect directors at the meeting.

The act recognizes that an individual may become a director of a nonprofit corporation in one of three different ways:

(1) The individual may be elected a director, whether by the members, the incumbent board, or a designated body. Election by the board may be to fill a vacancy or in a regular election if the corporation does not have members.
(2) The individual may be appointed in the manner provided in the articles of incorporation or bylaws. For example, the bylaws of a religious corporation may provide that the leader of a superior religious order may appoint directors of the corporation.

(3) The individual may be become a director because the individual is designated as a director in the articles of incorporation or bylaws. For example, the bylaws of a religious corporation may provide that the individual serving at the time as the leader of a superior religious order is designated as a director of the corporation.

§ 8.06. STAGGERED TERMS FOR DIRECTORS

The articles of incorporation or bylaws may provide for staggering the terms of directors by dividing the total number of directors into groups of one or more directors. The terms of office and number of directors in each group do not need to be uniform.

Source Note: Derived from Model Nonprofit Corporation Act (1987) § 8.06. Compare Model Business Corporation Act, 3d Ed. (2002) § 8.06.

CROSS-REFERENCES

Annual members meeting, see § 7.01.

Election of directors generally, see § 7.27.

Number of directors, see § 8.03.

Removal, see §§ 8.08 and 8.09.

Resignation, see § 8.07.

Terms of directors generally, see § 8.05.

Vacancies, see § 8.10.

OFFICIAL COMMENT

This section validates the practice of "classifying" the board or "staggering" the terms of directors so that fewer than all of the directors are elected each year. Unlike the case with business corporations, where each class of directors must be as nearly equal in number as possible, this section permits classes of directors to vary in size from each other. This section also does not limit the number of classes that may be created.

§ 8.07. RESIGNATION OF DIRECTORS

(a) A director may resign at any time by delivering a signed notice in the form of a record to the chair of the board of directors or to an executive officer or the secretary of the corporation.

(b) A resignation is effective when the notice is delivered unless the notice specifies a later effective time.

Source Note: Patterned after Model Business Corporation Act, 3d Ed. (2002) § 8.07. Substantially a reenactment of Model Nonprofit Corporation Act (1987) § 8.07, except that the last sentence of subsection (b) is omitted as supplied by § 8.10(c).

CROSS-REFERENCES

"Deliver" defined, see § 1.40.

Notice, see § 1.41.

"Secretary" defined, see § 1.40.

Vacancies, see § 8.10.

OFFICIAL COMMENT

The resignation of a director is effective when the resignation notice is delivered unless the notice specifies a later effective time, in which case the director continues to serve until that later time. Since the director giving the notice is still a member of the board, he or she may participate in all decisions until the specified time, including the choice of a successor under Section 8.10.

Vacancies created by a resignation effective at a later time may be filled before that date under Section 8.10.

§ 8.08. REMOVAL OF DIRECTORS BY MEMBERS OR OTHER PERSONS

(a) Removal of directors of a membership corporation is subject to the following provisions:

(1) The members may remove, with or without cause, one or more directors who have been elected by the

members, unless the articles of incorporation or bylaws provide that directors may be removed only for cause. The articles or bylaws may specify what constitutes cause for removal. See Section 10.22(a) (bylaw amendments requiring member approval).

(2) Except as provided in the articles of incorporation or bylaws, if a director is elected by a voting group of members, or by a chapter or other organizational unit, or by a region or other geographic grouping, only the members of that voting group or chapter, unit, region, or grouping may participate in the vote to remove the director.

(3) The notice of a meeting of members at which removal of a director is to be considered must state that the purpose, or one of the purposes, of the meeting is removal of the director.

(4) The board of directors of a membership corporation may not remove a director except as provided in subsection (c) or in the articles of incorporation or bylaws.

(b) The board of directors may remove a director of a nonmembership corporation:

(1) With or without cause, unless the articles of incorporation or bylaws provide that directors may be removed only for cause. The articles or bylaws may specify what constitutes cause for removal.

(2) As provided in subsection (c).

(c) The board of directors of a membership corporation or nonmembership corporation may remove a director who:

(1) has been declared of unsound mind by a final order of court;

(2) has been convicted of a felony;

(3) has been found by a final order of court to have breached a duty as a director under [Subchapter] 8C;

(4) has missed the number of board meetings specified in the articles of incorporation or bylaws, if the articles or bylaws at the beginning of the director's current term

provided that a director may be removed for missing the specified number of board meetings; or

(5) does not satisfy at the time any of the qualifications for directors set forth in the articles of incorporation or bylaws at the beginning of the director's current term, if the decision that the director fails to satisfy a qualification is made by the vote of a majority of the directors who meet all of the required qualifications.

(d) A director who is designated in the articles of incorporation or bylaws may be removed by an amendment to the articles or bylaws deleting or changing the designation. See Section 10.30 (approval of amendments by third persons).

(e) Except as provided in the articles of incorporation or bylaws, a director who is appointed by persons other than the members may be removed with or without cause by those persons.

Source Note: Subsection (a) is derived from Model Nonprofit Corporation Act (1987) § 8.08. Compare Model Business Corporation Act, 3d Ed. (2002) § 8.08. Subsection (c) is patterned after CAL. CORP. CODE § 5221(a) and (b) (2008). Subsections (d) and (e) are derived from Model Nonprofit Corporation Act (1987) § 8.09.

CROSS-REFERENCES

Court-ordered removal, see § 8.09.

Director standards of conduct, see § 8.30.

Election of directors generally, see § 7.27.

Meeting notice, see § 7.05.

Member meetings, see §§ 7.01–7.03.

"Membership corporation" defined, see § 1.40.

"Nonmembership corporation" defined, see § 1.40.

Quorum for voting group, see §§ 7.24 and 7.26.

"Voting group" defined, see § 1.40.

OFFICIAL COMMENT

Section 8.08(a) adopts the view that the members should normally have the power to change at will the directors elected by them. This section reverses the common law position that directors have a statutory entitlement to their office and can be removed only for cause—fraud, criminal conduct, gross abuse of office amounting to a breach of trust, or similar conduct. The power to remove directors of a membership corporation is subject to certain restrictions set forth in Section 8.08:

(1) The power to remove a director without cause may be eliminated by a provision in the articles of incorporation or bylaws.

(2) If the articles of incorporation provide that a voting group of members or other group is entitled to elect a director (see Section 8.04), only that group may participate in the vote whether or not to remove that director. But that director may be removed by court proceeding under Section 8.09 despite this section.

§ 8.09. REMOVAL OF DIRECTORS BY JUDICIAL PROCEEDING

(a) The [*name or describe*] court of the county where the principal office of a nonprofit corporation (or, if none in this state, its registered office) is located may remove a director from office in a proceeding commenced by or in the right of the corporation if the court finds that:

   (1) the director engaged in fraudulent conduct with respect to the corporation or its members, grossly abused the position of director, or intentionally inflicted harm on the corporation; and

   (2) considering the director's course of conduct and the inadequacy of other available remedies, removal would be in the best interest of the corporation.

(b) A member, individual director, or member of a designated body proceeding on behalf of the nonprofit corporation under subsection (a) shall comply with all of the requirements of [Chapter] 13.

(c) The court, in addition to removing the director, may bar the director from being reelected, redesignated, or reappointed for a period prescribed by the court.

(d) Nothing in this section limits the equitable powers of the court to order other relief.

(e) If a proceeding is commenced under this section to remove a director of a charitable corporation, the plaintiff must give the attorney general notice in record form of the commencement of the proceeding.

Source Note: Patterned after Model Business Corporation Act, 3d Ed. (2002) § 8.09. Derived from Model Nonprofit Corporation Act (1987) § 8.10.

CROSS-REFERENCES

Derivative proceedings, see Ch. 13.

Director standards of conduct, see § 8.30.

"Member" defined, see § 1.40.

"Principal office":
- defined, see § 1.40.
- designated in annual report, see § 16.21.

"Proceeding" defined, see § 1.40.

Registered office:
- designated in annual report, see § 16.21.
- required, see §§ 2.02, 5.01, and 15.07.

Removal by members, see § 8.08.

OFFICIAL COMMENT

Section 8.09 is designed to operate in the limited circumstance where other remedies are inadequate to address serious misconduct by a director and it is impracticable for members to invoke the usual remedy of removal under Section 8.08. In recognition that director election and removal are principal prerogatives of members, Section 8.09 authorizes judicial removal of a director who is found to have engaged in serious misconduct as described in subsection (a)(1) if the court also finds that, taking into consideration the director's course of conduct and the inadequacy of other available remedies, removal of the director would be in the best interest of the nonprofit corporation. Misconduct serious enough to justify the extraordinary remedy of judicial removal does not involve any matter falling within an individual director's lawful exercise of business judgment, no matter how unpopular the director's views may be with the other members of the board. Policy and personal differences among the members of the board of directors should be left to be resolved by the members.

Section 8.09(d) makes it clear that the court is not restricted to the removal remedy in actions under this section but may order any other equitable relief. Where, for example, the complaint concerns an ongoing course of conduct that is harmful to the nonprofit corporation, the court may enjoin the director from continuing that conduct. In another instance, the court may determine that the director's continuation in office is inimical to the best interest of the corporation.

A proceeding under this section may be brought directly by the board of directors. A proceeding may also be brought by a member or an individual director or member of a designated body suing derivatively. If an action is brought derivatively, all of the provisions of Chapter 13, including dismissal under Section 13.05, are applicable to the action.

Section 8.09 is designed to interfere as little as possible with the usual mechanisms of corporate governance. Accordingly, except for limited circumstances such as those described above, where members have reelected or declined to remove a director with full knowledge of the director's misbehavior, the court should decline to entertain an action for removal under Section 8.09. It is not intended to permit judicial resolution of internal corporate disputes involving issues other than those specified in subsection (a).

§ 8.10. VACANCY ON BOARD

(a) Except as otherwise provided in subsection (b), the articles of incorporation, or the bylaws, if a vacancy occurs on the board of directors, including a vacancy resulting from an increase in the number of directors, the vacancy may be filled by a majority of the directors remaining in office even if they constitute less than a quorum.

(b) Except as provided in the articles of incorporation or bylaws, a vacancy in the position of a director who is:

 (1) elected by a voting group of members, by a chapter or other organizational unit of members, or by a region or other geographic grouping of members, may be filled during the first three months after the vacancy occurs only by that voting group or chapter, unit, region, or grouping;

 (2) appointed by persons other than the members, may be filled only by those persons; or

 (3) designated in the articles of incorporation or bylaws, may not be filled by action of the board of directors.

(c) A vacancy that will occur at a specific later time (by reason of a resignation effective at a later time under Section 8.07(b) or otherwise) may be filled before the vacancy occurs but the new director may not take office until the vacancy occurs.

Source Note: Subsection (a) is patterned after 15 PA. CONS. STAT. § 5725(c) (2008). Derived from Model Nonprofit Corporation Act (1987) § 8.11. Compare Model Business Corporation Act, 3d Ed. (2002) § 8.11.

CROSS-REFERENCES

Number of directors, see § 8.03.

Quorum and voting of directors, see § 8.24.

Removal of directors, see §§ 8.08 and 8.09.

Resignation of directors, see § 8.07.

Terms of directors generally, see § 8.05.

Voting by voting group, see §§ 7.24 and 7.25.

"Voting group" defined, see § 1.40.

OFFICIAL COMMENT

Section 8.10(a) allows a majority of the directors remaining in office to fill vacancies even though they are fewer than a quorum. For example, on a board of six directors where a quorum is four, if there are two vacancies, they may be filled by action of three of the remaining directors.

Section 8.10(b)(1) protects the special rights of groups of members to elect directors by restricting the ability of the board of directors to fill a vacancy of a director elected by the group. The group is given the exclusive opportunity to fill the vacancy for an initial period, but the board is then given the power to fill the vacancy if the group does not act. The board of directors never has the power, however, to fill a vacancy in the case of a director designated or appointed in a manner other than election. Only the persons authorized to appoint a director may fill a vacancy in the appointed board seat. A vacancy in a designated board seat will only be filled when an individual satisfies the requirements of the designation.

Section 8.10(c) permits vacancies that will arise on a specific later time to be filled in advance of that time so long as the designee does not actually take office until the vacancy occurs. The director in the office that will become vacant may participate in the selection of the successor. A vacancy arising at a later time is most likely to arise because of a resignation effective at a later time; it may also arise in connection with retirements or with prospective amendments to bylaws.

§ 8.11. COMPENSATION OF DIRECTORS

Unless the articles of incorporation or bylaws provide otherwise, the board of directors may fix the compensation of directors.

Source Note: Patterned after Model Business Corporation Act, 3d Ed. (2002) § 8.11. Reenactment of Model Nonprofit Corporation Act (1987) § 8.12.

CROSS-REFERENCES

Committees of board of directors, see § 8.25.

Director standards of conduct, see § 8.30.

OFFICIAL COMMENT

This section overrules the common law doctrine that prohibited directors from setting their own compensation.

Most nonprofit corporations do not compensate individuals for serving as directors. In some nonprofit corporations, however, compensation may be appropriate as a result of the time and effort needed to serve as a director, the responsibilities undertaken, and other relevant factors. This section allows the board to set the compensation of directors for serving as directors. As a result of its power under Section 8.01, the board also has the power to set the compensation of directors who serve as officers or in some other capacity. When exercising their power under this section, the directors must comply with their duties as directors under Subchapter 8C.

Reimbursement of expenses incurred as a director in accordance with expense reimbursement policies of the corporation, or as approved by the board, does not constitute compensation under this section.

§ 8.12. DESIGNATED BODY

(a) Some, but less than all, of the powers, authority, or functions of the board of directors of a nonprofit corporation under this [act] may be vested by the articles of incorporation or bylaws in a designated body. If such a designated body is created:

(1) The provisions of this [chapter] and other provisions of law on the rights, duties, and liabilities of the board of directors or directors individually also apply to the designated body and to the members of the designated body individually. The provisions of this [chapter] and other provisions of law on meetings, notice, and the manner of acting of the board of directors also apply to the designated body in the absence of an applicable rule in the articles of incorporation, bylaws, or internal operating rules of the designated body.

(2) To the extent the powers, authority, or functions of the board of directors have been vested in the designated body, the directors are relieved from their duties and liabilities with respect to those powers, authority, and functions.

(3) A provision of the articles of incorporation regarding indemnification of directors or limiting the liability of directors adopted pursuant to Section 2.02(b)(8) or (c) applies to members of the designated body, except as otherwise provided in the articles.

(b) Some, but less than all, of the rights or obligations of the members of a nonprofit corporation under this [act] may be vested by the articles of incorporation or bylaws in a designated body. If such a designated body is created:

(1) The provisions of this [chapter] and other provisions of law on the rights and obligations of members also apply to the designated body and to the members of the designated body individually. The provisions of this [chapter] and other provisions of law on meetings, notice, and the manner of acting of members also apply to the designated body in the absence of an applicable provision in the articles of incorporation, bylaws, or internal operating rules of the designated body.

(2) To the extent the rights or obligations of the members have been vested in the designated body, the members are relieved from responsibility with respect to those rights and obligations.

(c) The articles of incorporation or bylaws may prescribe qualifications for members of a designated body. Except as otherwise provided by the articles or bylaws, a member of a designated body does not need to be:
   (1) an individual,
   (2) a director, officer, or member of the nonprofit corporation, or
   (3) a resident of this state.

(d) See Section 10.22(a) (bylaw amendments requiring member approval).

Source Note: Derived from Model Nonprofit Corporation Act (1987) § 8.01(c). Patterned in part after 15 PA. CONS. STAT. § 5734 (2008).

CROSS-REFERENCES

"Board of directors" defined, see § 1.40.

Functions of the board, see § 8.01.

"Member" defined, see § 1.40.

OFFICIAL COMMENT

"Designated bodies" were not referred to as such in the prior version of the act, although it did authorize a nonprofit corporation to adopt analogous governance arrangements. More detail has been provided in the current act to give nonprofit corporations greater certainty when using the flexibility inherent in the concept of a designated body to organize their affairs.

It is not necessary for a designated body to be referred to by that name, and designated bodies are typically referred to by the name they have for other purposes.

If all the powers, authority, and functions of the board of directors are vested in a body, it is not a designated body but has instead the status of the board of directors. Similarly, if all the rights and obligations of the members are vested in a group of persons, the group is not a designated body and its members instead have the status of members.

If all the members of a group of individuals that have some of the powers, authority, or functions of the board of directors are directors and the group is established by action of the board, the group will be a committee of the board rather than a designated body. If at least one member of a group is not a director, however, the group will be a designated body.

Use of a designated body does not reduce accountability because this section makes clear that members of a designated body have the duties and liabilities of directors when discharging functions that would otherwise be within the purview of the board.

See Section 10.30 with respect to special requirements for approval of amendments of the articles of incorporation or bylaws.

[Subchapter] B
MEETINGS AND ACTION OF THE BOARD

§ 8.20. MEETINGS

(a) The board of directors may hold regular or special meetings in or out of this state.

(b) Unless the articles of incorporation or bylaws provide otherwise, the board of directors may permit any or all directors to participate in a regular or special meeting by, or conduct the meeting through the use of, any means of communication by which all directors participating may simultaneously hear each other during the meeting. A director participating in a meeting by this means is considered to be present in person at the meeting.

Source Note: Patterned after Model Business Corporation Act, 3d Ed. (2002) § 8.20. Substantially a reenactment of Model Nonprofit Corporation Act (1987) § 8.20(b)–(c).

CROSS-REFERENCES

Action without meeting, see § 8.21.

Notice of meeting, see § 8.22.

Quorum and voting, see § 8.24.

Waiver of meeting notice, see § 8.23.

OFFICIAL COMMENT

This section authorizes meetings of directors anywhere. No distinction is made between meetings in-state and out-of-state. It also authorizes the board of directors to permit any or all directors to participate in a meeting by the use of any means of communication by which all directors participating may simultaneously hear each other. This decision is discretionary with the board of directors, and a person participating in this fashion is considered to be present in person at the meeting for purposes of quorum and voting requirements. If a director is hearing-impaired, participation by that director or other directors in a meeting by means of communications technology will still be permissible if reasonable accommodations are made to permit the hearing-impaired director to follow the discussion.

With the development of modern electronic technology, it is possible that the advantages of the traditional meeting, at which all members are present at a single place, may be obtained even though the participants are physically dispersed and no two directors are present at the same place. The advantage of the traditional meeting is the opportunity for interchange that is permitted by a meeting in a single room at which participants are physically present. If this opportunity for interchange is thought to be available by the board of directors, a meeting may be conducted by electronic means although no two directors are physically present at the same place and no specific place for the meeting is designated.

The provisions of this section also apply to meetings of a designated body. See Section 8.12(a)(1).

§ 8.21. ACTION WITHOUT MEETING

(a) Except to the extent that the articles of incorporation or bylaws require that action by the board of directors be taken at a meeting, action required or permitted by this [act] to be taken by the board of directors may be taken without a meeting if each director signs a consent in the form of a record describing the action to be taken and delivers it to the nonprofit corporation.

(b) Action taken under this section is the act of the board of directors when one or more consents signed by all the directors are delivered to the nonprofit corporation. The consent may specify the time at which the action taken in the consent is to be effective. A director's consent may be withdrawn by a revocation in the form of a record signed by the director and delivered to the corporation prior to delivery to the corporation of unrevoked consents signed by all the directors.

(c) A consent signed under this section has the effect of action taken at a meeting of the board of directors and may be described as such in any document.

Source Note: Patterned after Model Business Corporation Act, 3d Ed. (2002) § 8.21. Substantially a reenactment of Model Nonprofit Corporation Act (1987) § 8.21.

CROSS-REFERENCES

Notice generally, see § 1.41.

Notice of meeting, see § 8.22.

"Record" defined, see § 1.40.

"Sign" defined, see § 1.40.

Waiver of meeting notice, see § 8.23.

OFFICIAL COMMENT

The power of the board of directors to act unanimously without a meeting is based on the pragmatic consideration that in many situations a formal meeting is not needed. The consent may specify the time at which the action taken thereunder is to become effective.

Under Section 8.21 the requirement of unanimous consent precludes the possibility of stifling or ignoring opposing argument. A director opposed to an action that is proposed to be taken by unanimous consent, or uncertain about the desirability of that action, may compel the holding of a directors' meeting to discuss the matter simply by withholding consent.

A designated body may act without a meeting pursuant to this section. See Section 8.12(a)(1).

§ 8.22. CALL AND NOTICE OF MEETING

(a) Unless the articles of incorporation or bylaws provide otherwise, regular meetings of the board of directors may be held without notice of the date, time, place, or purpose of the meeting.

(b) Unless the articles of incorporation or bylaws provide for a longer or shorter period, special meetings of the board of directors must be preceded by at least two days' notice of the date, time, and place of the meeting. The notice need not describe the purpose of the special meeting unless required by the articles of incorporation or bylaws.

(c) Unless the articles of incorporation or bylaws provide otherwise, the chair of the board, the highest ranking officer of the corporation, or 20% of the directors then in office may call and give notice of a meeting of the board of directors.

(d) The articles of incorporation or bylaws may authorize oral notice of meetings of the board of directors.

Source Note: Patterned after Model Business Corporation Act, 3d Ed. (2002) § 8.22. Derived from Model Nonprofit Corporation Act (1987) § 8.22(a), (b), and (d).

CROSS-REFERENCES

Action without meeting, see § 8.21.

Meetings of board of directors, see §§ 8.20 and 8.21.

Notice, see § 1.41.

Waiver of notice, see § 8.23.

OFFICIAL COMMENT

Regular meetings of the board of directors may be held without notice and special meetings require only two days' notice unless other requirements are imposed by the articles of incorporation or bylaws. The notice may be in the form of a record or oral. See Section 1.41(a). If the notice of a special meeting is mailed, it must be deposited with the U.S. Mail at least seven days before the meeting because Section 1.41(e)(2) provides that notice by mail is effective five days after mailing.

No statement of the purpose of either a regular or a special meeting is necessary unless required by the articles of incorporation or bylaws. These requirements differ from the requirements applicable to meetings of members because of fundamental differences in their roles: directors are a collegial body and meetings of directors are held more systematically and regularly than meetings of members.

The provisions of this section also apply to meetings of a designated body. See Section 8.12(a)(1).

§ 8.23. WAIVER OF NOTICE

(a) A director may waive any notice required by this [act], the articles of incorporation, or the bylaws before or after the date and time stated in the notice. Except as provided by subsection (b), the waiver must be in the form of a record, signed by the director entitled to the notice, and filed with the minutes or corporate records.

(b) A director's attendance at or participation in a meeting waives any required notice to the director of the meeting, unless the director at the beginning of the meeting (or promptly upon arrival) objects to holding the meeting or transacting business at the meeting and does not thereafter vote for or assent to action taken at the meeting.

Source Note: Patterned after Model Business Corporation Act, 3d Ed. (2002) § 8.23. Substantially a reenactment of Model Nonprofit Corporation Act (1987) § 8.23.

CROSS-REFERENCES

Action without meeting, see § 8.21.

Meetings of board of directors, see § 8.20.

Notice generally, see § 1.41.

Notice of meeting, see § 8.22.

"Record" defined, see § 1.40.

"Secretary" defined, see § 1.40.

"Sign" defined, see § 1.40.

OFFICIAL COMMENT

Section 8.23(a) reverses the common law rule that invalidates waivers of notice by directors after the date and time of the meeting. In modern practice notice is often a technical requirement and waivers should be freely permitted.

Section 8.23(b) recognizes that the function of notice is to inform directors of a meeting. If a director actually appears at the meeting the director has probably had notice of it and generally should not be able to raise a technical objection about lack of notice.

In cases where actual prejudice occurs because of the lack of notice, as may be indicated by the absence of one or more other directors, the director must call attention to the defect at the outset of the meeting or promptly upon arrival. That director, or a director who did not receive notice and was not present at the meeting, may then attack the validity of the action taken for want of notice. If a director properly objects to the meeting being held, the director is not presumed to have assented to actions taken thereafter, but if the director thereafter votes for or assents to action taken at the meeting, an objection as to lack of notice is waived. See Section 8.24(d).

A member of a designated body may waive notice in the manner provided in this section. See Section 8.12(a)(1).

§ 8.24. QUORUM AND VOTING

(a) Except as provided in subsection (b), the articles of incorporation, or the bylaws, a quorum of the board of directors consists of a majority of the directors in office before a meeting begins.

(b) The articles of incorporation or bylaws may authorize a quorum of the board of directors to consist of no fewer than the greater of 1/3 of the number of directors in office or two directors.

(c) If a quorum is present when a vote is taken, the affirmative vote of a majority of directors present is the act of the board of directors unless a greater vote is required by the articles of incorporation or bylaws.

(d) A director who is present at a meeting of the board of directors when corporate action is taken is considered to have assented to the action taken unless one of the following applies:
   (1) The director objects at the beginning of the meeting (or promptly upon arrival) to holding it or transacting business at the meeting.
   (2) The director dissents or abstains from the action and:
      (i) the dissent or abstention is entered in the minutes of the meeting; or
      (ii) the director delivers notice in the form of a record of the director's dissent or abstention to the presiding officer of the meeting before its adjournment or to the corporation promptly after adjournment of the meeting.

(e) The right of dissent or abstention is not available to a director who votes in favor of the action taken.

Source Note: Patterned after Model Business Corporation Act, 3d Ed. (2002) § 8.24. Derived from Model Nonprofit Corporation Act (1987) § 8.24.

CROSS-REFERENCES

Action without meeting, see § 8.21.

Committees of board of directors, see § 8.25.

Director standards of conduct, see § 8.30.

Meetings of board of directors, see § 8.20.

Notice, see § 1.41.

Number of directors, see § 8.03.

"Secretary" defined, see § 1.40.

OFFICIAL COMMENT

Section 8.24(a) allows the articles of incorporation or bylaws to increase the quorum up to and including unanimity or to reduce it to not less than 1/3 (or at least two directors). Section 8.24(c) generally requires a majority vote of those directors present for action by the board, but allows the articles or bylaws to increase the vote necessary for the board to take action.

The phrase "when a vote is taken" in Section 8.24(c) is designed to make clear that the board of directors may act only when a quorum is present. If directors leave during the course of a meeting, the board of directors may not act after the number of directors present is reduced to less than a quorum.

Under Section 8.24(d) directors who object or abstain with respect to action taken by the board of directors or a committee of the board of directors must make their position clear in one of the ways described in this subsection. The objection serves the important purpose of forcefully bringing the position of the dissenting member to the attention of the balance of the board of directors. The requirement of an objection in the form of a record also prevents a director from later seeking to avoid responsibility because of secret doubts about the wisdom of the action taken. The right of dissent or abstention is not available to a director who voted in favor of the action taken.

Section 8.24(d) applies only to directors who are present at the meeting. Directors who are not present are not considered to have assented to any action taken at the meeting in their absence.

This section applies to meetings of a designated body. See Section 8.12(a)(1).

§ 8.25. BOARD AND ADVISORY COMMITTEES

(a) Unless this [act], the articles of incorporation, or the bylaws provide otherwise, a board of directors may create one or more committees of the board that consist of one or more directors.

(b) Unless this [act] otherwise provides, the creation of a committee and appointment of directors to it must be approved by the greater of:

  (1) a majority of all the directors in office when the action is taken; or

  (2) the number of directors required by the articles of incorporation or bylaws to take action under Section 8.24.

(c) Sections 8.20 through 8.24 apply both to committees of the board and to their members.

(d) To the extent specified by the board of directors or in the articles of incorporation or bylaws, each committee may exercise the powers of the board of directors under Section 8.01 except as limited by subsection (e).

(e) A committee may not, however:

  (1) authorize distributions;

  (2) in the case of a membership corporation, approve or propose to members action that this [act] requires be approved by members;

  (3) fill vacancies on the board of directors or, subject to subsection (g), on any of its committees; or

  (4) adopt, amend, or repeal bylaws.

(f) The creation of, delegation of authority to, or action by a committee does not alone constitute compliance by a director with the standards of conduct described in Section 8.30.

(g) The board of directors may appoint one or more directors as alternate members of any committee to replace any absent or disqualified member during the member's absence or disqualification.

(h) A nonprofit corporation may create or authorize the creation of one or more advisory committees whose members need not be directors. An advisory committee:

  (1) is not a committee of the board; and

  (2) may not exercise any of the powers of the board.

Source Note: Patterned after Model Business Corporation Act, 3d Ed. (2002) § 8.25. Derived from Model Nonprofit Corporation Act (1987) § 8.25. Subsection (h) is new.

CROSS-REFERENCES

Derivative proceedings, see Ch. 13.

Director standards of conduct, see § 8.30.

Distributions, see § 6.40.

Duties of board of directors, see § 8.01.

"Membership corporation" defined, see § 1.40.

Quorum and voting, see § 8.24.

Vacancies on board, see § 8.10.

OFFICIAL COMMENT

Section 8.25 makes explicit the common law power of a board of directors to act through committees of directors and specifies the powers of the board of directors that are nondelegable, that is, powers that only the full board of directors may exercise.

Section 8.25(b) provides that, unless this act otherwise provides, a committee of the board of directors may be created only by the affirmative vote of a majority of the board of directors then in office, or, if greater, by the number of directors required to take action by the articles of incorporation or bylaws. This supermajority requirement reflects the importance of the decision to invest board committees with power to act under Section 8.25. Section 13.05(b) requires that a special litigation committee, to consider whether the maintenance of a derivative action is in the corporation's best interest, be appointed by a majority vote of independent directors present at a meeting of the board. Section 8.55(b) contains a generally similar requirement with regard to the appointment of a committee to consider whether indemnification is permissible.

Section 8.25(a) permits a committee to consist of a single director. This accommodates situations in which only one director may be present or available to make a decision on short notice, as well as situations in which it is unnecessary or inconvenient to have more than one member on a committee. Committees also are often employed to decide matters in which other members of the board have a conflict of interest; in such a case, a court will typically scrutinize with care the committee's decision when it is the product of a lone director. *See, e.g., Lewis v. Fuqua*, 502 A.2d 962, 967 (Del. Ch. 1985).

Section 8.25 limits the role of board committees in light of competing policies: on the one hand, it seems clear that appropriate committee action is not only desirable but is also likely to improve the functioning of larger and more diffuse boards of directors; on the other hand, wholesale delegation of authority to a board committee, to the point of abdication of director responsibility as a board of directors, is manifestly inappropriate and undesirable. Overbroad delegation also increases the potential, where the board of directors is divided, for usurpation of basic board functions by means of delegation to a committee dominated by one faction.

The statement of nondelegable functions set out in Section 8.25(e) is based on the principle that prohibitions against delegation to board committees should be limited generally to actions that substantially affect the rights of members or are fundamental to the governance of the corporation. As a result, delegation of authority to committees under Section 8.25(e) may be broader than mere authority to act with respect to matters arising within the ordinary course of business.

Section 8.25(e) prohibits delegation of authority with respect to most mergers, sales of substantially all the assets, amendments to articles of incorporation, and voluntary dissolution since these require member action. In addition, Section 8.25(e) prohibits delegation to a board committee of authority to fill board vacancies, subject to subsection (g), or to amend the bylaws. On the other hand, under Section 8.25(e) many actions of a material nature, such as the authorization of long-term debt and capital investment, may properly be made the subject of committee delegation.

Section 8.25(f) makes clear that although the board of directors may delegate to a committee the authority to take action, the designation of the committee, the delegation of authority to it, and action by the committee do not alone constitute compliance by a noncommittee board member with the director's responsibility under Section 8.30. On the other hand, a noncommittee director also does not automatically incur personal risk should the action of the particular committee fail to meet the standard of conduct set out in Section 8.30. The noncommittee member's liability in these cases will depend upon whether the director's conduct was actionable under Section 8.31. Factors to be considered in this regard will include the care used in the delegation to and supervision over the committee, the extent to which the delegation was required by applicable law, and the amount of knowledge regarding the actions being taken by the committee that is available to the noncommittee director. Care in delegation and supervision may be facilitated, in the usual case, by review of minutes and receipt of other reports concerning committee activities. The enumeration of these factors is intended to emphasize that directors may not abdicate their responsibilities and avoid liability simply by delegating authority to board committees. Rather, a director against whom liability is asserted based upon acts of a committee of which the director is not a member avoids liability under Section 8.31 by an appropriate measure of monitoring—particularly if the director met the standards contained in Section 8.30 with respect to the creation and supervision of the committee.

Section 8.25(f) has no application to a member of the committee itself. The standards of conduct applicable to a committee member are set forth in Section 8.30.

Section 8.25(g) is a rule of convenience that permits the board of directors to replace an absent or disqualified member during the time that the member is absent or disqualified. Unless otherwise provided, replacement of an absent or disqualified member is not necessary to permit the other committee members to continue to perform their duties.

Section 8.25(h) recognizes that the board of directors or management may establish nonboard committees to perform functions that are not required to be exercised by the board of directors. Those committees are sometimes purely advisory, but may also perform functions that would otherwise be performed by officers, employees, or agents. If a nonboard committee exercises any of the powers of the board, it will have the status of a designated body and its members will have fiduciary duties under Section 8.12(b).

[Subchapter] C
DIRECTORS

INTRODUCTORY COMMENT TO SUBCHAPTER C

The provisions of this act with respect to the duties and liabilities of directors of nonprofit corporations closely follow the provisions of the Model Business Corporation Act on the same subjects. This is consistent with the view that the relationship of directors to a nonprofit corporation is more akin to that of directors of business corporations than to that of trustees to their beneficiaries. *Stern v. Lucy Webb Hayes National Training School for Deaconesses and Missionaries*, 381 F. SUPP. 1003 (D.D.C. 1974). See *Duties of Charitable Trust Trustees and Charitable Corporation Directors*, REAL PROPERTY, PROBATE AND TRUST JOURNAL 545 (1967).

Depending on the status of a particular state's law, Sections 8.30 and 8.31 will replace, modify, clarify, or set forth the basic standards that govern the conduct of directors of nonprofit corporations. States may have statutory or common law rules that apply a trust rule to director conduct. Those states should consider repealing those rules so that this act will replace those rules even though the corporation, as distinguished from its directors, may hold or be deemed to hold property in trust or subject to restrictions.

§ 8.30. STANDARDS OF CONDUCT FOR DIRECTORS

(a) Each member of the board of directors, when discharging the duties of a director, shall act:
   (1) in good faith, and
   (2) in a manner the director reasonably believes to be in the best interests of the nonprofit corporation.

(b) The members of the board of directors or a committee of the board, when becoming informed in connection with their decision-making function or devoting attention to their oversight function, must discharge their duties with the care that a person in a like position would reasonably believe appropriate under similar circumstances.

(c) In discharging board or committee duties a director must disclose, or cause to be disclosed, to the other board or committee members information not already known by them but known by the director to be material to the discharge of their decision-making or oversight function, except that disclosure is not required to the extent that the director reasonably believes that doing so would violate a duty imposed by law, a legally enforceable obligation of confidentiality, or a professional ethics rule.

(d) In discharging board or committee duties a director who does not have knowledge that makes reliance unwarranted may rely on the performance by any of the persons specified in subsection (f)(1), (3), or (4) to whom the board may have delegated, formally or informally by course of conduct, the authority or duty to perform one or more of the board's functions that are delegable under applicable law.

(e) In discharging board or committee duties, a director who does not have knowledge that makes reliance unwarranted may rely on information, opinions, reports, or statements, including financial statements and other financial data, prepared or presented by any of the persons specified in subsection (f).

(f) A director may rely, in accordance with subsection (d) or (e), on:

(1) one or more officers, employees, or volunteers of the nonprofit corporation whom the director reasonably believes to be reliable and competent in the functions performed or the information, opinions, reports, or statements provided;

(2) legal counsel, public accountants, or other persons retained by the corporation as to matters involving skills or expertise the director reasonably believes are matters:

(i) within the particular person's professional or expert competence, or

(ii) as to which the particular person merits confidence;

(3) a committee of the board of directors of which the director is not a member if the director reasonably believes the committee merits confidence; or

(4) in the case of a corporation engaged in religious activity, religious authorities and ministers, priests, rabbis, imams, or other persons whose positions or duties the director reasonably believes justify reliance and confidence and whom the director believes to be reliable and competent in the matters presented.

(g) A director is not a trustee with respect to the nonprofit corporation or with respect to any property held or administered by the corporation, including property that may be subject to restrictions imposed by the donor or transferor of the property.

Source Note: Subsections (a)–(e) and (f)(1)–(3) are patterned after Model Business Corporation Act, 3d Ed. (2002) § 8.30; those provisions and subsection (f)(4) are derived from Model Nonprofit Corporation Act (1987) § 8.30(a)–(c). Subsection (g) is a reenactment of Model Nonprofit Corporation Act (1987) § 8.30 (e).

CROSS-REFERENCES

Committees of board of directors, see § 8.25.
Conflict of interest, see Subch. 8F.
Derivative proceedings, see Ch. 13.
Functions of board of directors, see § 8.01.
Indemnification, see §§ 8.50–8.58.
Meetings of board of directors, see § 8.20.
Officer standards of conduct, see § 8.42.
Officers, see §§ 8.40 and 8.41.
Removal of directors, see §§ 8.08 and 8.09.
Standards of liability for directors, see § 8.31.
Unlawful distributions, see § 8.33.

OFFICIAL COMMENT

Section 8.30 defines the general standards of conduct for directors. Under subsection (a), each board member must always perform a director's duties in good faith and in a manner reasonably believed to be in the best interests of the nonprofit corporation. Although each director also has a duty to comply with its requirements, the focus of subsection (b) is on the discharge of those duties by the board as a collegial body. Under subsection (b), the members of the board or a board committee are to perform their duties with the care that a person in a like position would reasonably believe appropriate under similar circumstances. This standard of conduct is often characterized as a duty of care. Subsection (c) sets out the responsibility of each director, in discharging board or committee duties, to disclose or cause to be disclosed to the other members of the board or board committee information, of which they are unaware, known by the director to be material to their decision-making or oversight responsibilities, subject to countervailing confidentiality duties and appropriate action with respect thereto.

Section 8.30 sets forth the standards of conduct for directors by focusing on the manner in which directors perform their duties, not the correctness of the decisions made. These standards of conduct are based on former Section 35 of the 1969 Model Business Corporation Act, a number of state statutes, and judicial formulations of the standards of conduct applicable to directors. Section 8.30 should be read in light of the basic role of directors set forth in Section 8.01(b), which provides that the "activities and affairs of the corporation must be managed by or under the direction, and subject to the oversight, of" the board, as supplemented by various provisions of the act assigning specific powers or responsibilities to the board. Relevant thereto, directors often act collegially in performing their functions and discharging their duties. If the observance of the directors' conduct is called into question, courts will typically evaluate the conduct of the entire board (or committee). Deficient performance of Section 8.30 duties on the part of a particular director may be overcome, absent unusual circumstances, by acceptable conduct (meeting, for example, subsection (b)'s standard of care) on the part of other directors sufficient in number to perform the function or discharge the duty in question. While not thereby remedied, the deficient performance becomes irrelevant in any evaluation of the action taken. (This contrasts with a director's duties of loyalty, fair dealing, and disclosure which will be evaluated on an individual basis and will also implicate discharge of the director's duties under subsection (a).) Further relevant thereto, the board may delegate or assign to appropriate officers, employees, or agents of the nonprofit corporation the authority or duty to exercise powers that the law does not require it to retain. Since the directors are entitled to rely thereon absent knowledge making reliance unwarranted, deficient performance of the directors' Section 8.30 duties will not result from their delegatees' actions or omissions so long as the board acted in good faith and complied with the other standards of conduct set forth in Section 8.30 in delegating responsibility and, where appropriate, monitoring performance of the duties delegated.

In the prior version of the act the duty of care element was included in subsection (a), with the text reading: "[a] director shall discharge his duties . . . with the care an ordinarily prudent person in a like position would exercise under similar circumstances." The use of the phrase "ordinarily prudent person" in a basic guideline for director conduct, suggesting caution or circumspection vis-à-vis danger or risk, has long been problematic given the fact that risk-taking decisions are central to the directors' role. When coupled with the exercise of "care," the prior text had a familiar resonance long associated with the field of tort law. See the Official Comment to Section 8.31. The further coupling with the verb "shall discharge" added to the inference that former Section 8.30(a)'s standard of conduct involved a negligence standard, with resultant confusion. In order to facilitate its understanding, and analysis, independent of the other general standards of conduct for directors, the duty of care element has been set forth as a separate standard of conduct in subsection (b).

Long before statutory formulations of directors' standards of conduct, courts would invoke the business judgment rule in evaluating directors' conduct and determining whether to impose liability in a particular case. The elements of the business judgment rule and the circumstances for its application are continuing to be developed by the courts. Section 8.30 does not try to codify the business judgment rule or to delineate the differences between that defensive rule and the section's standards of director conduct. Section 8.30 deals only with standards of conduct—the level of performance expected of every director entering into the service of a nonprofit corporation and undertaking the role and responsibilities of the office of director. The section does not deal directly with the liability of a director—although exposure to liability will usually result from a failure to honor the standards of conduct required to be observed by subsection (a). See Section 8.31(a)(1) and clauses (i) and (ii)(A) of Section 8.31(a)(2). The issue of director liability is addressed in Sections 8.31 and 8.33 of this subchapter. Section 8.30 does, however, play an important role in evaluating a director's conduct and the effectiveness of board action. It has relevance in assessing, under Section 8.31, the reasonableness of a director's belief. Similarly, it has relevance in assessing a director's timely attention to appropriate inquiry when particular facts and circumstances of significant concern materialize. It serves as a frame of reference for determining, under Section 8.33(a), liability for an unlawful distribution. Finally, Section 8.30 compliance may have a direct bearing on a court's analysis where transactional justification (*e.g.*, a suit to enjoin a pending merger) is at issue.

A director complying with the standard of care expressed in subsection (b) is entitled to rely (under subsection (d)) upon board functions performed pursuant to delegated authority by, and to rely (under subsection (e)) upon information, opinions, reports, or statements, including financial statements and other financial data, provided by, the persons or committees specified in the relevant parts of subsection (f). Within this authorization, the right to rely applies to the entire range of matters for which the board of directors is responsible. However, a director so relying must be without knowledge that would cause that reliance to be unwarranted. Section 8.30 expressly prevents a director from "hiding his or her head in the sand" and relying on the delegation of board functions, or on information, opinions, reports, or statements, when the director has actual knowledge that makes (or has a measure of knowledge that would cause a person, in a like position under similar circumstances, to undertake reasonable inquiry that would lead to information making) reliance unwarranted. The standards in subsection (a) of good faith and reasonable belief in the best interests of the corporation also apply to a director's reliance under subsections (d), (e), and (f).

1. Section 8.30(a)

Section 8.30(a) establishes the basic standards of conduct for all directors. Its command is to be understood as peremptory (its obligations are to be observed by every director) and at the core of the subsection's mandate is the requirement that, when performing director duties, a director shall act in good faith coupled with conduct reasonably believed to be in the best interests of the nonprofit corporation. This mandate governs all aspects of director duties: the duty of care, the duty to become informed, the duty of inquiry, the duty of informed judgment, the duty of attention, the duty of disclosure, the duty of loyalty, the duty of fair dealing and, finally, the broad concept of fiduciary duty that the courts often use as a frame of reference when evaluating a director's conduct. These duties do not necessarily compartmentalize and, in fact, tend to overlap. For example, the duties of care, inquiry, becoming informed, attention, disclosure, and informed judgment all relate to the board's decision-making function, whereas the duties of attention, disclosure, becoming informed, and inquiry relate to the board's oversight function.

Two of the phrases chosen to specify the manner in which a director's duties are to be discharged deserve further comment:

(1) The phrase "reasonably believes" is both subjective and objective in character. Its first level of analysis is geared to what the particular director, acting in good faith, actually believes—not what objective analysis would lead another director (in a like position and acting in similar circumstances) to

conclude. The second level of analysis is focused specifically on "reasonably." While a director has wide discretion in marshalling the evidence and reaching conclusions, whether a director's belief is reasonable (*i.e.*, could (not would) a reasonable person in a like position and acting in similar circumstances have arrived at that belief) ultimately involves an overview that is objective in character.

(2) The phrase "best interests of the nonprofit corporation" is key to an explication of a director's duties. The term "corporation" is a surrogate for the enterprise as well as a frame of reference encompassing the body of members. In determining the corporation's "best interests," the director has wide discretion in deciding how to weigh near-term opportunities versus long-term benefits as well as in making judgments where the interests of various groups within the body of members or having other cognizable interests in the enterprise may differ.

As a generalization, Section 8.30 operates as a "baseline" principle governing director conduct "when discharging the [ongoing] duties of a director" in circumstances uncomplicated by self-interest taint. The act recognizes, however, that personal interests of directors may not always align with the nonprofit corporation's best interests and provides procedures by which interest-conflict transactions can be processed. See Subchapter E (indemnification) and Subchapter F (conflicting interest transactions) of this Chapter 8 and Chapter 13 (derivative proceedings). Those procedures generally contemplate that the interested director will not be involved in taking action on the interest-conflict transaction. And the common law has recognized that other interest-conflict situations may arise which do not entail a "transaction" by or with the corporation. See Subchapter G of this Chapter 8 (business opportunities). The interested director is relieved of the duty to act in connection with the matter on behalf of the corporation (specifically, the traditional mandate to act in the corporation's best interests), given the inherent conflict. However, the interested director is still expected to act in good faith, and that duty is normally discharged by observing the obligation of fair dealing. In the case of interest-conflict transactions, where there is a conflicting interest with respect to the corporation under Section 8.60, the interested director's conduct is governed by Subchapter F of this Chapter 8. In other cases, Section 8.30's standards of conduct are overlaid by various components of the duty to act fairly, the particular thrusts of which will depend upon the kind of interested director's conduct at issue and the circumstances of the case. As a general rule, the duty of fair dealing is normally discharged by the interested director through appropriate disclosure to the other directors considering the matter followed by abstention from participation in any decision-making relevant thereto. If and to the extent that the interested director's action respecting the matter goes further, the reasonableness of the director's belief as to the corporation's best interests, in respect of the action taken, should be evaluated not only on the basis of the director's honest and good faith belief but also on considerations bearing on the fairness of the transaction or conduct to the corporation.

2. Section 8.30(b)

Section 8.30(b) establishes a general standard of care for directors in the context of their dealing with the board's decision-making and oversight functions. While certain aspects will involve individual conduct (*e.g.*, preparation for meetings), these functions are generally performed by the board through collegial action, as recognized by the reference in subsection (b) to board and committee "members" and "their duties." In contrast with the individual conduct mandate in Section 8.30(a), Section 8.30(b) has a twofold thrust: it provides a standard of conduct for individual action and, more broadly, it states a conduct obligation—"must discharge their duties"—concerning the degree of care to be collegially used by the directors when performing those functions. It provides that directors have a duty to exercise "the care that a person in a like position would reasonably believe appropriate under similar circumstances."

The traditional formulation for a director's standard (or duty) of care has been geared to the "ordinarily prudent person." For example, the act's prior formulation (in former Section 8.30(a)(2)) referred to "the care an ordinarily prudent person in a like position would exercise under similar circumstances," and almost all state statutes that include a standard of care reflect parallel language. The phrase "ordinarily prudent person" constitutes a basic frame of reference grounded in the field of tort law and provides a primary benchmark for determining negligence. For this reason, its use in the standard of care for directors, suggesting that negligence is the proper determinant for measuring deficient (and thus actionable) conduct, has caused confusion and misunderstanding. Accordingly, the phrase "ordinarily prudent person" has been removed from the act's standard of care and in its place "a person in a like position" has been substituted. The standard is not what care a particular director might believe appropriate in the circumstances but what a person in a like position and acting under similar circumstances would reasonably believe to be appropriate. Thus, the degree of care that directors should employ, under subsection (b), involves an objective standard.

Some state statutes have used the words "diligence," "care," and "skill" to define the duty of care. There is very little authority as to what "skill" and "diligence," as distinguished from "care," can be required or properly expected of corporate directors in the performance of their duties. "Skill," in the sense of technical competence in a particular field, should not be a qualification for the office of director. The concept of "diligence" is sufficiently subsumed within the concept of "care." Accordingly, the words "diligence" and "skill" are not used in Section 8.30's standard of care.

The process by which a director becomes informed in carrying out the decision-making and oversight functions will vary. The directors' oversight function is established under Section 8.01. In relying on the performance by management of delegated or assigned Section 8.01 duties (including, for example, matters of law and legal compliance), as authorized by subsection (d), directors may depend upon the presumption of regularity absent knowledge or notice to the contrary. In discharging the Section 8.01 duties associated with the board's oversight function, the standard of care entails primarily a duty of attention. In contrast with the board's decision-making function, which generally involves informed action at a point in time, the oversight function is concerned with a continuum and the duty of attention accordingly involves participatory performance over a period of time.

Several of the phrases chosen to define the standard of conduct in Section 8.30(b) deserve specific mention:

(1) The phrase "becoming informed," in the context of the decision-making function, refers to the process of gaining sufficient familiarity with the background facts and circumstances in order to make an informed judgment. Unless the circumstances would permit a reasonable director to conclude that he or she is already sufficiently informed, the standard of care requires every director to take steps to become informed about the background facts and circumstances before taking action on the matter at hand. The process typically involves review of materials provided before or at the meeting and attention to/participation in the deliberations leading up to a vote. It can involve consideration of information and data generated by persons other than legal counsel, public accountants, etc., retained by the corporation, as contemplated by subsection (f)(2); for example, review of industry studies or research articles prepared by unrelated parties could be very useful. It can also involve direct communications, outside of the boardroom, with members of management or other directors. There is no one way for "becoming informed," and both the method and measure—"how to" and "how much"—are matters of reasonable judgment for the director to exercise.

(2) The phrase "devoting attention," in the context of the oversight function, refers to concern with the information and reporting systems of the nonprofit corporation and not to proactive inquiry searching out system inadequacies or noncompliance. While directors typically give attention to future plans and trends as well as current activities, they should not

be expected to anticipate the problems that the corporation may face except in those circumstances where something has occurred to make it obvious to the board that the corporation should be addressing a particular problem. The standard of care associated with the oversight function involves gaining assurances from management and advisers that systems believed appropriate have been established, coupled with ongoing monitoring of the systems in place, such as those concerned with legal compliance or internal controls—followed up with a proactive response when alerted to the need for inquiry.

(3) The reference to "person," without embellishment, is intended to avoid implying any qualifications, such as specialized expertise or experience requirements, beyond the basic director attributes of common sense, practical wisdom, and informed judgment.

(4) The phrase "reasonably believe appropriate" refers to the array of possible options that a person possessing the basic director attributes of common sense, practical wisdom, and informed judgment would recognize to be available, in terms of the degree of care that might be appropriate, and from which a choice by such person would be made. The measure of care that such person might determine to be appropriate, in a given instance, would normally involve a selection from the range of options and any choice within the realm of reason would be an appropriate decision under the standard of care called for under subsection (b). However, a decision that is so removed from the realm of reason, or is so unreasonable, that it falls outside the permissible bounds of sound discretion, and thus is an abuse of discretion, will not satisfy the standard.

(5) The phrase "in a like position" recognizes that the "care" under consideration is that which would be used by the "person" if he or she were a director of the particular nonprofit corporation.

(6) The combined phrase "in a like position—under similar circumstances" is intended to recognize that (a) the nature and

extent of responsibilities will vary, depending upon such factors as the size, complexity, urgency, and location of activities carried on by the particular nonprofit corporation, (b) decisions must be made on the basis of the information known to the directors without the benefit of hindsight, and (c) the special background, qualifications, and management responsibilities of a particular director may be relevant in evaluating that director's compliance with the standard of care. Even though the combined phrase is intended to take into account the special background, qualifications, and management responsibilities of a particular director, it does not excuse a director lacking business experience or particular expertise from exercising the basic director attributes of common sense, practical wisdom, and informed judgment.

3. Section 8.30(c)

A duty to disclose information that a director knows to be material to the oversight or decision-making function of the board or committee has always been embraced in the standards of conduct set forth in subsections (a) and (b). Subsection (c) makes explicit this existing duty of disclosure among directors. Thus, for example, when a member of the board knows information that the director recognizes is material to a decision by the board to approve financial statements of the nonprofit corporation, the director is obligated to see to it that such information is provided to the other members of the board. So long as that disclosure is accomplished, the action required of the director can occur through direct statements in meetings of the board, or by any other timely means, including, for example, communicating the information to the chairman of the board or the chairman of a committee, or to the corporation's general counsel, and requesting that the recipient inform the other board or committee members of the disclosed information.

Subsection (c) recognizes that a duty of confidentiality can override a director's obligation to share with other directors information pertaining to a current corporate matter, and that a director is not required to make such disclosure to the extent the director reasonably believes that such a duty of confidentiality prohibits it. In some circumstances, a duty of confidentiality may even prohibit disclosure of the nature or the existence of the duty itself. Ordinarily, however, a director who withholds material information based on a reasonable belief that a duty of confidentiality prohibits disclosure should advise the other directors of the existence and nature of that duty. Under the standards of conduct set forth in Section 8.30(a), the director may also be required to take other action in light of the confidentiality restraint. The precise nature of that action must, of necessity, depend on the specific circumstances. Depending on the nature of the material information and of the matter before the board of directors or committee of the board, such action may include abstention or absence from all or a portion of the other directors' deliberation or vote on the matter to which the undisclosed information is material, or even resignation as a director. Finally, a duty of confidentiality may not form the basis for the limitation on disclosure unless it is entered into and relied upon in good faith.

4. Section 8.30(d)

The delegation of authority and responsibility under subsection (d) may take the form of formal action through a board resolution, implicit action through the election of corporate officers (*e.g.*, chief financial officer or controller), the appointment of corporate managers (*e.g.*, credit manager), or a course of conduct (*e.g.*, the discharge by the board chair of a board function such as oversight of actions by the president). A director may properly rely on those to whom authority has been delegated pursuant to subsection (d) respecting particular matters calling for specific action or attention in connection with the directors' decision-making function as well as matters on the board's agenda, such as legal compliance and internal control, in connection with the directors' oversight function. Delegation should be carried out in accordance with the standard of care set forth in Section 8.30(b) and is subject to limitations in the articles, bylaws, resolutions of the board, or other law.

By identifying those upon whom a director may rely in connection with the discharge of duties, Section 8.30(d) does not limit the ability of directors to delegate their powers under Section 8.01(b) except where delegation is expressly prohibited by the act or otherwise by applicable law (see, *e.g.*, Section 8.25(e)). See Section 8.25 and its Official Comment for detailed consideration of delegation to board committees of the authority of the board under Section 8.01 and the duty to perform one or more of the board's functions. And by employing the concept of delegation, Section 8.30(d) does not limit the ability of directors to establish baseline principles as to management responsibilities. Specifically, Section 8.01(b) provides that "all corporate powers must be exercised by or under the authority of" the board, and a basic board function involves the allocation of management responsibilities and the related assignment (or delegation) of corporate powers. For example, a board can properly decide to retain a third party to assume responsibility for the administration of designated aspects of risk management for the nonprofit corporation (*e.g.*, health insurance or disability claims). This would involve the directors in the exercise of judgment in connection with the decision-making function pursuant to subsection (b) (*i.e.*, the assignment of authority to exercise corporate powers to an agent). See the Official Comment to Section 8.01. It would not entail impermissible delegation—to a person specified in subsection (f)(2) pursuant to subsection (d)—of a board function for which the directors by law have a duty to perform. They have the corporate power (under Section 8.01(b)) to perform the task but administration of risk management is not a board function coming within the ambit of director duties; together with many similar management responsibilities, they may assign the task in the context of the allocation of corporate powers exercised under the authority of the board. This illustration highlights the distinction between delegation of a board function and assignment of authority to exercise corporate powers.

Although the board may delegate the authority or duty to perform one or more of its functions, reliance on delegation under subsection (d) may not alone constitute compliance with Section

8.30 and reliance on the action taken by the delegatee may not alone constitute compliance by the directors or a noncommittee board member with Section 8.01 responsibilities. On the other hand, should the board committee or the corporate officer or employee performing the function delegated fail to meet Section 8.30's standard of care, noncompliance by the board with Section 8.01 will not automatically result. Factors to be considered, in this regard, will include the care used in the delegation to and supervision over the delegatee, and the amount of knowledge regarding the particular matter that is available to the particular director. Care in delegation and supervision includes appraisal of the capabilities and diligence of the delegatee in light of the subject and its relative importance and may be facilitated, in the usual case, by receipt of reports concerning the delegatee's activities. The enumeration of these factors is intended to emphasize that directors may not abdicate their responsibilities and avoid accountability simply by delegating authority to others. Rather, a director charged with accountability based upon acts of others will fulfill the director's duties if the standards contained in Section 8.30 are met.

5. Section 8.30(e)

Reliance under subsection (e) on a report, statement, opinion, or other information is permitted only if the director has read the information, opinion, report, or statement in question, or was present at a meeting at which it was orally presented, or took other steps to become generally familiar with it. A director must comply with the general standard of care of Section 8.30(b) in making a judgment as to the reliability and competence of the source of information upon which the director proposes to rely or, as appropriate, that it otherwise merits confidence.

6. Section 8.30(f)

Reliance on one or more of the corporation's officers or employees, pursuant to the intracorporate frame of reference of subsection (f)(1), is conditioned upon a reasonable belief as to the reliability and competence of those who have undertaken the functions performed or who prepared or communicated the information, opinions, reports, or statements presented. In determining whether a person is "reliable," the director would typically consider (i) the individual's background experience and scope of responsibility within the nonprofit corporation in gauging the individual's familiarity and knowledge respecting the subject matter, and (ii) the individual's record and reputation for honesty, care, and ability in discharging responsibilities which he or she undertakes. In determining whether a person is "competent," the director would normally take into account the same considerations and, if expertise should be relevant, the director would consider the individual's technical skills as well. Recognition in the statute of the right of one director to rely on the expertise and experience of another director, in the context of board or committee deliberations, is unnecessary, for the group's reliance on shared experience and wisdom is an implicit underpinning of director conduct. In relying on another member of the board, a director would quite properly take advantage of the colleague's knowledge and experience in becoming informed about the matter at hand before taking action; however, the director would be expected to exercise independent judgment when it comes time to vote.

Subsection (f)(2), which has an extracorporate frame of reference, permits reliance on outside advisers retained by the nonprofit corporation, including persons specifically engaged to advise the board or a board committee. Possible advisers include not only those in the professional disciplines customarily supervised by state authorities, such as lawyers, accountants, and engineers, but also those in other fields involving special experience and skills, such as investment bankers, geologists, management consultants, actuaries, and real estate appraisers. The adviser could be an individual or an organization, such as a law firm. Reliance on a nonmanagement director who is specifically engaged to undertake a special assignment or a particular consulting role would fall within this outside adviser frame of reference. In addition, a director may also rely on outside advisers where skills or expertise of a technical nature is not a prerequisite, or where the person's professional or expert competence has not been established, so long as the director reasonably believes the person merits confidence. For example, a board might choose to assign to a private investigator the duty of inquiry (*e.g.*, follow-up on rumors about a senior executive's "grand lifestyle") and properly rely on the private investigator's report. And it would be appropriate for a director to rely on advice from a lawyer in the corporation's outside law firm, without due inquiry concerning that particular lawyer's technical competence, where the director reasonably believes the lawyer giving the advice is appropriately informed (by reason of resources known to be available from that adviser's legal organization or through other means) and therefore merits confidence.

Subsection (f)(3) permits reliance on a board committee when it is submitting recommendations for action by the full board of directors as well as when it is performing supervisory or other functions in instances where neither the full board of directors nor the committee takes dispositive action. For example, the compensation committee typically reviews proposals and makes recommendations for action by the full board of directors. In contrast, there may be reliance upon an investigation undertaken by a board committee and reported to the full board, which forms the basis for a decision by the board of directors not to take dispositive action. Another example is reliance on a committee of the board of directors, such as an audit committee with respect to the board's ongoing role of oversight of the accounting and auditing functions of the corporation. In addition, where reliance on information or materials prepared or presented by a board committee is not involved, in connection with board action, a director may properly rely on oversight monitoring or dispositive action by a board committee (of which the director is not a member) empowered to act pursuant to authority delegated under Section 8.25 or acting with the acquiescence of the board of directors. See the Official Comment to Section 8.25. A director may similarly rely on committees not created under Section 8.25 which have nondirector members. In parallel with subsection (f)(2)(ii), the concept of "confidence" is substituted for "competence" in order to avoid any inference that technical skills are a prerequisite. In the usual case, the appointment of committee members or the reconstitution of the membership of a standing committee (*e.g.*, the audit committee), following an annual meeting of the members, would alone manifest the noncommittee members' belief that the committee "merits confidence." However, the reliance contemplated by subsection (f)(3) is geared to the point in time when the board takes action or the period of time over which a committee is engaged in an oversight function; consequently, the judgment to be made (*i.e.*, whether a committee "merits confidence") will arise at varying points in time. After making an initial judgment that a committee (of which a director is not a member) merits confidence, the director may depend upon the presumption of regularity, absent knowledge or notice to the contrary.

Subsection (f)(4) provides a special rule for religious corporations that permits directors to rely on superior authorities within a religious organization of which the corporation is a part.

7. *Application to Officers*

Section 8.30 generally deals only with directors and, pursuant to Section 8.12(a), with members of designated bodies. Section 8.42 and its Official Comment explain the extent to which the provisions of Section 8.30 apply to officers.

8. *Trust Property*

Section 8.30(g) is not found in the Model Business Corporation Act because it is only relevant in the context of nonprofit corporations. It provides that a director is not a trustee with respect to the corporation or any property held by it. Absent Section 8.30(g), it might be possible to argue that a director meeting his or her duties under Section 8.30 was liable for a breach of trust by improperly using, disposing of, or otherwise dealing with assets held by the corporation in trust. As a result of Section 8.30(g), this argument has no validity. A director who satisfies Subchapter 8C, but improperly acts or fails to act in regard to property held in trust, will not be liable. Depending on a particular state's law, if a corporation holds trust property, the corporation itself may be liable for breach of trust.

§ 8.31. STANDARDS OF LIABILITY FOR DIRECTORS

(a) A director is not liable to the nonprofit corporation or its members for any decision to take or not to take action, or any failure to take any action, as a director, unless the party asserting liability in a proceeding establishes that:
 (1) none of the following, if interposed as a bar to the proceeding by the director, precludes liability:
  (i) subsection (d) or a provision in the articles of incorporation authorized by Section 2.02(c);
  (ii) satisfaction of the requirements in Section 8.60 for validating a conflicting interest transaction; or
  (iii) satisfaction of the requirements in Section 8.70 for disclaiming a business opportunity; and
 (2) the challenged conduct consisted or was the result of:
  (i) action not in good faith; or
  (ii) a decision:
   (A) which the director did not reasonably believe to be in the best interests of the corporation, or
   (B) as to which the director was not informed to an extent the director reasonably believed appropriate in the circumstances; or
  (iii) a lack of objectivity due to the director's familial, financial, or business relationship with, or a lack of independence due to the director's domination or control by, another person having a material interest in the challenged conduct:
   (A) which relationship or which domination or control could reasonably be expected to have affected the director's judgment respecting the challenged conduct in a manner adverse to the corporation, and
   (B) after a reasonable expectation to such effect has been established, the director has not estab-

lished that the challenged conduct was reasonably believed by the director to be in the best interests of the corporation; or

(iv) a sustained failure of the director to devote attention to ongoing oversight of the activities and affairs of the corporation, or a failure to devote timely attention, by making (or causing to be made) appropriate inquiry, when particular facts and circumstances of significant concern materialize that would alert a reasonably attentive director to the need therefor; or

(v) receipt of a financial benefit to which the director was not entitled or any other breach of the director's duties to deal fairly with the corporation and its members that is actionable under applicable law.

(b) The party seeking to hold the director liable:

(1) for money damages, also has the burden of establishing that:

(i) harm to the nonprofit corporation or its members has been suffered, and

(ii) the harm suffered was proximately caused by the director's challenged conduct; or

(2) for other money payment under a legal remedy, such as compensation for the unauthorized use of corporate assets, also has whatever persuasion burden may be called for to establish that the payment sought is appropriate in the circumstances; or

(3) for other money payment under an equitable remedy, such as profit recovery by or disgorgement to the corporation, also has whatever persuasion burden may be called for to establish that the equitable remedy sought is appropriate in the circumstances.

(c) Nothing contained in this section:

(1) in any instance where fairness is at issue, such as consideration of the fairness of a transaction to the nonprofit corporation under Section 8.60(a)(3), alters the burden of proving the fact or lack of fairness otherwise applicable;

(2) alters the fact or lack of liability of a director under another section of this [act], such as the provisions governing the consequences of an unlawful distribution under Section 8.33, a conflicting interest transaction under Section 8.60, or taking advantage of a business opportunity under Section 8.70; or

(3) affects any rights to which the corporation or a director or member may be entitled under another statute of this state or the United States.

(d) Notwithstanding any other provision of this section, a director of a charitable corporation shall not be liable to the corporation or its members for money damages for any action taken, or any failure to take any action, as a director, except liability for:

(1) the amount of a financial benefit received by the director to which the director is not entitled;

(2) an intentional infliction of harm;

(3) a violation of Section 8.33; or

(4) an intentional violation of criminal law.

Source Note: Patterned after Model Business Corporation Act, 3d Ed. (2002) § 8.31, except that conforming changes have been made to subsections (a) and (c) with respect to §§ 8.60 and 8.70. Derived from Model Nonprofit Corporation Act (1987) § 8.30(d). Subsection (d) is new; cf. 42 U.S.C. § 14503 (2008) and 42 Pa. Cons. Stat. § 8332.1 (2008).

CROSS-REFERENCES

Article provision limiting or eliminating director liability, see § 2.02(c).

Article provision permitting expanded indemnification, see § 2.02(b)(8).

Derivative proceedings, see Ch. 13.

Director's conflicting interest transaction, see Subch. 8F.

Duty of board of directors, see § 8.01.

Indemnification, see §§ 8.50–8.58.

Judicial removal of directors, see § 8.09.

Standards of conduct for directors, see § 8.30.

Unlawful distributions, see § 8.33.

OFFICIAL COMMENT

Subsections (a) and (b) of Section 8.30 establish standards of conduct that are central to the role of directors. Section 8.30(b)'s standard of conduct is frequently referred to as a director's duty of care. The employment of the concept of "care," if considered in the abstract, suggests a tort-law/negligence-based analysis looking toward a finding of fault and damage recovery where the duty of care has not been properly observed and loss has been suffered. But the act's desired level of director performance, with its objectively based standard of conduct ("the care that a person in a like position would reasonably believe appropriate under similar circumstances"), does not carry with it the same type of result-oriented liability analysis. The courts recognize that boards of directors and corporate managers make numerous decisions that involve the balancing of risks and benefits for the enterprise. Although some decisions turn out to be unwise or the result of a mistake of judgment, it is not reasonable to reexamine an unsuccessful decision with the benefit of hindsight. As observed in *Joy v. North*, 692 F.2D 880, 885 (2d Cir. 1982):

> Whereas an automobile driver who makes a mistake in judgment as to speed or distance injuring a pedestrian will likely be called upon to respond in damages, a corporate [director or] officer who makes a mistake in judgment as to economic conditions, consumer tastes or production line efficiency will rarely, if ever, be found liable for damages suffered by the corporation.

Therefore, as a general rule, a director is not exposed to personal liability for injury or damage caused by an unwise decision. While a director is not personally responsible for unwise decisions or mistakes of judgment—and conduct conforming with the standards of Section 8.30 will almost always be protected—a director can be held liable for misfeasance or nonfeasance in performing the duties of a director. And while a director whose performance meets the standards of Section 8.30 should have no liability, the fact that a director's performance fails to reach that level does not automatically establish personal liability for damages that the nonprofit corporation may have suffered as a consequence.

****

Note on Directors' Liability

A director's financial risk exposure (*e.g.*, in a lawsuit for money damages suffered by the nonprofit corporation or its members claimed to have resulted from misfeasance or nonfeasance in connection with the performance of the director's duties) can be analyzed as follows:

(1) Liability limitation. If the nonprofit corporation is a charitable corporation (and its directors are accordingly entitled to the benefits of subsection (d)), or if the corporation's articles of incorporation contain a provision eliminating its directors' liability to the corporation or its members for money damages, adopted pursuant to Section 2.02(c), there is no liability unless the director's conduct involves one of the prescribed exceptions in subsection (d) or Section 2.02(c) that preclude the elimination of liability. See Section 2.02 and its Official Comment.

(2) Director's conflicting interest transaction safe harbor. If the matter at issue involves a director's conflicting interest transaction and one of the procedures in Section 8.60 has been followed to approve the transaction, there is no liability for the interested director arising out of the transaction.

(3) Business judgment rule. If none of (i) subsection (d), (ii) a provision of the articles of incorporation adopted pursuant to Section 2.02(c), or (iii) one of the procedures under Section 8.60 does not shield the director's conduct from liability, the business judgment rule standard of judicial review for director conduct—deeply rooted in the case law—presumes that, absent self-dealing or other breach of the duty of loyalty, directors' decision-making satisfies the applicable legal

requirements. A plaintiff challenging the director's conduct in connection with a corporate decision, and asserting liability by reason thereof, encounters certain procedural barriers. In the first instance, many jurisdictions have special pleading requirements that condition the ability to pursue the challenge on the plaintiff's bringing forward specific factual allegations that put in question the availability of the business judgment presumption. Assuming the suit survives a motion to dismiss for failure to state (in satisfaction of such a condition) an actionable claim, the plaintiff has the burden of overcoming that presumption of regularity.

(4) Damages and proximate cause. If the business judgment rule does not shield the directors' decision-making from liability, as a general rule it must be established that money damages were suffered by the nonprofit corporation or its members and those damages resulted from and were legally caused by the challenged act or omission of the director.

(5) Other liability for money payment. Aside from a claim for damages, the director may be liable to reimburse the nonprofit corporation pursuant to a claim under quantum meruit (the reasonable value of services) or quantum valebant (the reasonable value of goods and materials) if corporate resources have been used without proper authorization.

(6) Equitable profit recovery or disgorgement. An equitable remedy compelling the disgorgement of the director's improper financial gain or entitling the nonprofit corporation to recovery of financial gains, where directors' duties have been breached, may require the payment of money by the director to the corporation.

(7) Corporate indemnification. If the court determines that the director is liable, the director may be indemnified by the nonprofit corporation for any payments made and expenses incurred, depending upon the circumstances, if a third-party suit is involved. If the proceeding is by or in the right of the corporation, the director may be reimbursed for reasonable expenses incurred in connection with the proceeding if ordered by a court under Section 8.54(a)(3).

(8) Insurance. To the extent that corporate indemnification is not available, the director may be reimbursed for the money damages for which the director is accountable, together with proceeding-related expenses, if the claim/grounds for liability come within the coverage under directors' and officers' liability insurance that has been purchased by the corporation pursuant to Section 8.57.

****

Section 8.31 includes steps (1) through (6) in the analysis of a director's liability exposure set forth in the above Note. In establishing general standards of director liability under the act, the section also serves the important purpose of providing clarification that the general standards of conduct set forth in Section 8.30 are not intended to codify the business judgment rule—a point as to which there has been confusion on the part of some courts.

A board member's obligation to a nonprofit corporation and its members has two prongs, generally characterized as the duty of care and the duty of loyalty. The duty of care refers to the responsibility of a corporate fiduciary to exercise, in the performance of his tasks, the care that a reasonably prudent person in a similar position would use under similar circumstances. See New York Business Corporation Law Section 717. In evaluating a manager's compliance with the duty of care, New York courts adhere to the business judgment rule, which "bars judicial inquiry into actions of corporate directors taken in good faith and in the exercise of honest judgment in the lawful and legitimate furtherance of corporate purposes." *Norlin Corp. v. Rooney, Pace Inc.*, 744 F.2d 255, 264 (2d Cir. 1984) [quoting *Auerbach v. Bennett*, 47 N.Y.2d 619, 629 (1979)].

Sections 8.30 and 8.31 adopt the approach to director conduct and director liability taken in the *Norlin* decision. See Section 8.30 and its Official Comment with respect to the standards of conduct for directors. For a detailed analysis of how and why standards of conduct and standards of liability diverge in corporate law, see Melvin A. Eisenberg, *The Divergence of Standards of*

Conduct and Standards of Review in Corporate Law, 62 FORDHAM LAW REVIEW 437 (1993).

The act does not undertake to prescribe detailed litigation procedures. However, it does deal with requirements applicable to derivative suits (see Chapter 13) and Section 8.31 builds on those requirements. If none of (i) subsection (d), (ii) a liability-eliminating provision included in the corporation's articles of incorporation, pursuant to Section 2.02(c), or (iii) protection for a director's conflicting interest transaction afforded by Section 8.60 is interposed by a defendant director as a bar to the challenge of his or her conduct, the plaintiff's role in satisfying the requirement of subsection (a)(1)—*i.e.*, establishing that the articles of incorporation provision or the conflicting interest approval provision interposed does not apply—would be governed by the court's procedural rules. Consistent with the general rules of civil procedure, the plaintiff generally has the burden under subsection (b) of proving that the director's deficient conduct caused harm resulting in monetary damage or calls for monetary reimbursement; in the alternative, the circumstances may justify or require an equitable remedy.

1. Section 8.31(a)

If subsection (d) or a provision in the corporation's articles of incorporation adopted pursuant to Section 2.02(c) shelters a director from liability for money damages, or if approval under Section 8.60 shelters the director's conduct in connection with a conflicting interest transaction, there is no need to consider further the application of Section 8.31's standards of liability. In either case, the court would presumably grant the defendant director's motion for dismissal or summary judgment (or the equivalent) and the proceeding would be ended. Termination of the proceeding will not automatically follow, however, if the party challenging the director's conduct can assert any of the valid bases for contesting the availability of the liability shelter. In the absence thereof, the relevant shelter provision is self-executing and the individual director's exoneration from liability is automatic.

If a claim of liability arising out of a challenged act or omission of a director is not resolved and disposed of under subsection (a)(1), subsection (a)(2) provides the basis for evaluating whether the conduct in question can be challenged.

****

Note on the Business Judgment Rule

Over the years, the courts have developed a broad common law concept geared to business judgment. In basic principle, a board of directors enjoys a presumption of sound business judgment and its decisions will not be disturbed (by a court substituting its own notions of what is or is not sound business judgment) if they can be attributed to any rational business purpose. See *Sinclair Oil Corp. v. Levien*, 280 A.2D 717, 720 (Del. 1971). Relatedly, it is presumed that, in making a business decision, directors act in good faith, on an informed basis, and in the honest belief that the action taken is in the best interests of the nonprofit corporation. See *Aronson v. Lewis*, 473 A.2D 805, 812 (Del. 1983). When applied, this principle operates as both a procedural rule of evidence and a substantive rule of law, in that if the plaintiff fails to rebut the presumption that the directors acted in good faith, in the corporation's best interest, and on an informed basis, the business judgment standard protects both the directors and the decisions they make. *See Citron v. Fairchild Camera & Instrument Corp.*, 569 A.2D 53, 64 (Del. 1989).

Some have suggested that, within the business judgment standard's broad ambit, a distinction might usefully be drawn between that part which protects directors from personal liability for the decision they make and the part which protects the decision itself from attack. *See Revlon, Inc. v. MacAndrews & Forbes Holdings, Inc.*, 506 A.2D 173, 180 n.10 (Del. 1986). While these two objects of the business judgment standard's protection are different, and judicial review might result in the decision being enjoined but no personal liability (or vice versa), their operative elements are identical (*i.e.*, good faith, disinterest, informed judgment, and "best interests"). As a consequence, the courts have not observed any distinction in terminology and have generally followed the practice of referring only to the business judgment rule, whether dealing with personal liability issues or transactional justification matters.

While, in substance, the operative elements of the standard of judicial review commonly referred to as the business judgment rule have been widely recognized, courts have used a number of different word formulations to articulate the concept. The formulation adopted in Section 4.01(c) of The American Law Institute's PRINCIPLES OF CORPORATE GOVERNANCE: ANALYSIS AND RECOMMENDATIONS (1994) provides that a director who makes a business judgment in good faith (an obvious prerequisite) fulfills the duty of care standard if the director:

(1) is not interested [as defined] in the subject of the business judgment;
(2) is informed with respect to the subject of the business judgment to the extent the director . . . reasonably believes to be appropriate under the circumstances; and
(3) rationally believes that the business judgment is in the best interests of the corporation.

Referring to clause (2) above, the decision-making process is to be reviewed on a basis that is to a large extent individualized in nature ("informed . . . to the extent the director . . . reasonably believes to be appropriate under the circumstances")—as contrasted with the traditional objectively based duty-of-care standard (*e.g.*, the "care . . . an ordinarily prudent person . . . would exercise"). An "ordinarily prudent person" might do more to become better informed, but if a director believes, in good faith, that he or she can make a sufficiently informed business judgment, the director will be protected so long as that belief is within the bounds of reason. Referring to clause (3) above, the phrase "rationally believes" is stated in the PRINCIPLES to be a term having "both an objective and subjective content. A director . . . must actually believe that the business judgment is in the best interests of the corporation and that belief must be rational," 1 PRINCIPLES at 179. Others see that aspect to be primarily geared to the process employed by a director in making the decision as opposed to the substantive content of the board decision made. *See Aronson v. Lewis* at 812 ("The business judgment rule is . . . a presumption that in making a business decision the directors of a corporation acted on an informed basis, in good faith and in the honest belief that the action taken was in the best interests of the company. . . . Absent an abuse of discretion, that judgment will be respected by the courts.") In practical application, an irrational belief would in all likelihood constitute an abuse of discretion. Compare *In re Caremark International Inc. Derivative Litigation*, Civ. A. No. 13670, 1996 Del. Ch. LEXIS 125, at *27 (Del. Ch. Sept. 25, 1996): "whether a judge or jury considering the matter after the fact . . . believes a decision substantively wrong, or degrees of wrong extending through "stupid" to "egregious" or "irrational," provides no ground for director liability, so long as the court determines that the process employed was either rational or employed in a good faith effort to advance corporate interests . . . the business judgment rule is process oriented and informed by a deep respect for all good faith board decisions.")

****

Section 8.31 does not codify the business judgment rule as a whole. The section recognizes the common law doctrine and provides guidance as to its application in dealing with director liability claims. Because the elements of the business judgment rule and the circumstances for its application are continuing to be developed by the courts, it would not be desirable to freeze the concept in a statute. For example, in recent years the Delaware Supreme Court has established novel applications of the concept to various transactional justification matters, such as the role of special litigation committees. *See Zapata Corporation v. Maldonado*, 430 A.2D 779 (Del. 1981). Under *Zapata*, a rule that applies where there is no disinterested majority on the board appointing the special litigation committee, there is no presumption of regularity and the corporation must bear the burden of proving the independence of the committee, the reasonableness of its investigation, and the reasonableness of the bases of its determination that dismissal of the derivative litigation is in the best interests of the corporation. The business judgment concept has been employed in countless legal decisions and is a topic that has received a great deal of scholarly attention. For an exhaustive treatment of the subject, see D. Block, N. Barton and S. Radin, The Business Judgment Rule: Fiduciary Duties of Corporate Directors (4th ed. 1993 & Supp. 1995). While codification of the business judgment rule in Section 8.31 is expressly disclaimed, its principal elements, relating to personal liability issues, are embedded in subsection (a)(2).

A. GOOD FAITH

The expectation that a director's conduct will be in good faith is an overarching element of his or her baseline duties. Relevant thereto, it has been stated that a lack of good faith is presented where a board "lacked an actual intention to advance corporate welfare" and "bad faith" is presented where "a transaction . . . is authorized for some purpose other than a genuine attempt to advance corporate welfare or is known to constitute a violation of applicable positive law." *See Gagliardi v. TriFoods International Inc.*, 683 A.2d 1049 (Del. Ch. 1996). If a director's conduct can be successfully challenged pursuant to other clauses of subsection (a)(2), there is a substantial likelihood that the conduct in question will also present an issue of good faith implicating clause 2(i). Conduct involving knowingly illegal conduct that exposes the corporation to harm will constitute action not in good faith, and belief that decisions made (in connection with such conduct) were in the best interests of the corporation will be subject to challenge as well. If subsection (a)(2) included only clause 2(i), much of the conduct with which the other clauses are concerned could still be considered pursuant to the subsection, on the basis that such conduct evidenced the actor's lack of good faith. Accordingly, the canon of construction known as eiusdem generis has substantial relevance in understanding the broad overlap of the good faith element with the various other subsection (a)(2) clauses. Where conduct has not been found deficient on other grounds, decision-making outside the bounds of reasonable judgment—an abuse of discretion perhaps explicable on no other basis—can give rise to an inference of bad faith. That form of conduct (characterized by the court as "constructive fraud" or "reckless indifference" or "deliberate disregard" in the relatively few case precedents) giving rise to an inference of bad faith will also raise a serious question whether the director could have reasonably believed that the best interests of the corporation would be served.

B. REASONABLE BELIEF

A director should reasonably believe that his or her decision will be in the best interests of the nonprofit corporation and a director should become sufficiently informed, with respect to any action taken or not taken, to the extent he or she reasonably believes appropriate in the circumstances. In each case, the director's reasonable belief calls for a subjective belief and, so long as it is his or her honest and good faith belief, a director has wide discretion. However, in the rare case where a decision respecting the corporation's best interests is so removed from the realm of reason (*e.g.*, corporate waste), or a belief as to the sufficiency of the director's preparation to make an informed judgment is so unreasonable as to fall outside the permissible bounds of sound discretion (*e.g.*, a clear case is presented if the director has undertaken no preparation and is woefully uninformed), the director's judgment will not be sustained.

C. LACK OF OBJECTIVITY OR INDEPENDENCE

If a director has a familial, financial, or business relationship with another person having a material interest in a transaction or other conduct involving the nonprofit corporation, or if the director is dominated or controlled by another person having such a material interest, there is a potential for that conflicted interest or divided loyalty to affect the director's judgment. If the matter at issue involves a conflicting interest transaction, it will be governed by Section 8.60; otherwise, the lack of objectivity due to a relationship's influence on the director's judgment will be evaluated, in the context of the pending conduct challenge, under Section 8.31. If the matter at issue involves lack of independence, the proof of domination or control and its influence on the director's judgment will typically entail different (and perhaps more convincing) evidence than what may be involved in a lack of objectivity case. The variables are manifold, and the facts must be sorted out and weighed on a case-by-case basis. If that other person is the director's spouse or employer, the concern that the director's judgment might be improperly influenced would be substantially greater than if that person is the spouse of the director's step-grandchild or the director's partner in a vacation time-share. When the party challenging the director's conduct can establish that the relationship or the domination or control in question could reasonably be expected to affect the director's judgment respecting the matter at issue in a manner adverse to the corporation, the director will then have the opportunity to establish that the action taken by him or her was reasonably believed to be in the best interests of the corporation. The reasonableness of the director's belief as to the corporation's best interests, in respect of the action taken, should be evaluated on the basis of not only the director's honest and good faith belief but also on considerations bearing on the fairness to the corporation of the transaction or other conduct involving the corporation that is at issue.

D. IMPROPER FINANCIAL BENEFIT

Subchapter 8F of the act deals with conflicting interest transactions. Its coverage of those interests is exclusive and its procedures for approval of conflicting interest transactions will establish a director's entitlement to any financial benefit gained from the transactional event. A director's conflicting interest transaction that is not protected by the fairness standard set forth in Section 8.60(a)(3), pursuant to which the conflicted director may establish the transaction to have been fair to the nonprofit corporation, would often involve receipt of a financial benefit to which the director was not entitled (*i.e.*, the transaction was not "fair" to the corporation).

E. FINANCIAL BENEFIT/MATERIAL INTEREST

A director is expected to observe an obligation of undivided loyalty to the corporation and, while the law will not concern itself with trifling deviations (de minimis non curat lex), there is no materiality threshold that applies to a financial benefit to which a director is not properly entitled. The act observes this principle in several places (*e.g.*, the exception to liability elimination prescribed in Section 2.02(c)(1) and the indemnification restriction in Section 8.51(d)(2), as well as the liability standard in subsection (a)(2)(v)). In contrast, there is a materiality threshold for the interest of another in a transaction or conduct where a director's lack of objectivity or lack of independence has been asserted under subsection (a)(2)(iii). In the typical case, analysis of another's interest would first consider the materiality of the transaction or conduct at issue—in most cases, any transaction or other action involving the attention of the board or one of its committees will cross the materiality threshold, but not always—and would then consider the materiality of that person's interest therein. The possibility that another's interest in a transaction or conduct that is not material, or that an immaterial interest of another in a transaction or conduct, would adversely affect a director's judgment is sufficiently remote that it should not be made subject to judicial review.

F. SUSTAINED INATTENTION

The director's role involves two fundamental components: the decision-making function and the oversight function. In contrast with the decision-making function, which generally involves action taken at a point in time, the oversight function under Section 8.01(b) involves ongoing monitoring of the nonprofit corporation's activities and affairs over a period of time. This involves the duty of ongoing attention, when actual knowledge of particular facts and circumstances arouse suspicions which indicate a need to make inquiry. As observed by the Supreme Court of New Jersey in *Francis v. United Jersey Bank*, 432 A.2D 814, 822 (Sup. Ct. 1981):

> Directors are under a continuing obligation to keep informed about the activities of the corporation. . . . Directors may not shut their eyes to corporate misconduct and then claim that because they did not see the misconduct, they did not have a

> duty to look. The sentinel asleep at his post contributes nothing to the enterprise he is charged to protect. . . . Directorial management does not require a detailed inspection of day-to-day activities, but rather a general monitoring of corporate affairs and policies.

While the facts will be outcome-determinative, deficient conduct involving a sustained failure to exercise oversight—where found actionable—has typically been characterized by the courts in terms of abdication and continued neglect of a director's duty of attention, not a brief distraction or temporary interruption. However, embedded in the oversight function is the need to inquire when suspicions are aroused. This duty is not a component of ongoing oversight, and does not entail proactive vigilance, but arises when, and only when, particular facts and circumstances of material concern (*e.g.*, evidence of embezzlement at a high level or the discovery of significant inventory shortages) suddenly surface.

G. OTHER BREACHES OF A DIRECTOR'S DUTIES

Subsection (a)(2)(v) is, in part, a catchall provision that implements the intention to make Section 8.31 a generally inclusive provision but, at the same time, to recognize the existence of other breaches of common law duties that can give rise to liability for directors. A doctrine of corporate governance, well-established in the case law, is that a director owes a duty of loyalty to the nonprofit corporation; relatedly, the courts impose a duty of fair dealing on directors when their conduct affects the interests of the corporation. It has long been recognized that a director must first offer a "corporate opportunity" to the corporation before taking advantage of it. The term "corporate opportunity" can be readily stated in principle but, when determining the doctrine's application, the facts will often be outcome-determinative. It has been defined in Section 5.05(b)(1) of PRINCIPLES OF CORPORATE GOVERNANCE to mean, insofar as a director is concerned:

> Any opportunity to engage in a business activity of which a director . . . becomes aware, either:

> (A) In connection with the performance of functions as a director . . . , or under circumstances that should reasonably lead the director . . . to believe that the person offering the opportunity expects it to be offered to the corporation; or
>
> (B) Through the use of corporate information or property, if the resulting opportunity is one that the director . . . should reasonably be expected to believe would be of interest to the corporation. . . .

The application of the corporate opportunity doctrine, in cases where it is operative, is typically conditioned on the nonprofit corporation's financial ability to exploit the opportunity, although some courts have held that it is up to the corporation to judge that ability and the opportunity should therefore always be offered. Relatedly, a formal offer is not essential, so long as the surrounding circumstances indicate an awareness of, and afford the corporation reasonable access to, the opportunity and there is indicated disinterest, manifested by inaction or due to financial inability. *See Broz v. Cellular Information Systems, Inc.*, 673 A.2D 148 (Del. 1996). Failure to observe this obligation first to refer a corporate opportunity to the corporation results in a breach of a director's duty. See Subchapter G of this Chapter 8 for a procedure under which the taking of a corporate opportunity by a director may be approved.

A related duty obligates the director to refrain from gaining a pecuniary benefit by engaging in competition with the corporation that would cause reasonably foreseeable harm to it; unless authorized by the corporation, that conduct will constitute a breach of the director's duties.

H. FAIRNESS

Pursuant to Section 8.60(a)(3), an interested director (or the nonprofit corporation, if it chooses) can gain protection for a director's conflicting interest transaction by establishing that it was fair to the corporation. (The concept of "fair" and "fairness," in this and various other contexts, can take into account both fair price and fair dealing on the part of the interested director.)

Under case law, personal liability as well as transactional justification issues will be subject to a fairness standard of judicial review if the plaintiff makes out a credible claim of breach of the duty of loyalty or if the presumptions of the business judgment standard (*e.g.*, an informed judgment) are overcome, with the burden of proof shifting from the plaintiff to the defendant. In this respect, the issue of fairness is relevant to both subsection (a) and subsection (b). Within the ambit of subsection (a)(2), a director can often respond to the challenge that his or her conduct was deficient by establishing that the transaction or conduct at issue was fair to the corporation. *See Kahn v. Lynch Communications Systems, Inc.*, 669 A.2D 79 (Del. 1995). *Cf. Cede & Co. v. Technicolor Inc.*, 634 A.2D 345 (Del. 1993) (when the business judgment rule is rebutted—procedurally—the burden shifts to the defendant directors to prove the "entire fairness" of the challenged transaction). It is to be noted, however, that fairness may not be relevant to the matter at issue (see, *e.g.*, clause (iv) of subsection (a)(2)). If the director is successful in establishing fairness, where the issue of fairness is relevant, then it is unlikely that the complainant can establish legal liability or the appropriateness of an equitable remedy under subsection (b).

I. DIRECTOR CONDUCT

Subsection (a)(2) deals, throughout, with a director's action that is taken or not taken. To the extent that the director's conduct involves a breach of his or her duty of care or duty of attention within the context of collegial action by the board or one of its committees, proper performance of the relevant duty through the action taken by the director's colleagues can overcome the consequences of his or her deficient conduct. For example, where a director's conduct can be challenged under subsection (a)(2)(ii)(B) by reason of having been uninformed about the decision—he or she did not read the merger materials distributed prior to the meeting, arrived late at the board meeting just in time for the vote but, nonetheless, voted for the merger solely because the others were in favor—the favorable action by a quorum of properly informed directors would ordinarily protect the director against liability. When the director's conduct involves the duty of fair dealing within the context of action taken by the board or one of its committees, the wiser choice will usually be for the director not to participate in the collegial action. That is to say, where a director may have a conflicting interest or a divided loyalty, or even where there may be grounds for the issue to be raised, the better course to follow is usually for the director to disclose the conduct-related facts and circumstances posing the possible compromise of his or her independence or objectivity, and then to withdraw from the meeting (or, in the alternative, to abstain from the deliberations and voting).

2. Section 8.31(b)

After satisfying the burden of establishing that the conduct of the director is challengeable under subsection (a), the plaintiff, in order to hold the director liable for money damages under clause (b)(1), has the further burden of establishing that: (i) harm (measurable in money damages) has been suffered by the nonprofit corporation or its members, and (ii) the director's challenged conduct was the proximate cause of that harm. The concept of "proximate cause" is a term of art that is basic to tort law, and the cases providing content to the phrase represent well-developed authority to which a court will undoubtedly refer. A useful approach for the concept's application, for purposes of subsection (b)(1), would be that the challenged conduct must have been a "substantial factor in producing the harm." *See Francis v. United Jersey Bank*, 432 A.2D at 829. Similarly, the plaintiff has the burden of establishing that money payment is due from the director pursuant to clause (b)(2). If, while challengeable, the conduct at issue caused no harm under clause (b)(1) or does not provide the basis for other legal remedy under clause (b)(2), but may provide the basis for an equitable remedy under clause (b)(3), the plaintiff must satisfy whatever further burden of persuasion may be indicated to establish that imposition of the remedy sought is appropriate in the circumstances. In *Brophy v. Cities Service Co.*, 70 A.2D 5, 8 (Del. Ch. 1949), an employee was required to account for profits derived from the use of the corporation's confidential plans to reacquire its securities through open-market purchases. Notwithstanding the fact that harm to the corporation had not been established, the Chancellor observed: "[p]ublic policy will not permit an employee occupying a position of trust and confidence toward his employer to abuse that relation to his own profit, regardless of whether his employer suffers a loss." Once actionable conduct that provides the basis for an equitable remedy under clause (b)(3) has been established, its appropriateness will often be clear and, if so, no further advocacy on the part of the plaintiff will be required.

3. Section 8.31(c)

While Section 8.31 addresses director liability to the nonprofit corporation or its members under the act—and related case law dealing with corporate governance concepts coming within the common law's ambit—it does not limit any liabilities or foreclose any rights expressly provided for under other law. Subsection (c) merely acknowledges that those rights are unaffected by Section 8.31. And directors can have liability to persons other than the corporation and its members, such as (i) employee benefit plan participants and beneficiaries, if the directors are determined to be fiduciaries under the Employee Retirement Income Security Act of 1974, 29 U.S.C. Sections 1001–1461 (1988 & Supp. IV 1992), (ii) government agencies for regulatory violations, or (iii) individuals claiming damages for injury governed by tort law concepts (*e.g.*, libel or slander).

As discussed above in the Official Comment to Section 8.31(a), the concept of "fairness" is often relevant to whether a director will have liability if his or her conduct is challenged. Specifically, a director can successfully defend a financial interest in a transaction with the corporation by establishing that it was fair to the corporation. See Section 8.60 and its Official Comment. More generally, the courts have resorted to a fairness standard of review where the business judgment rule has been inapplicable. *See Weinberger v. UOP, Inc.*, 457 A.2D 701 (Del. 1983). In the usual case, the defendant seeking to justify challenged conduct, on the basis of fairness, has the burden of proving that it was fair to the nonprofit corporation. Subsection (c) expressly disclaims any intention to shift the burden of proof otherwise applicable where the question of the fairness of a transaction or other challenged conduct is at issue.

§ 8.32. LOANS TO OR GUARANTEES FOR DIRECTORS AND OFFICERS [*OPTIONAL*]

(a) A nonprofit corporation may not lend money to or guarantee the obligation of a director or officer of the corporation.

(b) This section does not apply to:

  (1) an advance to pay reimbursable expenses reasonably expected to be incurred by a director or officer;

  (2) an advance to pay premiums on life insurance if the advance is secured by the cash value of the policy;

  (3) advances pursuant to [Subchapter] 8E;

  (4) loans or advances pursuant to employee benefit plans;

  (5) a loan secured by the principal residence of an officer; or

  (6) a loan to pay relocation expenses of an officer.

(c) The fact that a loan or guarantee is made in violation of this section does not affect the borrower's liability on the loan.

Source Note: Subsections (a) and (c) are a reenactment of Model Nonprofit Corporation Act (1987) § 8.32. Subsection (b) is new.

OFFICIAL COMMENT

Section 8.32 is an optional section that prohibits all loans to and guarantees for directors and officers. Whether the potential abuse in this area is so great as to warrant prohibiting all loans and guarantees for the benefit of directors and officers is a policy judgment that individual states will need to make. Some members of the drafting committee for the act believe that having the ability to make loans and guarantees may be beneficial to a nonprofit corporation, such as when they are used to facilitate the recruitment of an executive from another area of the country who will have substantial moving expenses. Other members of the drafting committee believe that the potential abuses justify prohibiting all loans and guarantees notwithstanding the possible benefits under certain circumstances.

If this section is not adopted in a particular state, the making of loans and guarantees will still be subject to scrutiny under Sections 8.31 and 8.60.

§ 8.33. DIRECTORS' LIABILITY FOR UNLAWFUL DISTRIBUTIONS

(a) A director who votes for or assents to a distribution made in violation of this [act] is personally liable to the nonprofit corporation for the amount of the distribution that exceeds what could have been distributed without violating this [act] if the party asserting liability establishes that, when taking the action, the director did not comply with Section 8.30.

(b) A director held liable under subsection (a) for an unlawful distribution is entitled to:

  (1) contribution from every other director who could be held liable under subsection (a) for the unlawful distribution; and

  (2) recoupment from each person of the pro rata portion of the amount of the unlawful distribution the person received, whether or not the person knew the distribution was made in violation of this [act].

(c) A proceeding to enforce:

  (1) the liability of a director under subsection (a) is barred unless it is commenced within two years after the date on which the distribution was made; or

  (2) contribution or recoupment under subsection (b) is barred unless it is commenced within one year after the liability of the claimant has been finally adjudicated under subsection (a).

Source Note: Patterned after Model Business Corporation Act, 3d Ed. (2002) § 8.33. Subsections (a) and (b) are substantially a reenactment of Model Nonprofit Corporation Act (1987) § 8.33.

CROSS-REFERENCES

Article provision limiting liability, see § 2.02.

Director duties in dissolution, see § 14.09.

Director standards of conduct, see § 8.30.

Distributions prohibited generally, see § 6.40.

Indemnification, see §§ 2.02 and 8.50–8.58.

Permissible distributions, see § 6.41.

OFFICIAL COMMENT

A director who is compelled to restore the amount of an unlawful distribution to the nonprofit corporation is entitled to contribution from every other director who could have been held liable for the unlawful distribution. The director may also recover a pro rata portion of the amount of the unlawful distribution from any person who accepted the distribution. Although no attempt has been made in the act to work out in detail the relationship between the right of recoupment from other persons and the right of contribution from directors, it is expected that a court will equitably apportion the obligations and benefits arising from the application of the principles set forth in this section.

Section 8.33(c) limits the time within which a proceeding may be commenced against a director for an unlawful distribution to two years after the date on which the effect of the distribution was measured. Section 8.33(c) also limits the time within which a proceeding for contribution or recoupment may be made to one year after the date on which the liability of the claimant has been finally determined and adjudicated. This one-year period specified in clause (2) may end within or extend beyond the two-year period specified in clause (1).

This section also applies to a designated body pursuant to Section 8.12.

[Subchapter] D
OFFICERS

§ 8.40. OFFICERS

(a) The officers of a nonprofit corporation are the individuals who hold the offices described in its articles of incorporation or bylaws, or are appointed or elected in accordance with the articles and bylaws or as authorized by the board of directors.

(b) The articles of incorporation or bylaws or the board of directors must assign to one of the officers responsibility for preparing or supervising the preparation of the minutes of the meetings of the board of directors and the members, if any, and for maintaining and authenticating the records of the corporation required to be kept under Sections 16.01(a) and 16.01(e).

(c) The same individual may simultaneously hold more than one office in a nonprofit corporation.

Source Note: Patterned after Model Business Corporation Act, 3d Ed. (2002) § 8.40. Derived from Model Nonprofit Corporation Act (1987) § 8.40.

CROSS-REFERENCES

Agents of corporation, see § 3.02.

Contract rights of officers, see § 8.44.

"Designated body" defined, see § 1.40.

Duties of officers, see § 8.41.

Officer as employee of corporation, see § 1.40.

Removal of officers, see § 8.43.

"Secretary" defined, see § 1.40.

Tenure of officers, see § 8.44.

OFFICIAL COMMENT

Section 8.40 permits every nonprofit corporation to designate the officers it wants. The designation may be made in the articles of incorporation or bylaws or by the board of directors consistent with the articles and bylaws.

Section 8.40(a) indicates that, while it is generally the responsibility of the board of directors to elect officers, an officer may appoint one or more officers if authorized by the articles of incorporation or bylaws or the board of directors.

The board of directors, as well as duly authorized officers, employees, or agents, may also appoint other agents for the nonprofit corporation. Nothing in this section is intended to limit the authority of a board of directors to organize its own internal affairs, including designating officers of the board.

The articles of incorporation or bylaws or the board of directors must assign to an officer the responsibility for preparation of minutes and authentication of the corporate records referred to in Sections 16.01(a) and (e); the person performing this function is referred to as the "secretary" of the nonprofit corporation throughout the act. See Section 1.40. Under the act, a corporation may have this and all other corporate functions performed by a single individual.

The person who is designated by the articles of incorporation, bylaws, or board to have responsibility for preparing minutes of meetings and maintaining the corporate records has authority to bind the nonprofit corporation by that officer's authentication under this section. This assignment of authority, traditionally vested in the corporate "secretary," allows third persons to rely on authenticated records without inquiry as to their truth or accuracy.

The powers of the board of directors under this section may be vested by the articles of incorporation or bylaws in a designated body. See Sections 2.02(b)(2) and 8.12.

§ 8.41. DUTIES OF OFFICERS

Each officer has the authority and must perform the duties set forth in the articles of incorporation or bylaws or, to the extent consistent with the articles and bylaws, the duties prescribed by the board of directors or by direction of an officer authorized by the board of directors to prescribe the duties of other officers.

Source Note: Patterned after Model Business Corporation Act, 3d Ed. (2002) § 8.41. Substantially a reenactment of Model Nonprofit Corporation Act (1987) § 8.41.

CROSS-REFERENCES

Assistant officers, see § 8.40.

Officer as employee, see § 1.40.

"Secretary" defined, see § 1.40.

OFFICIAL COMMENT

Section 8.41 recognizes that persons designated as officers have the formal authority set forth for that position (1) by its description in the articles of incorporation or bylaws, (2) by specific resolution of the board of directors, or (3) by direction of another officer authorized by the board of directors to prescribe the duties of other officers.

These methods of investing officers with formal authority do not exhaust the sources of an officer's actual or apparent authority. Many cases state that specific corporate officers, particularly the chief executive officer, may have implied authority merely by virtue of their positions. This authority, which may overlap the express authority granted by the articles of incorporation or bylaws, generally has been viewed as extending only to transactions in the ordinary course of operations, although some cases have recognized unusually broad implied authority of the chief executive officer or have created a presumption that corporate officers have broad authority, thereby placing on the nonprofit corporation the burden of showing lack of authority. Corporate officers may also be vested with apparent (or ostensible) authority by reason of corporate conduct on which third persons reasonably rely.

In addition to express, implied, or apparent authority, a nonprofit corporation is normally bound by unauthorized acts of officers if the unauthorized acts are ratified by the board of directors. Generally, ratification extends only to acts that could have been authorized as an original matter. Ratification may itself be express or implied and may in some cases serve as the basis of apparent (or ostensible) authority.

The powers of the board of directors under this section may be vested by the articles of incorporation or bylaws in a designated body. See Sections 2.02(b)(2) and 8.12.

§ 8.42. STANDARDS OF CONDUCT FOR OFFICERS

(a) An officer with discretionary authority must discharge his or her duties under that authority:
   (1) in good faith;
   (2) with the care an ordinarily prudent person in a like position would exercise under similar circumstances; and
   (3) in a manner the officer reasonably believes to be in the best interests of the corporation.

(b) The duty of an officer includes the obligation to inform:
   (1) the superior officer to whom, or the board of directors or the committee thereof to which, the officer reports, of information about the affairs of the nonprofit corporation known to the officer, within the scope of the officer's functions, and known to the officer to be material to the superior officer, board, or committee; and
   (2) his or her superior officer, or another appropriate person within the nonprofit corporation, or the board of directors, or a committee thereof, of any actual or probable material violation of law involving the corporation or material breach of duty to the corporation by an officer, employee, or agent of the corporation, that the officer believes has occurred or is likely to occur.

(c) In discharging his or her duties, an officer who does not have knowledge that makes reliance unwarranted may rely on information, opinions, reports, or statements, including financial statements and other financial data, if prepared or presented by:
   (1) one or more officers or employees of the nonprofit corporation whom the officer reasonably believes to be reliable and competent in the functions performed or the information, opinions, reports, or statements provided;
   (2) legal counsel, public accountants, or other persons retained by the corporation as to matters involving skills or expertise the officer reasonably believes are matters:
      (i) within the particular person's professional or expert competence, or
      (ii) as to which the particular person merits confidence;
   (3) in the case of a corporation engaged in religious activity, religious authorities and ministers, priests, rabbis, imams, or other persons whose positions or duties the officer reasonably believes justify reliance and confidence and whom the officer believes to be reliable and competent in the matters presented.

Source Note: Patterned after Model Business Corporation Act, 3d Ed. (2002) § 8.42. Derived from Model Nonprofit Corporation Act (1987) § 8.42.

CROSS-REFERENCES

Appointment of officers, see § 8.40.

Duties of officers, see § 8.41.

Indemnification, see §§ 8.50–8.58.

Removal of officers, see § 8.43.

Standards of liability for directors, see § 8.31.

OFFICIAL COMMENT

Subsection (a) provides that an officer must meet standards of conduct generally similar to those expected of directors under

Section 8.30. Consistent with the principles of agency, which generally govern the conduct of corporate employees, an officer is expected to observe the duties of obedience and loyalty and to act with the care that a person in a like position would reasonably exercise under similar circumstances. *See* RESTATEMENT OF (SECOND) AGENCY Section 379(1) (1958) ("Unless otherwise agreed, a paid agent is subject to a duty to the principal to act with standard care and with the skill which is standard in the locality for the kind of work which he is employed to perform and, in addition, to exercise any special skill that he has"). This section is not intended to modify, diminish, or qualify the duties or standards of conduct that may be imposed upon specific officers by other law or regulation.

The common law, including the law of agency, has recognized a duty on the part of officers and key employees to disclose to their superiors material information relevant to the affairs of the agency entrusted to them. *See* RESTATEMENT OF (SECOND) AGENCY Section 381; A. Gilchrist Sparks, III and Lawrence A. Hamermesh, *Common Law Duties of Non-Director Corporate Officers*, 48 BUSINESS LAWYER 215, 226–29 (1992). This duty is implicit in, and embraced under, the broader standard of subsection (a). Subsection (b) sets forth explicitly this disclosure obligation by confirming that the officer's duty includes the obligation (i) to keep superior corporate authorities informed of material information within the officer's sphere of functional responsibilities, and (ii) to inform the relevant superior authority, or other appropriate person within the nonprofit corporation, of violations of law or breaches of duty that the officer believes have occurred or are about to occur (*i.e.*, more likely than not to occur) and are or would be material to the corporation. Subsection (b)(1) specifies that business information must be transmitted through the officer's regular reporting channels. Subsection (b)(2) specifies the reporting responsibility differently with respect to actual or probable material violations of law or material breaches of duty. The use of the term "appropriate" in subsection (b)(2) is intended to accommodate both the normative standard that may have been set up by the corporation for reporting potential violations of law or duty to a specified person, such as an ombudsperson, ethics officer, internal auditor, general counsel, or the like, and situations where there is no designated person but the officer's immediate superior is not appropriate (for example, because the officer believes that individual is implicit in the unlawful activity or breach of duty).

Subsection (b)(1) should not be interpreted so broadly as to discourage efficient delegation of functions. It addresses the flow of information to the board of directors and to superior officers necessary to enable them to perform their decision-making and oversight functions. See the Official Comment to Section 8.31. The officer's duties under subsection (b) may not be negated by agreement; however, their scope under subsection (b)(1) may be shaped by prescribing the scope of an officer's functional responsibilities.

With respect to the duties under subsection (b)(2), codes of conduct or codes of ethics, such as those adopted by many large corporations, may prescribe the circumstances in which and mechanisms by which officers and employees may discharge their duty to report material information to superior officers or the board of directors, or to other designated persons.

The term "material" modifying violations of law or breaches of duty in subsection (b)(2) denotes a qualitative as well as quantitative standard. It relates not only to the potential direct financial impact on the nonprofit corporation, but also to the nature of the violation or breach. For example, an embezzlement of $10,000, or even less, would be material because of the seriousness of the offense, even though the amount involved might not be material to the financial position or results of operations of the corporation.

The duty under subsection (b)(2) is triggered by an officer's subjective belief that a material violation of law or breach of duty actually or probably has occurred or is likely to occur. This duty is not triggered by objective knowledge concepts, such as whether the officer should have concluded that such misconduct was occurring. The subjectivity of the trigger under subsection (b)(2), however, does not excuse officers from their obligations under subsection (a) to act in good faith and with due care in the performance of the functions assigned to them, including oversight duties within their respective areas of responsibility. There may be occasions when the principles applicable under Section 8.30(c) limiting the duty of disclosure by directors where a duty of confidentiality is overriding may also apply to officers. See the Official Comment to Section 8.30(c).

An officer's ability to rely on others in meeting the standards prescribed in Section 8.42 may be more limited, depending upon the circumstances of the particular case, than the measure and scope of reliance permitted a director under Section 8.30, in view of the greater obligation the officer may have to be familiar with the affairs of the nonprofit corporation. The proper delegation of responsibilities by an officer, separate and apart from the exercise of judgment as to the delegatee's reliability and competence, is concerned with the procedure employed. This will involve, in the usual case, sufficient communication to the end that the delegatee understands the scope of the assignment and, in turn, manifests to the officer a willingness and commitment to undertake its performance. The entitlement to rely upon employees assumes that a delegating officer will maintain a sufficient level of communication with the officer's subordinates to fulfill his or her supervisory responsibilities. The definition of "employee" in Section 1.40 includes an officer who is otherwise employed by the corporation; accordingly, Section 8.42 contemplates the delegation or responsibilities to other officers as well as to nonofficer employees.

In some cases, failure to observe relevant standards of conduct can give rise to an officer's liability to the nonprofit corporation or its members. A court review of challenged conduct will involve an evaluation of the particular facts and circumstances in light of applicable law. In this connection, subsection (d) recognizes that relevant principles of Section 8.31, such as duties to deal fairly with the corporation and its members and the challenger's burden of establishing proximately caused harm, should be taken into account. In addition, the business judgment rule will normally apply to decisions within an officer's discretionary authority. Liability to others can also arise from an officer's own acts or omissions (*e.g.*, violations of law or tort claims) and, in some cases, an officer with supervisory responsibilities can have risk exposure in connection with the acts or omissions of others.

The Official Comment to Section 8.30 supplements this Official Comment to the extent that it can be appropriately viewed as generally applicable to officers as well as directors.

§ 8.43. RESIGNATION AND REMOVAL OF OFFICERS

(a) An officer may resign at any time by delivering notice to the nonprofit corporation. A resignation is effective when the notice is delivered unless the notice specifies a later effective time. If a resignation is made effective at a later time and the board of directors or the appointing officer accepts the future effective time, the board or the appointing officer may designate a successor before the effective time if the board or the appointing officer provides that the successor does not take office until the effective time.

(b) Except as provided in the articles of incorporation or bylaws, an officer may be removed at any time with or without cause by:
   (i) the board of directors;
   (ii) the officer who appointed the officer being removed, unless the board provides otherwise; or
   (iii) any other officer authorized by the articles, the bylaws, or the board.

(c) In this section, "appointing officer" means the officer (including any successor to that officer) who appointed the officer resigning or being removed.

Source Note: Patterned after Model Business Corporation Act, 3d Ed. (2002) § 8.43. Derived from Model Nonprofit Corporation Act (1987) § 8.43.

CROSS-REFERENCES

Contract rights of officers, see § 8.44.

"Deliver" defined, see § 1.40.

Effective date of notice, see § 1.41.

Notice to the corporation, see § 1.41.

OFFICIAL COMMENT

Section 8.43(a) is consistent with current practice and declaratory of current law. It recognizes: that corporate officers may resign; that, with the consent of the board of directors or the appointing officer, they may resign effective at a later time; and that a future vacancy may be filled to become effective as of the effective time of the resignation.

In part because of the unlimited power of removal confirmed by Section 8.43(b), a board of directors may enter into an employment agreement with the holder of an office that extends beyond the term of the board of directors. This type of contract is binding on the nonprofit corporation even if the articles of incorporation or bylaws provide that officers are elected for a term shorter than the period of the employment contract. If a later board of directors refuses to reelect that person as an officer, the person has the right to sue for damages but not for specific performance of the contract.

Section 8.43(b) is consistent with current practice and declaratory of current law. It recognizes that the officers of the nonprofit corporation are subject to removal by the board of directors and, in certain instances, by other officers. It provides the corporation with the flexibility to determine when, if ever, an officer will be permitted to remove another officer. To the extent that the corporation wishes to permit an officer, other than the appointing officer, to remove another officer, the articles of incorporation or bylaws or a board resolution should set forth clearly the persons having removal authority.

A person may be removed from office irrespective of contract rights or the presence or absence of "cause" in a legal sense. Section 8.44 provides that removal from office of a holder who has contract rights is without prejudice to whatever rights the former officer may assert in a suit for damages for breach of contract.

The powers of the board of directors under this section may be vested by the articles of incorporation or bylaws in a designated body. See Sections 2.02(b)(2) and 8.12.

§ 8.44. CONTRACT RIGHTS OF OFFICERS

(a) The appointment of an officer does not itself create contract rights.

(b) An officer's removal does not affect the officer's contract rights, if any, with the nonprofit corporation. An officer's resignation does not affect the corporation's contract rights, if any, with the officer.

Source Note: Patterned after Model Business Corporation Act, 3d Ed. (2002) § 8.44. Substantially a reenactment of Model Nonprofit Corporation Act (1987) § 8.44.

CROSS-REFERENCES

Appointment of officers and assistant officers, see § 8.40.

Resignation or removal of officers, see § 8.43.

OFFICIAL COMMENT

Section 8.44 makes clear that the appointment of an officer does not itself create contract rights in the officer. The removal of an officer with contract rights is without prejudice to the later enforcement by the officer of contract rights in a suit for damages for breach of contract. See the Official Comment to Section 8.43. Similarly, an officer with an employment contract who prematurely resigns may be in breach of the employment contract. The mere appointment of an officer for a term does not create a contractual obligation on the part of the officer to complete the term.

[Subchapter] E
INDEMNIFICATION AND ADVANCE FOR EXPENSES

INTRODUCTORY COMMENT TO SUBCHAPTER E

The substance of this subchapter is based almost entirely on an amendment to the 1969 Model Business Corporation Act adopted in 1980 and substantially revised in 1994 (the "MBCA"). Thus, the act closely follows the law with respect to indemnification of directors and officers of business corporations and advancement of their litigation expenses. This is consistent with the view that the relationship of directors to a nonprofit corporation is more akin to that of directors of business corporations than to that of trustees to their beneficiaries. *Stern v. Lucy Webb Hayes National Training School for Deaconesses and Missionaries*, 381 F. Supp. 1003 (D.D.C. 1974). *See Duties of Charitable Trust Trustees and Charitable Corporation Directors*, Real Property, Probate and Trust Journal 545 (1967).

The only differences in the area of indemnification between this act and the MBCA are that this act (i) changes the rule in Section 8.52, (ii) omits Section 8.59 of the MBCA, and (iii) treats members of a designated body as directors. The change in Section 8.52 is explained in the Official Comment to that section. Omitted Section 8.59 of the MBCA provides that a business corporation "may provide indemnification or advance expenses to a director or officer only as permitted by" Sections 8.50 through

8.59. The omission from this act of a provision analogous to Section 8.59 of the MBCA means that the provisions of this Subchapter 8E will not be the exclusive basis for providing indemnification and advance of expenses to directors and officers of nonprofit corporations. Defining "director" in Section 8.50(2) to include a member of a designated body is consistent with the role of designated bodies as provided in Section 8.12.

1. Policy Issues Raised by Indemnification and Advance for Expenses

Indemnification (including advance for expenses) provides financial protection by the nonprofit corporation for its directors against exposure to expenses and liabilities that may be incurred by them in connection with legal proceedings based on an alleged breach of duty in their service to or on behalf of the corporation. Today, when both the volume and the cost of litigation have increased dramatically, it would be difficult to persuade responsible persons to serve as directors if they were compelled to bear personally the cost of vindicating the propriety of their conduct in every instance in which it might be challenged. While reasonable people may differ as to what constitutes a meritorious case, almost all would agree that corporate directors should have appropriate protection against personal risk and that the rule of *New York Dock Co. v. McCollom*, 173 Misc. 106, 16 N.Y.S.2d 844 (Sup. Ct. 1939), which denied reimbursement to directors who successfully defended their case on the merits, should as a matter of policy be overruled by statute.

The concept of indemnification recognizes that there will be situations in which the director does not satisfy all of the elements of the standard of conduct set forth in Section 8.30(a) or the requirements of some other applicable law, but where the nonprofit corporation should nevertheless be permitted (or required) to absorb the economic costs of any ensuing litigation. A carefully constructed indemnification statute should identify these situations.

If permitted too broadly, however, indemnification may violate equally basic tenets of public policy. It is inappropriate to permit management to use corporate funds to avoid the consequences of certain conduct. For example, a director who intentionally inflicts harm on the nonprofit corporation should not expect to receive assistance from the corporation for legal or other expenses and should be required to satisfy from his personal assets not only any adverse judgment but also expenses incurred in connection with the proceeding. Any other rule would tend to encourage socially undesirable conduct.

A further policy issue is raised in connection with indemnification against liabilities or sanctions imposed under state or federal civil or criminal statutes. A shift of the economic cost of these liabilities from the individual director to the nonprofit corporation by way of indemnification may in some instances frustrate the public policy of those statutes.

The fundamental issue that must be addressed by an indemnification statute is the establishment of policies consistent with these broad principles: to ensure that indemnification is permitted only where it will further sound corporate policies and to prohibit indemnification where it might protect or encourage wrongful or improper conduct. As phrased by one commentator, the goal of indemnification is to "seek the middle ground between encouraging fiduciaries to violate their trust, and discouraging them from serving at all." Joseph F. Johnston, *Corporate Indemnification and Liability Insurance for Directors and Officers*, 33 BUSINESS LAWYER 1993, 1994 (1978). The increasing number of suits against directors, the increasing cost of defense, and the increasing emphasis on diversifying the membership of boards of directors all militate in favor of workable arrangements to protect directors against liability to the extent consistent with established principles.

Some of the same policy considerations apply to the indemnification of officers and, in many cases, employees and agents. The indemnification of officers, whose duties are specified in Section 8.41, is dealt with separately in Section 8.56. However, other considerations apply to employees and agents, who have significantly different roles and responsibilities and as to whom the specter of structural bias (sympathetic directors approving indemnification for themselves or for colleagues on the board or for officers, who may work closely with board members) is not present. The indemnification of employees and agents, whose duties are prescribed by sources of law other than corporation law (*e.g.*, contract and agency law), is beyond the scope of this subchapter. Section 8.58(e), however, makes clear that the absence in Subchapter E of provisions concerning employees and agents is not intended to limit a nonprofit corporation's power to indemnify or advance expenses to them in accordance with applicable law.

2. *Relationship of Indemnification to Other Policies Established in the Act*

Indemnification is closely related to the standards of conduct for directors and officers established elsewhere in Chapter 8. The structure of the act is based on the assumption that if a director acts consistently with the standards of conduct described in Section 8.30 or with the standards of a liability-limitation provision in the articles of incorporation (as authorized by Section 2.02(c)), the director will not have exposure to liability to the nonprofit corporation or to members and any expenses necessary to establish his defense will be borne by the corporation (under Section 8.52). But the converse is not necessarily true. The basic standards for indemnification set forth in this subchapter for a civil action, in the absence of an indemnification provision in the corporation's articles (as authorized by Section 2.02(b)(8)), are good faith and reasonable belief that the conduct was in or not opposed to the best interests of the corporation. See Section 8.51. In some circumstances, a director or officer may be found to have violated a statutory or common law duty and yet be able to establish eligibility for indemnification under these standards of conduct. In addition, this subchapter permits a director or officer who is held liable for violating a statutory or common law duty, but who does not meet the relevant standard of conduct, to petition a court to order indemnification under Section 8.54(a)(3) on the ground that it would be fair and reasonable to do so.

3. Application of Amendments to Prior Conduct

Each jurisdiction adopting amendments to its indemnification statutes should consider the extent to which the statutes, as amended, should apply to conduct occurring prior to the effective time of the amendments. Absent constitutional or statutory provisions dealing generally with retroactivity of statutory amendments, resolution of this issue may be made to depend upon whether a claim for indemnification was made prior to (and was pending at) the effective time of the amendment. Alternatively, the amended statute can specifically provide that it applies to conduct occurring before or after the effective time.

§ 8.50. SUBCHAPTER DEFINITIONS

In this [subchapter]:

(1) "Corporation" includes any domestic or foreign predecessor entity of a nonprofit corporation in a merger, conversion, or domestication.

(2) "Director" or "officer" means an individual who is or was a director or officer, respectively, of a nonprofit corporation or who, while a director or officer of the corporation, is or was serving at the corporation's request as a director, officer, partner, trustee, employee, or agent of another domestic or foreign corporation, partnership, joint venture, trust, employee benefit plan, or other entity. A director or officer is considered to be serving an employee benefit plan at the corporation's request if the individual's duties to the corporation also impose duties on, or otherwise involve services by, the individual to the plan or to participants in or beneficiaries of the plan. "Director" includes a member of a designated body. "Director" or "officer" includes, unless the context requires otherwise, the estate or personal representative of a director or officer.

(3) "Disinterested director" means a director who, at the time of a vote referred to in Section 8.53(c) or a vote or selection referred to in Section 8.55(b) or (c), is not:

(i) a party to the proceeding, or

(ii) an individual having a familial, financial, professional, or employment relationship with the director whose indemnification or advance for expenses is the subject of the decision being made, which relationship would, in the circumstances, reasonably be expected to exert an influence on the director's judgment when voting on the decision being made.

(4) "Expenses" includes counsel fees.

(5) "Liability" means the obligation to pay a judgment, settlement, penalty, fine (including an excise tax assessed with respect to an employee benefit plan), or reasonable expenses incurred with respect to a proceeding.

(6) "Official capacity" means:

(i) when used with respect to a director, the office of director in a nonprofit corporation; and

(ii) when used with respect to an officer, as contemplated in Section 8.56, the office in a corporation held by the officer.

"Official capacity" does not include service for any other domestic or foreign corporation or any partnership, joint venture, trust, employee benefit plan, or other entity.

(7) "Party" means an individual who was, is, or is threatened to be made, a defendant or respondent in a proceeding.

(8) "Proceeding" includes a threatened, pending, or completed proceeding.

Source Note: Patterned after Model Business Corporation Act, 3d Ed. (2002) § 8.50. Substantially a reenactment of Model Nonprofit Corporation Act (1987) § 8.50.

CROSS-REFERENCES

Act definitions, see § 1.40.

Officers, see § 8.40.

"Proceeding" defined, see § 1.40.

Witness indemnification, see § 8.58.

OFFICIAL COMMENT

The definitions set forth in Section 8.50 apply only to Subchapter E and have no application elsewhere in the act (except as set forth in Section 2.02(b)(8)).

1. Corporation

A special definition of "corporation" is included in Subchapter E to make it clear that predecessor entities that have been absorbed in mergers are included within the definition. It is probable that the same result would be reached for many transactions under Section 11.07(a) (effect of merger), which provides for the assumption of liabilities by operation of law upon a merger. The express responsibility of successor entities for the liabilities of their predecessors under this subchapter is broader than under Section 11.07(a) and may impose liability on a successor although Section 11.07(a) does not. Section 8.50(1) is thus an essential aspect of the protection provided by this subchapter for persons eligible for indemnification. The definition of "corporation" similarly makes clear that predecessor entities in a conversion or domestication are included within the definition.

2. Director and Officer

A special definition of "director" and "officer" is included in Subchapter E to cover individuals who are made parties to proceedings because they are or were directors or officers or, while serving as directors or officers, also serve or served at the nonprofit corporation's request in another capacity for another entity. The purpose of the latter part of this definition is to give directors and officers the benefits of the protection of this subchapter while serving at the corporation's request in a responsible position for employee benefit plans, trade associations, nonprofit or charitable entities, domestic or foreign entities, or other kinds of profit or nonprofit ventures. To avoid misunderstanding, it is good practice from both the corporation's and director's or officer's viewpoint for this type of request to be evidenced by resolution, memorandum, or other writing. The definition covers an individual who is or was either a director or officer so that further references in the remainder of Subchapter E to an individual who is a director or officer necessarily include former directors or officers.

The second sentence of Section 8.50(2) addresses the question of liabilities arising under the Employee Retirement Income Security Act of 1974 (ERISA), 29 U.S.C. §§ 1001–1461. It makes clear that a director or officer who is serving as a fiduciary of an employee benefit plan is automatically viewed for purposes of this subchapter as having been requested by the nonprofit corporation to act in that capacity. Special treatment is believed necessary because of the broad definition of "fiduciary" in Section 3(21) of ERISA, 29 U.S.C. § 1002(21), and the requirement of Section 404 (29 U.S.C. § 1104(a)) that a "fiduciary" must discharge his or her duties "solely in the interest" of the participants and beneficiaries of the employee benefit plan. Decisions by a director or officer serving as a fiduciary under the plan on questions regarding eligibility for benefits, investment decisions, and interpretation of plan provisions regarding qualifying service, years of service, and retroactivity are all subject to the protections of this subchapter. See also Sections 8.50(5) and 8.51(b) of this subchapter.

The last sentence of Section 8.50(2) provides that the estate or personal representative of a director or officer is entitled to the rights of indemnification possessed by the director or officer himself. The phrase "unless the context requires otherwise" was added to make clear that the estate or personal representative does not have the right to participate in directorial decisions authorized in this subchapter.

3. Disinterested Director

This term identifies, for purposes of Subchapter E, those members of the board who are eligible to make, in the first instance, the authorizations and determinations required in connection with decisions on advance for expenses and indemnification. It is used only in Sections 8.53(c) and 8.55(b) and (c) and is not applicable to any other sections of the act.

To be a "disinterested director," a member of the board must not be a party to the proceeding at the time the board makes the determination or authorization and he must not be the subject of the request for advance or indemnification with respect to which action is being taken. He must also not have a familial, financial, professional, or employment relationship that could reasonably be expected to influence his decision. The fact that a director was nominated for the board by directors who are parties to the proceeding or are interested in the request or that a director is also a director of another corporation of which the director who is a party to the proceeding or is interested in the request is also a director should not, absent unusual circumstances, constitute a disqualifying relationship.

4. Expenses

"Expenses" is defined to include counsel fees in order to avoid repeated references to such fees every time "expenses" appears throughout the subchapter. "Expenses" does not include the other items listed in the definition of "liability," such as judgments or amounts paid in settlement.

5. Liability

"Liability" is defined for convenience in order to avoid repeated references to recoverable items throughout the subchapter. Even though the definition of "liability" includes amounts paid in settlement or to satisfy a judgment, indemnification against certain types of settlements and judgments is not allowed under several provisions of Subchapter E. For example, indemnification in suits brought by or in the right of the nonprofit corporation is limited to expenses (see Section 8.51(d)(1)), unless indemnification for a settlement is ordered by a court under Section 8.54(a)(3).

The definition of "liability" permits the indemnification only of "reasonable expenses incurred." The intention is that any portion of expenses falling outside the perimeter of reasonableness should not be advanced or indemnified. In contrast, unlike earlier versions of the act and statutes of many states, Section 8.50(5) provides that amounts paid to settle or satisfy substantive claims are not subject to a reasonableness test.

"Penalties" and "fines" are expressly included within the definition of "liability" so that, in appropriate cases, these items may also be indemnified. The purpose of this definition is to cover every type of monetary obligation that may be imposed upon a director, including civil penalties, restitution, and obligations to give notice. This definition also expressly includes as a "fine" the levy of excise taxes under the Internal Revenue Code pursuant to ERISA.

6. *Official Capacity*

The definition of "official capacity" is necessary because the term determines which of the two alternative standards of conduct set forth in Section 8.51(a)(1)(ii) applies: If action is taken in an "official capacity," the person to be indemnified must have reasonably believed he was acting in the best interests of the nonprofit corporation, while if the action in question was not taken in his "official capacity," he need only have reasonably believed that the conduct was not opposed to the best interests of the corporation. See also the Official Comment to Section 8.51(a).

7. *Party*

The definition of "party" includes every "individual who was, is, or is threatened to be made, a defendant or respondent in a proceeding." Thus, the definition includes present and former parties in addition to individuals currently or formerly threatened with being made a party. An individual who is only called as a witness is not a "party" within this definition and, as specifically provided in Section 8.58(d), payment or reimbursement of his expenses is not limited by this subchapter.

8. *Proceeding*

The definition of "proceeding" in this section supplements the definition of the same term in Section 1.40. Both definitions are nonexclusive and are intended to have an identical and very broad scope. The term is redefined in this section because corporate indemnification statutes have traditionally included a definition that emphasizes that its application is not restricted by the time a proceeding is commenced or resolved. The broad definition of "proceeding" ensures that the benefits of this subchapter will be available to directors in new and unexpected, as well as traditional, types of litigation or other adversarial matters, whether civil, criminal, administrative, or investigative. It also includes arbitration and other dispute resolution proceedings, lawsuit appeals, and petitions to review administrative actions.

§ 8.51. PERMISSIBLE INDEMNIFICATIONS

(a) Except as otherwise provided in this section, a nonprofit corporation may indemnify an individual who is a party to a proceeding because he or she is or was a director against liability incurred in the proceeding if:

  (1) the individual:

    (i) acted in good faith; and

    (ii) reasonably believed:

      (A) in the case of conduct in an official capacity, that the conduct was in the best interests of the corporation, and

      (B) in all other cases, that the individual's conduct was at least not opposed to the best interests of the corporation; and

    (iii) in the case of any criminal proceeding, had no reasonable cause to believe his or her conduct was unlawful; or

  (2) the individual engaged in conduct for which broader indemnification has been made permissible or obligatory under a provision of the articles of incorporation (as authorized by Section 2.02(b)(8)).

(b) A director's conduct with respect to an employee benefit plan for a purpose the director reasonably believed to be in the interests of the participants in and the beneficiaries of the plan is conduct that satisfies the requirement of subsection (a)(1)(ii)(B).

(c) The termination of a proceeding by judgment, order, settlement, or conviction, or upon a plea of nolo contendere or its equivalent, is not, of itself, determinative that the director did not meet the relevant standard of conduct described in this section.

(d) Unless ordered by a court under Section 8.54(a)(3), a nonprofit corporation may not indemnify a director:

(1) in connection with a proceeding by or in the right of the corporation, except for reasonable expenses incurred in connection with the proceeding if it is determined that the director has met the relevant standard of conduct under subsection (a); or

(2) in connection with any proceeding with respect to conduct for which the director was adjudged liable on the basis that the director received a financial benefit to which the director was not entitled, whether or not involving action in an official capacity.

Source Note: Patterned after Model Business Corporation Act, 3d Ed. (2002) § 8.51. Substantially a reenactment of Model Nonprofit Corporation Act (1987) § 8.51.

CROSS-REFERENCES

Advance for expenses, see § 8.53.

"Corporation" defined, see § 8.50.

Court-ordered indemnification, see § 8.54.

Derivative proceedings, see Ch. 13.

Determination of indemnification, see § 8.55.

"Director" defined, see § 8.50.

Director's conflicting interest transaction, see § 8.60.

"Expenses" defined, see § 8.50.

"Liability" defined, see § 8.50.

Liability-limitation provisions, see §§ 2.02 and 8.31.

Limits on indemnification, see § 8.58.

Mandatory indemnification, see § 8.52.

Obligatory indemnification, see §§ 2.02 and 8.58.

Officer indemnification, see § 8.56.

"Official capacity" defined, see § 8.50.

"Party" defined, see § 8.50.

"Proceeding" defined, see §§ 1.40 and 8.50.

Standards of conduct for directors, see § 8.30.

Standards of liability for directors, see § 8.31.

OFFICIAL COMMENT

1. Section 8.51(a)

Subsection 8.51(a) permits, but does not require, a nonprofit corporation to indemnify directors if the standards of subsection (a)(1) or of a provision of the articles referred to in subsection (a)(2) are met. This authorization is subject to any limitations set forth in the articles of incorporation pursuant to Section 8.58(c). Conduct that does not meet one of these standards is not eligible for permissible indemnification under the act, although court-ordered indemnification may be available under Section 8.54(a)(3). Conduct that falls within these limits does not automatically entitle directors to indemnification, although a corporation may obligate itself to indemnify directors to the maximum extent permitted by applicable law. See Section 8.58(a). Absent such an obligatory provision, Section 8.52 defines much narrower circumstances in which directors are entitled as a matter of right to indemnification.

Some state statutes provide separate, but usually similarly worded, standards for indemnification in third-party suits and indemnification in suits brought by or in the right of the corporation. Section 8.51 makes clear that the standards of conduct for which indemnification is permitted should not be dependent on the type of proceeding in which the claim arises. To prevent circularity in recovery, however, Section 8.51(d)(1) limits indemnification in connection with suits brought by or in the right of the corporation to expenses incurred and excludes amounts paid to settle such suits or to satisfy judgments. In addition, to discourage wrongdoing, Section 8.51(d)(2) bars indemnification where the director has been adjudged to have received a financial benefit to which the director is not entitled. Nevertheless, a court may order certain relief from these limitations under Section 8.54(a)(3).

The standards of conduct described in subsections (a)(1)(i) and (a)(1)(ii)(A) that must be met in order to permit the nonprofit corporation to indemnify a director are closely related, but not identical, to the standards of conduct imposed by Section 8.30 on members of the board of directors when discharging the duties of a director: good faith, reasonable belief that the best interests of the corporation are being served, and appropriate care (*i.e.*, that which a person in a like position would reasonably believe appropriate under similar circumstances). Unless authorized by a charter provision adopted pursuant to subsection (a)(2), it would be difficult to justify indemnifying a director who has not met any of these standards. It would not, however, make sense to require a director to meet all these standards in order to be indemnified because a director who does so would normally have no liability, at least to the corporation or its shareholders, under the terms of Section 8.31.

Section 8.51(a) adopts a middle ground by authorizing discretionary indemnification in the case of a failure to meet the appropriate care standard of Section 8.30(b) because public policy would not be well served by an absolute bar. A director's potential liability for conduct which does not on each and every occasion satisfy the appropriate care requirement of Section 8.30(b), or which with the benefit of hindsight could be so viewed, would in all likelihood deter qualified individuals from serving as directors and inhibit some who serve from taking risks. Permitting indemnification against such liability tends to counter these undesirable consequences. Accordingly, Section 8.51(a) authorizes indemnification at the nonprofit corporation's option even though Section 8.30's appropriate care requirement is not met, but only if the director satisfies the "good faith" and "corporation's best interests" standards. This reflects a judgment that, balancing public policy considerations, the nonprofit corporation may indemnify a director who does not satisfy the appropriate care test but not one who fails either of the other two standards.

As in the case of Section 8.30, where the concept of good faith is also used, no attempt is made in Section 8.51 to provide a definition. The concept involves a subjective test, which would permit indemnification for "a mistake of judgment," in the words of the Official Comment to Section 8.31, even though made unwisely or negligently by objective standards. Section 8.51 also requires, as does Section 8.30, a "reasonable" belief that conduct when acting in the director's official capacity was in the nonprofit corporation's best interests. It then adds a provision, not found in Section 8.30, relating to criminal proceedings that requires the director to have had no "reasonable cause" to believe that the conduct was unlawful. These both involve objective standards applicable to the director's belief concerning the effect of the conduct in question. Conduct includes both acts and omissions.

Section 8.51(a)(1)(ii)(B) requires, if not acting in the director's official capacity, that the action be "at least not opposed to" the nonprofit corporation's best interests. This standard is applicable to the director when serving another entity at the request of the corporation or when sued simply because of the director's status. The words "at least" qualify "not opposed to" in order to make it clear that this standard is an outer limit for conduct other than in an official capacity. While this subsection is directed at the interests of the indemnifying (*i.e.*, the requesting) corporation, a director serving another entity by request remains subject to the provisions of the law governing service to that entity, including provisions dealing with conflicts of interest. Should indemnification from the requesting corporation be sought by a director for acts done while serving another entity, which acts involved breach of the duty of loyalty owed to that entity, nothing in Section 8.51(a)(1)(ii)(B) would preclude the requesting corporation from considering, in assessing its own best interests, whether the fact that its director had engaged in a violation of the duty owed to the other entity was in fact "opposed to" the interests of the indemnifying corporation. Receipt of an improper financial benefit from a subsidiary would normally be opposed to the best interests of the parent.

Section 8.51 also permits indemnification in connection with a proceeding involving an alleged failure to satisfy legal standards other than the standards of conduct in Section 8.30, *e.g.*, violations of environmental laws.

In addition to indemnification under Section 8.51(a)(1), Section 8.51(a)(2) permits indemnification under the standard of conduct set forth in a charter provision adopted pursuant to Section 2.02(b)(8). Based on such a charter provision, Section 8.51(a)(2) permits indemnification in connection with claims by third parties and, through Section 8.56, applies to officers as well as directors. (This goes beyond the scope of a charter provision adopted pursuant to Section 2.02(c), which can only limit liability of directors against claims by the corporation or its members.) Section 8.51(a)(2) is subject to the prohibition of subsection (d)(1) against indemnification of settlements and judgments in derivative suits. It is also subject to the prohibition of subsection (d)(2) against indemnification for receipt of an improper financial benefit; however, this prohibition is already subsumed in the exception contained in Section 2.02(b)(8)(i).

2. Section 8.51(b)

As discussed in the Official Comment to Section 8.50(2), ERISA requires that a "fiduciary" (as defined in ERISA) discharge the fiduciary's duties "solely in the interest" of the participants in and beneficiaries of an employee benefit plan. Section 8.51(b) makes clear that a director who is serving as a trustee or fiduciary for an employee benefit plan under ERISA meets the standard for indemnification under Section 8.51(a) if the director reasonably believes the conduct while serving in that capacity was in the best interests of the participants in and beneficiaries of the plan.

This standard is arguably an exception to the more general standard that conduct not in an official corporate capacity is indemnifiable if it is "at least not opposed to" the best interests of the nonprofit corporation. However, a corporation that causes a director to undertake fiduciary duties in connection with an employee benefit plan should expect the director to act in the best interests of the plan's beneficiaries or participants. Thus, subsection (b) establishes and provides a standard for indemnification that is consistent with the statutory policies embodied in ERISA. See Official Comment to Section 8.50(2).

3. Section 8.51(c)

The purpose of Section 8.51(c) is to reject the argument that indemnification is automatically improper whenever a proceeding has been concluded on a basis that does not exonerate the director claiming indemnification. Even though a final judgment or conviction is not automatically determinative of the issue of whether the minimum standard of conduct was met, any judicial determination of substantive liability would in most instances be entitled to considerable weight. By the same token, it is clear that the termination of a proceeding by settlement or plea of nolo contendere should not of itself create a presumption that conduct either met or did not meet the relevant standard of subsection (a) since a settlement or nolo plea may be agreed to for many reasons unrelated to the merits of the claim. On the other hand, a final determination of nonliability (including one based on a liability-limitation provision adopted under Section 2.02(c) or an acquittal in a criminal case) automatically entitles the director to indemnification of expenses under Section 8.52.

Section 8.51(c) applies to the indemnification of expenses in derivative proceedings (as well as to indemnification in third-party suits). The most likely application of this subsection in connection with a derivative proceeding will be to a settlement since a judgment or order would normally result in liability to the nonprofit corporation and thereby preclude indemnification under Section 8.51(d)(1), unless ordered by a court under Section 8.54(a)(3). In the rare event that a judgment or order entered against the director did not include a determination of liability to the corporation, the entry of the judgment or order would not be determinative that the director failed to meet the relevant standard of conduct.

4. Section 8.51(d)

This subsection makes clear that indemnification is not permissible under Section 8.51 in two situations: (i) a proceeding brought by or in the right of a nonprofit corporation that results in a settlement or a judgment against the director and (ii) a proceeding that results in a judgment that an improper financial benefit was received as a result of the director's conduct.

Permitting indemnification of settlements and judgments in derivative proceedings would give rise to a circularity in which the nonprofit corporation receiving payment of damages by the director in the settlement or judgment (less attorneys' fees) would then immediately return the same amount to the director (including attorneys' fees) as indemnification. Thus, the corporation would be in a poorer economic position than if there had been no proceeding. This situation is most egregious in the case of a judgment against the director. Even in the case of a settlement, however, prohibiting indemnification is not unfair. Under the revised procedures of Chapter 13, upon motion by the corporation, the court must dismiss any derivative proceeding which independent directors (or a court-appointed panel) determine in good faith, after a reasonable inquiry, is not in the best interests of the corporation. The liability of directors of a charitable corporation is limited by Section 8.31(d). Furthermore, under Section 2.02(c), the directors of a corporation which is not a charitable corporation have the opportunity to propose to members adoption of a provision similarly limiting the liability of directors in derivative proceedings. In view of these considerations, it is unlikely that directors will be unnecessarily exposed to meritless actions. In addition, if directors were to be indemnified for amounts paid in settlement, the dismissal procedures in Chapter 13 might not be fully employed since it could be less expensive for the corporation to indemnify the directors immediately for the amount of the claimed damages rather than bear the expense of the inquiry required by Chapter 13. The result could increase the filing of meritless derivative proceedings in order to generate small but immediately paid attorneys' fees. Despite the prohibition on indemnification of a settlement or a judgment in a derivative proceeding, subsection (d)(1) permits indemnification of the related reasonable expenses incurred in the proceeding so long as the director meets the relevant standard of conduct set forth in Section 8.51(a). In addition, indemnification of derivative proceeding expenses and amounts paid in settlement where the relevant standard was not met may be ordered by a court under Section 8.54(a)(3).

Indemnification under Section 8.51 is also prohibited if there has been an adjudication that a director received an improper financial benefit (*i.e.*, a benefit to which the director is not entitled), even if, for example, the director acted in a manner not opposed to the best interests of the nonprofit corporation. For example, improper use of inside information for financial benefit should not be an action for which the corporation may elect to provide indemnification, even if the corporation was not thereby harmed. Given the express language of Section 2.02(b)(8) establishing the outer limit of an indemnification provision contained in the articles of incorporation, a director found to have received an improper financial benefit would not be permitted indemnification under subsection (a)(2). Although it is unlikely that a director found to have received an improper financial benefit could meet the standard in subsection (a)(1)(ii)(B), this limitation is made explicit in Section 8.51(d)(2). Section 8.54(a)(3) permits a director found liable in a proceeding referred to in subsection (d)(2) to petition a court for a judicial determination of entitlement to indemnification for reasonable expenses. The language of Section 8.51(d)(2) is based on Section 2.02(c)(1) and, thus, the same standards should be used in interpreting the application of both provisions. Although a settlement may create an obligation to pay money, it should not be construed for purposes of this subchapter as an adjudication of liability.

§ 8.52. MANDATORY INDEMNIFICATION

A nonprofit corporation must indemnify a director to the extent the director was successful, on the merits or otherwise, in the defense of any proceeding to which the director was a party because the director was a director of the corporation against reasonable expenses incurred by the director in connection with the proceeding.

> *Source Note:* Patterned in part after Model Business Corporation Act, 3d Ed. (2002) § 8.52. Derived from Model Nonprofit Corporation Act (1987) § 8.52.

CROSS-REFERENCES

"Corporation" defined, see § 8.50.

Court-ordered indemnification, see § 8.54.

"Director" defined, see § 8.50.

"Expenses" defined, see § 8.50.

Limits on indemnification, see § 8.58.

"Party" defined, see § 8.50.

Permissible indemnification, see § 8.51.

"Proceeding" defined, see §§ 1.40 and 8.50.

OFFICIAL COMMENT

Section 8.51 determines whether indemnification may be made voluntarily by a nonprofit corporation if it elects to do so. Section 8.52 determines whether a nonprofit corporation must indemnify a director for his expenses; in other words, Section 8.52 creates a statutory right of indemnification in favor of the director who meets the requirements of the section. Enforcement of this right by judicial proceeding is specifically contemplated by Section 8.54(a)(1). Section 8.54(b) gives the director a statutory right to recover expenses incurred by him in enforcing his statutory right to indemnification under Section 8.52.

This section is consistent with the argument accepted in *Merritt-Chapman & Scott Corp. v. Wolfson*, 321 A.2D 138 (Del. Super. 1974), that a defendant may be entitled to partial mandatory indemnification if, by plea bargaining or otherwise, he was able to obtain the dismissal of some but not all counts of an indictment. In contrast, Section 8.52 of the Model Business Corporation Act provides that indemnification is mandatory only if a defendant is "wholly successful," in other words only if the entire proceeding is disposed of on a basis that does not involve a finding of liability.

The language in earlier versions of the act and in many other state statutes that the basis of success may be "on the merits or otherwise" is retained. While this standard may result in an occasional defendant becoming entitled to indemnification because of procedural defenses not related to the merits, *e.g.*, the statute of limitations or disqualification of the plaintiff, it is unreasonable to require a defendant with a valid procedural defense to undergo a possibly prolonged and expensive trial on the merits in order to establish eligibility for mandatory indemnification.

§ 8.53. ADVANCE FOR EXPENSES

(a) A nonprofit corporation may, before final disposition of a proceeding, advance funds to pay for or reimburse the reasonable expenses incurred by an individual who is a party to a proceeding because he or she is or was a director if the individual delivers to the corporation:

(1) an affirmation in the form of a record of his or her good faith belief that he or she has met the relevant standard of conduct described in Section 8.51 or that the proceeding involves conduct for which liability has been eliminated by Section 8.31(d) or under a provision of the articles of incorporation as authorized by Section 2.02(c); and

(2) an undertaking in the form of a record to repay any funds advanced if the individual is not entitled to mandatory indemnification under Section 8.52 and it is ultimately determined under Section 8.54 or 8.55 that the

individual has not met the relevant standard of conduct described in Section 8.51.

(b) The undertaking required by subsection (a)(2) must be an unlimited general obligation of the director, but need not be secured and may be accepted without reference to the financial ability of the director to make repayment.

(c) Authorizations under this section must be made:

(1) by the board of directors:

(i) if there are two or more disinterested directors, by a majority vote of all the disinterested directors (a majority of whom will constitute a quorum for that purpose) or by a majority of the members of a committee of two or more disinterested directors appointed by such a vote; or

(ii) if there are fewer than two disinterested directors, by the vote necessary for action by the board in accordance with Section 8.24(c), in which authorization directors who do not qualify as disinterested directors may participate; or

(2) by the members.

Source Note: Patterned after Model Business Corporation Act, 3d Ed. (2002) § 8.53. Derived from Model Nonprofit Corporation Act (1987) § 8.53.

CROSS-REFERENCES

Committees of the board, see § 8.25.

"Corporation" defined, see § 8.50.

Court-ordered indemnification, see § 8.54.

Determination of indemnification, see § 8.55.

"Director" defined, see § 8.50.

"Disinterested director" defined, see § 8.50.

"Expenses" defined, see § 8.50.

Limits on advance for expenses, see § 8.58.

"Party" defined, see § 8.50.

"Proceeding" defined, see §§ 1.40 and 8.50.

Quorum of directors, see § 8.24.

Standard for indemnification, see § 8.51.

OFFICIAL COMMENT

Section 8.53 authorizes, but does not require, a nonprofit corporation to pay for or reimburse, in advance, a director's reasonable expenses if two conditions are met. This authorization is subject to any limitations set forth in the articles of incorporation pursuant to Section 8.58(c).

Section 8.53 recognizes an important difference between indemnification and an advance for expenses: indemnification is retrospective and, therefore, enables the persons determining whether to indemnify to do so on the basis of known facts, including the outcome of the proceeding. An advance for expenses is necessarily prospective and the individuals making the decision whether to advance expenses generally have fewer known facts on which to base their decision. Indemnification may include reimbursement for nonadvanced expenses.

Section 8.53 reflects a determination that it is sound public policy to permit the nonprofit corporation to advance (by direct payment or by reimbursement) the defense expenses of a director so long as the director believes in good faith that he or she was acting in accordance with the relevant standard for indemnification set forth in Section 8.51 or that the proceeding involves conduct for which liability has been eliminated by Section 8.31(d) or pursuant to Section 2.02(c) and agrees to repay any amounts advanced if it is ultimately determined that the director is not entitled to indemnification. This policy is based upon the view that a person who serves an entity in a representative capacity should not be required to finance his or her own defense. Moreover, adequate legal representation often requires substantial expenses during the proceeding and many individuals are willing to serve as directors only if they have the assurance that the corporation has the power to advance these expenses. In fact, many corporations contractually obligate themselves (by a provision in the articles or bylaws or otherwise) to advance expenses for directors. See Section 8.58(a).

Section 8.53(a) requires an affirmation in record form by the director of his or her good faith belief that he or she has met the relevant standard of conduct necessary for indemnification by the nonprofit corporation and a written undertaking by the director to repay any funds advanced if it is ultimately determined that he or she has not met the standard of conduct. A single undertaking may cover all funds advanced in connection with the proceeding. Under Section 8.53(b), the undertaking need not be secured and financial ability to repay is not a prerequisite. The theory underlying this subsection is that wealthy directors should not be favored over directors whose financial resources are modest. The undertaking must be made by the director and not by a third party. If the director or the corporation wishes some third party to be responsible for the director's obligation in this regard, either of them is free to make those arrangements separately with the third party.

In the absence of an obligatory provision established pursuant to Section 8.58(a), the decision to advance expenses must be made in accordance with Section 8.53(c). Section 8.53 does not address the question of the standard by which the decision to advance expenses is to be made. Accordingly, the standards of Section 8.30 should, in general, govern. The conditions for advance for expenses are different from the conditions for indemnification. Directors normally meet the standards of Section 8.30 in approving an advance for expenses if they limit their consideration to the financial ability of the nonprofit corporation to pay the amounts in question and do not have actual knowledge of facts sufficient to cause them to believe that the subsection (a)(1) affirmation was not made in good faith. The directors are not required by Section 8.30 to make any inquiry into the merits of the proceeding or the good faith of the belief stated in that affirmation. Thus, in the great majority of cases, no special inquiry will be required. The directors acting on a decision to advance expenses may, but are not required to, consider any additional matters they deem appropriate and may condition the advance of expenses upon compliance with any additional requirements they desire to impose.

Advance for expenses under Section 8.53 may be made obligatory upon a nonprofit corporation pursuant to Section 8.58(a) by a provision set forth in its articles of incorporation or bylaws, in a resolution of its members or board of directors, in a contract, or otherwise. However, any such provision must comply with the requirements of subsection (a) of Section 8.53 regarding furnishing of an affirmation and undertaking. No other procedures are contemplated, although obligatory provisions may include notice and other procedures in connection with advancement of expenses and indemnification requests.

At least one court has held that a general obligatory provision requiring indemnification to the extent permitted by law does not include advance for expenses if not specifically mentioned. *See, e.g.*, *Advanced Mining Systems, Inc. v. Fricke*, 623 A.2D 82 (Del. Ch. 1992). Section 8.58(a) requires the opposite result, unless provided otherwise.

The decision to advance expenses is required to be made only one time with respect to each proceeding rather than each time a request for payment of expenses is received by the nonprofit corporation. The directors are, however, free to reconsider the decision at any time, *e.g.*, upon a change in the financial ability of the corporation to pay the amounts in question. The decision as to the reasonableness of any expenses may be made by any officer or agent of the corporation duly authorized to do so.

The procedures set forth in subsection (c) for authorizing an advance for expenses parallel the procedures set forth in Section 8.55(b) for selecting the person or persons to make the determination that indemnification is permissible. Unless the authorization is made by the members under subsection (c)(2), first resort must be made to subsection (c)(1)(i). If it is unavailable, then resort may be made to subsection (c)(1)(ii).

Under subsection (c)(1)(i), the vote required when the disinterested directors act as a group is an absolute majority of their number. A majority of the disinterested directors constitutes a quorum for board action for this purpose.

The committee of two or more disinterested directors referred to in subsection (c)(1)(i) may include a standing committee of the board of directors to which the power to authorize advances for expenses has been delegated, so long as (1) the committee was appointed by a majority vote of directors who were, at the time of appointment of the committee, not parties to the proceeding in connection with which the advance is being sought, and (2) the advance is authorized by a majority vote of members of the committee who, at the time of the vote, are disinterested directors.

Under subsection (c)(1)(ii), which is available only if subsection (c)(1)(i) is not available, the board's action must be taken in accordance with Sections 8.20 or 8.21, as the case may be, and directors who are not disinterested directors may participate in the vote. Allowing non-disinterested directors to participate in the authorization decision, if there is no or only one disinterested director, is a principle of prudence that is based on the concept that if there are not at least two disinterested directors, then it is preferable to return the power to make the decision to the full board (even though it includes non-disinterested directors) rather than to leave it with one disinterested director. An interested director should absent himself from any meeting considering a request for advance for expenses by him or the appointment of a committee to consider such a request.

Illustration 1: The board consists of 15 directors, 4 of whom are interested. Of the 11 disinterested directors, 9 are present at the meeting at which the authorization is made or the committee is appointed.

Under subsection (c)(1)(i), a quorum is present and at least 6 of the 9 disinterested directors present at the board meeting must authorize any advance for expenses because 6 is an absolute majority of the 11 disinterested directors. Alternatively, 6 of the 9 disinterested directors present at the board meeting may appoint a committee of 2 to all (11) of the disinterested directors to decide whether to authorize the advance. Action by the committee requires an absolute majority of the members appointed.

Illustration 2: The board consists of 15 directors, 14 of whom are interested.

Subsection (c)(1)(i) is not available because the number of disinterested directors, 1, is less than 2. Accordingly, the decision must be made by the board under subsection (c)(1)(ii) (or, as is always permitted, by the members under subsection (c)(2)).

Authorizations by members rather than by directors are permitted by Section 8.53(c)(2), but memberships under the control of directors who at the time do not qualify as disinterested directors may not be voted on the authorizations of eligibility for indemnification. This does not affect rules governing the authorization as to the presence of a quorum at the meeting.

The fact that there has been an advance for expenses does not determine whether a director is entitled to indemnification. Repayment of any advance is required only if it is ultimately determined that the director did not meet the relevant standard of conduct in Section 8.51. A proceeding will often terminate without a judicial or other determination of whether the director's conduct met that standard. Nevertheless, the board of directors should make, or cause to be made, an affirmative determination of entitlement to indemnification at the conclusion of the proceeding. This decision should be made in accordance with the procedures set forth in Section 8.55.

Judicial enforcement of rights granted by or pursuant to Section 8.53 is specifically contemplated by Section 8.54.

§ 8.54. COURT-ORDERED INDEMNIFICATION AND ADVANCE FOR EXPENSES

(a) A director who is a party to a proceeding because he or she is or was a director may apply for indemnification or an advance for expenses to the court conducting the proceeding or to another court of competent jurisdiction. After receipt of an application and after giving any notice it considers necessary, the court must:

(1) order indemnification if the court determines that the director is entitled to mandatory indemnification under Section 8.52;

(2) order indemnification or advance for expenses if the court determines that the director is entitled to indemnification or advance for expenses pursuant to a provision authorized by Section 8.58(a); or

(3) order indemnification or advance for expenses if the court determines, in view of all the relevant circumstances, that it is fair and reasonable:

(i) to indemnify the director, or

(ii) to advance expenses to the director, even if the director has not met the relevant standard of conduct set forth in Section 8.51(a), failed to comply with Section 8.53, or was adjudged liable in a proceeding referred to in Section 8.51(d)(1) or (d)(2), but if the director was adjudged so liable his or her indemnification must be limited to reasonable expenses incurred in connection with the proceeding.

(b) If the court determines that the director is entitled to indemnification under subsection (a)(1) or to indemnification or advance for expenses under subsection (a)(2), it must also order the nonprofit corporation to pay the director's reasonable expenses incurred in connection with obtaining court-ordered indemnification or advance for expenses. If the court determines that the director is entitled to indemnification or advance for expenses under subsection (a)(3), it may also order the corporation to pay the director's reasonable expenses to obtain court-ordered indemnification or advance for expenses.

Source Note: Patterned after Model Business Corporation Act, 3d Ed. (2002) § 8.54. Derived from Model Nonprofit Corporation Act (1987) § 8.54.

CROSS-REFERENCES

Advance for expenses, see § 8.53.

"Corporation" defined, see § 8.50.

"Director" defined, see § 8.50.

"Expenses" defined, see § 8.50.

Limits on indemnification and advance for expenses, see § 8.58.

Mandatory indemnification, see § 8.52.

Obligatory indemnification, see § 8.58.

"Party" defined, see § 8.50.

Permissible indemnification, see § 8.51.

"Proceeding" defined, see §§ 1.40 and 8.50.

OFFICIAL COMMENT

Section 8.54(a) provides for court-ordered indemnification in three situations:

(1) A director is entitled to mandatory indemnification under Section 8.52. If so, the director may enforce that right by judicial proceeding.

(2) A director is entitled to indemnification or advance for expenses pursuant to a provision in the articles or bylaws, board or member resolution, or contract. If so, the director may enforce that right by judicial proceeding. To the extent that these rights are contractual, the nonprofit corporation may have contractual defenses. If the corporation has contracted to indemnify a director to the fullest extent permitted by law, a court may, nevertheless, deny an advance for expenses if it determines that the director did not have, at the time he delivered the affirmation required by Section 8.53(a)(1), a good faith belief that he met the relevant standard of conduct.

(3) A court in its discretion determines that it is fair and reasonable under all the relevant circumstances to order an advance for expenses or indemnification for the amount of a settlement or judgment (in addition to expenses), whether or not the director met the relevant standard of conduct in Section 8.51 or is otherwise ineligible for indemnification. However, there are two exceptions: an adverse judgment in a derivative proceeding (Section 8.51(d)(1)) and an adverse judgment in

a proceeding charging receipt of an improper financial benefit (Section 8.51(d)(2)), although in either case the court may order payment of expenses. Thus, with these exceptions, Section 8.54(a)(3) permits a court to order indemnification for amounts paid in settlement of and expenses incurred in connection with a derivative proceeding or a proceeding charging receipt of an improper financial benefit. Section 8.54(a)(3) applies to (a) a situation in which a provision in the articles of incorporation, bylaws, resolution, or contract obligates the nonprofit corporation to indemnify or to advance expenses but the relevant standard of conduct has not been met, and (b) a situation involving a permissive provision pursuant to which the board declines to exercise its authority to indemnify or to advance expenses. However, in determining whether indemnification or expense advance would be "fair and reasonable," a court should give appropriate deference to an informed decision of a board or committee made in good faith and based upon full information. Ordinarily, a court should not determine that it is "fair and reasonable" to order indemnification or expense advance where the director has not met conditions and procedures to which he agreed.

A director seeking court-ordered indemnification or expense advance under Section 8.54(a)(3) must show that there are facts peculiar to his situation that make it fair and reasonable to both the nonprofit corporation and to the director to override an intracorporate declination or any otherwise applicable statutory prohibition against indemnification, *e.g.*, Section 8.51(a) or (d).

Aside from the two exceptions noted above and other than the fairness and reasonableness requirement, there are no statutory outer limits on the court's power to order indemnification under Section 8.54(a)(3). In an appropriate case, a court may wish to refer to the provisions of Sections 2.02(c) and 8.31(d) establishing the outer limits of director exoneration. It would be an extraordinary situation in which a court would want to provide indemnification going beyond the limits of Sections 2.02(c) and 8.31(d), but if the court, as the independent decision-maker, finds that it is "fair and reasonable," then the court is permitted to do so. It should be emphasized again, however, that the director seeking indemnification must make a showing of fairness and reasonableness and that exercise of the power granted by Section 8.54(a)(3) is committed to the court's discretion.

Among the factors a court may want to consider are the gravity of the offense, the financial impact upon the nonprofit corporation, or, in the case of an advance for expenses, the inability of the director to finance his defense. A court may want to give special attention to certain other issues. First, has the corporation joined in the application to the court for indemnification or an advance for expenses? This factor may be particularly important where under Section 8.51(d) indemnification is not permitted for an amount paid in settlement of a proceeding brought by or in the right of the corporation. Second, in a case where indemnification would have been available under Section 8.51(a)(2) if the corporation had adopted a provision authorized by Section 2.02(b)(8), was the decision to adopt such a provision presented to and rejected by the members and, if not, would exculpation of the director's conduct have resulted under Section 8.31(d) or a charter provision adopted under Section 2.02(c)? Third, in connection with considering indemnification for expenses under Section 8.51(d)(2) in a proceeding in which a director was adjudged liable for receiving a financial benefit to which he or she was not entitled, was such financial benefit insubstantial—particularly in relation to the other aspects of the transaction involved—and what was the degree of the director's involvement in the transaction and the decision to participate?

Under Section 8.54(b), if a director successfully sues to enforce his or her right to indemnification of expenses under subsection (a)(1) or to indemnification or advance for expenses under subsection (a)(2), then the court must order the nonprofit corporation to pay the director's expenses in the enforcement proceeding. However, if a director successfully sues for indemnification or advance for expenses under subsection (a)(3), then the court may (but is not required to) order the corporation to pay the director's expenses in the proceeding under subsection (a)(3). The basis for the distinction is that the corporation breached its obligation in the first two cases but not in the third.

Application for indemnification under Section 8.54 may be made either to the court in which the proceeding was heard or to another court of appropriate jurisdiction. For example, a defendant in a criminal proceeding who has been convicted but believes that indemnification would be proper could apply either to the court which heard the criminal proceeding or bring an action against the nonprofit corporation in another forum.

A decision by the board of directors not to oppose the request for indemnification is governed by the general standards of conduct of Section 8.30. Even if the nonprofit corporation decided not to oppose the request, the court must satisfy itself that the person seeking indemnification is deserving of receiving it under Section 8.54.

As provided in Section 8.58(c), a nonprofit corporation may limit the rights of a director under Section 8.54 by a provision in its articles of incorporation. In the absence of such a provision, the court has general power to exercise the authority granted under this section.

§ 8.55. DETERMINATION AND AUTHORIZATION OF INDEMNIFICATION

(a) A nonprofit corporation may not indemnify a director under Section 8.51 unless authorized for a specific proceeding after a determination has been made that indemnification of the director is permissible because the director has met the relevant standard of conduct set forth in Section 8.51.

(b) The determination may be made:

(1) if there are two or more disinterested directors, by a majority vote of all the disinterested directors (a majority of whom will constitute a quorum for that purpose), or by a majority of the members of a committee of two or more disinterested directors appointed by such a vote;

(2) by special legal counsel:

(i) selected in the manner prescribed in subdivision (1), or

(ii) if there are fewer than two disinterested directors, selected by the board of directors (in which selection directors who do not qualify as disinterested directors may participate); or

(3) by the members.

(c) Authorization of indemnification must be made in the same manner as the determination that indemnification is permissible, except that if there are fewer than two disinterested directors or if the determination is made by special legal counsel, authorization of indemnification must be made by those entitled under subsection (b)(2)(ii) to select special legal counsel.

Source Note: Patterned after Model Business Corporation Act, 3d Ed. (2002) § 8.55. Derived from Model Nonprofit Corporation Act (1987) § 8.55.

CROSS-REFERENCES

Advance for expenses, see § 8.53.

Committees of the board, see § 8.25.

"Corporation" defined, see § 8.50.

"Director" defined, see § 8.50.

"Disinterested director" defined, see § 8.50.

"Party" defined, see § 8.50.

"Proceeding" defined, see §§ 1.40 and 8.50.

Quorum of directors, see § 8.24.

Standard for indemnification, see § 8.51.

OFFICIAL COMMENT

Section 8.55 provides the method for determining whether a nonprofit corporation should indemnify a director under Section 8.51. In this section a distinction is made between a "determination" and an "authorization." A "determination" involves a decision whether under the circumstances the person seeking indemnification has met the relevant standard of conduct under Section 8.51 and is therefore eligible for indemnification. This decision may be made by the individuals or groups described in Section 8.55(b). In addition, after a favorable "determination" has been made, the corporation must decide whether to "authorize" indemnification except to the extent that an obligatory provision under Section 8.58(a) is applicable. This decision includes a review of the reasonableness of the expenses, the financial ability of the corporation to make the payment, and the judgment whether limited financial resources should be devoted to this or some other use by the corporation. While special legal counsel may make the "determination" of eligibility for indemnification, counsel may not "authorize" the indemnification. The existence of an obligation to "authorize" indemnification is subject to the existence of an obligatory provision under Section 8.58(a).

Section 8.55(b) establishes procedures for selecting the person or persons who will make the determination of permissibility of indemnification. As indicated in the Official Comment to Section 8.53(c), the committee referred to in subsection (b)(1) may include a standing committee of the board to which the power to determine whether to indemnify a director has been delegated so long as the appointment and composition of the committee members comply with subsection (b)(1). In selecting special legal counsel under subsection (b)(2), directors who are parties to the proceeding may participate in the decision if there are insufficient disinterested directors to satisfy subsection (b)(1). Directors who do not qualify as disinterested directors may also participate in the decision to "authorize" indemnification on the basis of a favorable "determination" if necessary to permit action by the board of directors. The authorization of indemnification is the decision that results in payment of any amounts to be indemnified. This limited participation of interested directors in the authorization decision is justified by the principle of necessity.

Under subsection (b)(1), the vote required when the disinterested directors act as a group is an absolute majority of their number. A majority of the disinterested directors constitutes a quorum for board action for this purpose.

If there are not at least two disinterested directors, then the determination of entitlement to indemnification must be made by special legal counsel or by the members.

Legal counsel authorized to make the required determination is referred to as "special legal counsel." In earlier versions of the act, and in the statutes of many states, reference is made to "independent" legal counsel. The word "special" is felt to be more descriptive of the role to be performed; it is intended that the counsel selected should be independent in accordance with governing legal precepts. "Special legal counsel" normally should be counsel having no prior professional relationship with those seeking indemnification, should be retained for the specific occasion, and should not be or have been either inside counsel or regular outside counsel to the nonprofit corporation. Special legal counsel should also not have any familial, financial, or other relationship with any of those seeking indemnification that would, in the circumstances, reasonably be expected to exert an influence on counsel in making the determination. It is important that the process be sufficiently flexible to permit selection of counsel in light of the particular circumstances and so that unnecessary expense may be avoided. Hence the phrase "special legal counsel" is not defined in the statute.

Determinations by members rather than by directors or special legal counsel are permitted by Section 8.55(b)(3), but memberships under the control of directors who at the time do not qualify as disinterested directors may not be voted on the determination of eligibility for indemnification. This does not affect rules governing the determination as to the presence of a quorum at the meeting.

Section 8.55 is subject to Section 8.58(a), which permits the nonprofit corporation to obligate itself in advance to provide indemnification or to advance expenses.

§ 8.56. INDEMNIFICATION OF OFFICERS

(a) A nonprofit corporation may indemnify and advance expenses under this [subchapter] to an officer of the corporation who is a party to a proceeding because he or she is or was an officer of the corporation

(1) to the same extent as a director; and

(2) if he or she is an officer but not a director, to such further extent as may be provided by the articles of incorporation, the bylaws, a resolution of the board of directors, or contract except for:

   (i) liability in connection with a proceeding by or in the right of the corporation other than for reasonable expenses incurred in connection with the proceeding, or

   (ii) liability arising out of conduct that constitutes:

      (A) receipt by the officer of a financial benefit to which the officer is not entitled,

      (B) an intentional infliction of harm on the corporation or the members, or

      (C) an intentional violation of criminal law.

(b) The provisions of subsection (a)(2) apply to an officer who is also a director if the basis on which he or she is made a party to the proceeding is an act or omission solely as an officer.

(c) An officer of a corporation who is not a director is entitled to mandatory indemnification under Section 8.52, and may apply to a court under Section 8.54 for indemnification or an advance for expenses, in each case to the same extent to which a director may be entitled to indemnification or advance for expenses under those provisions.

Source Note: Patterned after Model Business Corporation Act, 3d Ed. (2002) § 8.56. Derived from Model Nonprofit Corporation Act (1987) § 8.56.

CROSS-REFERENCES

Advance for expenses, see § 8.53.

Agents, indemnification of and advance for expenses for, see § 8.58.

"Corporation" defined, see § 8.50.

"Director" defined, see § 8.50.

Employees, indemnification of and advance for expenses for, see § 8.58.

"Expenses" defined, see § 8.50.

"Liability" defined, see § 8.50.

Limits on rights to indemnification and advance for expenses, see § 8.58.

Obligatory indemnification, see §§ 2.02 and 8.58.

"Officer" defined, see § 8.50.

Officer standards of conduct, see § 8.42.

"Party" defined, see § 8.50.

"Proceeding" defined, see §§ 1.40 and 8.50.

Volunteers, indemnification of and advance of expenses for, see § 8.58.

OFFICIAL COMMENT

1. In General

Section 8.56 correlates the general legal principles relating to the indemnification of officers of the nonprofit corporation with the limitations on indemnification in Subchapter E. This correlation may be summarized in general terms as follows.

(1) An officer of a corporation who is not a director may be indemnified by the corporation on a discretionary basis to the same extent as though he were a director, and, in addition, may have additional indemnification rights apart from Subchapter E, but the outer limits of such rights are specified. See Section 8.56(a)(2) and (c).

(2) An officer who is also a director of the corporation is entitled to the indemnification rights of a director and of an officer who is not a director (see preceding paragraph) if his conduct that is the subject of the proceeding was solely in his capacity as an officer. See Section 8.56(b).

(3) An officer of a corporation who is not a director has the right of mandatory indemnification granted to directors under Section 8.52 and the right to apply for court-ordered indemnification under Section 8.54. See Section 8.56(c).

Section 8.56 does not deal with indemnification of employees and agents because the concerns of self-dealing that arise when directors provide for their own indemnification and expense advance (and sometimes for senior executive officers) are not present when directors (or officers) provide for indemnification and expense advance for employees and agents who are not directors or officers. Moreover, the rights of employees and agents to indemnification and advance for expenses derive from principles of agency, the doctrine of respondeat superior, collective bargaining or other contractual arrangements rather than from a corporation statute. It would be presumptuous for a corporation statute to seek to limit the indemnification bargain that a nonprofit corporation may wish to make with those it hires or retains. The same standard applicable to directors and officers may not be appropriate for office workers and hazardous-waste workers, brokers and custodians, engineers and farm workers. None of their roles or responsibilities are prescribed by the act.

Section 3.02 grants broad powers to nonprofit corporations, including powers to make contracts, appoint and fix the compensation of employees and agents, and make payments furthering the activities and affairs of the corporation. Many corporations provide for the exercise of these powers in the same provisions in the articles, bylaws, or otherwise in which they provide for expense advance and indemnification for directors and officers.

Indemnification may also be provided to protect employees or agents from liabilities incurred while serving at a nonprofit corporation's request as a director, officer, partner, trustee, or agent of another commercial, charitable, or nonprofit venture.

Although employees and agents are not covered by Subchapter E, the principles and procedures set forth in the subchapter for indemnification and advance for expenses for directors and officers may be helpful to counsel and courts in dealing with indemnification and expense advance for employees and agents.

Careful consideration should be given to extending mandatory maximum indemnification and expense advance to employees and agents. The same considerations that may favor mandatory maximum indemnification for directors and officers—*e.g.*, encouraging qualified individuals to serve—may not be present in the cases of employees and agents. Many nonprofit corporations may prefer to retain the discretion to decide, on a case-by-case basis, whether to indemnify and advance expenses to employees and agents (and perhaps even officers, especially nonexecutive officers) rather than binding themselves in advance to do so.

2. Officers Who Are Not Directors

While Section 8.56 does not prescribe the standards governing the rights of officers to indemnification, subsection (a) does set outer limits beyond which the nonprofit corporation may not indemnify. These outer limits for officers (see subsection (a)(2)) are substantially the same as the limits on the corporation's power to indemnify directors: (i) in a proceeding by or in the right of the corporation, indemnification is not allowed other than for reasonable expenses incurred in connection therewith, and (ii) in any proceeding, indemnification is not allowed in those situations in which directors' liability to the corporation or its members would not be eliminated by Section 8.31(d) or a provision included in the articles pursuant to Section 2.02(c), *i.e.*, where there has been receipt of a financial benefit to which the director is not entitled, intentional infliction of harm on the corporation or members, or intentional violation of criminal law. Since officers are held to substantially the same standards of conduct as directors (see Section 8.42), there does not appear to be any reasoned basis for granting officers greater indemnification rights as a substantive matter. Procedurally, however, there is an important difference. To permit greater flexibility, officers may be indemnified (within the above-mentioned outer limits) with respect to conduct that does not meet the standards set by Section 8.51(a)(1) simply by authorization of the board of directors, whereas directors' indemnification can reach beyond those standards, as contemplated by Section 8.51(a)(2), only with a member-approved provision included in the articles pursuant to Section 2.02(b)(8). This procedural difference reflects the reduced risk of self-dealing as to officers.

Section 8.56(c) grants nondirector officers the same rights to mandatory indemnification under Section 8.52 and to apply to a court for indemnification under Section 8.54 as are granted to directors. Since their substantive rights to indemnification are essentially the same as those of directors, it is appropriate to grant officers the same affirmative procedural rights to judicial relief as are provided to directors.

The broad authority in Section 8.56(a)(2) to grant indemnification may be limited by appropriate provisions in the articles of incorporation. See Section 8.58(c).

3. *Officers Who Are Also Directors*

Subsection (b) provides, in effect, that an officer of the nonprofit corporation who is also a director is subject to the same standards of indemnification as other directors and cannot avail himself of the provisions of subsection (a) unless he can establish that the act or omission that is the subject of the proceeding was committed solely in his capacity as officer. Thus, a vice president for sales who is also a director and whose actions failed to meet Section 8.51(a) standards could be indemnified provided that his conduct was within the outer limits of subsection (a)(2) and involved only his officer capacity.

This more flexible approach for situations where the individual is not acting as a director seems appropriate as a matter of fairness. There are many instances where officers who also serve as directors assume responsibilities and take actions in their nondirector capacities. It is hard to justify a denial of indemnification to an officer who failed to meet a standard applicable only to directors when the officer can establish that he did not act as a director. Nor are there likely to be complications or difficulties because some directors are treated differently than others where the high burden of proof—solely as officer—is met. Obviously, the burden will be especially difficult to meet where the roles of officer and director are closely intertwined.

For a director-officer to be indemnified under Section 8.51 for conduct in his capacity as a director when he has not satisfied the standards of Section 8.51(a), a provision in the articles under Section 2.02(b)(8) is required. If such a provision is included in the articles, the standards for indemnification are those specified in Section 2.02(b)(8). For a director-officer to be indemnified for conduct solely in his capacity as an officer, even though the director-officer has not satisfied the standards of Section 8.56(a), only a resolution of the board authorizing such indemnification is required, rather than a provision in the articles. If such a resolution is adopted, the standards for indemnification are those specified in subsection (a)(2). However, when a director-officer seeks indemnification or expense advance under subsections (b) and (a)(2) on the basis of having acted solely in his capacity as an officer, indemnification or expense advance must be approved through the same procedures as set forth in Sections 8.55 or 8.53(c), as the case may be, for approval of indemnification or expense advance for a director when acting in his capacity as a director.

§ 8.57. INSURANCE

A nonprofit corporation may purchase and maintain insurance on behalf of an individual who is or was a director or officer of the corporation, or who, while a director or officer of the corporation, serves or served at the corporation's request as a director, officer, partner, trustee, employee, or agent of another domestic or foreign corporation, partnership, joint venture, trust, employee benefit plan, or other entity, against liability asserted against or incurred by the individual in that capacity or arising from the individual's status as a director or officer, whether or not the corporation would have power to indemnify or advance expenses to the individual against the same liability under this [subchapter].

Source Note: Patterned after Model Business Corporation Act, 3d Ed. (2002) § 8.57. Substantially a reenactment of Model Nonprofit Corporation Act (1987) § 8.57.

CROSS-REFERENCES

"Corporation" defined, see § 8.50.

"Director" defined, see § 8.50.

Employees, agents, and volunteers, see § 8.58.

"Expenses" defined, see § 8.50.

"Liability" defined, see § 8.50.

"Officer" defined, see § 8.50.

"Official capacity" defined, see § 8.50.

Standard for indemnification, see § 8.51.

OFFICIAL COMMENT

Section 8.57 authorizes a nonprofit corporation to purchase and maintain insurance on behalf of directors and officers against liabilities imposed on them by reason of actions in their official capacity, or their status as such, or arising from their service to the corporation or another entity at the corporation's request. Insurance is not limited to claims against which a corporation is entitled to indemnify under this subchapter. This insurance, usually referred to as "D&O liability insurance," provides protection to directors and officers in addition to the rights of indemnification created by or pursuant to this subchapter (as well as typically protecting the individual insureds against the corporation's failure to pay indemnification required or permitted by this subchapter) and provides a source of reimbursement for corporations which indemnify directors and others for conduct covered by the insurance. On the other hand, policies typically do not cover uninsurable matters, such as actions involving dishonesty, self-dealing, bad faith, knowing violations of the securities acts, or other willful misconduct. Joseph F. Johnston, *Corporate Indemnification and Liability Insurance for Directors and Officers*, 33 Business Lawyer 1993, 2024–29 (1978). See also William E.

KNEPPER & DAN A. BAILEY, LIABILITY OF CORPORATE OFFICERS AND DIRECTORS, Section 21.07 (4th ed. 1988).

Although this section does not include employees and agents for the reasons stated in the Official Comment to Section 8.56, the nonprofit corporation has the power under Section 3.02 to purchase and maintain insurance on their behalf. This power is confirmed in Section 8.58(d).

This section is not intended to set the outer limits on the type of insurance that a nonprofit corporation may maintain or the persons to be covered. Rather, it is included to remove "any doubt as to the power to carry insurance and to maintain it on behalf of directors, officers, employees and agents." Orvel Sebring, *Recent Legislative Changes in the Law of Indemnification of Directors, Officers and Others*, 23 BUSINESS LAWYER 95, 106 (1967).

§ 8.58. VARIATION OF INDEMNIFICATION

(a) A nonprofit corporation may, by a provision in its articles of incorporation or bylaws or in a resolution adopted or a contract approved by its board of directors or members, obligate itself in advance of the act or omission giving rise to a proceeding to provide indemnification as permitted by Section 8.51 or advance funds to pay for or reimburse expenses as permitted by Section 8.53. An obligatory provision satisfies the requirements for authorization referred to in Sections 8.53(c) and 8.55(c). Any such provision that obligates the corporation to provide indemnification to the fullest extent permitted by law obligates the corporation to advance funds to pay for or reimburse expenses in accordance with Section 8.53 to the fullest extent permitted by law, unless the provision specifically provides otherwise.

(b) Any provision pursuant to subsection (a) may not obligate the nonprofit corporation to indemnify or advance expenses to a director of a predecessor of the corporation, pertaining to conduct with respect to the predecessor, unless otherwise specifically provided. Any provision for indemnification or advance for expenses in the organic records, articles of incorporation, bylaws, or a resolution of the governors, board of directors, members, or interest holders of a predecessor of the corporation in a fundamental transaction, or in a contract to which the predecessor is a party, existing at the time the fundamental transaction takes effect, is governed by:

(1) Section 9.23(a)(2) in the case of a domestication;
(2) Section 9.33(a)(2) in the case of a for-profit conversion;
(3) Section 9.42(a)(2) in the case of a foreign for-profit domestication and conversion;
(4) Section 9.54(a)(2) in the case of an entity conversion; or
(5) Section 11.07(a)(4) in the case of a merger.

(c) A nonprofit corporation may, by a provision in its articles of incorporation or bylaws, limit any of the rights to indemnification or advance for expenses created by or pursuant to this [subchapter].

(d) This [subchapter] does not limit a nonprofit corporation's power to pay or reimburse expenses incurred by a director or an officer in connection with appearance as a witness in a proceeding at a time when the director or officer is not a party.

(e) This [subchapter] does not limit a nonprofit corporation's power to indemnify, advance expenses to, or provide or maintain insurance on behalf of an employee, agent, or volunteer.

Source Note: Patterned after Model Business Corporation Act, 3d Ed. (2002) § 8.58. Derived from Model Nonprofit Corporation Act (1987) § 8.58.

CROSS-REFERENCES

Advance for expenses, see § 8.53.

"Corporation" defined, see § 8.50.

"Director" defined, see § 8.50.

"Expenses" defined, see § 8.50.

Indemnification generally, see §§ 8.51–8.56.

Insurance, power to provide, see § 8.57.

"Officer" defined, see § 8.50.

"Party" defined, see § 8.50.

Predecessor, see § 8.50.

"Proceeding" defined, see § 8.50.

OFFICIAL COMMENT

Section 8.58(a) authorizes a nonprofit corporation to make obligatory the permissive provisions of Subchapter E in advance of the conduct giving rise to the request for assistance. Many corporations have adopted such provisions, often with member approval. An obligatory provision satisfies the requirements for authorization in subsection (c) of Sections 8.53 and 8.55, but compliance is still required with subsections (a) and (b) of these sections.

Section 8.58(a) further provides that a provision requiring indemnification to the fullest extent permitted by law, absent an express statement to the contrary, includes an obligation to advance expenses under Section 8.53. This provision of the statute is intended to avoid a decision such as that of the Delaware Chancery Court in *Advanced Mining Systems, Inc. v. Fricke*, 623 A.2D 82 (Del. Ch. 1992). If a nonprofit corporation provides for obligatory indemnification and not for obligatory advance for expenses, the provision should be reviewed to ensure that it properly reflects the intent in light of the third sentence of Section 8.58(a). Also, a corporation should consider whether obligatory expense advance is intended for direct suits by the corporation as well as for derivative suits in the right of the corporation. In the former case, assuming compliance with subsections (a) and (b) of Section 8.53, the corporation could be required to fund the defense of a defendant director even where the board of directors has already concluded that he has engaged in significant wrongdoing. See Official Comment to Section 8.53.

Section 8.58(b) provides that an obligatory indemnification provision adopted after a fundamental transaction pursuant to subsection (a) does not, unless specific provision is made to the contrary, bind the corporation with respect to a predecessor in the transaction. An obligatory indemnification provision of a predecessor is treated as a liability (to the extent it is one) in a fundamental transaction.

Section 8.58(c) permits a nonprofit corporation to limit the right of the corporation to indemnify or advance expenses by a provision in its articles of incorporation. As provided in Section 10.09, no such limitation will affect rights in existence when the provision becomes effective pursuant to Section 1.23.

Section 8.58(d) makes clear that Subchapter E deals only with actual or threatened defendants or respondents in a proceeding, and that expenses incurred by a director in connection with appearance as a witness may be indemnified without regard to the limitations of Subchapter E. Indeed, most of the standards described in Sections 8.51 and 8.54(a) by their own terms can have no meaningful application to a director whose only connection with a proceeding is that he has been called as a witness.

Subchapter E does not regulate the power of the nonprofit corporation to indemnify or advance expenses to employees and agents. That subject is governed by the law of agency and related principles and frequently by contractual arrangements between the corporation and the employee or agent. Section 8.58(e) makes clear that, while indemnification, advance for expenses, and insurance for employees and agents are beyond the scope of this subchapter, the elaboration in Subchapter E of standards and procedures for indemnification, expense advance, and insurance for directors and officers is not in any way intended to cast doubt on the power of the corporation to indemnify or advance expenses to or purchase and maintain insurance for employees and agents under Section 3.02 or otherwise.

[Subchapter] F
CONFLICTING INTEREST TRANSACTIONS

§ 8.60. Conflicting interest transactions; voidability.

§ 8.60. CONFLICTING INTEREST TRANSACTIONS; VOIDABILITY

(a) A contract or transaction between a nonprofit corporation and one or more of its members, directors, members of a designated body, or officers or between a nonprofit corporation and any other entity in which one or more of its directors, members of a designated body, or officers are directors or officers, hold a similar position, or have a financial interest, is not void or voidable solely for that reason, or solely because the member, director, member of a designated body, or officer is present at or participates in the meeting of the board of directors that authorizes the contract or transaction, or solely because his or their votes are counted for that purpose, if:

(1) the material facts as to the relationship or interest and as to the contract or transaction are disclosed or are known to the board of directors and the board in good faith authorizes the contract or transaction by the affirmative votes of a majority of the disinterested directors even though the disinterested directors are less than a quorum;

(2) the material facts as to the relationship or interest of the member, director, or officer and as to the contract or transaction are disclosed or are known to the members entitled to vote thereon, if any, and the contract or transaction is specifically approved in good faith by vote of those members; or

(3) the contract or transaction is fair as to the corporation as of the time it is authorized, approved, or ratified by the board of directors or the members.

(b) Common or interested directors may be counted in determining the presence of a quorum at a meeting of the board that authorizes a contract or transaction specified in subsection (a).

(c) This section is applicable except as otherwise restricted in the articles of incorporation or bylaws.

Source Note: Patterned after 8 Del. Code § 144 (2008) and 15 Pa. Cons. Stat. § 5728 (2008). Compare Model Nonprofit Corporation Act (1987) § 8.31.

CROSS-REFERENCES

"Designated body" defined, see § 1.40.

"Director" defined, see § 1.40.

Director's liability for unlawful distributions, see § 8.33.

"Entity" defined, see § 1.40.

"Member" defined, see § 1.40.

Quorum requirements for board meetings, see § 8.24.

Standards of conduct for directors, see § 8.30.

Standards of liability for directors, see § 8.31.

OFFICIAL COMMENT

This section applies to all contracts and transactions between a nonprofit corporation and one or more of its members, directors, members of a designated body, or officers, or between a corporation and any other entity in which one or more of its members, directors, members of a designated body, or officers holds a similar position or has a financial interest. A contract or transaction subject to this section may be permissible under this act yet be prohibited as an excess benefit transaction or otherwise under standards applicable to charitable corporations under the Internal Revenue Code.

This section, like Subchapter 8C regarding the standards of conduct of directors, rejects the trustee standard regarding interested transactions in favor of the corporate standard. The trustee standard prohibits any transaction between a trust and a trustee. That standard was considered overly restrictive for nonprofit corporations. This section also rejects the concept that a director may not obtain any profit from a transaction involving his or her corporation. If the requirements of Section 8.60 are met, a director can make a profit from a transaction involving the corporation subject to other applicable provisions of law.

[Subchapter] G
BUSINESS OPPORTUNITIES

§ 8.70. BUSINESS OPPORTUNITIES

(a) The taking advantage, directly or indirectly, by a director of a business opportunity may not be the subject of equitable relief, or give rise to an award of damages or other sanctions against the director, in a proceeding by or in the right of the nonprofit corporation on the ground that the opportunity should have first been offered to the corporation, if before becoming legally obligated or entitled respecting the opportunity the director brings it to the attention of the corporation and action by the members or the directors disclaiming the corporation's interest in the opportunity is taken in compliance with the procedures set forth in Section 8.60, as if the decision being made concerned a conflicting interest transaction.

(b) In any proceeding seeking equitable relief or other remedies, based upon an alleged improper taking advantage of a business opportunity by a director, the fact that the director did not employ the procedure described in subsection (a) before taking advantage of the opportunity does not support an inference that the opportunity should have been first presented to the nonprofit corporation or alter the burden of proof otherwise applicable to establish that the director breached a duty to the corporation in the circumstances.

(c) As used in this section, "director" includes a member of a designated body.

Source Note: Patterned after Model Business Corporation Act, 3d Ed. (2002) § 8.70.

OFFICIAL COMMENT

Section 8.70 provides a safe harbor for a director weighing possible involvement with a prospective business opportunity that might constitute a "corporate opportunity." By action of the board of directors or members of the nonprofit corporation under Section 8.70, the director can receive a disclaimer of the corporation's interest in the matter before proceeding with such involvement. In the alternative, the corporation may (i) decline to disclaim its interest, (ii) delay a decision respecting granting a disclaimer pending receipt from the director of additional information (or for any other reason), or (iii) attach conditions to the disclaimer it grants under Section 8.70(a). The safe harbor granted to the director pertains only to the specific opportunity and does not have broader application, such as to a line of business or a geographic area.

The common law doctrine of "corporate opportunity" has long been recognized as a core part of the director's duty of loyalty. The doctrine stands for the proposition that the nonprofit corporation has a right prior to that of its director to act on certain business opportunities that come to the attention of the director. In such situations, a director who acts on the opportunity for the benefit of the director or another without having first presented it to the corporation can be held to have "usurped" or "intercepted" a right of the corporation. A defendant director who is found by a court to have violated the duty of loyalty in this regard is subject to damages or an array of equitable remedies, including injunction, disgorgement, or the imposition of a constructive trust in favor of the corporation. While the doctrine's concept is easily described, whether it will be found to apply in a given case depends on the facts and circumstances of the particular situation and is thus frequently unpredictable. Ultimately, the doctrine requires the court to balance the corporation's legitimate expectations that its directors will faithfully promote its best interests against the legitimate right of individual directors to pursue their own economic interests in other contexts and venues.

In response to this difficult balancing task, courts have developed several (sometimes overlapping) principles to cabin the doctrine. Although the principles applied have varied from state to state, courts have sought to determine, for example, whether a disputed opportunity presented a business opportunity that was:

- the same as, or similar to, the nonprofit corporation's current or planned activities ("line of business" test);
- one that the corporation had already formulated plans or taken steps to acquire for its own use ("expectancy" test);
- developed by the director through the use of the corporation's property, personnel, or proprietary information ("appropriation" test); or presented to the director with the explicit or implicit expectation that the director would present it to the corporation for its consideration or, in contrast, one that initially came to the director's attention in the director's individual capacity unrelated to the director's corporate role ("capacity" test).

Finally, in recognition that the nonprofit corporation need not pursue every business opportunity of which it becomes aware, an opportunity coming within the doctrine's criteria that has been properly presented to and declined by the corporation may then be pursued by the presenting director without breach of the director's duty of loyalty.

The fact-intensive nature of the corporate opportunity doctrine resists statutory definition. Instead, Subchapter G employs the broader notion of "business opportunity" that encompasses any opportunity, without regard to whether it would come within the judicial definition of a "corporate opportunity" as it may have been developed by courts in a jurisdiction. When properly employed, it provides a safe-harbor mechanism enabling a director to pursue an opportunity for his or her own account or for the benefit of another free of possible challenge claiming conflict with the director's duty of loyalty on the ground that the opportunity should first have been offered to the corporation.

Section 8.70(a) describes the safe harbor available to a director who elects to subject a business opportunity, regardless of whether the opportunity would be classified as a "corporate opportunity," to the disclosure and approval procedures set forth therein. The safe harbor provided is as broad as that provided for a director's conflicting interest transaction in Section 8.60: if the director makes required disclosure of the facts specified and the nonprofit corporation's interest in the opportunity is disclaimed by director action or member action, the director has foreclosed any claimed breach of the duty of loyalty and may not be subject to equitable relief, damages, or other sanctions if the director thereafter takes the opportunity for his or her own account or for the benefit of another person.

Section 8.70(c) extends the procedures of this section to members of a designated body.

CHAPTER 9

Domestication and Conversion

INTRODUCTORY OFFICIAL COMMENT TO CHAPTER 9

This chapter provides a series of procedures by which a domestic nonprofit corporation may become a different form of entity or, conversely, an entity that is not a domestic nonprofit corporation may become a domestic nonprofit corporation. These various types of procedures are as follows:

- *Domestication.* The procedures in Subchapter 9B permit a corporation to change its state of incorporation, thus allowing a domestic nonprofit corporation to become a foreign nonprofit corporation or a foreign nonprofit corporation to become a domestic nonprofit corporation.
- *For-Profit Conversion.* The procedures in Subchapter 9C permit a domestic nonprofit corporation to become either a domestic business corporation or a foreign business corporation.

- *Foreign For-Profit Domestication and Conversion.* The procedures in Subchapter 9D permit a foreign business corporation to become a domestic nonprofit corporation.
- *Entity Conversion.* The procedures in Subchapter 9E permit a domestic nonprofit corporation to become a domestic or foreign unincorporated entity, and also permit a domestic or foreign unincorporated entity to become a domestic nonprofit corporation.

The provisions of this chapter apply only if a domestic nonprofit corporation is present either immediately before or immediately after a transaction. Some states may wish to generalize the provisions of this chapter so that they are not limited to transactions involving a domestic nonprofit corporation—for example, to permit a domestic limited partnership to become a domestic limited liability company. The Model Entity Transactions Act prepared jointly by the American Bar Association Section of Business Law and the National Conference of Commissioners on Uniform State Laws is such a generalized statute.

The procedures of this chapter do not permit the combination of two or more entities into a single entity. Transactions of that type must continue to be conducted under Chapter 11 or 12 as a merger or transfer of assets, respectively.

[Subchapter] A
PRELIMINARY PROVISIONS

§ 9.01. DEFINITIONS

In this [chapter]:

(1) "Conversion" means a transaction authorized by [Subchapter] C, D, or E.
(2) "Converting corporation" means the domestic or foreign nonprofit or business corporation that approves a conversion pursuant to this [chapter] or its organic law.
(3) "Converting entity" means the domestic or foreign entity that approves a conversion pursuant to Section 9.50 or its organic law.
(4) "Domesticated corporation" means the domesticating corporation as it continues in existence after a domestication.
(5) "Domesticating corporation" means the domestic nonprofit corporation that adopts a plan of domestication pursuant to Section 9.21 or the foreign nonprofit corporation that approves a domestication pursuant to its organic law.
(6) "Domestication" means a transaction authorized by [Subchapter] B.
(7) "Surviving corporation" means the corporation as it continues in existence immediately after consummation of a for-profit conversion pursuant to [Subchapter] C, a foreign for-profit conversion and domestication pursuant to [Subchapter] D, or an entity conversion pursuant to [Subchapter] E.
(8) "Surviving entity" means the unincorporated entity as it continues in existence immediately after consummation of an entity conversion pursuant to [Subchapter] E.

Source Note: Patterned after Model Entity Transactions Act (2007) § 102(5), (6), (7), (9), (10), (11), and (37).

OFFICIAL COMMENT

This section supplies definitions applicable to Chapter 9. The definitions in Section 1.40 also apply to this chapter.

§ 9.02. EXCLUDED TRANSACTIONS

This [chapter] may not be used to effect a transaction that:

(1) [converts a nonprofit insurance company to a for-profit stock corporation;]
(2)
(3)

Source Note: Patterned after Model Business Corporation Act, 3d Ed. (2002) § 9.01.

OFFICIAL COMMENT

The purpose of this section is to prohibit certain transactions from being effectuated under Chapter 9. A state should use this section to (i) list all the situations in which the state has enacted specific legislation governing the conversion of domestic nonprofit corporations that are of a particular type or that do business in a regulated industry to any other form of corporation or to an unincorporated entity, or (ii) otherwise restrict conversions of domestic nonprofit corporations. The conversion of a nonprofit insurance company to a for-profit stock corporation has been listed as a possible example of such a transaction, since most states have separate statutes that govern such a conversion.

§ 9.03. RESTRICTIONS AND REQUIRED APPROVALS

(a) If a domestic or foreign nonprofit corporation or eligible entity may not be a party to a merger or sale of its assets without the approval of the [*attorney general*], the [*department of insurance*] or the [*public utility commission*], the corporation or eligible entity shall not be a party to a transaction under this [chapter] without the prior approval of that [*agency*].

(b) Property held in trust by an entity or otherwise dedicated to a charitable purpose may not be diverted from its purpose by any transaction under this [chapter] unless the entity obtains an appropriate order of [*court*] [*the attorney general*] specifying the disposition of the property to the extent required by and pursuant to the law of this state on cy pres or otherwise dealing with the nondiversion of charitable assets.

(c) Unless an entity that is a party to a transaction under this [chapter] obtains an appropriate order of [*court*] [*the attorney general*] under the law of this state on cy pres or otherwise dealing with the nondiversion of charitable assets, the transaction may not affect:

   (1) any restriction imposed upon the entity by its organic records that may not be amended by its board of directors, governors, members, or interest holders or by a designated body;

   (2) any restriction imposed upon property held by the entity by virtue of any trust under which it holds that property; or

   (3) the existing rights of persons other than members, shareholders, or interest holders of the entity.

(d) A person who is a member, interest holder, or otherwise affiliated with a charitable corporation or an unincorporated entity with a charitable purpose may not receive a direct or indirect financial benefit in connection with a transaction under this [chapter] to which the charitable corporation or unincorporated entity is a party unless the person is itself a charitable corporation or unincorporated entity with a charitable purpose. This subsection does not apply to the receipt of reasonable compensation for services rendered.

(e) A devise, bequest, gift, grant, or promise contained in a will or other instrument, in trust or otherwise, made before or after a transaction under this [chapter], to or for the entity that is the subject of the transaction, shall inure to the entity as it continues in existence after the transaction, subject to the express terms of the will or other instrument.

Source Note: Subsections (a)–(d) are patterned after Model Business Corporation Act, 3d Ed. (2002) § 9.02. Subsection (e) is patterned after Revised Model Nonprofit Corporation Act (1987) § 11.07.

CROSS-REFERENCES

Appeal from secretary of state's refusal to file document, see § 1.26.

"Domestic nonprofit corporation" defined, see § 1.40.

Filing duty of secretary of state, see § 1.25.

OFFICIAL COMMENT

Section 9.03(a) applies to those nonprofit corporations or other entities that are charitable and require approval before transferring restricted property or that conduct regulated activities such as insurance or the provision of public utility services and are incorporated or organized under general laws instead of under special laws applicable only to entities conducting the regulated activity. Examples of those types of nonprofit entities in many states include health maintenance organizations subject to regulation as insurance companies and rural electric cooperatives subject to regulation as public utilities. Because the provisions of Chapter 9 are new, there is a possibility that existing state laws that require regulatory approval of mergers by those types of entities may not be worded in a fashion that will include the transactions authorized by this chapter.

The purpose of Section 9.03(a) is to ensure that transactions under Chapter 9 will be subject to the same regulatory approval as mergers or sales of assets, in contrast to Section 9.02, which is an outright prohibition on conducting certain transactions under Chapter 9. The list of agencies in subsection (a) should be conformed to the laws of the enacting state. The consequences of violating subsection (a) will be the same as in the case of a merger consummated without the required approval.

As in the case of laws regulating particular industries, a state's laws governing the nondiversion of charitable property to other uses may not be worded in a fashion that will include all of the transactions authorized by this chapter. To prevent the procedures in this chapter from being used to avoid restrictions on the use of property held in trust by nonprofit entities or otherwise dedicated to charitable purposes, Section 9.03(b) requires approval of the effect of transactions under this chapter by the appropriate arm of government having supervision of nonprofit entities.

[Subchapter] B
DOMESTICATION

§ 9.20. DOMESTICATION

(a) A foreign nonprofit corporation may become a domestic nonprofit corporation only if the domestication is authorized by the law of the foreign jurisdiction.

(b) A domestic nonprofit corporation may become a foreign nonprofit corporation if the domestication is permitted by the laws of the foreign jurisdiction. Regardless of whether the laws of the foreign jurisdiction require the adoption of a plan of domestication, the domestication must be approved by the adoption by the corporation of a plan of domestication in the manner provided in this [subchapter].

(c) The plan of domestication must include:

(1) a statement of the jurisdiction in which the corporation is to be domesticated;

(2) the terms and conditions of the domestication;

(3) the manner and basis of canceling or reclassifying the memberships of the corporation following its domestication into memberships, obligations, rights to acquire memberships, cash, other property, or any combination of the foregoing; and

(4) any desired amendments to the articles of incorporation or bylaws of the corporation following its domestication.

(d) The plan of domestication may also include a provision that the plan may be amended prior to filing the document required by the laws of this state or the other jurisdiction to consummate the domestication; except that, subsequent to approval of the plan by the members, the plan may not be amended without the approval of the members to change:

(1) the amount or kind of memberships, obligations, rights to acquire memberships, cash, or other property to be received by the members under the plan;

(2) the articles of incorporation as they will be in effect immediately following the domestication, except for changes permitted by Section 10.05 or by comparable provisions of the laws of the other jurisdiction; or

(3) any of the other terms or conditions of the plan if the change would adversely affect any of the members in any material respect.

(e) Terms of a plan of domestication may be made dependent upon facts objectively ascertainable outside the plan in accordance with Section 1.20(c).

(f) If any debt security, note or similar evidence of indebtedness for money borrowed, whether secured or unsecured, or a contract of any kind, issued, incurred or executed by a domestic nonprofit corporation before [*the effective date of this subchapter*] contains a provision applying to a merger of the corporation and the document does not refer to a domestication of the corporation, the provision shall be deemed to apply to a domestication of the corporation until such time as the provision is amended subsequent to that date.

(g) See Sections 9.02 (prohibited transactions) and 9.03 (restrictions and required approvals).

Source Note: Patterned after Model Business Corporation Act, 3d Ed. (2002) § 9.20.

CROSS-REFERENCES

Abandonment of domestication, see § 9.24.

Approval of plan, see § 9.21.

Articles of domestication, see § 9.22.

Articles of incorporation following domestication, see § 9.22.

"Domestic nonprofit corporation" defined, see § 1.40.

Effect of domestication, see § 9.23.

Excluded transactions, see § 9.02.

"Foreign nonprofit corporation" defined, see § 1.40.

"Organic law" defined, see § 1.40.

OFFICIAL COMMENT

1. Applicability

This subchapter authorizes a foreign nonprofit corporation to become a domestic nonprofit corporation. It also authorizes a domestic nonprofit corporation to become a foreign nonprofit corporation. In each case, the domestication is authorized only if the laws of the foreign jurisdiction permit the domestication. Whether and on what terms a foreign nonprofit corporation is authorized to domesticate in this state are issues governed by the laws of the foreign jurisdiction, not by this subchapter.

A foreign corporation is not required to have in effect a valid certificate of authority under Chapter 15 in order to domesticate in this state.

If a domesticating corporation has established its exempt status with the Internal Revenue Service, the domesticated corporation may be considered a new entity by the IRS and may need to refile if its exempt status does not carry over.

2. Terms and Conditions of Domestication

This subchapter imposes virtually no restrictions or limitations on the terms and conditions of a domestication, except for those set forth in Section 9.20(d) concerning provisions in a plan of domestication for amendment of the plan after it has been approved by the members and those in Sections 9.02 and 9.03. Memberships in a domestic nonprofit corporation that domesticates in another jurisdiction may be reclassified into memberships, obligations, rights to acquire memberships, cash, or other property. The articles of incorporation may be amended by the articles of domestication in any way deemed appropriate. When a foreign nonprofit corporation domesticates in this state, the laws of the foreign jurisdiction determine which of the foregoing actions may be taken.

Section 9.20(c) requires that the terms and conditions of the domestication be set forth in the plan of domestication. The plan of domestication is not required to be publicly filed, and the articles of domestication that are filed with the secretary of state by a foreign nonprofit corporation domesticating in this state are not required to include a plan of domestication. See Section 9.22.

The list in Section 9.20(c) of required provisions in a plan of domestication is not exhaustive and the plan may include any other provisions that may be desired.

3. *Amendments of Articles of Incorporation*

A nonprofit corporation's articles of incorporation may be amended in a domestication. Under Section 9.20(c)(4), a plan of domestication of a domestic nonprofit corporation proposing to domesticate in a foreign jurisdiction may include amendments to the articles of incorporation and should include, at a minimum, any amendments required to conform the articles of incorporation to the requirements for articles of incorporation of a corporation incorporated in the foreign jurisdiction. It is assumed that the foreign jurisdiction will give effect to the articles of incorporation as amended to the same extent that it would if the articles had been independently amended before the domestication.

The laws of the foreign jurisdiction determine whether and to what extent a foreign nonprofit corporation may amend its articles of incorporation when domesticating in this state. Following the domestication of a foreign corporation in this state, of course, its articles of incorporation may be amended under Chapter 10.

4. *Adoption and Approval; Abandonment*

The domestication of a domestic nonprofit corporation in a foreign jurisdiction must be adopted and approved as provided in Section 9.21. Under Section 9.24, the board of directors of a domestic nonprofit corporation may abandon a domestication before its effective date even if the plan of domestication has already been approved by the corporation's members.

5. Transitional Rule

Because the concept of domestication is new, a person contracting with a nonprofit corporation or loaning it money who drafted and negotiated special rights relating to the transaction before the enactment of this subchapter should not be charged with the consequences of not having dealt with the concept of domestication in the context of those special rights. Section 9.20(f) accordingly provides a transitional rule that is intended to protect such special rights. If, for example, a corporation is a party to a contract that provides that the corporation cannot participate in a merger without the consent of the other party to the contract, the requirement to obtain the consent of the other party will also apply to the domestication of the corporation in another jurisdiction. If the corporation fails to obtain the consent, the result will be that the other party will have the same rights it would have if the corporation were to participate in a merger without the required consent.

The purpose of Section 9.20(f) is to protect the third party to a contract with the corporation, and Section 9.20(f) should not be applied in such a way as to impair unconstitutionally the third party's contract. As applied to the corporation, Section 9.20(f) is an exercise of the reserved power of the state legislature set forth in Section 1.02.

The transitional rule in Section 9.20(f) ceases to apply at such time as the provision of the agreement or debt instrument giving rise to the special rights is first amended after the effective date of this subchapter because at that time the provision may be amended to address expressly a domestication of the corporation.

A similar transitional rule governing the application to a domestication of special voting rights of directors and members and other internal corporate procedures is found in Section 9.21(7).

§ 9.21. ACTION ON A PLAN OF DOMESTICATION

In the case of a domestication of a domestic nonprofit corporation in a foreign jurisdiction:

(1) The plan of domestication must be adopted by the board of directors.

(2) After adopting the plan of domestication the board of directors must submit the plan to the members for their approval, if there are members entitled to vote on the plan. The board of directors must also transmit to the members a recommendation that the members approve the plan, unless the board of directors makes a determination that because of conflicts of interest or other special circumstances it should not make such a recommendation, in which case the board of directors must transmit to the members the basis for that determination.

(3) The board of directors may condition its submission of the plan of domestication to the members on any basis.

(4) If the approval of the members is to be given at a meeting, the corporation must notify each member, whether or not entitled to vote, of the meeting of members at which the plan of domestication is to be submitted for approval. The notice must state that the purpose, or one of the purposes, of the meeting is to consider the plan and must contain or be accompanied by a copy or summary of the plan. The notice must include or be accompanied by a copy of the articles of incorporation and bylaws as they will be in effect immediately after the domestication.

(5) Unless the articles of incorporation or bylaws, or the board of directors acting pursuant to paragraph (3), requires a greater vote or a greater number of votes to be present, the approval of the plan of domestication by the members requires the approval of the members at a meeting at which a quorum exists, and, if any class of members is entitled to vote as a separate group on the plan, the approval of each such separate voting group at a meeting at which a quorum of the voting group exists.

(6) Separate voting by voting groups is required by each class of members that:
   (i) are to be reclassified under the plan of domestication into a different class of memberships, or into obligations, rights to acquire memberships, cash, other property, or any combination of the foregoing;
   (ii) would be entitled to vote as a separate group on a provision of the plan that, if contained in a proposed amendment to articles of incorporation, would require action by separate voting groups under Section 10.04; or
   (iii) is entitled under the articles of incorporation or bylaws to vote as a voting group to approve an amendment of the articles.

(7) If any provision of the articles of incorporation, bylaws, or an agreement to which any of the directors, members of a designated body, or members are parties, adopted or entered into before [*the effective date of this subchapter*] applies to a merger of the corporation and that document does not refer to a domestication of the corporation, the provision shall be deemed to apply to a domestication of the corporation until such time as the provision is amended subsequent to that date.

Source Note: Patterned after Model Business Corporation Act, 3d Ed. (2002) § 9.21.

CROSS-REFERENCES

Abandonment of domestication, see § 9.24.

Contents of plan of domestication, see § 9.20.

"Domestic nonprofit corporation" defined, see § 1.40.

"Foreign nonprofit corporation" defined, see § 1.40.

OFFICIAL COMMENT

1. In General

This section sets forth the rules for adoption and approval of a plan of domestication of a domestic nonprofit corporation to a foreign jurisdiction. The manner in which the domestication of a foreign nonprofit corporation in this state must be adopted and approved will be controlled by the laws of the foreign jurisdiction. The provisions of this section follow generally the rules in Chapter 11 for adoption and approval of a plan of merger or membership exchange.

A plan of domestication must be adopted by the board of directors. Although Section 9.21(2) permits the board to refrain from making a recommendation to the members that they approve the plan, that does not change the underlying requirement that the board first adopt the plan before it is submitted to the members. Separate approval by the members of a plan of domestication is required if there are members entitled to vote on a domestication.

2. *Voting by Separate Groups*

Section 9.21(6) provides that a class of members has a right to vote on a plan of domestication as a separate voting group if, as part of the domestication, the class would be reclassified into other memberships, obligations, rights to acquire memberships, cash, or other property. A class of members also is entitled to vote as a separate voting group if the class would be entitled to vote as a separate group on a provision in the plan that, if contained in an amendment to the articles of incorporation, would require approval by that class under Section 10.04. In this latter case, a class will be entitled to vote as a separate voting group if the terms of that class are being changed, or if the memberships of that class are being reclassified into memberships of any other class. It is not intended that immaterial changes in the language of the articles of incorporation made to conform to the usage of the laws of the foreign jurisdiction will alone create an entitlement to vote as a separate group.

Under Section 10.04, and therefore under Section 9.21(6), if a change that requires voting by separate voting groups affects two or more classes in the same or a substantially similar way, the relevant classes will vote together, rather than separately, on the change. For the mechanics of voting where voting by voting groups is required under Section 9.21(6), see Sections 7.24 and 7.25.

If a domestication would amend the articles of incorporation to change the voting requirements on future amendments of the articles, the transaction must also be approved by the vote required by Section 7.26.

3. *Quorum and Voting*

Section 9.21(5) provides that approval of a plan of domestication requires approval of the members at a meeting at which there exists a quorum consisting of a majority of the votes entitled to be cast on the plan. Section 9.21(5) also provides that if any class of members are entitled to vote as a separate group on the plan, the approval of each such separate group must be given at a meeting at which there exists a quorum consisting of at least a majority of the votes entitled to be cast on the plan by that class. If a quorum is present, then under Sections 7.24 and 7.25 the plan will be approved if more votes are cast in favor of the plan than against it by each voting group entitled to vote on the plan.

In lieu of approval at a meeting of the members, approval can be given by the consent of all the members entitled to vote on the domestication, under the procedures set forth in Section 7.04.

4. *Transitional Rule*

Because the concept of domestication is new, persons who drafted and negotiated special rights for directors or members before the enactment of this subchapter should not be charged with the consequences of not having dealt with the concept of domestication in the context of those special rights. Section 9.21(7) accordingly provides a transitional rule that is intended to protect such special rights. If, for example, the articles of incorporation provide that the corporation cannot participate in a merger without a supermajority vote of the members, that supermajority requirement will also apply to the domestication of the corporation in another jurisdiction.

The purpose of Section 9.21(7) is to protect persons who negotiated special rights for directors or members whether in a contract with the corporation or in the articles of incorporation or bylaws, and Section 9.21(7) should not be applied in such a way as to impair unconstitutionally the rights of any party to a contract with the corporation. As applied to the corporation, Section 9.21(7) is an exercise of the reserved power of the state legislature set forth in Section 1.02.

The transitional rule in Section 9.21(7) ceases to apply at such time as the provision of the articles of incorporation, bylaws, or agreement giving rise to the special rights is first amended after the effective date of this subchapter because at that time the provision may be amended to address expressly a domestication of the corporation.

A similar transitional rule with regard to the application to a domestication of special contractual rights of third parties is found in Section 9.20(f).

§ 9.22. ARTICLES OF DOMESTICATION

(a) Articles of domestication must be signed on behalf of the domesticating corporation by any officer or other duly authorized representative. The articles must set forth:
  (1) the name and jurisdiction of incorporation of the domesticating corporation;
  (2) the name and jurisdiction of incorporation of the domesticated entity; and
  (3) if the domesticating corporation is a domestic nonprofit corporation, a statement that the plan of domestication was approved in accordance with this [subchapter] or, if the domesticating corporation is a foreign nonprofit corporation, a statement that the domestication was approved in accordance with the law of its jurisdiction of incorporation.

(b) If the domesticated corporation is a domestic nonprofit corporation, the articles of domestication either shall contain all of the provisions that Section 2.02(a) requires to be set forth in articles of incorporation and any other desired provisions that Section 2.02(b) and (c) permit to be included in articles of incorporation, or shall have attached articles of incorporation. In either case, provisions that would not be required to be included in restated articles of incorporation may be omitted, except that the name and address of the initial registered agent of the domesticated corporation must be included. The name of the domesticated corporation must satisfy the requirements of Section 4.01.

(c) The articles of domestication must be delivered to the secretary of state for filing, and take effect at the effective time provided in Section 1.23.

(d) If the domesticating corporation is a qualified foreign nonprofit corporation, its certificate of authority is cancelled automatically on the effective date of its domestication.

Source Note: Patterned after Model Business Corporation Act, 3d Ed. (2002) § 9.22.

CROSS-REFERENCES

"Deliver" defined, see § 1.40.

Effect of domestication, see § 9.23.

Filing fees, see § 1.22.

Filing requirements, see § 1.20.

"Foreign nonprofit corporation" defined, see § 1.40.

Restrictions and required approvals, see § 9.03.

OFFICIAL COMMENT

The filing of articles of domestication under this section makes the domestication a matter of public record. It also makes of public record the articles of incorporation of the domesticated corporation if it is a domestic nonprofit corporation. If a domesticating foreign corporation is authorized to transact business in this state, Section 9.22(d) automatically cancels its certificate of authority.

The filing requirements for articles of domestication are set forth in Section 1.20. Under Section 1.23, a document may specify a delayed effective time and date, and if it does so the document becomes effective at the time and date specified, except that a delayed effective date may not be later than the 90th day after the date the document is filed. The filing of articles of domestication terminates the status of a domesticating corporation that is a domestic corporation as a corporation incorporated under the laws of this state. Once the articles of domestication have become effective, the corporation will no longer be in good standing in this state. The domesticated corporation may, however, apply for a certificate of authority as a foreign corporation under Subchapter 15A.

Where a foreign nonprofit corporation domesticates in this state, the filing required to terminate its status as a corporation incorporated under the laws of the foreign jurisdiction is determined by the laws of that jurisdiction.

To avoid any question about a gap in the continuity of its existence, it is recommended that a corporation use a delayed effective date provision in its domestication filings in both this state and the foreign jurisdiction, or otherwise coordinate those filings, so that the filings become effective at the same time.

As Section 9.20(c)(4) makes clear, a corporation may amend its articles of incorporation in connection with a domestication. Because the articles of domestication will either contain or have attached to them an integrated set of articles of incorporation, the articles of domestication will have the effect of restating the articles of incorporation.

§ 9.23. EFFECT OF DOMESTICATION

(a) Except as otherwise provided in Section 9.03, when a domestication becomes effective:

   (1) the title to all real and personal property, both tangible and intangible, of the domesticating corporation remains in the domesticated corporation without reversion or impairment;

   (2) the liabilities of the domesticating corporation remain the liabilities of the domesticated corporation;

   (3) an action or proceeding pending against the domesticating corporation continues against the domesticated corporation as if the domestication had not occurred;

(4) the articles of domestication, or the articles of incorporation attached to the articles of domestication, constitute the articles of incorporation of a foreign corporation domesticating in this state;

(5) the memberships in the domesticating corporation are reclassified into memberships, obligations, rights to acquire memberships, or cash or other property in accordance with the terms of the domestication, and the members are entitled only to the rights provided by those terms; and

(6) the domesticating corporation is deemed to:

(i) be incorporated under and subject to the organic law of the domesticated corporation for all purposes; and

(ii) be the same corporation without interruption as the domesticating corporation.

(b) The interest holder liability of a member in a foreign nonprofit corporation that is domesticated in this state is as follows:

(1) The domestication does not discharge any interest holder liability under the laws of the foreign jurisdiction to the extent any such interest holder liability arose before the effective time of the articles of domestication.

(2) The member does not have interest holder liability under the laws of the foreign jurisdiction for any debt, obligation, or liability of the corporation that arises after the effective time of the articles of domestication.

(3) The provisions of the laws of the foreign jurisdiction continue to apply to the collection or discharge of any interest holder liability preserved by paragraph (1), as if the domestication had not occurred.

(4) The member has whatever rights of contribution from other members are provided by the laws of the foreign jurisdiction with respect to any interest holder liability preserved by paragraph (1), as if the domestication had not occurred.

Source Note: Patterned after Model Business Corporation Act, 3d Ed. (2002) § 9.24.

CROSS-REFERENCES

"Domestic nonprofit corporation" defined, see § 1.40.

"Foreign nonprofit corporation" defined, see § 1.40.

"Interest holder liability" defined, see § 1.40.

OFFICIAL COMMENT

When a nonprofit corporation is domesticated in this state under this subchapter, the corporation becomes a domestic corporation with the same status under this act as if it had been originally incorporated under this act. Thus, the domesticated corporation will have all of the powers, privileges, and rights granted to corporations originally incorporated in this state and will be subject to all of the duties, liabilities, and limitations imposed on domestic nonprofit corporations. Except as provided in Section 9.23(b), the effect of domesticating a corporation of this state in a foreign jurisdiction is governed by the laws of the foreign jurisdiction. See Section 9.20(b).

A domestication is not a conveyance, transfer, or assignment. It does not give rise to claims of reverter or impairment of title based on a prohibited conveyance, transfer, or assignment. Nor does it give rise to a claim that a contract with the corporation is no longer in effect on the ground of nonassignability, unless the contract specifically provides that it does not survive a domestication.

Section 9.23(a)(1)–(3) and (b) are similar to Section 11.07(a)(3)–(5) and (c) with respect to the effects of a merger. Although Section 9.23(a)(1)–(3) would be implied by the general rule stated in Section 9.23(a)(6) even if not stated expressly, those rules have been included to avoid any question as to whether a different result was intended.

Section 9.23(b) preserves liability only for interest holder liabilities to the extent they arise before the domestication. Interest holder liability is not preserved for subsequent changes in an underlying liability, regardless of whether a change is voluntary or involuntary.

§ 9.24. ABANDONMENT OF A DOMESTICATION

(a) Unless otherwise provided in a plan of domestication of a domestic nonprofit corporation, after the plan has been adopted and approved as required by this [subchapter], and at any time before the domestication has become effective, it may be abandoned by the board of directors without action by the members.

(b) If a domestication is abandoned under subsection (a) after articles of domestication have been filed with the secretary of state but before the domestication has become effective, a statement that the domestication has been abandoned in accordance with this section, signed by an officer or other duly authorized representative, must be delivered to the secretary of state for filing prior to the effective date of the domestication. The statement takes effect upon filing and the domestication is abandoned and does not become effective.

(c) If the domestication of a foreign nonprofit corporation in this state is abandoned in accordance with the laws of the foreign jurisdiction after articles of domestication have been filed with the secretary of state, a statement that the domestication has been abandoned, signed by an officer or other duly authorized representative, must be delivered to the secretary of state for filing. The statement takes effect upon filing and the domestication is abandoned and does not become effective.

Source Note: Patterned after Model Business Corporation Act, 3d Ed. (2002) § 9.25.

CROSS-REFERENCES

Approval of domestication, see § 9.21.

"Deliver" defined, see § 1.40.

"Domestic nonprofit corporation" defined, see § 1.40.

Effective time and date of filing, see § 1.23.

Filing requirements, see § 1.20.

"Foreign nonprofit corporation" defined, see §1.40.

OFFICIAL COMMENT

Unless otherwise provided in a plan of domestication, a domestic nonprofit corporation proposing to domesticate in another jurisdiction may abandon the transaction without member approval, even though the domestication has been previously approved by the members. Whether or not the domestication of a foreign nonprofit corporation in this state may be abandoned is determined by the laws of the foreign jurisdiction.

[Subchapter] C
FOR-PROFIT CONVERSION

§ 9.30. FOR-PROFIT CONVERSION

(a) A domestic nonprofit corporation may become a domestic business corporation pursuant to a plan of for-profit conversion.

(b) A domestic nonprofit corporation may become a foreign business corporation if the for-profit conversion is permitted by the laws of the foreign jurisdiction. Regardless of whether the laws of the foreign jurisdiction require the adoption of a plan of for-profit conversion, the foreign for-profit conversion shall be approved by the adoption by the domestic nonprofit corporation of a plan of for-profit conversion in the manner provided in this [subchapter].

(c) The plan of for-profit conversion must include:

(1) the terms and conditions of the conversion;

(2) the manner and basis of:

(i) issuing at least one share in the corporation following its conversion; and

(ii) otherwise reclassifying the memberships in the corporation, if any, following its conversion into shares and other securities, obligations, rights to acquire shares or other securities, cash, other property, or any combination of the foregoing;

(3) any desired amendments to the articles of incorporation or bylaws of the corporation following its conversion; and

(4) if the domestic nonprofit corporation is to be converted to a foreign business corporation, a statement of the jurisdiction in which the corporation will be incorporated after the conversion.

(d) The plan of for-profit conversion may also include a provision that the plan may be amended prior to filing articles of for-profit conversion, except that subsequent to approval of the plan by the members the plan may not be amended without the approval of the members to change:
   (1) the amount or kind of shares and other securities, obligations, rights to acquire shares or other securities, cash, or other property to be received by the members under the plan;
   (2) the articles of incorporation as they will be in effect immediately following the conversion, except for changes permitted by Section 10.05; or
   (3) any of the other terms or conditions of the plan if the change would adversely affect any of the members in any material respect.

(e) Terms of a plan of for-profit conversion may be made dependent upon facts objectively ascertainable outside the plan in accordance with Section 1.20(c).

(f) If any debt security, note, or similar evidence of indebtedness for money borrowed, whether secured or unsecured, or a contract of any kind, issued, incurred, or executed by a domestic nonprofit corporation before [*the effective date of this subchapter*] contains a provision applying to a merger of the corporation and the document does not refer to a for-profit conversion of the corporation, the provision shall be deemed to apply to a for-profit conversion of the corporation until such time as the provision is amended subsequent to that date.

(g) See Sections 9.02 (prohibited transactions) and 9.03 (restrictions and required approvals).

Source Note: Patterned after Model Business Corporation Act, 3d Ed. (2002) § 9.30.

CROSS-REFERENCES

Abandonment of for-profit conversion, see § 9.34.

Approval of plan, see § 9.31.

Articles of for-profit conversion, see § 9.32.

"Domestic business corporation" defined, see § 1.40.

"Domestic nonprofit corporation" defined, see § 1.40.

Effect of for-profit conversion, see § 9.33.

Excluded transactions, see § 9.02.

"Foreign business corporation" defined, see § 1.40.

"Membership" defined, see § 1.40.

OFFICIAL COMMENT

1. Applicability

This subchapter provides a procedure for a domestic nonprofit corporation to change its status from not-for-profit to for-profit and thus become a domestic business corporation.

This subchapter also provides a procedure for a domestic nonprofit corporation to become a foreign business corporation, which is in effect a combination of a domestication and a for-profit conversion. However, Section 9.30(b) permits a domestic nonprofit corporation to become a foreign business corporation only if the laws of the foreign jurisdiction permit the transaction.

A separate procedure is provided in Subchapter 9D for a foreign business corporation to become a domestic nonprofit corporation.

2. Terms and Conditions of For-Profit Conversion

This subchapter imposes virtually no restrictions or limitations on the terms and conditions of a for-profit conversion, except for (i) those set forth in Sections 9.02 and 9.03, (ii) the requirements in Section 9.30(d) concerning provisions in a plan of for-profit conversion for amendment of the plan after it has been approved by the members, and (iii) the requirement in Section 9.30(c)(2)(i) that at least one share be issued by the corporation in connection with the conversion. In addition, other law such as the Internal Revenue Code may limit or prohibit for-profit conversions.

So long as at least one share in the corporation is outstanding following the conversion, memberships in a domestic nonprofit corporation that converts to a business corporation may be reclassified into other securities, obligations, rights to acquire shares or other securities, cash, or other property.

Section 9.30(c) requires that the terms and conditions of the conversion be set forth in the plan of for-profit conversion. The plan of for-profit conversion is not required to be publicly filed, and the articles of for-profit conversion that are filed with the secretary of state are not required to include a plan of for-profit conversion. See Section 9.32.

The list in Section 9.30(c) of required provisions in a plan of for-profit conversion is not exhaustive and the plan may include any other provisions that may be desired.

3. Amendments of Articles of Incorporation

A nonprofit corporation's articles of incorporation will need to be amended in its conversion to a business corporation so that the articles satisfy the requirements for articles of a business corporation. See Section 9.32(b). Similarly, where a domestic nonprofit corporation converts to a foreign business corporation, the articles of incorporation will need to be amended to conform to the law of the foreign jurisdiction on the contents of articles of incorporation for a nonprofit business corporation.

4. Adoption and Approval; Abandonment

The conversion of a domestic nonprofit corporation to a business corporation must be adopted and approved as provided in Section 9.31. Under Section 9.34, the board of directors of a domestic nonprofit corporation may abandon a conversion to for-profit status before its effective date even if the plan of for-profit conversion has already been approved by the corporation's members.

5. Transitional Rule

Because the concept of for-profit conversion is new, a person contracting with a corporation or loaning it money who drafted and negotiated special rights relating to the transaction before the enactment of this subchapter should not be charged with the consequences of not having dealt with the concept of for-profit conversion in the context of those special rights. Section 9.30(f) accordingly provides a transitional rule that is intended to protect such special rights. If, for example, a corporation is a party to a contract that provides that the corporation cannot participate in a merger without the consent of the other party to the contract, the requirement to obtain the consent of the other party will also apply to the conversion of the corporation to a domestic or foreign business corporation. If the corporation fails to obtain the consent, the result will be that the other party will have the same rights it would have if the corporation were to participate in a merger without the required consent.

The purpose of Section 9.30(f) is to protect the third party to a contract with the corporation, and Section 9.30(f) should not be applied in such a way as to impair unconstitutionally the third party's contract. As applied to the corporation, Section 9.30(f) is an exercise of the reserved power of the state legislature set forth in Section 1.02.

The transitional rule in Section 9.30(f) ceases to apply at such time as the provision of the agreement or debt instrument giving rise to the special rights is first amended after the effective date of this subchapter because at that time the provision may be amended to address expressly a for-profit conversion of the corporation.

A similar transitional rule governing the application to a for-profit conversion of special voting rights of directors and members and other internal corporate procedures is found in Section 9.31(6).

§ 9.31. ACTION ON A PLAN OF FOR-PROFIT CONVERSION

In the case of a conversion of a domestic nonprofit corporation to a domestic or foreign business corporation:

(1) The plan of for-profit conversion must be adopted by the board of directors.
(2) After adopting the plan of for-profit conversion, the board of directors must submit the plan to the members for their approval if there are members entitled to vote on the plan. The board of directors must also transmit to the members a recommendation that the members approve the plan, unless the board of directors makes a determination that because of conflicts of interest or other special circumstances it should not make such a recommendation, in which case the board of directors must transmit to the members the basis for that determination.
(3) The board of directors may condition its submission of the plan of for-profit conversion to the members on any basis.
(4) If the approval of the members is to be given at a meeting, the corporation must notify each member of the meeting of members at which the plan of for-profit conversion is to be submitted for approval. The notice must state that the purpose, or one of the purposes, of the meeting is to consider the plan and must contain or be accompanied by a copy or summary of the plan. The notice shall include or be accompanied by a copy of the articles of incorporation as they will be in effect immediately after the for-profit conversion.
(5) Unless the articles of incorporation, or the board of directors acting pursuant to paragraph (3), require a greater vote or a greater number of votes to be present, the approval of the plan of for-profit conversion by the members requires the approval of each class of members of the corporation voting as a separate voting group at a meeting at which a quorum of the voting group exists.
(6) If any provision of the articles of incorporation, bylaws, or an agreement to which any of the directors or members are parties, adopted or entered into before [the effective date of this subchapter], applies to a merger of the corporation and the document does not refer to a for-profit conversion of the corporation, the provision shall be deemed to apply to a

for-profit conversion of the corporation until such time as the provision is amended subsequent to that date.

Source Note: Patterned after Model Business Corporation Act, 3d Ed. (2002) § 9.31.

CROSS-REFERENCES

Abandonment of for-profit conversion, see § 9.34.

Contents of plan of for-profit conversion, see § 9.30.

"Domestic business corporation" defined, see § 1.40.

"Domestic nonprofit corporation" defined, see § 1.40.

"Foreign business corporation" defined, see § 1.40.

OFFICIAL COMMENT

1. In General

This section sets forth the rules for adoption and approval of a plan of for-profit conversion of a domestic nonprofit corporation to a domestic or foreign business corporation.

A plan of for-profit conversion must be adopted by the board of directors. Although Section 9.31(2) permits the board to refrain from making a recommendation to the members that they approve the plan, that does not change the underlying requirement that the board first adopt the plan before it is submitted to the members. Separate approval by the members of a plan of for-profit conversion is required if there are members entitled to vote on the transaction.

2. Quorum and Voting

Section 9.31(5) provides that if the corporation has more than one class of members, approval of a for-profit conversion requires the approval of each class voting as a separate voting group at a meeting at which there exists a quorum consisting of at least a majority of the votes entitled to be cast on the plan by that class. If a quorum is present, then under Sections 7.24 and 7.25 the plan will be approved if more votes are cast in favor of the plan than against it by each voting group entitled to vote on the plan. If the members of a corporation are not divided into two or more classes or series, all of the members together will constitute a single class for purposes of Section 9.31(5).

In lieu of approval at a meeting of the members, approval can be given by the consent of all the members entitled to vote on the conversion, under the procedures set forth in Section 7.04.

3. *Transitional Rule*

Because the concept of for-profit conversion is new, persons who drafted and negotiated special rights for directors or members before the enactment of this subchapter should not be charged with the consequences of not having dealt with the concept of for-profit conversion in the context of those special rights. Section 9.31(6) accordingly provides a transitional rule that is intended to protect such special rights. If, for example, the articles of incorporation provide that the corporation cannot participate in a merger without a supermajority vote of the members, that supermajority requirement will also apply to the conversion of the corporation to a domestic or foreign business corporation.

The purpose of Section 9.31(6) is to protect persons who negotiated special rights for directors or members whether in a contract with the corporation or in the articles of incorporation or bylaws, and Section 9.31(6) should not be applied in such a way as to impair unconstitutionally the rights of any party to a contract with the corporation. As applied to the corporation, Section 9.31(6) is an exercise of the reserved power of the state legislature set forth in Section 1.02.

The transitional rule in Section 9.31(6) ceases to apply at such time as the provision of the articles of incorporation, bylaws, or agreement giving rise to the special rights is first amended after the effective date of this subchapter because at that time the provision may be amended to address expressly a for-profit conversion of the corporation.

A similar transitional rule with regard to the application to a for-profit conversion of special contractual rights of third parties is found in Section 9.30(f).

§ 9.32. ARTICLES OF FOR-PROFIT CONVERSION

(a) Articles of for-profit conversion must be signed on behalf of the converting corporation by any officer or other duly authorized representative. The articles must set forth:

(1) if the surviving corporation is a domestic business corporation, the name of the corporation immediately before the filing of the articles of for-profit conversion and if that name does not satisfy the requirements of [*the Model Business Corporation Act*], or the corporation desires to change its name in connection with the conversion, a name that satisfies the requirements of [*the Model Business Corporation Act*];

(2) if the surviving corporation is a foreign business corporation, its name after the conversion and its jurisdiction of incorporation; and

(3) a statement that the plan of for-profit conversion was duly approved by the members in the manner required by this [act] and the articles of incorporation.

(b) If the surviving corporation is a domestic business corporation, the articles of for-profit conversion either shall contain all of the provisions that [*the Model Business Corporation Act*] requires to be set forth in articles of incorporation of a domestic business corporation and any other desired provisions permitted by [*the Model Business Corporation Act*], or shall have attached articles of incorporation that satisfy the requirements of [*the Model Business Corporation Act*]. In either case, provisions that would not be required to be included in restated articles of incorporation of a domestic business corporation may be omitted, except that the name and address of the initial registered agent of the business corporation must be included.

(c) The articles of for-profit conversion must be delivered to the secretary of state for filing, and take effect at the effective time provided in Section 1.23.

Source Note: Patterned after Model Business Corporation Act, 3d Ed. (2002) § 9.32.

CROSS-REFERENCES

"Deliver" defined, see § 1.40.

"Domestic business corporation" defined, see § 1.40.

"Domestic nonprofit corporation" defined, see § 1.40.

Effect of nonprofit conversion, see § 9.33.

Filing fees, see § 1.22.

Filing requirements, see § 1.20.

Restrictions and required approvals, see § 9.03.

OFFICIAL COMMENT

The filing of articles of for-profit conversion makes the conversion of a domestic nonprofit corporation to a domestic or foreign business corporation a matter of public record. Where a domestic nonprofit corporation is converting to a foreign business corporation, the filing required in the foreign jurisdiction is determined by the laws of that jurisdiction. When a conversion to a foreign business corporation is effective, the converting corporation will no longer be a domestic nonprofit corporation in good standing in this state.

The filing requirements for articles of for-profit conversion are set forth in Section 1.20. Under Section 1.23, a document may specify a delayed effective time and date, and if it does so the document becomes effective at the time and date specified, except that a delayed effective date may not be later than the 90th day after the date the document is filed.

The articles of incorporation that must be included in or attached to the articles of for-profit conversion will satisfy the requirements of [*the Model Business Corporation Act*] for incorporating a business corporation.

This section assumes that all business corporations are incorporated under the same law. If that is not the case, appropriate changes must be made to this section so that the type of business corporation that will result from the conversion is made clear.

§ 9.33. EFFECT OF FOR-PROFIT CONVERSION

[(a)] Except as otherwise provided in Section 9.03, when a conversion of a domestic nonprofit corporation to a domestic or foreign business corporation becomes effective:

(1) the title to all real and personal property, both tangible and intangible, of the corporation remains in the corporation without reversion or impairment;

(2) the liabilities of the corporation remain the liabilities of the corporation;

(3) an action or proceeding pending against the corporation continues against the corporation as if the conversion had not occurred;

(4) the articles of incorporation of the domestic or foreign business corporation become effective;

(5) the memberships of the corporation are reclassified into shares or other securities, obligations, rights to acquire shares or other securities, or into cash or other property in accordance with the plan of conversion, and the members are entitled only to the rights provided in the plan of for-profit conversion; and

(6) the corporation is deemed to:

(i) be a domestic or foreign business corporation for all purposes; and

(ii) be the same corporation without interruption as the nonprofit corporation.

[(b) The interest holder liability of a member in a domestic nonprofit corporation that converts to a domestic business corporation is as follows:

(1) The conversion does not discharge any interest holder liability of the member as a member of the nonprofit corporation to the extent any such interest holder liability arose before the effective time of the articles of for-profit conversion.

(2) The member does not have interest holder liability for any debt, obligation, or liability of the business corporation that arises after the effective time of the articles of for-profit conversion.

(3) *The laws of this state continue to apply to the collection or discharge of any interest holder liability preserved by paragraph (1), as if the conversion had not occurred.*

(4) *The member has whatever rights of contribution from other members are provided by the laws of this state with respect to any interest holder liability preserved by paragraph (1), as if the conversion had not occurred.*

(c) A member who becomes subject to interest holder liability for some or all of the debts, obligations, or liabilities of the business corporation has interest holder liability only for those debts, obligations, or liabilities of the business corporation that arise after the effective time of the articles of for-profit conversion.]

Source Note: Patterned after Model Business Corporation Act, 3d Ed. (2002) § 9.33.

CROSS-REFERENCES

"Domestic business corporation" defined, see § 1.40.

"Domestic nonprofit corporation" defined, see § 1.40.

"Interest holder liability" defined, see § 1.40.

"Membership" defined, see § 1.40.

OFFICIAL COMMENT

When a nonprofit corporation is converted under this subchapter to a domestic business corporation, the corporation has the same status as if it had been originally incorporated under [*the Model Business Corporation Act*]. Thus, the converted corporation will have all of the powers, privileges, and rights granted to business corporations originally incorporated as such in this state and will be subject to all of the duties, liabilities, and limitations imposed on domestic business corporations.

A for-profit conversion is not a conveyance, transfer, or assignment. It does not give rise to claims of reverter or impairment of title based on a prohibited conveyance, transfer, or assignment. Nor does it give rise to a claim that a contract with the corporation is no longer in effect on the ground of nonassignability, unless the contract specifically provides that it does not survive a conversion.

Section 9.33(a)(1)–(3) are similar to Section 11.07(a)(3)–(5) with respect to the effects of a merger. Although Section 9.33(a)(1)–(3) would be implied by the general rule stated in Section 9.33(a)(6) even if not stated expressly, those rules have been included to avoid any question as to whether a different result was intended.

Section 9.33(b) and (c) are optional provisions that will not be needed in most states. Those provisions should be included only when the statutory laws of a state impose some form of personal liability on the shareholders of a business corporation that is not imposed on members of a nonprofit corporation, or the reverse. Section 9.33(c) preserves liability only for interest holder liabilities to the extent they arise before the conversion. Interest holder liability is not preserved for subsequent changes in an underlying liability, regardless of whether a change is voluntary or involuntary.

§ 9.34. ABANDONMENT OF A FOR-PROFIT CONVERSION

(a) Unless otherwise provided in a plan of for-profit conversion of a domestic nonprofit corporation, after the plan has been adopted and approved as required by this [subchapter], and at any time before the for-profit conversion has become effective, it may be abandoned by the board of directors without action by the members.

(b) If a for-profit conversion is abandoned under subsection (a) after articles of for-profit conversion have been filed with the secretary of state but before the for-profit conversion has become effective, a statement that the for-profit conversion has been abandoned in accordance with this section, signed by an officer or other duly authorized representative, must be delivered to the secretary of state for filing prior to the effective date of the for-profit conversion. The statement takes effect upon filing and the for-profit conversion is abandoned and does not become effective.

Source Note: Patterned after Model Business Corporation Act, 3d Ed. (2002) § 9.34.

CROSS-REFERENCES

Approval of for-profit conversion, see § 9.31.

"Deliver" defined, see § 1.40.

"Domestic business corporation" defined, see § 1.40.

Effective time and date of filing, see §§ 1.23 and 9.32.

Filing requirements, see § 1.20.

OFFICIAL COMMENT

Unless otherwise provided in a plan of for-profit conversion, a domestic nonprofit corporation proposing to convert to for-profit status may abandon the transaction without member approval, even though the conversion has been previously approved by the members.

[Subchapter] D
FOREIGN FOR-PROFIT DOMESTICATION AND CONVERSION

§ 9.40. FOREIGN FOR-PROFIT DOMESTICATION AND CONVERSION

A foreign business corporation may become a domestic nonprofit corporation if the domestication and conversion is permitted by the law of the foreign jurisdiction.

Source Note: Patterned after Model Business Corporation Act, 3d Ed. (2002) § 9.40.

CROSS-REFERENCES

Abandonment of foreign for-profit domestication and conversion, see § 9.43.

Articles of domestication and conversion, see § 9.41.

Articles of incorporation following domestication and conversion, see § 9.41.

"Domestic nonprofit corporation" defined, see § 1.40.

Effect of foreign for-profit domestication and conversion, see § 9.42.

Excluded transactions, see § 9.02.

"Foreign business corporation" defined, see § 1.40.

OFFICIAL COMMENT

This subchapter authorizes a foreign business corporation to become a domestic nonprofit corporation. The manner in which a foreign business corporation may be domesticated in this state and converted to a domestic nonprofit corporation must be adopted and approved will be controlled by the laws of the foreign jurisdiction.

The domestication of a foreign nonprofit corporation in this state as a domestic business corporation is outside the scope of this act. Similarly, the conversion of a foreign nonprofit corporation to a domestic unincorporated entity is also outside the scope of this act.

§ 9.41. ARTICLES OF DOMESTICATION AND CONVERSION

(a) After the conversion of a foreign business corporation to a domestic nonprofit corporation has been authorized as required by the laws of the foreign jurisdiction, articles of domestication and conversion shall be signed by any officer or other duly authorized representative. The articles shall set forth:

(1) the name of the corporation immediately before the filing of the articles of domestication and conversion and, if that name is unavailable for use in this state or the corporation desires to change its name in connection with the domestication and conversion, a name that satisfies the requirements of Section 4.01;

(2) the jurisdiction of incorporation of the corporation immediately before the filing of the articles of domestication and conversion and the date the corporation was incorporated in that jurisdiction; and

(3) a statement that the domestication and conversion of the corporation in this state was duly authorized as required by the laws of the jurisdiction in which the corporation was incorporated immediately before its domestication and conversion in this state.

(b) The articles of domestication and conversion either shall contain all of the provisions that Section 2.02(a) requires to be set forth in articles of incorporation and any other desired provisions that Section 2.02(b) and (c) permit to be included in articles of incorporation, or shall have attached articles of incorporation. In either case, provisions that would not be required to be included in restated articles of incorporation may be omitted, except that the name and address of the initial registered agent of the domestic business corporation must be included.

(c) The articles of domestication and conversion must be delivered to the secretary of state for filing, and take effect at the effective time provided in Section 1.23.

(d) If the foreign business corporation is authorized to transact business in this state under [the foreign qualification provision of the Model Business Corporation Act], its certificate of authority shall be cancelled automatically on the effective date of its domestication and conversion.

Source Note: Patterned after Model Business Corporation Act, 3d Ed. (2002) § 9.41.

CROSS-REFERENCES

"Deliver" defined, see § 1.40.

"Domestic nonprofit corporation" defined, see § 1.40.

Effect of domestication and conversion, see § 9.42.

Filing fees, see § 1.22.

Filing requirements, see § 1.20.

"Foreign business corporation" defined, see § 1.40.

OFFICIAL COMMENT

The filing of articles of domestication and conversion under this section makes the domestication of a foreign business corporation in this state and its conversion to nonprofit status a matter of public record. It also makes of public record the articles of incorporation of the corporation as a corporation of this state. If the foreign corporation is authorized to transact business in this state, Section 9.41(d) automatically cancels its certificate of authority.

This section only applies in the situation where a foreign business corporation is domesticating in this state and converting to nonprofit status. The domestication of a foreign business corporation in this state as a domestic business corporation is not within the scope of this act.

The filing requirements for articles of domestication and conversion are set forth in Section 1.20. Under Section 1.23, a document may specify a delayed effective time and date, and if it does so the document becomes effective at the time and date specified, except that a delayed effective date may not be later than the 90th day after the date the document is filed. To avoid any question about a gap in the continuity of its existence, it is recommended that a corporation use a delayed effective date provision in its domestication and conversion filings in both this state and the foreign jurisdiction, or otherwise coordinate those filings, so that the filings become effective at the same time.

§ 9.42. EFFECT OF FOREIGN FOR-PROFIT DOMESTICATION AND CONVERSION

(a) When a domestication and conversion of a foreign business corporation to a domestic nonprofit corporation becomes effective:

  (1) the title to all real and personal property, both tangible and intangible, of the corporation remains in the corporation without reversion or impairment;

  (2) the liabilities of the corporation remain the liabilities of the corporation;

  (3) an action or proceeding pending against the corporation continues against the corporation as if the domestication and conversion had not occurred;

  (4) the articles of domestication and conversion, or the articles of incorporation attached to the articles of domestication and conversion, constitute the articles of incorporation of the corporation;

  (5) memberships, securities, obligations, rights to acquire memberships or securities of the corporation, or cash or

other property shall be issued or paid as provided pursuant to the laws of the foreign jurisdiction; and

(6) the corporation is deemed to:

(i) be a domestic corporation for all purposes; and

(ii) be the same corporation without interruption as the foreign business corporation.

(b) The interest holder liability of a shareholder of the foreign business corporation who becomes a member of the domestic nonprofit corporation in the domestication and conversion is as follows:

(1) The domestication and conversion does not discharge any interest holder liability under the laws of the foreign jurisdiction to the extent any such interest holder liability arose before the effective time of the articles of domestication and conversion.

(2) The member does not have interest holder liability under the laws of the foreign jurisdiction for any debt, obligation, or liability of the corporation that arises after the effective time of the articles of domestication and conversion.

(3) The provisions of the laws of the foreign jurisdiction continue to apply to the collection or discharge of any interest holder liability preserved by paragraph (1), as if the domestication and conversion had not occurred.

(4) The member has whatever rights of contribution from other members are provided by the laws of the foreign jurisdiction with respect to any interest holder liability preserved by paragraph (1), as if the domestication and conversion had not occurred.

[(c) A shareholder of a foreign business corporation who becomes subject to interest holder liability for some or all of the debts, obligations, or liabilities of the corporation as a result of its domestication and conversion in this state has interest holder liability only for those debts, obligations, or liabilities of the corporation that arise after the effective time of the articles of domestication and conversion.]

Source Note: Patterned after Model Business Corporation Act, 3d Ed. (2002) § 9.42.

CROSS-REFERENCES

"Domestic nonprofit corporation" defined, see § 1.40.

"Foreign business corporation" defined, see § 1.40.

"Interest holder liability" defined, see § 1.40.

OFFICIAL COMMENT

When a corporation is domesticated in this state and converted to nonprofit status under this subchapter, the corporation becomes a domestic nonprofit corporation with the same status as if it had been originally incorporated under this act. Thus, the domesticated nonprofit corporation will have all of the powers, privileges, and rights granted to corporations originally incorporated in this state and will be subject to all of the duties, liabilities, and limitations imposed on domestic nonprofit corporations.

A domestication and conversion under this subchapter is not a conveyance, transfer, or assignment. It does not give rise to claims of reverter or impairment of title based on a prohibited conveyance, transfer, or assignment. Nor does it give rise to a claim that a contract with the corporation is no longer in effect on the ground of nonassignability, unless the contract specifically provides that it does not survive a domestication or conversion.

Section 9.42(a)(1)–(3) are similar to Section 11.07(a)(3)–(5) with respect to the effects of a merger. Although Section 9.42(a)(1)–(3) would be implied by the general rule stated in Section 9.42(a)(6) even if not stated expressly, those rules have been included to avoid any question as to whether a different result was intended.

Section 9.42(b) preserves liability only for interest holder liabilities to the extent they arise before the domestication and conversion. Interest holder liability is not preserved for subsequent changes in an underlying liability, regardless of whether a change is voluntary or involuntary.

Section 9.42(c) is an optional provision that will not be needed in most states. It should be included only when the statutory laws of a state impose personal liability on the members of a nonprofit corporation that is not imposed on the shareholders of a business corporation.

§ 9.43. ABANDONMENT OF A FOREIGN FOR-PROFIT DOMESTICATION AND CONVERSION

If the domestication and conversion of a foreign business corporation to a domestic nonprofit corporation is abandoned in accordance with the laws of the foreign jurisdiction after articles of domestication and conversion have been filed with the secretary of state, a statement that the domestication and conversion has been abandoned, signed by an officer or other duly authorized representative, must be delivered to the secretary of state for filing. The statement takes effect upon filing and the domestication and conversion is abandoned and does not become effective.

Source Note: Patterned after Model Business Corporation Act, 3d Ed. (2002) § 9.43.

CROSS-REFERENCES

"Deliver" defined, see § 1.40.

"Domestic nonprofit corporation" defined, see § 1.40.

Effective time and date of filing, see § 1.23.

Filing requirements, see § 1.20.

"Foreign business corporation" defined, see § 1.40.

OFFICIAL COMMENT

Whether or not the domestication and conversion of a foreign business corporation may be abandoned is determined by the laws of the foreign jurisdiction.

[Subchapter] E
ENTITY CONVERSION

§ 9.50. ENTITY CONVERSION AUTHORIZED

(a) A domestic nonprofit corporation may become a domestic unincorporated entity pursuant to a plan of entity conversion.

(b) A domestic nonprofit corporation may become a foreign unincorporated entity if the entity conversion is permitted by the laws of the foreign jurisdiction.

(c) A domestic unincorporated entity may become a domestic nonprofit corporation. If the organic law of a domestic unincorporated entity does not provide procedures for the approval of an entity conversion, the conversion must be adopted and approved, and the entity conversion effectuated, in the same manner as a merger of the unincorporated entity, and its interest holders will be entitled to appraisal rights if appraisal rights are available upon any type of merger under the organic law of the unincorporated entity. If the organic law of a domestic unincorporated entity does not provide procedures for the approval of either an entity conversion or a merger, a plan of entity conversion must be adopted and approved, the entity conversion effectuated, and appraisal rights exercised, in accordance with the procedures in this [subchapter]. Without limiting the provisions of this subsection, a domestic unincorporated entity whose organic law does not provide procedures for the approval of an entity conversion is subject to subsection (e) and Section 9.52(7). For purposes of applying this [subchapter]:

(1) the unincorporated entity, its interest holders, interests, and organic records taken together, are deemed to be a domestic nonprofit corporation, members, memberships, and articles of incorporation, respectively and vice versa, as the context may require; and

(2) if the business and affairs of the unincorporated entity are managed by a group of persons that is not identical to the interest holders, that group is deemed to be the board of directors.

(d) A foreign unincorporated entity may become a domestic nonprofit corporation if the law of the foreign jurisdiction authorizes it to become a nonprofit corporation in another jurisdiction.

(e) If any debt security, note, or similar evidence of indebtedness for money borrowed, whether secured or unsecured, or a contract of any kind, issued, incurred, or executed by a domestic nonprofit corporation before [*the effective date of this subchapter*], applies to a merger of the corporation and the document does not refer to an entity conversion of the corporation, the provision shall be deemed to apply to an entity conversion of the corporation until such time as the provision is amended subsequent to that date.

(f) See Sections 9.02 (prohibited transactions) and 9.03 (restrictions and required approvals).

Source Note: Patterned after Model Business Corporation Act, 3d Ed. (2002) § 9.50.

CROSS-REFERENCES

"Domestic nonprofit corporation" defined, see § 1.40.

"Domestic unincorporated entity" defined, see § 1.40.

Excluded transactions, see § 9.02.

"Foreign unincorporated entity" defined, see § 1.40.

"Interest" defined, see § 1.40.

"Interest holder" defined, see § 1.40.

"Organic document" defined, see § 1.40.

"Organic law" defined, see § 1.40.

OFFICIAL COMMENT

1. Scope of Subchapter

Subject to certain restrictions that are discussed below, this subchapter authorizes the following types of conversion:

(1) a domestic nonprofit corporation to a domestic unincorporated entity,
(2) a domestic nonprofit corporation to a foreign unincorporated entity,
(3) a domestic unincorporated entity to a domestic nonprofit corporation,
(4) a foreign unincorporated entity to a domestic nonprofit corporation.

This subchapter provides for the conversion of a domestic unincorporated entity only to a domestic nonprofit corporation because the conversion of a domestic unincorporated entity to another form of unincorporated entity or to a domestic or foreign business corporation would be outside of the scope of this act. This subchapter similarly does not provide for the conversion of a foreign corporation or unincorporated entity to a domestic unincorporated entity. States may nonetheless wish to consider generalizing the provisions of this subchapter to authorize those types of conversions.

2. Procedural Requirements

The concept of entity conversion as authorized by this subchapter is not found in many laws governing the incorporation or organization of corporations and unincorporated entities. In recognition of that fact, the rules in this section vary depending on whether the corporation or unincorporated entity desiring to convert pursuant to this subchapter is incorporated or organized under the laws of this state or of some other jurisdiction.

If the organic law of a domestic unincorporated entity does not expressly authorize it to convert to a domestic nonprofit corporation, it is intended that the first sentence of subsection (c) will provide the necessary authority. Until such time as the various organic laws of each form of unincorporated entity have been amended to provide procedures for adopting and approving a plan of entity conversion, subsection (c) provides those procedures by reference to the procedures for mergers under the organic law of the unincorporated entity or, if there are no such merger provisions, by reference to the provisions of this subchapter applicable to domestic nonprofit corporations.

Subsection (d) provides that a foreign unincorporated entity may convert to a domestic nonprofit corporation pursuant to this subchapter only if the law under which the foreign unincorporated entity is organized permits the conversion. This rule avoids issues that could arise if this state authorized a foreign unincorporated entity to participate in a transaction in this state that its home jurisdiction did not authorize. This subchapter does not specify the procedures that a foreign unincorporated entity must follow to authorize a conversion under this subchapter on the assumption that if the organic law of the foreign unincorporated entity authorizes the conversion that law will also provide the applicable procedures and any safeguards considered necessary to protect the interest holders of the unincorporated entity.

3. *Transitional Rule*

Because the concept of entity conversion is new, a person contracting with a corporation or loaning it money who drafted and negotiated special rights relating to the transaction before the enactment of this subchapter should not be charged with the consequences of not having dealt with the concept of entity conversion in the context of those special rights. Section 9.50(e) accordingly provides a transitional rule that is intended to protect such special rights. If, for example, a corporation is a party to a contract that provides that the corporation cannot participate in a merger without the consent of the other party to the contract, the requirement to obtain the consent of the other party will also apply to the conversion of the corporation to a domestic or foreign unincorporated entity. If the corporation fails to obtain the consent, the result will be that the other party will have the same rights it would have if the corporation were to participate in a merger without the required consent.

The purpose of Section 9.50(e) is to protect the third party to a contract with the corporation, and Section 9.50(e) should not be applied in such a way as to impair unconstitutionally the third party's contract. As applied to the corporation, Section 9.50(e) is an exercise of the reserved power of the state legislature set forth in Section 1.02.

The transitional rule in Section 9.50(e) ceases to apply at such time as the provision of the agreement or debt instrument giving rise to the special rights is first amended after the effective date of this subchapter because at that time the provision may be amended to address expressly an entity conversion of the corporation.

Section 9.50(e) will also apply in the case of an unincorporated entity whose organic law does not provide procedures for the approval of an entity conversion because Section 9.50(c) treats such an unincorporated entity as a nonprofit corporation for purposes of Section 9.50(e).

A similar transitional rule governing the application to an entity conversion of special voting rights of directors and members and other internal corporate procedures is found in Section 9.52(6).

§ 9.51. PLAN OF ENTITY CONVERSION

(a) A plan of entity conversion must include:
   (1) a statement of the type of unincorporated entity the surviving entity will be and, if it will be a foreign unincorporated entity, its jurisdiction of organization;
   (2) the terms and conditions of the conversion;
   (3) the manner and basis of converting the memberships in the domestic nonprofit corporation following its conversion into interests or other securities, obligations, rights to acquire interests or other securities, cash, other property, or any combination of the foregoing; and

(4) the full text, as it will be in effect immediately following the conversion, of the organic documents of the surviving entity.

(b) The plan of entity conversion may also include a provision that the plan may be amended prior to filing articles of entity conversion, except that subsequent to approval of the plan by the members the plan may not be amended to change:

(1) the amount or kind of memberships or other securities, interests, obligations, rights to acquire memberships, securities or interests, cash, or other property to be received under the plan by the members;

(2) the organic documents that will be in effect immediately following the conversion, except for changes permitted by a provision of the organic law of the surviving entity comparable to Section 10.05; or

(3) any of the other terms or conditions of the plan if the change would adversely affect any of the members in any material respect.

(c) Terms of a plan of entity conversion may be made dependent upon facts objectively ascertainable outside the plan in accordance with Section 1.20(c).

Source Note: Patterned after Model Business Corporation Act, 3d Ed. (2002) § 9.51.

CROSS-REFERENCES

Abandonment of entity conversion, see § 9.55.

Application to domestic unincorporated entities, see § 9.50.

Approval of plan, see § 9.52.

"Domestic nonprofit corporation" defined, see § 1.40.

"Domestic unincorporated entity" defined, see § 1.40.

Effect of entity conversion, see §9.54.

"Foreign unincorporated entity" defined, see § 1.40.

"Interest" defined, see § 1.40.

"Interest holder" defined, see § 1.40.

"Organic document" defined, see § 1.40.

"Surviving entity" defined, see § 9.50.

"Unincorporated entity" defined, see § 1.40.

OFFICIAL COMMENT

1. Terms and Conditions of Entity Conversion

This subchapter imposes virtually no restrictions or limitations on the terms and conditions of an entity conversion, except for those set forth in Section 9.51(b) concerning provisions in a plan of entity conversion for amendment of the plan after it has been approved by the members and those imposed under Section 9.03. Memberships in a domestic nonprofit corporation that converts to an unincorporated entity may be reclassified into interests or other securities, obligations, rights to acquire interests or other securities, cash, or other property. The capitalization of the entity will need to be restructured in the conversion and its organic documents or articles of incorporation may be amended by the articles of entity conversion in any way deemed appropriate. When a foreign unincorporated entity converts to a domestic nonprofit corporation, the laws of the foreign jurisdiction determine which of the foregoing actions may be taken.

Section 9.51(a) requires that the terms and conditions be set forth in the plan of entity conversion. The plan of entity conversion is not required to be publicly filed, and the articles of entity conversion that are filed with the secretary of state are not required to include a plan of entity conversion. See Section 9.53.

The list in Section 9.51(a) of required provisions in a plan of entity conversion is not exhaustive and the plan may include any other provisions that may be desired.

2. Adoption and Approval; Abandonment

The conversion of a domestic nonprofit corporation to a foreign unincorporated entity must be adopted and approved as provided in Section 9.52. Under Section 9.55, the board of directors of a domestic nonprofit corporation may abandon an entity conversion before its effective date even if the plan of entity conversion has already been approved by the corporation's members.

§ 9.52. ACTION ON A PLAN OF ENTITY CONVERSION

In the case of an entity conversion of a domestic nonprofit corporation to a domestic or foreign unincorporated entity:

(1) The plan of entity conversion must be adopted by the board of directors.

(2) After adopting the plan of entity conversion, the board of directors must submit the plan to the members for their approval if there are members entitled to vote on the plan. The board of directors must also transmit to the members a recommendation that the members approve the plan, unless the board of directors makes a determination that because of conflicts of interest or other special circumstances it should not make such a recommendation, in which case the board of directors must transmit to the members the basis for that determination.

(3) The board of directors may condition its submission of the plan of entity conversion to the members on any basis.

(4) If the approval of the members is to be given at a meeting, the corporation must notify each member, whether or not entitled to vote, of the meeting of members at which the plan of entity conversion is to be submitted for approval. The notice must state that the purpose, or one of the purposes, of the meeting is to consider the plan and must contain or be accompanied by a copy or summary of the plan. The notice shall include or be accompanied by a copy of the organic documents as they will be in effect immediately after the entity conversion.

(5) Unless the articles of incorporation, or the board of directors acting pursuant to paragraph (3), requires a greater vote or a greater number of votes to be present, the approval of the plan of entity conversion by the members requires the

approval of each class of members of the corporation voting as a separate voting group at a meeting at which a quorum of the voting group exists.

(6) If any provision of the articles of incorporation, bylaws, or an agreement to which any of the directors or members are parties, adopted or entered into before [*the effective date of this subchapter*], applies to a merger of the corporation and the document does not refer to an entity conversion of the corporation, the provision shall be deemed to apply to an entity conversion of the corporation until such time as the provision is subsequently amended.

(7) If as a result of the conversion one or more members of the corporation would become subject to interest holder liability for the debts, obligations, or liabilities of any other person or entity, approval of the plan of conversion shall require the execution, by each such member, of a separate written consent to become subject to such interest holder liability.

Source Note: Patterned after Model Business Corporation Act, 3d Ed. (2002) § 9.52.

CROSS-REFERENCES

Abandonment of entity conversion, see § 9.54.

Application to domestic unincorporated entities, see § 9.50.

Contents of plan of entity conversion, see § 9.51.

"Domestic nonprofit corporation" defined, see § 1.40.

"Domestic unincorporated entity" defined, see § 1.40.

"Foreign unincorporated entity" defined, see § 1.40.

"Interest holder liability" defined, see § 1.40.

"Organic record" defined, see § 1.40.

OFFICIAL COMMENT

1. In General

This section sets forth the rules for adoption and approval of a plan of entity conversion by a domestic nonprofit corporation.

The manner in which a domestic unincorporated entity must adopt and approve a plan of entity conversion will be controlled by its organic law or by the application of the provisions of this subchapter by analogy as provided in Section 9.50(c). The manner in which the conversion of a foreign unincorporated entity to a domestic nonprofit corporation must be adopted and approved will be controlled by the laws of the foreign jurisdiction. The provisions of this section follow generally the rules in Chapter 11 for adoption and approval of a plan of merger or membership exchange.

A plan of entity conversion must be adopted by the board of directors. Although Section 9.52(2) permits the board to refrain from making a recommendation to the members that they approve the plan, that does not change the underlying requirement that the board adopt the plan before it is submitted to the members. Separate approval by the members of a plan of entity conversion is required if there are members entitled to vote on the conversion.

2. Quorum and Voting

Section 9.52(5) provides that if the corporation has more than one class of members, approval of an entity conversion requires the approval of each class of members voting as a separate voting group at a meeting at which there exists a quorum consisting of at least a majority of the votes entitled to be cast on the plan by that class. If a quorum is present, then under Sections 7.24 and 7.25 the plan will be approved if more votes are cast in favor of the plan than against it by each voting group entitled to vote on the plan. If the members of a corporation are not divided into two or more classes, all of the members together will constitute a single class for purposes of Section 9.52(5).

In lieu of approval at a meeting of the members, approval can be given by the consent of all the members entitled to vote on the domestication, under the procedures set forth in Section 7.04.

3. Transitional Rule

Because the concept of entity conversion is new, persons who drafted and negotiated special rights for directors or members before the enactment of this subchapter should not be charged with the consequences of not having dealt with the concept of entity conversion in the context of those special rights. Section 9.52(7) accordingly provides a transitional rule that is intended to protect such special rights. If, for example, the articles of incorporation provide that the corporation cannot participate in a merger without a supermajority vote of the members, that supermajority requirement will also apply to the conversion of the corporation to a domestic or foreign unincorporated entity.

The purpose of Section 9.52(6) is to protect persons who negotiated special rights for directors or members whether in a contract with the corporation or in the articles of incorporation or bylaws, and Section 9.52(6) should not be applied in such a way as to impair unconstitutionally the rights of any party to a contract with the corporation. As applied to the corporation, Section 9.52(6) is an exercise of the reserved power of the state legislature set forth in Section 1.02.

The transitional rule in Section 9.52(6) ceases to apply at such time as the provision of the articles of incorporation, bylaws, or agreement giving rise to the special rights is first amended after the effective date of this subchapter because at that time the provision may be amended to address expressly an entity conversion of the corporation.

Section 9.52(6) will also apply in the case of an unincorporated entity whose organic law does not provide procedures for the approval of an entity conversion because Section 9.50(c) treats such an unincorporated entity as a nonprofit corporation for purposes of Section 9.52(6).

A similar transitional rule with regard to the application to an entity conversion of special contractual rights of third parties is found in Section 9.50(e).

§ 9.53. ARTICLES OF ENTITY CONVERSION

(a) After the conversion of a domestic nonprofit corporation to a domestic or foreign unincorporated entity has been adopted and approved as required by this [act], articles of entity conversion must be signed on behalf of the converting corporation by any officer or other duly authorized representative. The articles must:

(1) set forth the name of the corporation immediately before the filing of the articles of entity conversion and the name to which the name of the corporation is to be changed, which shall be a name that satisfies the organic law of the surviving entity if the surviving entity is a domestic entity;

(2) state the type of unincorporated entity that the surviving entity will be and its jurisdiction of organization;

(3) state that the plan of entity conversion was duly approved in the manner required by this [act];

(4) if the surviving entity is a domestic filing entity, either contain all of the provisions required to be set forth in its public organic record and any other desired provisions that are permitted, or have attached a public organic record.

(b) After the conversion of a domestic unincorporated entity to a domestic nonprofit corporation has been adopted and approved as required by the organic law of the unincorporated entity, articles of entity conversion must be signed on behalf of the unincorporated entity by any officer or other duly authorized representative. The articles must:

(1) set forth the name of the unincorporated entity immediately before the filing of the articles of entity conversion and the name to which the name of the unincorporated entity is to be changed, which shall be a name that satisfies the requirements of Section 4.01;

(2) set forth a statement that the plan of entity conversion was duly approved in accordance with the organic law of the unincorporated entity;

(3) either contain all of the provisions that Section 2.02(a) requires to be set forth in articles of incorporation and any other desired provisions that Section 2.02(b) and (c) permit to be included in articles of incorporation, or have attached articles of incorporation.

(c) After the conversion of a foreign unincorporated entity to a domestic nonprofit corporation has been authorized as required by the laws of the foreign jurisdiction, articles of entity conversion shall be executed on behalf of the foreign unincorporated entity by any officer or other duly authorized representative. The articles must:

(1) set forth the name of the unincorporated entity immediately before the filing of the articles of entity conversion and the name to which the name of the unincorporated entity is to be changed, which shall be a name that satisfies the requirements of Section 4.01;

(2) set forth the jurisdiction under the laws of which the unincorporated entity was organized immediately before the filing of the articles of entity conversion and the date on which the unincorporated entity was organized in that jurisdiction;

(3) set forth a statement that the conversion of the unincorporated entity was duly approved in the manner required by the law of the foreign jurisdiction; and

(4) either contain all of the provisions that Section 2.02(a) requires to be set forth in articles of incorporation and any other desired provisions that Section 2.02(b) and (c) permit to be included in articles of incorporation, or have attached articles of incorporation; except that, in either case, provisions that would not be required to be included in restated articles of incorporation of a domestic nonprofit corporation may be omitted.

(d) The articles of entity conversion must be delivered to the secretary of state for filing, and take effect at the effective time provided in Section 1.23. Articles of entity conversion filed under Section 9.53(a) or (b) may be combined with any required conversion filing under the organic law of the domestic unincorporated entity if the combined filing satisfies the requirements of both this section and the other organic law.

(e) If the converting entity is a foreign unincorporated entity that is authorized to transact business in this state under a provision of law similar to [Chapter] 15, its certificate of authority or other type of foreign qualification is cancelled automatically on the effective date of its conversion.

Source Note: Patterned after Model Business Corporation Act, 3d Ed. (2002) § 9.53.

CROSS-REFERENCES

"Deliver" defined, see § 1.40.

"Domestic nonprofit corporation" defined, see § 1.40.

"Domestic unincorporated entity" defined, see § 1.40.

Effect of entity conversion, see § 9.55.

"Filing entity" defined, see § 1.40.

Filing fees, see § 1.22.

Filing requirements, see § 1.20.

"Foreign unincorporated entity" defined, see § 1.40.

"Organic law" defined, see § 1.40.

"Public organic record" defined, see § 1.40.

Restrictions and required approvals, see § 9.03.

"Surviving entity" defined, see § 9.50.

"Unincorporated entity" defined, see § 1.40.

OFFICIAL COMMENT

The filing of articles of entity conversion makes the conversion a matter of public record. Where the surviving entity is organized under the laws of this state, the filing also makes of public record its articles of incorporation or public organic record. If the converting entity is a foreign unincorporated entity that is authorized to transact business in this state, Section 9.53(e) automatically cancels its certificate of authority.

The filing requirements for articles of entity conversion are set forth in Section 1.20. Under Section 1.23, a document may specify a delayed effective time and date, and if it does so the document becomes effective at the time and date specified, except that a delayed effective date may not be later than the

90th day after the date the document is filed. In cases where an entity is changing the jurisdiction in which it is incorporated or otherwise organized, it is recommended that the entity use a delayed effective date provision in its entity conversion filings in both this state and the foreign jurisdiction, or otherwise coordinate those filings, so that the filings become effective at the same time. This will avoid any question about a gap in the continuity of its existence that might otherwise arise as a result of those filings taking effect at different times.

If a conversion involves a domestic unincorporated entity whose organic law also requires a filing to effectuate the conversion, Section 9.53(d) permits the filings under that organic law and this act to be combined so that only one document need be filed with the secretary of state.

§ 9.54. EFFECT OF ENTITY CONVERSION

(a) Except as otherwise provided in Section 9.03, when a conversion under this [subchapter] becomes effective:

(1) the title to all real and personal property, both tangible and intangible, of the converting entity remains in the surviving entity without reversion or impairment;

(2) the liabilities of the converting entity remain the liabilities of the surviving entity;

(3) an action or proceeding pending against the converting entity continues against the surviving entity as if the conversion had not occurred;

(4) in the case of a surviving entity that is a filing entity, its articles of incorporation or public organic record and its private organic rules become effective;

(5) in the case of a surviving entity that is a nonfiling entity, its private organic rules become effective;

(6) the memberships or interests of the converting entity are reclassified into memberships, interests, other securities, obligations, rights to acquire memberships, interests or securities, or into cash or other property in accordance with the plan of conversion; and the members or interest

holders of the converting entity are entitled only to the rights provided to them under the terms of the conversion and to any appraisal rights they may have under the organic law of the converting entity; and

(7) the surviving entity is deemed to:

(i) be incorporated or organized under and subject to the organic law of the converting entity for all purposes; and

(ii) be the same nonprofit corporation or unincorporated entity without interruption as the converting entity.

(b) A member who becomes subject to interest holder liability for some or all of the debts, obligations, or liabilities of the surviving entity has interest holder liability only for those debts, obligations, or liabilities of the surviving entity that arise after the effective time of the articles of entity conversion.

(c) The interest holder liability of an interest holder in an unincorporated entity that converts to a domestic nonprofit corporation is as follows:

(1) The conversion does not discharge any interest holder liability under the organic law of the unincorporated entity to the extent any such interest holder liability arose before the effective time of the articles of entity conversion.

(2) The interest holder does not have interest holder liability under the organic law of the unincorporated entity for any debt, obligation, or liability of the corporation that arises after the effective time of the articles of entity conversion.

(3) The provisions of the organic law of the unincorporated entity continue to apply to the collection or discharge of any interest holder liability preserved by paragraph (1), as if the conversion had not occurred.

(4) The interest holder has whatever rights of contribution from other interest holders are provided by the organic law of the unincorporated entity with respect to any

interest holder liability preserved by paragraph (1), as if the conversion had not occurred.

Source Note: Patterned after Model Business Corporation Act, 3d Ed. (2002) § 9.54.

CROSS-REFERENCES

"Converting entity" defined, see § 9.50.

"Domestic nonprofit corporation" defined, see § 1.40.

"Domestic unincorporated entity" defined, see § 1.40.

"Filing entity" defined, see § 1.40.

"Foreign unincorporated entity" defined, see § 1.40.

"Interest" defined, see § 1.40.

"Interest holder" defined, see § 1.40.

"Nonfiling entity" defined, see § 1.40.

"Organic law" defined, see § 1.40.

"Private organic rules" defined, see § 1.40.

"Public organic record" defined, see § 1.40.

"Surviving entity" defined, see § 9.50.

"Unincorporated entity" defined, see § 1.40.

OFFICIAL COMMENT

This section provides for the effect of an entity conversion. An entity conversion is not a conveyance, transfer, or assignment. It does not give rise to claims of reverter or impairment of title based on a prohibited conveyance, transfer, or assignment. Nor does it give rise to a claim that a contract with the converting entity is no longer in effect on the ground of nonassignability, unless the contract specifically provides that it does not survive an entity conversion.

Section 9.54(a)(1)–(3) and (b) are similar to Section 11.07(a)(3)–(5) and (c) with respect to the effects of a merger. Although Section 9.54(a)(1)–(3) would be implied by the general rule stated in Section 9.54(a)(7) even if not stated expressly, those rules have been included to avoid any question as to whether a different result was intended.

Section 9.54(c) preserves liability only for interest holder liabilities to the extent they arise before the conversion. Interest holder liability is not preserved for subsequent changes in an underlying liability, regardless of whether a change is voluntary or involuntary.

This section does not address the issue that could arise in an entity conversion where a person who had authority to bind the converting entity loses that authority because of the conversion and yet purports to act to bind the surviving entity. For example, in a conversion of a general partnership into a corporation, a person who is a general partner but does not become an officer of the corporation will lose the authority of a general partner to bind the business to obligations incurred in the ordinary course, but might purport to commit the corporation to such an obligation in dealing with a person who does not have knowledge of the conversion. Instances in which this occurs will be rare and, in the limited instances in which it does occur, general principles of agency law are sufficient to resolve the problems created.

§ 9.55. ABANDONMENT OF AN ENTITY CONVERSION

(a) Unless otherwise provided in a plan of entity conversion of a domestic nonprofit corporation, after the plan has been adopted and approved as required by this [subchapter], and at any time before the entity conversion has become effective, it may be abandoned by the board of directors without action by the members.

(b) If an entity conversion is abandoned after articles of entity conversion have been filed with the secretary of state but before the entity conversion has become effective, a statement that the entity conversion has been abandoned in accordance with this section, signed by an officer or other duly authorized representative, must be delivered to the secretary of state for filing prior to the effective date of the entity conversion. Upon filing, the statement takes effect and the entity conversion is abandoned and does not become effective.

Source Note: Patterned after Model Business Corporation Act, 3d Ed. (2002) § 9.55.

CROSS-REFERENCES

Approval of entity conversion, see § 9.52.

"Deliver" defined, see § 1.40.

"Domestic nonprofit corporation" defined, see § 1.40.

Effective time and date of filing, see § 1.23.

Filing requirements, see § 1.20.

OFFICIAL COMMENT

Unless otherwise provided in a plan of entity conversion, a domestic nonprofit corporation proposing to convert to an unincorporated entity may abandon the transaction without member approval, even though it has been previously approved by the members. Whether or not the conversion of an unincorporated entity to a domestic nonprofit corporation may be abandoned is determined by the law under which the unincorporated entity is organized, except that the rule of this section will apply to the extent provided in Section 9.50(c).

CHAPTER 10

Amendment of Articles of Incorporation and Bylaws

[Subchapter] A
AMENDMENT OF ARTICLES OF INCORPORATION

§ 10.01. AUTHORITY TO AMEND

A nonprofit corporation may amend its articles of incorporation at any time to add or change a provision that is required or permitted in the articles as of the effective date of the amendment or to delete a provision that is not required to be contained in the articles.

Source Note: Patterned after Model Business Corporation Act, 3d Ed. (2002) § 10.01. Derived from Revised Model Nonprofit Corporation Act (1987) § 10.01.

CROSS-REFERENCES

Amendment:
- before issuance of memberships, see § 10.02.
- by board of directors and members, see § 10.03.
- by directors, see § 10.05.
- pursuant to court-ordered reorganization, see § 10.08.

Articles of incorporation, see § 2.02.

Duration of corporation existence, see § 3.02.

Effective date of amendment, see § 1.23.

Powers of corporation, see § 3.02.

Procedure for amendment, see §§ 10.02–10.07.

Purposes of corporation, see § 3.01.

Restatement of articles, see § 10.07.

Voting by voting groups, see §§ 7.24, 7.25, and 10.04.

"Voting group" defined, see § 1.40.

OFFICIAL COMMENT

Section 10.01 authorizes a nonprofit corporation to amend its articles of incorporation by adding a new provision to its articles of incorporation, modifying an existing provision, or deleting a provision in its entirety. The sole test for the validity of an amendment is whether the provision could lawfully have been included in (or in the case of a deletion, omitted from) the articles as of the effective date of the amendment.

The power of amendment must be exercised pursuant to the procedures set forth in Chapter 10. Section 10.03 requires most amendments to be approved by a majority of the votes cast on the proposed amendment at a meeting at which a quorum consisting of at least a majority of the votes entitled to be cast is present. This requirement is supplemented by Section 10.04, which governs voting by voting groups on amendments that directly affect a single class of members, and by Section 7.26, which governs amendments that change the voting requirements for future amendments.

A provision in the articles of incorporation is subject to amendment under Section 10.01 even though the provision is described, referred to, or stated in a membership certificate or other document issued by the corporation that reflects provisions of the articles of incorporation.

However, Section 10.01 does not concern obligations of a corporation to its members based upon contracts independent of the articles of incorporation. An amendment permitted by this section may constitute a breach of such a contract or of a contract between the members themselves. A member with contractual rights (or who otherwise is concerned about possible onerous amendments) may obtain complete protection against these amendments by establishing procedures in the articles or bylaws that limit the power of amendment without the member's consent. In appropriate cases, a member may be able to enjoin an amendment that constitutes a breach of a contract.

Because of the broad power of amendment contained in this section, it is unnecessary to make any reference to, or reserve, an express power to amend in the articles of incorporation.

§ 10.02. AMENDMENT BEFORE ISSUANCE OF MEMBERSHIPS

If a membership corporation has not yet issued memberships, its board of directors, or its incorporators if it has no board of directors, may adopt one or more amendments to the articles of incorporation.

Source Note: Patterned after Model Business Corporation Act, 3d Ed. (2002) § 10.02. Derived from Revised Model Nonprofit Corporation Act (1987) § 10.02(b) (first sentence).

CROSS-REFERENCES

Articles of amendment, see § 10.06.

Effective date of amendment, see § 1.23.

Incorporators, see § 2.01.

"Membership corporation" defined, see § 1.40.

Organization of corporation, see § 2.05.

Restated articles of incorporation, see § 10.07.

OFFICIAL COMMENT

Section 10.02 provides that, before any memberships are issued, amendments may be made by the persons empowered to complete the organization of a membership corporation. Under Section 2.05 the organizers may be either the incorporators or the initial board of directors or designated body named in the articles of incorporation.

The authority of the board of directors under this section to amend the articles of incorporation may be vested by the articles or bylaws in a designated body. See Section 8.12.

§ 10.03. AMENDMENT OF ARTICLES OF MEMBERSHIP CORPORATION

(a) An amendment to the articles of incorporation of a membership corporation must be adopted in the following manner:
   (1) Except as provided in paragraph (5), the proposed amendment must be adopted by the board of directors.
   (2) Except as provided in Sections 10.05, 10.07, and 10.08, a proposed amendment must be submitted to the members entitled to vote for their approval.
   (3) The board of directors must transmit to the members a recommendation that the members approve the amendment, unless the board of directors makes a determination that because of conflicts of interest or other special circumstances it should not make such a recommendation, in which case the board of directors must transmit to the members the basis for that determination.
   (4) The board of directors may condition its submission of the amendment to the members on any basis.
   (5) Except as provided in the articles of incorporation or bylaws, an amendment may be proposed by 10% or more of the members entitled to vote on the amendment or by such greater or lesser number of members as is specified in the articles. Paragraphs (1), (3), and (4) do not apply to an amendment proposed by the members under this paragraph.
   (6) If the amendment is required to be approved by the members, and the approval is to be given at a meeting, the corporation must give notice to each member entitled to vote on the amendment of the meeting of members at which the amendment is to be submitted for approval. The notice must state that the purpose, or one of the purposes, of the meeting is to consider the

amendment and must contain or be accompanied by a copy of the amendment.

(7) Unless the articles of incorporation or bylaws, or the board of directors acting pursuant to paragraph (4), requires a greater vote or a greater number of members to be present, the approval of an amendment requires the approval of the members at a meeting at which a quorum exists, and, if any class of members is entitled to vote as a separate group on the amendment, the approval of each such separate voting group at a meeting at which a quorum of the voting group exists.

(8) In addition to the adoption and approval of an amendment by the board of directors and members as required by this section, an amendment must also be approved by a designated body whose approval is required by the articles of incorporation or bylaws.

(b) Unless the articles of incorporation provide otherwise, the board of directors of a membership corporation may adopt amendments to the corporation's articles of incorporation without approval of the members to:

(1) extend the duration of the corporation if it was incorporated at a time when limited duration was required by law;

(2) delete the names and addresses of the initial directors or members of a designated body;

(3) delete the name and address of the initial registered agent or registered office, if a statement of change is on file with the secretary of state;

(4) change the corporation name by substituting or deleting the word "corporation," "incorporated," "company," or "limited," or the abbreviation "corp.," "inc.," "co.," or "ltd.," for a similar word or abbreviation in the name;

(5) restate without change all of the then operative provisions of the articles.

Source Note: Subsection (a) is patterned after Model Business Corporation Act, 3d Ed. (2002) § 10.03 and derived from Revised Model Nonprofit Corporation Act (1987) § 10.03.

Required vote of the members is reduced from 2/3 of the votes cast or an absolute majority of the outstanding voting power to a majority of the votes cast. Paragraph (a)(5) is new. Subsection (b) is patterned after Model Business Corporation Act, 3d Ed. (2002) § 10.05(1)–(4).

CROSS-REFERENCES

Articles of amendment, see § 10.06.

Designated body, see § 8.12.

Director standards of conduct, see § 8.30.

"Membership corporation" defined, see § 1.40.

Notice, see § 1.41.

Notice of members' meeting, see § 7.05.

Quorum at members' meeting, see § 7.24.

Restatement of articles of incorporation, see § 10.07.

Supermajority quorum and voting requirements, see § 7.26.

Voting by voting group, see §§ 7.24, 7.25, and 10.04.

Voting entitlement of members generally, see § 7.21.

"Voting group" defined, see § 1.40.

OFFICIAL COMMENT

1. In General

Under Section 10.03, if a nonprofit corporation has issued memberships, a proposed amendment to the articles of incorporation must be adopted by the board. Thereafter, the board must submit the amendment to the members for their approval, except as provided in Sections 10.05, 10.07, and 10.08.

The functions and powers of the board of directors under this section may be vested by the articles of incorporation or bylaws in a designated body.

2. Submission to the Members

Section 10.03 requires the board of directors, after having adopted an amendment, to submit the amendment to the members for approval except as otherwise provided by Sections 10.05, 10.07, and 10.08. When submitting the amendment, the board of directors must make a recommendation to the members that the amendment be approved, unless the board of directors makes a determination that because of conflicts of interest or other special circumstances it should make no recommendation. For example, the board of directors may make such a determination where there is not a sufficient number of directors free of a conflicting interest to approve the amendment or because the board of directors is evenly divided as to the merits of an amendment but is able to agree that members should be permitted to consider the amendment. If the board of directors makes such a determination, it must describe the conflict of interest or special circumstances, and communicate the basis for the determination, when submitting the amendment to the members. The exception for conflicts of interest or other special circumstances is intended to be available sparingly. Generally, members should not be asked to act on an amendment in the absence of a recommendation by the board of directors. The exception is not intended to relieve the board of directors of its duty to consider carefully the amendment and the interests of members.

Section 10.03(4) permits the board of directors to condition its submission of an amendment on any basis. Among the conditions that a board might impose are that the amendment will not be deemed approved unless it is approved by a specified vote of the members, or by one or more specified classes of members, voting as a separate voting group, or by a specified percentage of disinterested members. The board of directors is not limited to conditions of these types.

3. Quorum and Voting

Section 10.03(7) provides that approval of an amendment requires approval of the members at a meeting at which a quorum consisting of at least a majority of the votes entitled to be cast on the amendment exists, including, if any class of members is entitled to vote as a separate group, at a meeting at which a similar quorum of the voting group exists. If a quorum exists, then under Sections 7.24 and 7.25 the amendment will be approved if more votes are cast in favor of the amendment than against it by the voting group or separate voting groups entitled to vote on the plan. This represents a change from the act's previous higher voting rule for amendments, which required approval by 2/3 of the votes cast or an absolute majority of the outstanding voting power.

If an amendment would affect the voting requirements on future amendments, it must be approved by the vote required by Section 7.26.

4. Approval by Board of Directors Alone

The amendments described in Section 10.03(b) are so routine and "housekeeping" in nature as not to require approval by the members. None affects substantive rights in any meaningful way.

§ 10.04. VOTING ON AMENDMENTS BY VOTING GROUPS

(a) Except as provided in the articles of incorporation or bylaws, if a nonprofit corporation has more than one class of members, the members of each class are entitled to vote as a separate voting group (if member voting is otherwise required by this [act]) on a proposed amendment to the articles of incorporation if the amendment would:

(1) effect an exchange or reclassification of all or part of the memberships of the class into memberships of another class;

(2) effect an exchange or reclassification, or create the right of exchange, of all or part of the memberships of another class into memberships of the class;

(3) change the rights, preferences, or limitations of all or part of the memberships of the class in a manner different than the amendment would affect another class;

(4) change the rights, preferences, or limitations of all or part of the memberships of the class by changing the rights, preferences, or limitations of another class;

(5) increase or decrease the number of memberships authorized for that class;
(6) increase the number of memberships authorized for another class; or
(7) authorize a new class of memberships.

(b) If a class of members will be divided into two or more classes by an amendment to the articles of incorporation, the amendment must be approved by a majority of the members of each class that will be created.

Source Note: Subsection (a) is patterned after Model Business Corporation Act, 3d Ed. (2002) § 10.04(a), except subsection (a)(5)–(8), and derived from Revised Model Nonprofit Corporation Act (1987) § 10.04. Subsection (b) is patterned after Revised Model Nonprofit Corporation Act (1987) § 10.22(d).

CROSS-REFERENCES

Classes of members, see § 6.01.

Quorum for members' meeting to amend articles, see § 10.03.

Voting by voting groups generally, see §§ 7.24 and 7.25.

"Voting group" defined, see § 1.40.

OFFICIAL COMMENT

Section 10.04(a)(1) requires separate approval by voting groups for certain types of amendments to the articles of incorporation where the nonprofit corporation has more than one class of members.

Members are entitled to vote as separate voting groups under this section even though they are designated as nonvoting members in the articles of incorporation or bylaws, unless the articles or bylaws specifically deny them the right to vote on a proposed amendment that would otherwise give them the right to vote under this section.

This section does not make the right to vote by separate voting group dependent on an evaluation of whether the amendment is detrimental to the class; if the amendment is one of those described, the class is automatically entitled to vote as a separate voting group on the amendment. The question whether an amendment is detrimental is often a question of judgment, and approval by the affected class is required irrespective of whether the board or other members believe it is beneficial or detrimental to the affected class.

Sections 7.24 and 7.25 set forth the mechanics of voting by multiple voting groups.

The functions and powers of the board of directors under this section may be vested by the articles or bylaws in a designated body.

§ 10.05. AMENDMENT OF ARTICLES OF NONMEMBERSHIP CORPORATION

Except as otherwise provided in the articles of incorporation, the board of directors of a nonmembership corporation may adopt amendments to the corporation's articles. An amendment adopted by the board of directors under this subsection must also be approved:

(1) by a designated body whose approval is required by the articles of incorporation or bylaws;
(2) if the amendment changes or deletes a provision regarding the appointment of a director by persons other than the board, by those persons as if they constituted a voting group; and
(3) if the amendment changes or deletes a provision regarding the designation of a director, by the individual designated at the time as that director.

Source Note: Derived from Revised Model Nonprofit Corporation Act (1987) § 10.02(a).

CROSS-REFERENCES

Action by board of directors, see §§ 8.20–8.24.

Articles of amendment, see § 10.06.

Duration of corporate existence, see § 3.02.

Effective date of amendment, see § 1.23.

Extrinsic facts, see § 1.20.

Name of corporation, see Ch. 4.

"Nonmembership corporation" defined, see § 1.40.

Registered office and agent, see Ch. 5.

Restatement of articles, see § 10.07.

OFFICIAL COMMENT

This section only applies to nonmembership corporations. The procedures for amending the articles of incorporation of a membership corporation are found in Sections 10.02 through 10.04.

Amendments provided for in this section may be included in restated articles of incorporation under Section 10.07 or in the various types of articles filed to effectuate fundamental transactions under Chapter 9 or 11.

The authority of the board of directors under this section to amend the articles of incorporation may be vested by the articles of incorporation or bylaws in a designated body.

§ 10.06. ARTICLES OF AMENDMENT

After an amendment to the articles of incorporation has been adopted and approved in the manner required by this [act] and by the articles of incorporation, the nonprofit corporation must deliver to the secretary of state, for filing, articles of amendment, which must set forth:

(1) the name of the corporation;
(2) the text of the amendment adopted;
(3) if the amendment provides for an exchange, reclassification, or cancellation of memberships, provisions for implementing the amendment if not contained in the amendment itself (which may be made dependent upon facts objectively ascertainable outside the articles of amendment in accordance with Section 1.20(c));

(4) the date of the amendment's adoption; and
(5) if the amendment:
  (i) was adopted by the incorporators, board of directors, or a designated body without member approval, a statement that the amendment was adopted by the incorporators or by the board of directors or designated body, as the case may be, and that member approval was not required; or
  (ii) required approval by the members, a statement that the amendment was duly approved by the members in the manner required by this [act] and by the articles of incorporation and bylaws.

Source Note: Patterned after Model Business Corporation Act, 3d Ed. (2002) § 10.06. Derived from Revised Model Nonprofit Corporation Act (1987) § 10.05, except that the requirement that the articles of amendment state the number of votes cast for and against an amendment by the members has been omitted.

CROSS-REFERENCES

Amendment by:
  board of directors, see § 10.05.
  incorporators or initial directors, see § 10.02.
  members, see §§ 10.03 and 10.04.

Deliver" defined, see § 1.40.

Effective date of amendment, see § 1.23.

Extrinsic facts, see § 1.20.

Filing fees, see § 1.22.

"Voting group" defined, see § 1.40.

OFFICIAL COMMENT

Section 10.06(3) requires the articles of amendment to contain a statement of the manner in which an exchange, reclassification, or cancellation of memberships is to be put into effect, if not set forth in the amendment itself. This requirement avoids any possible confusion that may arise as to how the amendment is to be put into effect and also permits the amendment itself to be limited to provisions of permanent applicability, with transitional provisions having no long-range effect appearing only in the articles of amendment.

§ 10.07. RESTATED ARTICLES OF INCORPORATION

(a) The board of directors of a nonprofit corporation may restate its articles of incorporation at any time, without approval by the members or any other person, to consolidate all amendments into a single document without substantive change.

(b) If restated articles of a membership corporation include one or more new amendments that require member approval, the amendments must be adopted and approved as provided in Sections 10.03 and 10.04.

(c) A nonprofit corporation that restates its articles of incorporation must deliver to the secretary of state for filing articles of amendment under Section 10.06 which include a statement that the articles of amendment are a restatement that consolidates all amendments into a single record.

(d) Duly adopted restated articles of incorporation supersede the original articles of incorporation and all amendments thereto.

(e) The secretary of state shall certify restated articles of incorporation as the articles of incorporation currently in effect.

Source Note: Patterned after Model Business Corporation Act, 3d Ed. (2002) § 10.07. Derived from Revised Model Nonprofit Corporation Act (1987) § 10.06.

CROSS-REFERENCES

Amendment of articles of incorporation:
- before issuance of memberships, see § 10.02.
- by board of directors, see § 10.05.
- by board of directors and by members, see § 10.03.

Certified copies, see § 1.22.

"Deliver" defined, see § 1.40.

Effective date of restatement, see § 1.23.

Filing fees, see § 1.22.

Filing requirements, see § 1.20.

"Membership corporation" defined, see § 1.40.

OFFICIAL COMMENT

Restated articles of incorporation serve the useful purpose of permitting articles of incorporation that have been amended from time to time, or are being concurrently amended, to be consolidated into a single document.

A restatement of a nonprofit corporation's articles of incorporation is not an amendment of the articles of incorporation, but only a consolidation of amendments into a single document. A corporation that is restating its articles may concurrently amend the articles, and include the new amendments in the restated articles. In such a case, the provisions of this chapter that govern amendments of the articles of incorporation would apply to the new amendments. In case of doubt whether a provision of a restatement of the articles of incorporation might be deemed to be an amendment, rather than a consolidation, the prudent course for the corporation is to treat that provision as an amendment, and follow the procedures that apply to amendments under this chapter.

Where the articles of incorporation are amended at the same time they are restated, a combined articles of amendment and restatement may be filed.

The authority of the board of directors under this section to restate the articles of incorporation may be vested by the articles or bylaws in a designated body.

§ 10.08. AMENDMENT PURSUANT TO REORGANIZATION

(a) A nonprofit corporation's articles of incorporation may be amended without action by the board of directors, a designated body, or the members to carry out a plan of reorganization ordered or decreed by a court of competent jurisdiction under the authority of a law of the United States.

(b) An individual designated by the court shall deliver to the secretary of state for filing articles of amendment setting forth:
   (1) the name of the corporation;
   (2) the text of each amendment approved by the court;
   (3) the date of the court's order or decree approving the articles of amendment;
   (4) the title of the reorganization proceeding in which the order or decree was entered; and
   (5) a statement that the court had jurisdiction of the proceeding under federal statute.

(c) This section does not apply after entry of a final decree in the reorganization proceeding even though the court retains jurisdiction of the proceeding for limited purposes unrelated to consummation of the reorganization plan.

Source Note: Patterned after Model Business Corporation Act, 3d Ed. (2002) § 10.08. Substantially a reenactment of Revised Model Nonprofit Corporation Act (1987) § 10.07.

CROSS-REFERENCES

Deliver" defined, see § 1.40.

Effective date of amendment, see § 1.23.

Filing fees, see § 1.22.

Filing requirements, see § 1.20.

OFFICIAL COMMENT

Section 10.08 provides a simplified method of conforming corporate documents filed under state law with the federal statutes relating to corporate reorganization. If a federal court confirms a plan of reorganization that requires articles of amendment to be filed, those amendments may be prepared and filed by an individual designated by the court and no approval is required from the members, the board of directors, or a designated body.

This section applies only to amendments in articles of incorporation approved before the entry of a final decree in the reorganization.

§ 10.09 EFFECT OF ARTICLES AMENDMENT

(a) Except as provided in subsections (b), (c), and (d), an amendment to the articles of incorporation does not affect a cause of action existing against or in favor of the nonprofit corporation, a proceeding to which the corporation is a party, or the existing rights of persons other than members of the corporation or persons referred to in the articles. An amendment changing a corporation's name does not abate a proceeding brought by or against the corporation in its former name.

(b) Property held in trust by a nonprofit corporation or otherwise dedicated to a charitable purpose may not be diverted from its purpose by an amendment of its articles of incorporation unless the corporation obtains an appropriate order of [*court*] [*the attorney general*] to the extent required by and pursuant to the law of this state on cy pres or otherwise dealing with the nondiversion of charitable assets.

(c) Unless a nonprofit corporation obtains an appropriate order of [*court*] [*the attorney general*] under the law of this state on cy pres or otherwise dealing with the nondiversion of charitable assets, an amendment of its articles of incorporation may not affect:

  (1) any restriction imposed upon property held by the corporation by virtue of any trust under which it holds that property; or

  (2) the existing rights of persons other than its members.

(d) A person who is a member or otherwise affiliated with a charitable corporation may not receive a direct or indirect financial benefit in connection with an amendment of the articles of incorporation unless the person is itself a charitable corporation or an unincorporated entity with a charitable purpose. This subsection does not apply to the receipt of reasonable compensation for services rendered.

Source Note: Subsection (a) is patterned after Model Business Corporation Act, 3d Ed. (2002) § 10.09. Derived from Revised Model Nonprofit Corporation Act (1987) § 10.08. Subsections (b)–(d) are new.

CROSS-REFERENCES

Amendment after issuance of shares, see §§ 10.03–10.05.

Amendment before issuance of memberships, see § 10.02.

Delayed effective date, see § 1.23.

Effective time and date of filing, see § 1.23.

"Proceeding" defined, see § 1.40.

OFFICIAL COMMENT

Provision is made in Section 10.09 to prevent the diversion of property held in trust by a nonprofit corporation or otherwise dedicated to a charitable purpose without appropriate review. The section also prohibits the receipt of direct or indirect financial benefit by a member or person otherwise affiliated with a charitable corporation as a result of an amendment of the articles of incorporation. The only exception is if the member or person otherwise affiliated with a charitable corporation is itself a charitable corporation or an unincorporated entity with a charitable purpose. Reasonable compensation for services rendered to the charitable corporation is not within the scope of Section 10.09(d).

Under Section 10.09, amendments to articles of incorporation do not interrupt the corporate existence and do not abate a proceeding by or against the nonprofit corporation even though the amendment changes the name of the corporation.

Amendments are effective when filed unless a delayed effective date is elected. See Section 1.23.

[Subchapter] B
AMENDMENT OF BYLAWS

§ 10.20. AMENDMENT BY BOARD OF DIRECTORS OR MEMBERS

(a) Except as provided in the articles of incorporation or bylaws, the members of a membership corporation may amend or repeal the corporation's bylaws.

(b) The board of directors of a membership corporation or nonmembership corporation may amend or repeal the corporation's bylaws, unless the articles of incorporation or bylaws or Sections 10.21 or 10.22 reserve that power exclusively to the members or a designated body in whole or part.

Source Note: Patterned after Model Business Corporation Act, 3d Ed. (2002) § 10.20. Derived generally from Revised Model Nonprofit Corporation Act (1987) §§ 10.20 and 10.21.

CROSS-REFERENCES

Action by:

board of directors, see §§ 8.20–8.24.

members, see §§ 7.24 and 7.25.

"Membership corporation" defined, see § 1.40.

"Nonmembership corporation" defined, see § 1.40.

Supermajority requirements for directors or designated body, see § 10.21.

OFFICIAL COMMENT

The power to amend or repeal bylaws is shared by the board of directors and the members in a membership corporation, unless that power is reserved exclusively to the members by an appropriate provision in the articles of incorporation. Section 10.20(b) provides that the power to amend or repeal the bylaws may be reserved to the members "in whole or in part." This language permits the reservation of power to be limited to specific articles or sections of the bylaws or to specific subjects or topics addressed in the bylaws. The powers of the board of directors under this section may be vested by the articles or bylaws in a designated body.

Section 10.21 limits the power of directors of a membership corporation to adopt or amend supermajority provisions in the bylaws. See Section 10.21 and the Official Comment thereto.

This section follows the simplified style of the Model Business Corporation Act. In contrast, the provisions on bylaw amendments in the prior version of this act largely followed the provisions on articles amendments, including, among other things, a detailed set of provisions requiring class voting on bylaw amendments in a membership corporation.

§ 10.21. BYLAW INCREASING QUORUM OR VOTING REQUIREMENT FOR BOARD OF DIRECTORS OR DESIGNATED BODY

(a) A bylaw that increases a quorum or voting requirement for the board of directors or a designated body may be amended or repealed:
  (1) if originally adopted by the members, only by the members, unless the bylaws otherwise provide;
  (2) if adopted by the board of directors or designated body, either by the members or by the board of directors or designated body.

(b) A bylaw adopted or amended by the members that increases a quorum or voting requirement for the board of directors or a designated body may provide that it can be amended or repealed only by a specified vote of either the members or the board of directors or designated body.

(c) Action by the board of directors or a designated body under subsection (a) to amend or repeal a bylaw that changes the quorum or voting requirement for the board of directors or a designated body must meet the same quorum requirement and be adopted by the same vote required to take action under the quorum and voting requirement then in effect or proposed to be adopted, whichever is greater.

Source Note: Patterned after Model Business Corporation Act, 3d Ed. (2002) § 10.21.

CROSS-REFERENCES

Increased quorum and voting requirements for members, see § 7.26.

Quorum and voting of directors, see § 8.24.

OFFICIAL COMMENT

Provisions that increase a quorum or voting requirement for the board of directors or a designated body over the requirement that would otherwise apply under this act or that was previously set forth in the bylaws ("supermajority requirements") may be placed in the bylaws of the nonprofit corporation without specific authorization in the articles of incorporation. See Section 8.24(a) and (c). Like other bylaw provisions, they may be adopted either by the members or by the board of directors or a designated body. See Section 10.20. Such provisions may be amended or repealed as provided in this section.

Section 10.21(a)(1) provides that if a supermajority requirement is imposed by a bylaw adopted by the members, only the members may amend or repeal it. Under Section 10.21(b), such a bylaw may impose restrictions on the manner in which it may be thereafter amended or repealed by the members. If a supermajority requirement is imposed in a bylaw adopted by the board of directors or a designated body, the bylaw may be amended either by the members or the board of directors or designated body (see Section 10.21(a)(2)). However, if such an amendment is amended by the board of directors or a designated body, Section 10.21(c) requires approval by the supermajority requirement then in effect or proposed to be adopted, whichever is greater. Compare Section 7.26.

§ 10.22. BYLAW AMENDMENTS REQUIRING MEMBER APPROVAL

(a) Except as provided in the articles of incorporation or bylaws, the board of directors or designated body of a membership corporation that has one or more members at the time may not adopt or amend a bylaw under:
- (1) Section 6.10 providing that some of the members shall have different rights or obligations than other members with respect to voting, dissolution, transfer of memberships, or other matters;
- (2) Section 6.13 levying dues, assessments, or fees on some or all of the members;
- (3) Section 6.21 relating to the termination or suspension of members;
- (4) Section 6.22 authorizing the purchase of memberships;
- (5) Section 8.08(a):
  - (i) requiring cause to remove a director; or
  - (ii) specifying what constitutes cause to remove a director;
- (6) Section 8.08(e) relating to the removal of a director who is designated in a manner other than election or appointment; or
- (7) Section 8.12.

(b) The board of directors or designated body of a membership corporation may not amend the articles of incorporation or bylaws to vary the application of subsection (a) to the corporation.

(c) If a nonprofit corporation has more than one class of members, the members of a class are entitled to vote as a separate voting group on an amendment to the bylaws that:

(1) is described in subsection (a) if the amendment would affect the members of that class differently than the members of another class; or
(2) has any of the effects described in Section 10.04.

(d) If a class of members will be divided into two or more classes by an amendment to the bylaws, the amendment must be approved by a majority of the members of each class that will be created.

Source Note: Subsection (d) is derived from Revised Model Nonprofit Corporation Act (1987) § 10.22(d).

CROSS-REFERENCES

Class voting by members, see § 7.24.

"Designated body" defined, see § 1.40.

"Member" defined, see § 1.40.

OFFICIAL COMMENT

Section 10.22(a) prohibits the board of directors or a designated body from amending bylaws on certain subjects without the approval of the members except as otherwise permitted by the articles of incorporation or bylaws. The subjects requiring member approval were considered so important to members that their consent should be required, unless the members have in effect agreed that they will not have a vote by accepting membership in a nonprofit corporation whose articles or bylaws dispense with the required vote.

§ 10.23. EFFECT OF BYLAW AMENDMENT

(a) Property held in trust by a nonprofit corporation or otherwise dedicated to a charitable purpose may not be diverted from its purpose by an amendment of its bylaws unless the corporation obtains an appropriate order of [*court*] [*the attorney general*] to the extent required by and pursuant to the law of this state on cy pres or otherwise dealing with the nondiversion of charitable assets.

(b) Unless a nonprofit corporation obtains an appropriate order of [*court*] [*the attorney general*] under the law of this state on cy pres or otherwise dealing with the nondiversion of charitable assets, an amendment of its bylaws may not affect:
   (1) any restriction imposed upon property held by the corporation by virtue of any trust under which it holds that property; or
   (2) the existing rights of persons other than its members.

(c) A person who is a member or otherwise affiliated with a charitable corporation may not receive a direct or indirect financial benefit in connection with an amendment of the bylaws unless the person is itself a charitable corporation or an unincorporated entity with a charitable purpose. This subsection does not apply to the receipt of reasonable compensation for services rendered.

Source Note: New.

OFFICIAL COMMENT

Because the act generally permits the bylaws to contain the same types of provisions for the governance of a nonprofit corporation as the articles of incorporation, this section makes applicable to amendments of the bylaws the same restrictions that apply to amendments of the articles under Section 10.09.

[Subchapter] C
SPECIAL RIGHTS

§ 10.30. APPROVAL BY THIRD PERSONS

(a) The articles of incorporation may require that an amendment to the articles be approved in the form of a record by a specified person or group of persons in addition to the board of directors and members.

(b) The articles of incorporation or bylaws may require that an amendment to the bylaws be approved in the form of a record by a specified person or group of persons in addition to the board of directors and members.

(c) A requirement in the articles of incorporation or bylaws described in subsection (a) or (b) may only be amended with the approval in the form of a record of the specified person or group of persons.

Source Note: Derived from Revised Model Nonprofit Corporation Act (1987) § 10.30.

CROSS-REFERENCES

Amendment of articles of incorporation, see Subch. 10A.

Amendment of bylaws, see Subch. 10B.

"Designated body" defined, see § 1.40.

"Member" defined, see § 1.40.

"Person" defined, see § 1.40.

OFFICIAL COMMENT

This section provides a nonprofit corporation flexibility in control over amendments to the articles of incorporation or bylaws by allowing parent or affiliated corporations, government bodies, and others to exercise a veto power over such amendments.

A person given the right to approve an amendment under this section is not a designated body because the approval required under this section is in addition to the otherwise required approvals by the board of directors and members. A situation where a person other than the board of directors is given the power to approve an amendment and approval by the board is not also required, does not implicate this section because in that situation the person will be a designated body.

The act also provides that a person or group of persons whose approval must be obtained to amend the articles of incorporation or bylaws must also consent to a merger, membership exchange, or a sale of all, or substantially all, of the property of a nonprofit corporation other than in the regular course of its activities. See Sections 11.04 and 12.02.

CHAPTER 11

Mergers and Membership Exchanges

§ 11.01. PRELIMINARY PROVISIONS AND RESTRICTIONS

(a) As used in this [chapter]:

(1) "Exchanging entity" means the domestic or foreign nonprofit corporation or eligible entity in which all of one or more classes of memberships or classes or series of eligible interests are to be acquired in a membership exchange.

(2) "Membership exchange" means a transaction pursuant to Section 11.03.

(3) "Merger" means a transaction pursuant to Section 11.02.

(4) "Party to a merger" or "party to a membership exchange" means any domestic or foreign nonprofit corporation or eligible entity that:

(i) will merge under a plan of merger;

(ii) will acquire memberships or eligible interests of another corporation or an eligible entity in a membership exchange; or

(iii) is an exchanging entity.

(5) "Survivor" in a merger means the corporation or eligible entity into which one or more other corporations or eligible entities are merged. A survivor of a merger may preexist the merger or be created by the merger.

(b) Property held in trust by an entity or otherwise dedicated to a charitable purpose may not be diverted from its purpose by a transaction under this [chapter] unless the entity obtains an appropriate order of [*court*] [*the attorney general*] to the extent required by and pursuant to the law of this state on cy pres or otherwise dealing with the nondiversion of charitable assets.

(c) Unless an entity that is a party to a transaction under this [chapter] obtains an appropriate order of [*court*] [*the attorney general*] under the law of this state on cy pres or otherwise dealing with the nondiversion of charitable assets, the transaction may not affect:

(1) any restriction imposed upon the entity by its organic documents that may not be amended by its governors, members, or interest holders;
(2) any restriction imposed upon property held by the entity by virtue of any trust under which it holds that property; or
(3) the existing rights of persons other than members, shareholders, or interest holders of the entity.

(d) A person that is a member, an interest holder, or otherwise affiliated with a charitable corporation or an unincorporated entity with a charitable purpose may not receive a direct or indirect financial benefit in connection with a transaction under this [chapter] to which the charitable corporation or unincorporated entity is a party unless the person is itself a charitable corporation or unincorporated entity with a charitable purpose. This subsection does not apply to the receipt of reasonable compensation for services rendered.

Source Note: Subsection (a) is patterned after Model Business Corporation Act, 3d Ed. (2002) § 11.01. Subsection (b) is patterned after 15 PA. CONS. STAT. § 5547(b) (2008). Subsection (c) is patterned in part after Revised Model Nonprofit Corporation Act (1987) § 10.08. Subsection (d) is new.

CROSS-REFERENCES

"Eligible entity" defined, see § 1.40.

"Eligible interests" defined, see § 1.40.

"Interest holder" defined, see § 1.40.

"Member" defined, see § 1.40.

"Shareholder" defined, see § 1.40.

OFFICIAL COMMENT

1. *Eligible Entities*

The definition of what constitutes an "eligible entity" in Section 1.40 determines the kinds of entities, other than nonprofit corporations, with which a nonprofit corporation may merge or engage in a membership exchange.

2. Interests

The term “interests” as defined in Section 1.40 includes such interests as general and limited partnership interests in limited partnerships, equity interests in limited liability companies, and any other form of equity or ownership interests in an unincorporated entity, as defined in Section 1.40, however denominated. The definition of “eligible interests” in Section 1.40 also includes shares in a domestic or foreign business corporation.

3. Survivor

The term “survivor” is used in Chapter 11 as a defined technical term and therefore is not always used in a manner that is equivalent to the ordinary meaning of the term. For example, a corporation may be the “survivor” of a merger within the meaning of Section 11.01(5) even if it is created by the merger, and therefore had no existence before the merger.

4. Restrictions

This chapter permits mergers of domestic nonprofit corporations with foreign nonprofit corporations, for-profit corporations, or unincorporated entities; and also permits membership exchanges involving those types of entities. Section 11.01(b) protects property held in trust or dedicated to a charitable purpose from being diverted by a merger or membership exchange from its trust purposes. Section 11.01(c) similarly protects other restrictions applicable to a nonprofit corporation. A state adopting Section 11.01(b) and (c) should consider what restrictions and procedures should apply in a proceeding under those provisions.

§ 11.02. MERGER

(a) One or more domestic nonprofit corporations may merge with one or more domestic or foreign nonprofit corporations or eligible entities pursuant to a plan of merger, or two or more foreign nonprofit corporations or domestic or foreign eligible entities may merge into a new domestic nonprofit corporation to be created in the merger in the manner provided in this [chapter].

(b) A foreign nonprofit corporation, or a foreign eligible entity, may be a party to a merger with a domestic nonprofit corporation, or may be created by the terms of the plan of merger, only if the merger is permitted by the organic law of the corporation or eligible entity.

(c) If the organic law of a domestic eligible entity does not prohibit a merger with a nonprofit corporation but does not provide procedures for the approval of such a merger, a plan of merger may be adopted and approved, and the merger may be effectuated, in accordance with the procedures in this [chapter]. For the purposes of applying this [chapter]:

(1) the eligible entity, its interest holders, eligible interests, and organic records, shall be deemed to be a domestic nonprofit corporation, members, memberships, and articles of incorporation and bylaws, respectively, as the context may require; and

(2) if the business and affairs of the eligible entity are managed by a group of persons that is not identical to the interest holders, that group shall be deemed to be the board of directors.

(d) The plan of merger must be in the form of a record and include:

(1) the name of each domestic or foreign nonprofit corporation or eligible entity that will merge and the name of the domestic or foreign nonprofit corporation or eligible entity that will be the survivor of the merger;

(2) the terms and conditions of the merger;

(3) the manner and basis of converting the memberships of each merging domestic or foreign nonprofit membership corporation and the eligible interests of each merging domestic or foreign eligible entity into memberships, eligible interests, securities, or obligations; rights

to acquire memberships, eligible interests, securities, or obligations; cash; other property or other consideration; or any combination of the foregoing;

(4) the articles of incorporation and bylaws of any corporation, or the organic records of any eligible entity, to be created by the merger; or if a new corporation or eligible entity is not to be created by the merger, any amendments to the survivor's articles or bylaws or organic records; and

(5) any other provisions relating to the merger that the parties desire be included in the plan of merger.

(e) The plan of merger may also include a provision that the plan may be amended prior to filing articles of merger, but if the members of a domestic corporation that is a party to the merger are required or permitted to vote on the plan, the plan must provide that subsequent to approval of the plan by such members the plan may not be amended to change:

(1) the amount or kind of memberships, eligible interests, securities, or obligations; rights to acquire memberships, eligible interests, securities, or obligations; cash; or other property or other consideration to be received by the members of or owners of eligible interests in any party to the merger;

(2) the articles of incorporation or bylaws of any corporation, or the organic records of any unincorporated entity, that will survive or be created as a result of the merger, except for changes permitted by Section 10.05 or by comparable provisions of the organic law of any such foreign nonprofit or business corporation or domestic or foreign unincorporated entity; or

(3) any of the other terms or conditions of the plan, if the change would adversely affect such members in any material respect.

(f) Terms of a plan of merger may be made dependent on facts objectively ascertainable outside the plan in accordance with Section 1.20(c).

(g) See Section 11.01(b), (c), and (d) (restrictions).

Source Note: Patterned after Model Business Corporation Act, 3d Ed. (2002) § 11.02. Subsection (a) is derived from Revised Model Nonprofit Corporation Act (1987) § 11.01(a). Subsection (b) is derived from Revised Model Nonprofit Corporation Act (1987) § 11.06. Subsection (d) is derived from Revised Model Nonprofit Corporation Act (1987) § 11.01(b) and (c).

CROSS-REFERENCES

Abandonment of merger, see § 11.08.

Amendment of articles by board of directors, see § 10.05.

Amendment of articles of incorporation, see § 11.06.

Approval of plan, see § 11.03.

Articles of merger, see § 11.06.

Effect of merger, see § 11.07.

"Eligible entity" defined, see § 1.40.

Membership exchange, see § 11.03.

Merger between parent and subsidiary or between subsidiaries, see § 11.05.

OFFICIAL COMMENT

1. In General

Section 11.02 authorizes mergers between one or more domestic nonprofit corporations, or between one or more domestic nonprofit corporations and one or more foreign nonprofit corporations or domestic or foreign eligible entities. Upon the effective date of the merger the survivor becomes vested with all the assets of the corporations or other entities that merge into the survivor and becomes subject to their liabilities, as provided in Section 11.07.

Section 11.02 of the previous version of the act imposed restrictions on the types of entities with which certain nonprofit corporations could merge. If a nonprofit corporation that is an exempt organization were to merge into an entity that is not an exempt organization, the merger would have adverse tax consequences for the nonprofit corporation, but those tax consequences are a separate issue from the power of a nonprofit corporation to be a party to such a merger. Most existing state nonprofit corporation laws do not contain restrictions analogous to former Section 11.02, and those restrictions have been omitted from the act. It is the general approach of the act to provide an enabling statute that imposes the minimum restrictions necessary on transactions involving nonprofit corporations, with appropriate public policy limitations being imposed by other provisions of substantive law addressed to particular situations where restrictions are considered necessary. The effect of such statutes is preserved by Section 1.03 with respect to mergers. Some states, however, may wish to include restrictions similar to those in former Section 11.02 on the power of certain types of nonprofit corporations to engage in certain mergers.

2. Applicability to Foreign Corporations and Eligible Entities

A merger of a domestic nonprofit corporation with a foreign nonprofit corporation or a foreign eligible entity is authorized by Chapter 11 only if the merger is permitted by the laws under which the foreign corporation or the foreign eligible entity is organized. Whether and on what terms a foreign corporation or a foreign eligible entity is authorized to merge with a domestic corporation is a matter that is governed by the laws under which that corporation or eligible entity is organized or by which it is governed, not by Chapter 11.

Nevertheless, certain provisions of Chapter 11 have an indirect effect on a foreign corporation or eligible entity that proposes to or does merge with a domestic corporation, because they set conditions concerning the effectiveness and effect of the merger. For example, Section 11.02(d) sets forth certain requirements for the contents of a plan of merger.

3. Applicability to Domestic Eligible Entities

If the organic law of a domestic eligible entity (including a domestic business corporation) does not expressly authorize it to engage in a merger with a nonprofit corporation, it is intended that the domestic eligible entity will nonetheless have that power pursuant to Section 11.02(a). *See Cole v. Kershaw*, No. 13904, 2000 Del. Ch. LEXIS 117 (Del Ch. Aug. 15, 2000) (Delaware general partnership could merge with Delaware limited liability company even though general partnership law was silent on mergers because limited liability company law authorized the merger). If the organic law of a domestic eligible entity provides procedures for the adoption, approval, and effectuation of a merger with any type of entity, those procedures will apply to a merger with a nonprofit corporation. If the organic law of a domestic eligible entity does not provide procedures for any type of merger, the procedures of this chapter will apply instead. Pursuant to Section 11.02(c)(1), the provisions of this chapter will apply to the entity simply by substituting in the provisions of this chapter the appropriate terms for the analogous concepts applicable to the entity. If the persons who manage the business and affairs of an eligible entity are the same as its interest holders, then a single approval by those persons will be sufficient under Section 11.02(c)(2).

4. *Terms and Conditions of Merger*

Chapter 11 imposes virtually no restrictions or limitations on the terms or conditions of a merger, except for those set forth in Section 11.02(e) concerning provisions in a plan of merger for amendment of the plan after it has been approved by members and those imposed by Section 11.01(b), (c), and (d). Subject to Section 11.01(d), members or owners of eligible interests in a party to the merger that merges into the survivor may receive memberships, eligible interests, securities or obligations of the survivor or any party other than the survivor, rights to acquire the same, or cash or other property. The memberships in the survivor may be restructured in the merger, and its articles or organic documents may be amended by the articles of merger, in any way deemed appropriate.

Section 11.02(d) requires that the terms and conditions be set forth in the plan of merger and that the plan of merger be in the form of a record. The plan of merger need not be set forth in the articles of merger that are to be delivered to the secretary of state for filing after the merger has been adopted and approved. See Section 11.06.

Section 11.02(d)(4) provides that a plan of merger must set forth the articles of incorporation of any nonprofit corporation, and the organic records of any eligible entity, to be created by the merger, or if a new corporation or eligible entity is not to be created by the merger, any amendments to the survivor's articles of incorporation or organic documents.

The terms of a merger involving a nonprofit corporation frequently provide for a contribution to be made by another party either to the nonprofit corporation itself or to another designated entity. That type of provision may be included in a plan of merger under Section 11.02(d)(2) and (5).

A plan of merger is not required to state who will be the directors and officers of the survivor, but those subjects are typically dealt with in a plan of merger.

5. *Amendments of Articles of Incorporation and Bylaws*

Under Section 11.02, a corporation's articles of incorporation or bylaws may be amended by a merger. Under Section 11.02(d)(4), a plan of merger must include any amendments to the survivor's articles or bylaws or organic records. If the plan of merger is approved, the amendments will be effective.

6. *Adoption and Approval; Abandonment*

A merger must be adopted and approved as set forth in Sections 11.04 and 11.05. Under Section 11.08, the board of directors or a designated body may abandon a merger before its effective date even if the plan of merger has already been approved by the corporation's members.

7. *Effective Date of Merger*

A merger takes effect on the date the articles of merger are filed, unless a later date, not more than 90 days after filing, is specified in the articles. See Section 11.06 and the Official Comment thereto.

§ 11.03. MEMBERSHIP EXCHANGE

(a) Through a membership exchange:

(1) a domestic nonprofit corporation may acquire, pursuant to a plan of membership exchange, all of the memberships of one or more classes of another domestic or foreign nonprofit corporation, or all of the eligible interests of one or more classes or series of eligible interests of a domestic or foreign eligible entity, in exchange for memberships, eligible interests, securities, or obligations; rights to acquire memberships, eligible interests, securities, or obligations; cash; other property or other consideration; or any combination of the foregoing;

(2) all of the memberships of one or more classes of a domestic nonprofit corporation may be acquired by another domestic or foreign nonprofit corporation or eligible entity, in exchange for memberships, eligible interests, securities, obligations; rights to acquire memberships, eligible interests, securities, or obligations; cash; other property or other consideration; or any combination of the foregoing, pursuant to a plan of membership exchange.

(b) A foreign nonprofit corporation or eligible entity may be a party to a membership exchange only if the membership exchange is permitted by the organic law of the corporation or eligible entity.

(c) If the organic law of a domestic eligible entity does not prohibit a membership exchange with a nonprofit corporation but does not provide procedures for the approval of an exchange of interests similar to a membership exchange, a plan of membership exchange may be adopted and approved, and the membership exchange effectuated, in accordance with the procedures, if any, for a merger. If the organic law of a domestic eligible entity does not provide procedures for either an interest exchange or a merger, a plan of membership exchange may be adopted and approved, and the membership exchange effectuated, in accordance with the procedures in this [chapter]. For the purposes of applying this [chapter]:

(1) the eligible entity, its interest holders, eligible interests, and organic documents shall be deemed to be a domestic nonprofit corporation, members, memberships, and articles of incorporation and bylaws, respectively, as the context may require; and
(2) if the business and affairs of the eligible entity are managed by a group of persons that is not identical to the interest holders, that group shall be deemed to be the board of directors.

(d) The plan of membership exchange must be in the form of a record and include:
(1) the name of each domestic or foreign nonprofit corporation or eligible entity whose memberships or eligible interests will be acquired and the name of the corporation or eligible entity that will acquire those memberships or eligible interests;
(2) the terms and conditions of the membership exchange;
(3) the manner and basis of exchanging the memberships of a corporation or the eligible interests in an eligible entity whose memberships or eligible interests will be acquired under the membership exchange into memberships, eligible interests, securities, or obligations; rights to acquire memberships, eligible interests, securities, or obligations; cash; other property or other consideration; or any combination of the foregoing;
(4) any changes desired to be made in the organic records of the exchanging entity; and
(5) any other provisions relating to the membership exchange that the parties desire be included in the plan of exchange.

(e) The plan of membership exchange may also include a provision that the plan may be amended prior to filing articles of membership exchange, but if the members of a domestic nonprofit corporation that is a party to the membership exchange are required or permitted to vote on the plan, the plan must provide that subsequent to approval of the plan by such members the plan may not be amended to change:

(1) the amount or kind of memberships, eligible interests, securities, or obligations; rights to acquire memberships, eligible interests, securities, or obligations; cash; or other property or other consideration to be issued by the domestic nonprofit corporation or to be received by its members, as the case may be; or

(2) any of the other terms or conditions of the plan if the change would adversely affect such members in any material respect.

(f) Terms of a plan of membership exchange may be made dependent on facts objectively ascertainable outside the plan in accordance with Section 1.20(c).

(g) Section 11.03 does not limit the power of a domestic nonprofit corporation to acquire memberships in another corporation or eligible interests in an eligible entity in a transaction other than a membership exchange.

(h) If any debt security, note or similar evidence of indebtedness for money borrowed, whether secured or unsecured, or a contract of any kind, issued, incurred, or signed by a domestic exchanging entity before [*the effective date of this section*] contains a provision applying to a merger or change in control of the exchanging entity that does not refer to a membership exchange, the provision shall be deemed to apply to a membership exchange of the exchanging entity until such time as the provision is amended subsequent to that date.

(i) See Section 11.01(b), (c), and (d) (restrictions).

Source Note: Patterned after Model Business Corporation Act, 3d Ed. (2002) § 11.03. Subsection (h) is patterned after Model Inter-Entity Transactions Act (2007), § 301(d).

CROSS-REFERENCES

Abandonment of membership exchange, see § 11.08.

Approval of plan, see § 11.04.

Articles of membership exchange, see § 11.06.

Classes of memberships, see § 6.01.

Effect of membership exchange, see § 11.07.

OFFICIAL COMMENT

1. In General

It is often desirable to structure a corporate combination so that the separate existence of one or more parties to the combination does not cease although another nonprofit corporation or eligible entity obtains ownership of the memberships or eligible interests of those parties. In the absence of the procedure authorized in Section 11.03, this kind of result often can be accomplished only by a reverse triangular merger, which involves the formation by a corporation, A, of a new subsidiary, followed by a merger of that subsidiary into another party to the merger, B, effected through the exchange of memberships in A for memberships in B. Section 11.03 authorizes a more straightforward procedure to accomplish the same result.

Under Section 11.03, the acquiring nonprofit corporation in a membership exchange must acquire all of the memberships or eligible interests of the class or series of memberships or eligible interests that are being acquired. The memberships or eligible interests of one or more other classes or series of the acquired corporation or eligible entity may be excluded from the membership exchange or may be included on different bases. After the plan of membership exchange is adopted and approved as required by Section 11.04, it is binding on all holders of the class of memberships or class or series of eligible interests to be acquired. Accordingly, a membership exchange may operate in a mandatory fashion on some holders of the class or series of memberships or eligible interests acquired.

Section 11.03(g) makes clear that the authorization of membership exchange combinations under Section 11.03 does not limit the power of nonprofit corporations to acquire memberships or eligible interests without using the membership exchange procedure, either as part of a corporate combination or otherwise.

This section does not apply, of course, to the acquisition of a nonprofit corporation without members. In such a case, control of the corporation can be transferred by means of an amendment to its articles of incorporation or bylaws changing the manner in which the directors are selected.

The previous version of the act did not authorize membership exchanges. In connection with mergers, however, Section 11.02 of the previous version of the act imposed restrictions on the types of entities with which certain nonprofit corporations could merge. As discussed in the Official Comment to Section 11.02. it is the general approach of the act to provide an enabling statute that imposes the minimum restrictions necessary on transactions involving nonprofit corporations, with appropriate public policy limitations being imposed by other provisions of substantive law addressed to particular situations where restrictions are considered necessary. The effect of such statutes is preserved by Section 1.03 and they will apply to membership exchanges. Some states, however, may wish to include restrictions similar to those in former Section 11.02 on the power of certain types of nonprofit corporations to engage in certain membership exchanges.

2. Applicability to Foreign Corporations and Foreign Eligible Entities

Whether and on what terms a foreign nonprofit corporation or a foreign eligible entity is authorized to enter into a membership exchange with a domestic nonprofit corporation is a matter that is governed by the laws under which that corporation or eligible entity is organized or by which it is governed, not by Chapter 11. Therefore, Section 11.04 applies only to adoption of a plan of membership exchange by a domestic nonprofit corporation (or a domestic eligible entity as provided in Section 11.03(c)).

Nevertheless, certain provisions of Chapter 11 have an indirect effect on a foreign corporation, or a foreign eligible entity, that proposes to or does engage in a membership exchange with a domestic corporation, because they set conditions concerning the effectiveness and effect of the membership exchange. For example, Section 11.03(d) sets forth certain requirements for the contents of a plan of membership exchange.

3. Applicability to Domestic Eligible Entities

If the organic law of a domestic eligible entity (including a domestic business corporation) does not expressly authorize it to engage in a membership exchange with a nonprofit corporation, the domestic eligible entity will nonetheless have that power pursuant to Section 11.02(a). If the organic law of a domestic eligible entity provides procedures for the adoption, approval, and effectuation of a merger with any type of entity, but not for a membership exchange or eligible interest exchange, the merger procedures will apply to a membership exchange with a nonprofit corporation. If the organic law of a domestic eligible entity does not provide procedures for any type of merger or share or interest exchange, the procedures of this chapter will apply pursuant to Section 11.03(c). If the persons who manage the business and affairs of an eligible entity are the same as its interest holders, then a single approval by those persons will be sufficient under Section 11.03(c)(2).

4. Terms and Conditions of Membership Exchange

Chapter 11 imposes virtually no restrictions or limitations on the terms or conditions of a membership exchange, except for those contained in Section 11.03(a) that the acquiring party must acquire all the memberships of the acquired class or series of memberships or eligible interests, in Section 11.03(e) concerning provisions in a plan of membership exchange for amendment of the plan after it has been approved by members, and those imposed by Section 11.01(b), (c), and (d). Members or owners of interests in a party whose memberships are acquired under Section 11.03(a)(2) may receive securities or eligible interests of the acquiring party, securities or eligible interests of a party other than the acquiring party, or cash or other property.

Section 11.03(d) requires that the terms and conditions be set forth in the plan of membership exchange and that the plan of membership exchange be in the form of a record. The plan of membership exchange need not be set forth in the articles of membership exchange that are to be delivered to the secretary of state for filing after the membership exchange has been adopted and approved. See Section 11.06.

The terms of a merger involving a nonprofit corporation frequently provide for a contribution to be made by another party either to the nonprofit corporation itself or to a related entity. It is anticipated that a similar practice will develop with respect to membership exchanges, and thus Section 11.03(d)(2) and (5) permits that type of provision to be included in a plan of membership exchange.

5. Adoption and Approvals; Abandonment

A membership exchange must be adopted and approved as set forth in Section 11.04. Under Section 11.08, the board of directors may abandon a membership exchange before its effective date even if the plan of membership exchange has already been approved by the nonprofit corporation's members.

6. Effective Date of Membership Exchange

A membership exchange takes effect on the date the articles of membership exchange are filed, unless a later date, not more than 90 days after filing, is specified in the articles. See Section 11.06 and the Official Comment thereto.

§ 11.04. ACTION ON A PLAN OF MERGER OR MEMBERSHIP EXCHANGE

In the case of a nonprofit corporation that is a party to a merger or membership exchange:

(1) The plan of merger or membership exchange must be adopted by the board of directors.

(2) Except as provided in paragraph (8), Section 11.05, or the articles of incorporation or bylaws, after adopting the plan of merger or membership exchange the board of directors must submit the plan to the members entitled to vote on the plan for their approval. The board of directors must also transmit to the members a recommendation that the mem-

bers approve the plan, unless the board of directors makes a determination that because of conflicts of interest or other special circumstances it should not make such a recommendation, in which case the board of directors must transmit to the members the basis for that determination.

(3) The board of directors may condition its submission of the plan of merger or membership exchange to the members on any basis.

(4) If the plan of merger or membership exchange is required to be approved by the members, and if the approval is to be given at a meeting, the nonprofit corporation must give notice to each member entitled to vote on the merger or membership exchange of the meeting of members at which the plan is to be submitted for approval. The notice must state that the purpose, or one of the purposes, of the meeting is to consider the plan and must contain or be accompanied by a copy or summary of the plan. If the corporation is to be merged into an existing corporation or eligible entity, the notice shall also include or be accompanied by a copy or summary of the articles of incorporation and bylaws or organic records of that corporation or eligible entity. If the corporation is to be merged into a corporation or eligible entity that is to be created pursuant to the merger, the notice shall include or be accompanied by a copy or a summary of the articles of incorporation and bylaws or organic records of the new corporation or eligible entity.

(5) Unless the articles of incorporation or bylaws, or the board of directors acting pursuant to paragraph (3), requires a greater vote or a greater number of votes to be present, the approval of the plan of merger or membership exchange by the members requires the approval of the members at a meeting at which a quorum exists, and, if any class of memberships is entitled to vote as a separate group on the plan of merger or membership exchange, the approval of each such separate voting group at a meeting at which a quorum of the voting group exists.

(6) Separate voting by voting groups is required:

(i) on a plan of merger, by each class of memberships that:
(A) are to be converted into memberships, eligible interests, securities, or obligations; rights to acquire memberships, eligible interests, securities, or obligations; cash; other property or other consideration; or any combination of the foregoing, or
(B) would be entitled to vote as a separate group on a provision in the plan that, if contained in a proposed amendment to articles of incorporation, would require action by separate voting groups under Section 10.04;
(ii) on a plan of membership exchange, by each class of memberships included in the exchange, with each class constituting a separate voting group; and
(iii) on a plan of merger or membership exchange, if the voting group is entitled under the articles of incorporation to vote as a voting group to approve a plan of merger or membership exchange.

(7) If as a result of a merger or membership exchange one or more members of a domestic nonprofit corporation would become subject to owner liability for the debts, obligations, or liabilities of any other person or entity, approval of the plan of merger or membership exchange requires the signature, by each such member, of a separate record consenting to become subject to such owner liability.

(8) If a domestic nonprofit corporation that is a party to a merger does not have any members entitled to vote thereon, a plan of merger shall be deemed adopted by the corporation when it has been adopted by the board of directors pursuant to paragraph (1).

(9) In addition to the adoption and approval of the plan of merger by the board of directors and members as required by this section, the plan of merger must also be approved in the form of a record by any person or group of persons whose approval is required under Section 10.30 to amend the articles of incorporation or bylaws.

Source Note: Paragraphs (1)–(7) are patterned after Model Business Corporation Act, 3d Ed. (2002) § 11.04. Paragraph (8) is patterned after 15 PA. CONS. STAT. § 5924(b) (2008). Derived from Revised Model Nonprofit Corporation Act (1987) § 11.03.

CROSS-REFERENCES

Abandonment of merger or membership exchange, see § 11.08.

Amendment of articles by board of directors, see § 10.05.

Director standards of conduct, see § 8.30.

Director standards of liability, see § 8.31.

Notice generally, see § 1.41.

Notice of members meeting, see § 7.05.

"Record" defined, see § 1.40.

Supermajority quorum and voting requirements, see § 7.26.

Voting by voting group on amendment of articles of incorporation, see § 10.04.

Voting by voting groups generally, see §§ 7.24 and 7.25.

Voting entitlement of members generally, see § 7.21.

"Voting group" defined, see § 1.40.

"Voting power" defined, see § 1.40.

OFFICIAL COMMENT

1. *In General*

Under Section 11.04, a plan of merger or membership exchange must be adopted by the board of directors. Thereafter, the board must submit the plan to the members for their approval, unless the conditions stated in Section 11.05 are satisfied. The functions of the board of directors under this section may be vested by the articles of incorporation or bylaws in a designated body either to the exclusion of, or jointly with, the board of directors.

A plan of membership exchange must always be approved by the members of the class that is being acquired in a membership exchange. Similarly, a plan of merger must always be approved by the members of a nonprofit corporation that is merged into another party in a merger, unless the corporation is a subsidiary and the merger falls within Section 11.05 or the articles of incorporation or bylaws provide that approval by the members is not required.

Section 11.04(6) provides that a class of members has a right to vote on a plan of merger as a separate voting group if the class is being converted in the merger or if the class would have the right to vote as a separate group on a provision in the plan that, if contained in an amendment to the articles of incorporation, would require approval by that class, voting as a separate voting group, under Section 10.04. Under Section 10.04, and therefore under Section 11.04(6), if a change that requires voting by separate voting groups affects two or more classes in the same or a substantially similar way, the relevant classes vote together, rather than separately, on the change. For the mechanics of voting where voting by voting groups is required under Section 11.04(6), see Sections 7.24 and 7.25 and the Official Comments thereto.

If a merger would amend the articles of incorporation in such a way as to affect the voting requirements on future amendments, the transaction must also be approved by the vote required by Section 7.26.

2. Submission to the Members

Section 11.04(2) requires the board of directors of a membership corporation, after having adopted the plan of merger or membership exchange, to submit the plan of merger or membership exchange to the members for approval, except as provided in Section 11.05 or the articles of incorporation or bylaws, or if there are no members entitled to vote on the plan. When submitting the plan of merger or membership exchange the board of directors must make a recommendation to the members that the plan be approved, unless the board of directors makes a determination that because of conflicts of interest or other special circumstances it should make no recommendation. For example, the board of directors may make such a determination where there is not a sufficient number of directors free of a conflicting interest to approve the transaction or because the board of directors is evenly divided as to the merits of a transaction but is able to agree that members should be permitted to consider the transaction. If the board of directors makes such a determination, it must describe the conflict of interest or special circumstances, and communicate the basis for the determination, when submitting the plan of merger or membership exchange to the members. The exception for conflicts of interest or other special circumstances is intended to be sparingly available. Generally, members should not be asked to act on a merger or membership exchange in the absence of a recommendation by the board of directors. The exception is not intended to relieve the board of directors of its duty to consider carefully the proposed transaction and the interests of members.

Section 11.04(3) permits the board of directors to condition its submission of a plan of merger or membership exchange on any basis. Among the conditions that a board might impose are that the plan will not be deemed approved unless it is approved by a specified vote of the members (which may be higher than the vote that would otherwise be required), or by one or more specified classes of members, voting as a separate voting group, or by a specified percentage of disinterested members. The board is not limited, however, to conditions of these types. If the members object to a condition imposed by the board, their remedy is to change the members of the board.

Section 11.04(4) provides that if the plan of merger or membership exchange is required to be approved by the members, and if the approval is to be given at a meeting, the corporation must notify each member entitled to vote on the plan of the meeting of members at which the plan is to be submitted. Requirements concerning the timing and content of a notice of meeting are set out in Section 7.05.

3. *Quorum and Voting*

Section 11.04(5) provides that approval of a plan of merger or membership exchange requires approval of the members at a meeting at which a quorum consisting of a majority of the votes entitled to be cast on the plan exists and, if any class of members is entitled to vote as a separate group on the plan, the approval of each such separate group at a meeting at which a quorum consisting of at least a majority of the votes entitled to be cast on the plan by that class exists. If a quorum is present, then under Sections 7.24 and 7.25 the plan will be approved if more votes are cast in favor of the plan than against it by the voting group or separate voting groups entitled to vote on the plan.

In lieu of approval at a member meeting, approval can be given by the consent of the members entitled to vote on the merger or membership exchange, under the procedures set forth in Section 7.04.

Section 11.04(7) requires any member who will become subject to owner liability to sign a record consenting to becoming subject to owner liability, which consent must be separate from the plan of merger or membership exchange. Although the transactions that produce this result will be infrequent, Section 11.04(7) is an important protective provision in those instances where owner liability may arise. An example of such a transaction is a merger of a nonprofit corporation into an unincorporated nonprofit association in a state where members of such an association are not protected from personal liability for debts or obligations of the association.

4. *Abandonment of Merger or Membership Exchange*

Under Section 11.08, the board of directors may abandon a merger or membership exchange before its effective date even if the plan of merger or membership exchange has already been approved by the corporation's members.

§ 11.05. MERGER WITH CONTROLLED CORPORATION OR BETWEEN CONTROLLED CORPORATIONS

(a) A domestic or foreign entity that holds a membership in a domestic nonprofit corporation that carries at least 80% of the voting power of each class of membership of the controlled corporation that has voting power may merge the controlled corporation into itself or into another such controlled corporation, or merge itself into the controlled corporation, without the approval of the board of directors, designated body or members of the controlled corporation, unless the articles of incorporation or bylaws of any of the corporations or the organic records of a controlling unincorporated entity otherwise provide.

(b) If under subsection (a) approval of a merger by the members of a controlled corporation is not required, the controlling entity shall, within ten days after the effective date of the merger, notify each of the members of the controlled corporation that the merger has become effective.

(c) Except as provided in subsections (a) and (b), a merger between a controlling entity and a controlled corporation is governed by the provisions of Chapter 11 applicable to mergers generally.

(d) A merger pursuant to this section must also be approved in a record by a designated body whose approval is required to amend the articles of incorporation of the controlled corporation.

Source Note: Patterned after Model Business Corporation Act, 3d Ed. (2002) § 11.05. Subsection (d) is derived from Revised Model Nonprofit Corporation Act (1987), § 11.03(a)(3).

CROSS-REFERENCES

Articles of merger, see § 11.06.

Director standards of conduct, see § 8.30.

Director standards of liability, see § 8.31.

"Record" defined, see § 1.40.

"Voting power" defined, see § 1.40.

OFFICIAL COMMENT

Under Section 11.05, if an entity holds 80% of the voting power of each class of memberships of a nonprofit corporation that has voting power, the controlled corporation may be merged into the controlling entity or another such controlled corporation, or the controlling entity may be merged into the controlled corporation, without the approval of the members, board of directors, or a designated body of the controlled corporation, subject to certain informational and notice requirements. Approval by the members of the controlled corporation is not required partly because if an entity already owns 80% or more of the voting power of each class of memberships, approval of a merger by the members would be a foregone conclusion, and partly to facilitate the simplification of corporate structure where only a small fraction of memberships is held by outside members. Approval by the board of directors or a designated body of the controlled corporation is not required because if an entity owns 80% or more of the voting power of each class of the outstanding memberships, the directors or designated body of the controlled corporation cannot be expected to be independent, so that the approval by the board of directors of the controlled corporation would also be a foregone conclusion. In other respects, mergers between controlling entities and 80%-owned corporations are governed by the provisions of Chapter 11.

Section 11.05 does not dispense with approval by the members of a nonprofit corporation that is the controlling entity in a merger subject to this section.

This section only applies to the approvals required with respect to a subsidiary that is a domestic nonprofit corporation because the approvals that would be required in the case of a subsidiary that is any other form of entity will be determined under the organic law of that entity.

§ 11.06. ARTICLES OF MERGER OR MEMBERSHIP EXCHANGE

(a) After a plan of merger or membership exchange has been adopted and approved as required by this [act], articles of merger or membership exchange shall be signed on behalf of each party to the merger or membership exchange by any officer or other duly authorized representative. The articles shall set forth:

(1) the names of the parties to the merger or membership exchange;

(2) if the articles of incorporation of the survivor of a merger or an exchanging nonprofit corporation are amended, or if a new corporation is created as a result of a merger, the amendments to the articles of incorporation of the survivor or exchanging corporation or the articles of incorporation of the new corporation;

(3) if the plan of merger or membership exchange required approval by the members of a domestic nonprofit corporation that was a party to the merger or membership exchange, a statement that the plan was duly approved by the members and, if voting by any separate voting group was required, by each such separate voting group, in the manner required by this [act] and the articles of incorporation or bylaws;

(4) if the plan of merger or membership exchange did not require approval by the members of a domestic nonprofit corporation that was a party to the merger or membership exchange, a statement to that effect; and

(5) as to each foreign nonprofit corporation or eligible entity that was a party to the merger or membership exchange, a statement that the participation of the foreign corporation or eligible entity was duly authorized as required by the organic law of the corporation or eligible entity.

(b) Terms of articles of merger or membership exchange may be made dependent on facts objectively ascertainable outside the articles in accordance with Section 1.20(c).

(c) Articles of merger or membership exchange must be delivered to the secretary of state for filing by the survivor of the merger or the acquiring corporation or eligible entity in a membership exchange and shall take effect at the effective time provided in Section 1.23. Articles of merger or membership exchange filed under this section may be combined with any filing required under the organic law of any domestic eligible entity involved in the transaction if the combined filing satisfies the requirements of both this section and the other organic law.

Source Note: Subsections (a) and (c) are patterned after Model Business Corporation Act, 3d Ed. (2002) § 11.06 and are derived from Revised Model Nonprofit Corporation Act (1987) § 11.04. Subsection (b) is new.

CROSS-REFERENCES

Approval of merger or share exchange, see § 11.04.

"Deliver" defined, see § 1.40.

Filing fees, see § 1.22.

Filing requirements, see § 1.20.

Short form merger, see § 11.05.

Voting by voting group, see §§ 7.24 and 7.25.

"Voting group" defined, see § 1.40.

OFFICIAL COMMENT

The filing of articles of merger or membership exchange makes the transaction a matter of public record. The requirements of filing are set forth in Sections 1.20 through 1.25. The effective time of the articles is the effective time of their filing, unless otherwise specified. Under Section 1.23, a document may specify a delayed effective time and date, and if it does so the document become effective at the time and date specified, except that a delayed effective date may not be later than the 90th day after the date the document is filed.

Some states require notice to the attorney general of transactions involving specific types of nonprofit entities, such as health care providers. *See, e.g.*, Model Act for Nonprofit Healthcare Conversion Transactions prepared by the National Association of Attorneys General. States with such notice requirements should make sure that they are adequately integrated with the procedures in the act.

§ 11.07. EFFECT OF MERGER OR MEMBERSHIP EXCHANGE

(a) Subject to Sections 11.01(b), (c), and (d), when a merger becomes effective:

  (1) the domestic or foreign nonprofit corporation or eligible entity that is designated in the plan of merger as the survivor continues or comes into existence, as the case may be;

  (2) the separate existence of every domestic or foreign nonprofit corporation or eligible entity that is merged into the survivor ceases;

  (3) all property owned by, and every contract and other right possessed by, each domestic or foreign nonprofit corporation or eligible entity that merges into the survivor is vested in the survivor without reversion or impairment;

  (4) all liabilities of each domestic or foreign nonprofit corporation or eligible entity that is merged into the survivor are vested in the survivor;

  (5) the name of the survivor may be, but need not be, substituted in any pending proceeding for the name of any party to the merger whose separate existence ceased in the merger;

  (6) the articles of incorporation and bylaws or organic records of the survivor are amended to the extent provided in the plan of merger;

(7) the articles of incorporation and bylaws or organic records of a survivor that is created by the merger become effective; and

(8) the memberships of each corporation that is a party to the merger, and the eligible interests in an eligible entity that is a party to a merger, that are to be converted under the plan of merger into memberships, eligible interests, securities, or obligations; rights to acquire memberships, eligible interests, securities, or obligations; cash; other property or other consideration; or any combination of the foregoing, are converted.

(b) Subject to Sections 11.01(b), (c), and (d), when a membership exchange becomes effective:

(1) the memberships or eligible interests in the exchanging entity that are to be exchanged under the plan of membership exchange into memberships, eligible interests, securities, or obligations; rights to acquire memberships, eligible interests, securities, or obligations; cash; other property or other consideration; or any combination of the foregoing, are exchanged; and

(2) the articles of incorporation and bylaws or organic records of the exchanging entity are amended to the extent provided in the plan of membership exchange.

(c) A person who becomes subject to owner liability for some or all of the debts, obligations, or liabilities of any entity as a result of a merger or membership exchange has owner liability only to the extent provided in the organic law of the entity and only for those debts, obligations, and liabilities that arise after the effective time of the articles of merger or membership exchange.

(d) The effect of a merger or membership exchange on the owner liability of a person who had owner liability for some or all of the debts, obligations, or liabilities of a party to the merger or membership exchange is as follows:

(1) The merger or membership exchange does not discharge any owner liability under the organic law of the entity in which the person was a member, shareholder, or interest

holder to the extent any such owner liability arose before the effective time of the articles of merger or membership exchange.

(2) The person does not have owner liability under the organic law of the entity in which the person was a member, shareholder, or interest holder prior to the merger or membership exchange for any debt, obligation, or liability that arises after the effective time of the articles of merger or membership exchange.

(3) The provisions of the organic law of any entity for which the person had owner liability before the merger or membership exchange continue to apply to the collection or discharge of any owner liability preserved by paragraph (1), as if the merger or membership exchange had not occurred.

(4) The person has whatever rights of contribution from other persons are provided by the organic law of the entity for which the person had owner liability with respect to any owner liability preserved by paragraph (1), as if the merger or membership exchange had not occurred.

(e) A devise, bequest, gift, grant, or promise contained in a will or other instrument, in trust or otherwise, made before or after a merger, to or for any of the parties to the merger, shall inure to the survivor, subject to the express terms of the will or other instrument.

Source Note: Patterned after Model Business Corporation Act, 3d Ed. (2002) § 11.07. Subsection (a) is derived from Revised Model Nonprofit Corporation Act (1987) § 11.05. Subsection (e) is derived from Revised Model Nonprofit Corporation Act (1987) § 11.07.

CROSS-REFERENCES

Effective time and date of merger or membership exchange, see § 1.23.

"Proceeding" defined, see § 1.40.

OFFICIAL COMMENT

Under Section 11.07(a), in the case of a merger the survivor and the parties that merge into the survivor become one. The survivor automatically becomes the owner of all real and personal property and becomes subject to all the liabilities, actual or contingent, of each party that is merged into it. A merger is not a conveyance, transfer, or assignment. It does not give rise to claims of reverter or impairment of title based on a prohibited conveyance, transfer, or assignment. It does not give rise to a claim that a contract with a party to the merger is no longer in effect on the ground of nonassignability, unless the contract specifically provides that it does not survive a merger. All pending proceedings involving either the survivor or a party whose separate existence ceased as a result of the merger are continued. The survivor has the right to pursue any claims that any of the parties to the merger had the right to pursue. Under Section 11.07(a)(5), the name of the survivor may be, but need not be, substituted in any pending proceeding for the name of a party to the merger whose separate existence ceased as a result of the merger. The substitution may be made whether the survivor is a complainant or a respondent, and may be made at the instance of either the survivor or an opposing party. Such a substitution has no substantive effect, because whether or not the survivor's name is substituted it succeeds to the claims of, and is subject to the liabilities of, any party to the merger whose separate existence ceased as a result of the merger.

In contrast to a merger, a membership exchange does not in and of itself affect the separate existence of the parties, vest in the acquiring entity the assets of the exchanging entity, or render the acquiring entity liable for the liabilities of the exchanging entity.

Under Section 11.07(a)(8), on the effective date of a merger the former members of a nonprofit corporation that is merged into the survivor are entitled only to the rights provided in the plan of merger, which would include any rights they have as holders of any consideration they properly acquire in the merger. Similarly, under Section 11.07(b), on the effective date of a membership exchange the former members of a corporation whose memberships are acquired are entitled only to the rights provided in the plan of membership exchange, including any rights they have as holders of the consideration they acquire. These provisions are not intended to preclude an otherwise proper question concerning the validity of the merger or membership exchange.

If a person becomes subject to owner liability as a result of a merger or membership exchange, Section 11.07(c) limits that owner liability to debts, obligations, and liabilities arising after the merger or membership exchange. Prior to that time, the personal liability of the person will be limited to the extent and as provided in the organic law applicable prior to the transaction. A person may always agree, of course, to assume greater personal liability than that imposed by this section.

Section 11.07(d) preserves liability only for owner liabilities to the extent they arise before the merger or membership exchange. Owner liability is not preserved for subsequent changes in an underlying liability, regardless of whether a change is voluntary or involuntary.

Under Section 11.04(g), a merger cannot have the effect of making any member of a domestic nonprofit corporation subject to owner liability for the obligations or liabilities of any other person or entity unless each such member has signed a separate record consenting to become subject to owner liability.

This section does not address the issue that could arise in a merger where a person who had authority to bind a party to the merger loses that authority because of the merger and yet purports to act to bind the survivor of the merger. For example, in a merger of a general partnership into a nonprofit corporation, a person who is a general partner but does not become an officer of the corporation will lose the authority of a general partner to bind the business to obligations incurred in the ordinary course, but might purport to commit the corporation to such an obligation in dealing with a person who does not have knowledge of the merger. Instances in which this occurs are rare and, in the limited instances in which it does occur, general principles of agency law are sufficient to resolve the problems created.

§ 11.08. ABANDONMENT OF MERGER OR MEMBERSHIP EXCHANGE

(a) Unless otherwise provided in a plan of merger or membership exchange or in the organic law of a foreign nonprofit corporation or a domestic or foreign eligible entity that is a party to a merger or a membership exchange, after the plan has been adopted and approved as required by this [chapter], and at any time before the merger or membership exchange has become effective, it may be abandoned by a domestic nonprofit corporation that is a party thereto without action by its members, in accordance with any procedures set forth in the plan of merger or membership exchange or, if no such procedures are set forth in the plan, in the manner determined by the board of directors, subject to any contractual rights of other parties to the merger or membership exchange.

(b) If a merger or membership exchange is abandoned under subsection (a) after articles of merger or membership exchange have been filed with the secretary of state but before the merger or membership exchange has become effective, a statement that the merger or membership exchange has been abandoned in accordance with this section, executed on behalf of a party to the merger or membership exchange by an officer or other duly authorized representative, shall be delivered to the secretary of state for filing prior to the effective date of the merger or membership exchange. Upon filing, the statement shall take effect and the merger or membership exchange shall be deemed abandoned and shall not become effective.

Source Note: Patterned after Model Business Corporation Act, 3d Ed. (2002) § 11.08.

CROSS-REFERENCES

Approval of merger or membership exchange, see § 11.04.

"Deliver" defined, see § 1.40.

Effective time and date of filing, see § 1.23.

Filing requirements, see § 1.20.

OFFICIAL COMMENT

Under Section 11.08, unless otherwise provided in the plan of merger or membership exchange, a party to a merger or membership exchange may abandon the transaction without member approval, even though the transaction has been previously approved by the party's members. The power of a party under Section 11.08 to abandon a transaction without member approval does not affect any contract rights that other parties may have.

The functions of the board of directors under this section may be vested by the articles of incorporation or bylaws in a designated body either to the exclusion of, or jointly with, the board of directors.

CHAPTER 12

Disposition of Assets

§ 12.01. DISPOSITION OF ASSETS NOT REQUIRING MEMBER APPROVAL

(a) Approval of the members of a nonprofit corporation is not required, unless the articles of incorporation or bylaws otherwise provide:

(1) to sell, lease, exchange, or otherwise dispose of any or all of the corporation's assets:

(i) in the usual and regular course of its activities; or

(ii) if the corporation and its consolidated subsidiaries retain an activity that represented or was supported by at least 33 percent of total assets at the end of the most recently completed fiscal year;

(2) to mortgage, pledge, dedicate to the repayment of indebtedness (whether with or without recourse), or otherwise encumber any or all of the corporation's assets, whether or not in the usual and regular course of its business activities; or

(3) to transfer any or all of the corporation's assets to one or more corporations or other entities all of the memberships or interests of which are owned by the corporation.

(b) See Section 12.03 (restrictions on dispositions of assets).

Source Note: Subsection (a) is patterned in part after Model Business Corporation Act, 3d Ed. (2002) § 12.01(1)–(3). Provision permitting distribution of assets pro rata to shareholders was omitted as inappropriate in the context of nonprofit corporations. Derived from Revised Model Nonprofit Corporation Act (1987) § 12.01. Subsection (b) is new.

CROSS-REFERENCES

Director standards of conduct, see § 8.30.

Distributions to members, see § 6.40.

Member approval of certain dispositions, see § 12.02.

OFFICIAL COMMENT

Section 12.01 provides that no approval of the members is required for dispositions of assets of the types described therein, unless the articles of incorporation or bylaws otherwise provide. Dispositions other than those described in Section 12.01 require member approval if they fall within Section 12.02.

Section 12.01(a) provides that member approval is not required for a sale, lease, exchange, or other disposition by a corporation that would leave the corporation with a significant continuing activity. The test employed in Section 12.01(a) for whether a disposition of assets requires member approval differs verbally from the prior test, which centered on whether a sale involves "all or substantially all" of a corporation's assets. In practice, courts have commonly employed a test comparable to that embodied in 12.01(a). For example, in *Gimbel v. Signal Cos.*, 316 A.2D 599 (Del. Ch.), *aff'd*, 316 A.2D 619 (Del. 1974), the court stated that "[w]hile it is true that [the all or substantially all] test does not lend itself to a strict mathematical standard to be applied in every case, the qualitative factor can be defined to some degree. . . . If the sale is of assets quantitatively vital to the operation of the corporation and is out of the ordinary [course] and substantially affects the existence and purpose of the corporation then it is beyond the power of the Board of Directors." In *Thorpe v. CERBCO, Inc.*, 676 A.2D 436 (Del. 1996), a major issue was whether the sale by a corporation, CERBCO, of one of its subsidiaries, East, would have been a sale of all or substantially all of the corporation's assets, and therefore would have required shareholder approval under the Delaware statute. The court, quoting *Oberly v. Kirby*, 592 A.2D 445 (Del. 1991), stated:

> [T]he rule announced in *Gimbel v. Signal Cos.*, Del. Ch., 316 A.2d 599, *aff'd*, Del. Supr., 316 A.2d 619 (1974), makes it clear that the need for shareholder . . . approval is to be measured not by the size of a sale alone, but also by its qualitative effect upon the corporation. Thus, it is relevant to ask whether a transaction "is out of the ordinary and substantially affects the existence and purpose of the corporation." [*Gimbel*, 316 A.2d] at 606.
>
> In the opinion below, the Chancellor determined that the sale of East would constitute a radical transformation of CERBCO.

> In addition, CERBCO's East stock accounted for 68 [percent] of CERBCO's assets in 1990 and this stock was its primary income generating asset. We therefore affirm the decision that East stock constituted "substantially all" of CERBCO's assets as consistent with Delaware law.

See also Katz v. Bregman, 431 A.2D 1274 (Del. Ch.), *appeal refused sub nom. Plant Industries, Inc. v. Katz*, 435 A.2D 1044 (Del. 1981); *Stiles v. Aluminum Products Co.*, 338 ILL. APP. 48, 86 N.E.2D 887 (1949); *Campbell v. Vose*, 515 F.2D 256 (10th Cir. 1975); *South End Improvement Group, Inc. v. Mulliken*, 602 So. 2d 1327 (Fla. App. 1992); *Schwadel v. Uchitel*, 455 So. 2D 401 (Fla. App. 1984).

Section 12.01(a)(1)(ii) provides a safe harbor under which member approval is not required if a nonprofit corporation retains a continuing activity that represents at least 25% of the total assets of the company and its subsidiaries on a consolidated basis for the most recent full fiscal year. Adoption of that safe harbor represents a policy judgment that a greater measure of certainty than is provided by interpretations of the current case law is highly desirable. The application of this bright-line safe-harbor test should, in most cases, produce a reasonably clear result substantially in conformity with the approaches taken in the better case law developing the "quantitative" and "qualitative" analyses. The test is to be applied to assets for the most recent fiscal year ended immediately before the decision by the board of directors to make the disposition in question.

If a nonprofit corporation disposes of assets for the purpose of reinvesting the proceeds of the disposition in substantially the same activity in a somewhat different form (for example, by selling the corporation's only building for the purpose of buying or building a replacement building), the disposition and reinvestment should be treated together, so that the transaction should not be deemed to leave the corporation without a significant continuing activity.

In determining whether member approval of a disposition of assets is required, the subsidiaries of a nonprofit corporation that are or should be consolidated with the parent under generally accepted accounting principles are included in the calculation of whether the safe harbor in Section 12.01(a)(1)(ii) is met.

The board of directors may base a determination that a retained activity falls within the 25% bright-line test of the safe harbor embodied in Section 12.01(a)(1)(ii) either on accounting principles and practices that are reasonable in the circumstances or on a fair valuation or other method that is reasonable in the circumstances.

The utilization of the specific 25% safe harbor test for purposes of this section should not be read as implying a standard for the test of significance or materiality for any other purposes under the act or otherwise.

Under Section 12.01(a)(1)(i), member approval is not required for a disposition of the corporation's assets in the usual and regular course of its activities, regardless of the size of the transaction.

Under Section 12.01(a)(2), member approval is not required before a nonprofit corporation encumbers its assets, whether or not in the usual and regular course of its business activities. Such a transaction often involves a bank or some other lender requiring a corporation to pledge its property as collateral for a loan. Subject to a contrary provision in a corporation's articles of incorporation, an encumbrance may be authorized by the board of directors alone.

Section 12.01(a)(3) provides that no approval of members is required to transfer any or all of the corporation's assets to a wholly owned subsidiary or other entity. This provision may not be used as a device to avoid a vote of members by a multistep transaction because of Section 12.02(h), which treats assets of subsidiaries as assets of their parent.

§ 12.02. MEMBER APPROVAL OF CERTAIN DISPOSITIONS

(a) Except as provided in the articles of incorporation or bylaws, a sale, lease, exchange, or other disposition of assets, other than a disposition described in Section 12.01, requires approval of the corporation's members.

(b) A disposition that requires approval of the members under subsection (a) must be initiated by a resolution by the board of directors authorizing the disposition. After adoption of the resolution, the board of directors must submit the proposed disposition to the members for their approval. The board of directors must also transmit to the members a recommendation that the members approve the proposed disposition, unless the board of directors makes a determination that because of conflicts of interest or other special circumstances it should not make such a recommendation, in which case the board of directors must transmit to the members the basis for that determination.
(c) The board of directors may condition its submission of a disposition to the members under subsection (b) on any basis.
(d) If a disposition is required to be approved by the members under subsection (a), and if the approval is to be given at a meeting, the nonprofit corporation must give notice to each member, whether or not entitled to vote, of the meeting of members at which the disposition is to be submitted for approval. The notice must state that the purpose, or one of the purposes, of the meeting is to consider the disposition and must contain a description of the disposition, including the terms and conditions thereof and the consideration to be received by the corporation.
(e) Unless the articles of incorporation or bylaws, or the board of directors acting pursuant to subsection (c), requires a greater vote, or a greater number of votes to be present, the approval of a disposition by the members requires the approval of the members at a meeting at which a quorum exists, and, if any class of members is entitled to vote as a separate group on the disposition, the approval of each such separate voting group at a meeting at which a quorum of the voting group exists.
(f) After a disposition has been approved by the members under subsection (e), and at any time before the disposition has been consummated, it may be abandoned by the nonprofit

corporation without action by the members, subject to any contractual rights of other parties to the disposition.

(g) A disposition of assets in the course of dissolution under [Chapter] 14 is not governed by this section.

(h) The assets of a direct or indirect consolidated subsidiary are deemed the assets of the parent nonprofit corporation for the purposes of this section.

(i) In addition to the approval of a disposition of assets by the board of directors and members as required by this section, the disposition must also be approved in the form of a record by any person or group of persons whose approval is required under Section 10.30 to amend the articles of incorporation or bylaws.

(j) See Section 12.03 (restrictions on dispositions of assets).

Source Note: Patterned after Model Business Corporation Act, 3d Ed. (2002) § 12.02. Derived from Revised Model Nonprofit Corporation Act (1987) § 12.02, except that the required vote of members has been reduced from 2/3 to a majority of the votes cast.

CROSS-REFERENCES

Director standards of conduct, see § 8.30.

Disposition of assets not requiring member approval, see § 12.01.

Dissolution, see Ch 14.

Notice generally, see § 1.41.

Notice of meeting of members, see § 7.05.

Supermajority quorum and voting requirements, see § 7.26.

Voting by voting group, see §§ 7.24 and 7.25.

Voting entitlement of members generally, see § 7.21.

"Voting group" defined, see § 1.40.

OFFICIAL COMMENT

Section 12.02(b) requires the board of directors, after having adopted a resolution authorizing a disposition that requires member approval, to submit the disposition to the members for approval. When submitting the disposition to the members, the board of directors must make a recommendation to the members that the disposition be approved, unless the board makes a determination that because of conflicts of interests or other special circumstances it should not make a recommendation. For example, the board of directors may make such a determination where there is not a sufficient number of directors free of a conflicting interest to approve the transaction or because the board of directors is evenly divided as to the merits of a transaction but is able to agree that members should be permitted to consider the transaction. If the board of directors makes such a determination, it must describe the conflicts of interest or special circumstances, and communicate the basis for the determination, when submitting the disposition to the members. The exception for conflicts of interest or other special circumstances is intended to be sparingly available. Generally, members should not be asked to act on a disposition in the absence of a recommendation by the board of directors. The exception is not intended to relieve the board of directors of its duty to consider carefully the proposed transaction and the interests of members.

Section 12.02(c) permits the board of directors to condition its submission of a proposed disposition to the members. Among the conditions that a board might impose are that the disposition will not be deemed approved unless it is approved by a specified percentage of the members, or by one or more specified classes of members voting as separate voting groups, or by a specified percentage of disinterested members.

Section 12.02(e) provides that approval of a disposition requires approval of the members at a meeting at which at least a majority of the votes entitled to be cast on the disposition is present. In lieu of approval at a meeting of the members, approval can be given by the consent of all the members entitled to vote on the transaction, under the procedures set forth in Section 7.04.

The term "subsidiary" or "subsidiaries," as used in Section 12.02, includes both corporate and noncorporate subsidiaries.

Accordingly, for example, a limited liability company or a partnership may be a subsidiary for purposes of Section 12.02.

§ 12.03. RESTRICTIONS ON DISPOSITIONS OF ASSETS

(a) Property held in trust or otherwise dedicated to a charitable purpose may not be diverted from its purpose by a transaction described in Section 12.01 or 12.02 unless the nonprofit corporation obtains an appropriate order from [*court*] [*the attorney general*] to the extent required by and pursuant to the law of this state on cy pres or otherwise dealing with the nondiversion of charitable assets.

(b) A person who is a member of or otherwise affiliated with a charitable corporation may not receive a direct or indirect financial benefit in connection with a disposition of assets unless the person is a charitable corporation or an unincorporated entity that has a charitable purpose. This subsection does not apply to the receipt of reasonable compensation for services rendered.

Source Note: Subsection (a) patterned after 15 PA. CONS. STAT. § 5547(b) (2008). Derived from Revised Model Nonprofit Corporation Act (1987) § 12.02(g).

CROSS-REFERENCES

"Charitable corporation" defined, see § 1.40.

OFFICIAL COMMENT

Section 12.03(a) protects property held in trust or dedicated to a charitable purpose from being diverted by a disposition of assets from its restricted purposes. Section 12.03(a) applies to all nonprofit corporations. A state adopting Section 12.03(a) should consider what restrictions and procedures should apply in a proceeding under that provision.

CHAPTER 13

Derivative Proceedings

§ 13.01. SCOPE OF [CHAPTER]

In this [chapter], "derivative proceeding" means a civil suit in the right of a domestic nonprofit corporation or, to the extent provided in Section 13.08, in the right of a foreign nonprofit corporation.

> *Source Note:* Patterned after Model Business Corporation Act, 3d Ed. (2002) § 7.40(1).

CROSS-REFERENCES

"Proceeding" defined, see § 1.40.

OFFICIAL COMMENT

The definition of "derivative proceeding" makes it clear that the chapter applies to foreign corporations only to the extent provided in Section 13.08, which provides that the law of the jurisdiction of incorporation governs except for Sections 13.04 (stay of proceedings), 13.06 (discontinuance or settlement), and 13.07 (payment of expenses). See the Official Comment to Section 13.08.

§ 13.02. STANDING

(a) A derivative proceeding may be brought by:
  (1) a member or members having 5% or more of the voting power, or by 50 members, whichever is less; or
  (2) any director or member of a designated body.

(b) The plaintiff in a derivative proceeding must be a member, director, or member of a designated body at the time of bringing the proceeding. A plaintiff who is a member must also have been a member at the time of any action complained of in the derivative proceeding.

> *Source Note:* Substantially a reenactment of Revised Model Nonprofit Corporation Act (1987) § 6.30(a) and (b), except last sentence of subsection (b) which is new. Compare Model Business Corporation Act, 3d Ed. (2002) § 7.41.

CROSS-REFERENCES

"Derivative proceeding" defined, see § 13.01.

OFFICIAL COMMENT

The act and the statutes of many states have long required that a plaintiff must have been a member at the time of the transaction in question. This rule has been criticized as being unduly narrow and technical and unnecessary to prevent the transfer or purchase of lawsuits.

The decision to retain the rule of contemporaneous status as a member in Section 13.02(b) was based primarily on the view that it was simple, clear, and easy to apply. Further, there has been no persuasive showing that the contemporaneous membership rule has prevented the litigation of substantial suits. Where the plaintiff is a director or member of a designated body, however, the plaintiff need only have that status at the time the proceeding is commenced.

Section 13.02 does not permit a creditor to commence a derivative proceeding.

§ 13.03. DEMAND

A person may not commence a derivative proceeding until:

(1) a demand in the form of a record has been delivered to the nonprofit corporation to take suitable action; and
(2) 90 days have expired from the date the demand was effective unless the person has earlier been notified that the demand has been rejected by the corporation or unless irreparable injury to the corporation would result by waiting for the expiration of the 90-day period.

Source Note: Patterned after Model Business Corporation Act, 3d Ed. (2002) § 7.42. Compare Revised Model Nonprofit Corporation Act (1987) § 6.30(c).

CROSS-REFERENCES

"Derivative proceeding" defined, see § 13.01.

OFFICIAL COMMENT

Section 13.03 requires a demand on the nonprofit corporation in all cases. The demand must be made at least 90 days before commencement of suit unless irreparable injury to the corporation would result. This approach has been adopted for two reasons. First, even though no director may be independent, the demand will give the board of directors the opportunity to re-examine the act complained of in the light of a potential lawsuit and take corrective action. Secondly, the provision eliminates the time and expense of the litigants and the court involved in litigating the question whether demand is required. It is believed that requiring a demand in all cases does not impose an onerous burden since a relatively short waiting period of 90 days is provided and this period may be shortened if irreparable injury to the corporation would result by waiting for the expiration of the 90-day period. Moreover, the cases in which demand is excused are relatively rare. Many plaintiffs' counsel as a matter of practice make a demand in all cases rather than litigate the issue whether demand is excused.

1. Form of Demand

Section 13.03 specifies only that the demand must be in the form of a record. The demand should, however, set forth the facts concerning membership and be sufficiently specific to apprise the nonprofit corporation of the action sought to be taken and the ground for that action so that the demand can be evaluated. *See Allison v. General Motors Corp.*, 604 F. SUPP. 1106, 1117 (D. Del. 1985). Detailed pleading is not required since the corporation can contact the member for clarification if there are any questions. In keeping with the spirit of this section, the specificity of the demand should not become a new source of dilatory motions.

2. Upon Whom Demand Should Be Made

Section 13.03 states that demand shall be made upon the nonprofit corporation. Reference is not made specifically to the board of directors since there may be instances, such as a decision to sue a third party for an injury to the corporation, in which the taking of, or refusal to take, action would fall within the authority of an officer of the corporation. Nevertheless, it is expected that in most cases the board of directors will be the appropriate body to review the demand and only in relatively rare cases will a designated body have been given the role of reviewing a demand.

To ensure that the demand reaches the appropriate person for review, it should be addressed to the board of directors, chief executive officer, or corporate secretary of the nonprofit corporation at its principal office.

3. *The 90-Day Period*

Section 13.03(2) provides that a derivative proceeding may not be commenced until 90 days after demand has been made. Ninety days has been chosen as a reasonable minimum time within which the board of directors can meet, direct the necessary inquiry into the charges, receive the results of the inquiry, and make its decision. In many instances a longer period may be required. *See, e.g., Mozes v. Welch*, 638 F. SUPP. 215 (D. Conn. 1986) (eight-month delay in responding to demand not unreasonable). However, a fixed time period eliminates further litigation over what is not a reasonable time. The nonprofit corporation may request counsel for the plaintiff to delay filing suit until the inquiry is completed or, if suit is commenced, the corporation can apply to the court for a stay under Section 13.04.

Two exceptions are provided to the 90-day waiting period. The first exception is the situation where the plaintiff has been notified of the rejection of the demand prior to the end of the 90 days. The second exception is where irreparable injury to the nonprofit corporation would otherwise result if the commencement of the proceeding is delayed for the 90-day period. The standard to be applied is intended to be the same as that governing the entry of a preliminary injunction. *Compare Gimbel v. Signal Cos.*, 316 A.2D 599 (Del. Ch. 1974) *with Gelco Corp. v. Coniston Partners*, 811 F.2D 414 (8th Cir. 1987). Other factors may also be considered, such as the possible expiration of the statute of limitations, although this would depend on the period of time during which the plaintiff was aware of the grounds for the proceeding.

It should be noted that the person bringing suit does not necessarily have to be the person making the demand. Only one demand need be made in order for the nonprofit corporation to consider whether to take corrective action.

4. *Response by the Corporation*

There is no obligation on the part of the nonprofit corporation to respond to the demand. However, if the corporation, after receiving the demand, decides to institute litigation or, after a derivative proceeding has commenced, decides to assume control of the litigation, the plaintiff's right to commence or control the proceeding ends unless it can be shown that the corporation will not adequately pursue the matter. As stated in *Lewis v. Graves*, 701 F.2d 245, 247–48 (2d Cir. 1983):

> The [demand] rule is intended "to give the derivative corporation itself the opportunity to take over a suit which was brought on its behalf in the first place, and thus to allow the directors the chance to occupy their normal status as conductors of the corporation's affairs." Permitting corporations to assume control over derivative suits also has numerous practical advantages. Corporate management may be in a better position to pursue alternative remedies, resolving grievances without burdensome and expensive litigation. Deference to directors' judgment may also result in the termination of meritless actions brought solely for their settlement or harassment value. Moreover, where litigation is appropriate, the derivative corporation will often be in a better position to bring or assume the suit because of superior financial resources and knowledge of the challenged transactions. [Citations omitted.]

§ 13.04. STAY OF PROCEEDINGS

(a) If the nonprofit corporation commences an inquiry into the allegations made in the demand or complaint, the court may stay any derivative proceeding for such period as the court deems appropriate.

(b) See Section 13.06 (applicability to foreign corporations).

Source Note: Patterned after Model Business Corporation Act, 3d Ed. (2002) § 7.43. Compare Revised Model Nonprofit Corporation Act (1987) § 6.30(c). Subsection (b) is new.

CROSS-REFERENCES

Demand, see § 13.03.

"Derivative proceeding" defined, see § 13.01.

OFFICIAL COMMENT

Section 13.04 provides that if the nonprofit corporation undertakes an inquiry, the court may in its discretion stay the proceeding for such period as the court deems appropriate. This might occur where the complaint is filed 90 days after demand but the inquiry into matters raised by the demand has not been completed or where a demand has not been investigated but the corporation commences the inquiry after the complaint has been filed. In either case, it is expected that the court will monitor the course of the inquiry to ensure that it is proceeding expeditiously and in good faith.

§ 13.05. DISMISSAL

(a) A derivative proceeding shall be dismissed by the court on motion by the nonprofit corporation if one of the groups specified in subsection (b) or (e) has determined in good faith after conducting a reasonable inquiry upon which its conclusions are based that the maintenance of the derivative proceeding is not in the best interests of the corporation.

(b) Unless a panel is appointed pursuant to subsection (e), the determination in subsection (a) shall be made by:

(1) a majority vote of independent directors present at a meeting of the board of directors if the independent directors constitute a quorum; or

(2) a majority vote of a committee consisting of two or more independent directors appointed by majority vote of

independent directors present at a meeting of the board of directors, whether or not such independent directors constituted a quorum.

(c) If a derivative proceeding is commenced after a determination has been made rejecting a demand by a member, the complaint must allege with particularity facts establishing either:

(1) that a majority of the board of directors did not consist of independent directors at the time the determination was made; or

(2) that the requirements of subsection (a) have not been met.

(d) If a majority of the board of directors does not consist of independent directors at the time the determination is made, the nonprofit corporation has the burden of proving that the requirements of subsection (a) have been met. If a majority of the board of directors consists of independent directors at the time the determination is made, the plaintiff has the burden of proving that the requirements of subsection (a) have not been met.

(e) The court may appoint a panel of one or more independent persons upon motion by the nonprofit corporation to make a determination whether the maintenance of the derivative proceeding is in the best interests of the corporation. In such case, the plaintiff shall have the burden of proving that the requirements of subsection (a) have not been met.

(f) A person is independent for purposes of this section if the person does not have:

(1) a material interest in the outcome of the proceeding, or

(2) a material relationship with a person who has such an interest.

(g) None of the following shall by itself cause a director to be considered not independent for purposes of this section:

(1) the nomination, election, or appointment of the director by persons who are defendants in the derivative proceeding or against whom action is demanded;

(2) the naming of the director as a defendant in the derivative proceeding or as a person against whom action is demanded; or

(3) the approval by the director of the act being challenged in the derivative proceeding or demand if the act resulted in no personal benefit to the director.

Source Note: Patterned after Model Business Corporation Act, 3d Ed. (2002) § 7.44.

CROSS-REFERENCES

Board of directors:

committees, see § 8.25.

meetings, see § 8.20.

quorum and voting, see § 8.24.

Demand, see § 13.03.

"Derivative proceeding" defined, see § 13.01.

"Material interest" defined, see § 1.40.

"Material relationship" defined, see § 1.40.

OFFICIAL COMMENT

When a board of directors properly rejects a demand to bring an action, judicial decisions indicate that the derivative action should be dismissed. *See Aronson v. Lewis*, 743 A.2D 805, 813 (Del. 1984). The prior version of the act was silent on the effect of a determination by a special litigation committee of independent directors that a previously commenced derivative action can be dismissed. Several state business corporation laws have been amended to provide for action by such a committee. *See, e.g.* IND. CODE ANN. § 23-1-32-4 (Burns 1984 & Supp. 1988); N.D. CENT. CODE § 10-19.149 (1985). This section adopts for nonprofit corporations those developments in business corporation law. Section 13.05(a) specifically provides that the proceeding shall be dismissed if there is a proper determination that the maintenance of the proceeding is not in the best interests of the corporation. This determination can be made prior to commencement of the suit in response to a demand or after the commencement upon examination of the allegations of the complaint.

The procedures set forth in Section 13.05 are not intended to be exclusive. As noted in the comment to Section 13.03, there may be instances where a decision to commence an action falls within the authority of an officer of the nonprofit corporation depending upon the amount of the claim and the identity of the potential defendants.

1. The Persons Making the Determination

Section 13.05(b) prescribes the persons by whom the determination in subsection (a) may be made. The subsection provides that the determination may be made by a majority vote of independent directors if there is a quorum of independent directors, or by a committee of independent directors appointed by a vote of the independent directors. These provisions parallel the mechanics for determining entitlement to indemnification in Section 8.55. In this respect this clause is an exception to Section 8.25 which required the approval of at least a majority of all the directors in office to create a committee and appoint members. This approach has been taken to respond to the criticism expressed in a few cases that special litigation committees suffer from a structural bias because of their appointment by a vote of non-independent directors. *See Hasan v. Cleve Trust Realty Investors*, 729 F.2D 372, 376–77 (6th Cir. 1984).

The decisions that have examined the qualifications of directors making the determination have required that the directors be both "disinterested" in the sense of not having a personal interest in the transaction being challenged (as opposed to a benefit which devolves upon the corporation or all shareholders generally) and "independent" in the sense of not being influenced in favor of the defendants by reason of personal or other relationships. *See, e.g., Aronson v. Lewis*, 743 A.2D 805, 812–16 (Del. 1984). Only the word "independent" has been used in Section 13.05(b) because it is believed that a person who has an interest in the transaction would not be independent. The concept of an independent director is not intended to be limited to nonofficer or "outside" directors but may in appropriate circumstances include directors who are also officers.

Many of the special litigation committees involved in the reported cases consisted of directors who were elected after the alleged wrongful acts by the directors who were named as defendants in the action. Section 13.05(g)(1) makes it clear that the participation of non-independent directors or members in the nomination, election, or appointment of a new director will not prevent the new director from being considered independent. This sentence therefore rejects the concept that the mere appointment of new directors by the non-independent directors makes the new directors not independent in making the necessary determination because of an inherent structural bias. Clauses (2) and (3) also confirm the decisions by a number of courts that the mere fact that a director has been named as a defendant or approved the action being challenged does not cause the director to be considered not independent. *See Aronson v. Lewis*, 743 A.2D 805, 816 (Del. 1984); *Lewis v. Graves*, 701 F.2D 245 (2d Cir. 1983). It is believed that a court will be able to assess any actual bias in deciding whether the director is independent without any presumption arising out of the method of the director's appointment, the mere naming of the director as a defendant, or the director's approval of the act where the director received no personal benefit from the transaction.

Section 13.05(e) also provides for a determination by a panel of one or more independent persons appointed by the court. *Cf.* VA. CODE ANN. § 13.1-672D (1987) (court may appoint a committee of two or more persons). The subsection provides for the appointment only upon motion by the nonprofit corporation. This would not, however, prevent the court on its own initiative from appointing a special master pursuant to applicable state rules of procedure.

This procedure may be desirable in a number of circumstances. If there are no independent directors available, the nonprofit corporation may not wish to enlarge the board to add independent directors or may be unable to find persons willing to serve as independent directors. In addition, if there are independent directors, they may not have the available time to conduct the inquiry in an expeditious manner.

Appointment by the court should also eliminate any question about the independence of the person making the determination. Although the nonprofit corporation may wish to suggest to the court possible appointees, the court will not be bound by these suggestions and, in any case, will want to satisfy itself with respect to independence at the same time the person is appointed.

Although subsection (b)(2) requires a committee of at least two directors, subsection (e) permits the appointment of only one person in recognition of the potentially increased costs to the nonprofit corporation for the fees and expenses of an outside person.

Under Section 8.12, a designated body may perform the functions of the board of directors under this section.

2. *Standards to Be Applied*

Section 13.05(a) requires that the determination be made by the appropriate persons in good faith after conducting a reasonable inquiry upon which their conclusions are based. The word "inquiry" rather than "investigation" has been used to make it clear that the scope of the inquiry will depend upon the issues raised and knowledge of the group making the determination with respect to the issues. In some cases, the issues may be so simple or the knowledge of the group so extensive that little additional inquiry is required. In other cases, the group may need to engage counsel and other professionals to make an investigation and assist the group in its evaluation of the issues.

The phrase "in good faith" modifies both the determination and inquiry. The test, which is also included in Section 8.30 (general standards of conduct for directors) and 8.51 (authority to indemnify), is a subjective one, meaning "honestly or in an honest manner." The American Bar Association, *The Corporate Director's Guidebook*, 33 Bus. Law. 1595, 1601 (1978). As stated in *Abella v. Universal Leaf Tobacco Co.*, 546 F. Supp. 795, 800 (E.D. Va. 1982), "the inquiry intended by this phrase goes to the spirit and sincerity with which the investigation was conducted, rather than the reasonableness of its procedures or basis for conclusions."

The phrase "upon which its conclusions are based" requires that the inquiry and the conclusions follow logically. This provision authorizes the court to examine the determination to ensure that it has some support in the findings of the inquiry. The burden of convincing the court about this issue lies with whichever party has the burden under Section 13.05(d). This phrase does not require the persons making the determination to prepare a report that sets forth their determination and the bases therefore, since circumstances will vary as to the need for such a report. There may, however, be many instances where good corporate practice will commend such a procedure.

Section 13.05 is not intended to modify the general standards of conduct for directors set forth in Section 8.30 of the act, but rather to make those standards somewhat more explicit in the derivative proceeding contest. In this regard, the independent directors making the determination would be entitled to rely on information and reports from other persons in accordance with Section 8.30(b).

Section 13.05 is similar in several respects and differs in certain other respects from the law as it has developed in Delaware and been followed in a number of other states. Under the Delaware cases, the role of the court in reviewing the board's determination varies depending upon whether the plaintiff is in a demand-required or demand-excused situation. Demand is excused only if the plaintiff pleads particularized facts that create a reasonable doubt that a majority of directors at the time demand would be made are independent or disinterested, or that the challenged transaction was the product of a valid exercise of business judgment by the approving board. *Aronson v. Lewis*, 743 A.2D 805, 814 (Del. 1984); *Levine v. Smith*, 591 A.2D 194 (Del. 1991). If the plaintiff fails to make these two showings, demand is required. Since the *Aronson* requirements are difficult to satisfy, the plaintiff normally must make demand on the board.

In the unusual case where the plaintiff's demand is excused under either of the *Aronson* tests, the plaintiff has standing to bring the derivative suit. If the nonprofit corporation seeks to reassert its right to control the litigation, the corporation will form a special litigation committee to determine if the litigation is in the best interests of the corporation. If the corporation files a motion to dismiss the litigation based upon the recommendation of the special committee, Delaware law requires the corporation to bear the burden of proving the independence of the committee, the reasonableness of its investigation, and the reasonableness of the bases of its decision reflected in the motion. *Zapata Corp. v. Maldonado*, 430 A.2D 779 (Del. 1981). *Zapata* also permits the court a discretionary second step to review the special committee's decision by invoking the court's "independent business judgment." *Id.* at 789.

In the usual scenario where demand is not excused, the member must demand that the board take action and the *Zapata* principles do not apply. The board or special committee of independent directors decides whether the nonprofit corporation should take the action the member requests or respond in some other way. As in the case of all board decisions, the board's response to the member's demand is presumptively protected by the traditional business judgment rule. *Allison v. General Motors Corp.*, 604 F. SUPP. 1106, 1122 (D. Del. 1985). As a result, the member in filing suit bears the normal burden of creating by particularized pleadings a reasonable doubt that the board's response to the demand was wrongful. *Levine v. Smith*, 591 A.2D 194, 210 (Del. 1991). The plaintiff must allege with particularity a lack of good faith, care, independence, or disinterestedness by the directors in responding to the demand.

In contrast to Delaware's approach, some jurisdictions have adopted uniform tests to judge both demand-required and demand-excused situations. For example, in New York, judicial review is always limited to an analysis of the independence and good faith of the board or committee and the reasonableness of the bases for the board's decision, and the court does not have the discretionary authority to use its independent business judgment. *Auerbach v. Bennett*, 47 N.Y.2D 619, 633–34, 419 N.Y.S. 2D 920, 928–29, 393 N.E.2D 994, 1002–03 (1979). In contrast, the

North Carolina Supreme Court has interpreted that state's statutory provisions on derivative actions as requiring the application of the *Zapata* criteria in both demand-required and demand-excused cases. *Alford v. Shaw*, 358 S.E.2D 323, 327 (N.C. 1987).

Since Section 13.03 requires demand in all cases, the distinction between demand-excused and demand-required cases does not apply. Subsections (c) and (d) of Section 13.05 carry forward the distinction, however, by establishing pleading rules and allocating the burden of proof depending on whether there is a majority of independent directions. Subsection (c), like Delaware law, assigns the plaintiff the threshold burden of alleging facts establishing that a majority of the board is not independent. If there is an independent majority, the burden remains with the plaintiff to plead and establish that the requirements of Section 13.05(a) have not been met. If there is no independent majority, the burden is on the nonprofit corporation on the issues delineated in Section 13.05(a). In this case, the corporation must prove both the independence of the decision makers and the propriety of the inquiry and determination.

Subsections (c) and (d) of Section 13.05 thus follow the first *Aronson* standard in allocating the burden of proof depending on whether the majority of the board is independent. The committee decided, however, not to adopt the second *Aronson* standard for excusing demand (and thus shifting the burden to the corporation) based on whether the decision of the board that decided the challenged transaction is protected by the business judgment rule. The committee believes that the only appropriate concern in the context of derivative litigation is whether the board considering the demand has a disabling conflict. *See Starrels v. First Nat'l Bank*, 870 F.2D 1168, 1172–76 (7th Cir. 1989) (Easterbrook, J. concurring).

Thus, the burden of proving that the requirements of Section 13.05(a) have not been met will remain with the plaintiff in several situations. First, in subsection (b)(1), the burden of proof will generally remain with the plaintiff since the subsection requires a quorum of independent directors and a quorum is normally a majority. See Section 8.24. The burden will also remain with the plaintiff if there is a majority of independent directors that appoints the committee under subsection (b)(2). Under Section 13.05(e), the burden of proof also remains with the plaintiff in the case of a determination by a panel appointed by the court.

The burden of proof will shift to the nonprofit corporation, however, where a majority of directors is not independent, and the determination is made by the group specified in subsection (b)(2). It can be argued that, if the directors making the determination under subsection (b)(2) are independent and have been delegated full responsibility for making the decision, the composition of the entire board is irrelevant. This argument is buttressed by the section's method of appointing the group specified in subsection (b)(2) since subsection (b)(2) departs from the general method of appointing committees and allows only independent directors, rather than a majority of the entire board, to appoint the committee which will make the determination. Nevertheless, despite the argument that the composition of the board is irrelevant in these circumstances, the committee adopted the provisions of subsections (b)(2) and (d) of Section 13.05 to response to concerns of structural bias.

Finally, Section 13.05 does not authorize the court to review the reasonableness of the determination. As discussed above, the phrase in Section 13.44(a) "upon which its conclusions are based" limits judicial review to whether the determination has some support in finding of the inquiry.

3. *Pleading*

Section 13.05(c) sets forth a modified pleading rule to cover the typical situation where a plaintiff makes demand on the board, the board rejects that demand, and the plaintiff commences an action. In that scenario, in order to state a cause of action, subsection (c) requires the complaint to allege facts with particularity demonstrating either (1) that no majority of independent directors exists or (2) why the determination does not meet the standards in subsection (a). Discovery is available to the plaintiff only after the plaintiff has successfully stated a cause of action by making either of these two showings.

§ 13.06. DISCONTINUANCE OR SETTLEMENT

(a) A derivative proceeding may not be discontinued or settled without the court's approval. If the court determines that a proposed discontinuance or settlement will substantially affect the interests of the members or a class of members of the nonprofit corporation, the court shall direct that notice be given to the members affected.

(b) See Section 13.08 (applicability to foreign corporations).

Source Note: Patterned after Model Business Corporation Act, 3d Ed. (2002) § 7.45. Subsection (b) is new.

CROSS-REFERENCES

"Derivative proceeding" defined, see § 13.01.

OFFICIAL COMMENT

Section 13.06 follows the Federal Rules of Civil Procedure and the statutes of a number of states, and requires that all proposed settlements and discontinuances must receive judicial approval. This requirement seems a natural consequence of the proposition that a derivative suit is brought for the benefit of all members and avoids many of the evils of the strike suit by preventing the individual member-plaintiff from settling privately with the defendants.

Section 13.06 also requires notice to all affected members if the court determines that the proposed settlement may substantially affect their interests. This provision permits the court to decide that no notice need be given if, in the court's judgment, the proceeding is frivolous or has become moot. The section also makes a distinction between classes of members, an approach which is not in Federal Rule of Civil Procedure 23.1, but is adapted from the New York and Michigan statutes.

Unlike the statutes of some states, Section 13.06 does not address the issue of which party should bear the cost of giving this notice. This is a matter left to the discretion of the court reviewing the proposed settlement.

§ 13.07. SECURITY FOR COSTS; PAYMENT OF EXPENSES

(a) In any derivative proceeding brought under Section 13.02(a)(1), the nonprofit corporation shall be entitled at any stage of the proceeding to seek an order requiring the plaintiffs to give security for reasonable expenses, including attorney fees and expenses, that may be incurred by the corporation in connection with the proceeding, to which security the corporation may have recourse in such amount as the court determines upon termination of the proceeding. The amount of security may be increased or decreased in the discretion of the court upon a showing that the security provided has or may become inadequate or excessive. Security may be denied or limited in the discretion of the court upon a preliminary showing, by application and upon such types of proof as may be required by the court, establishing prima facie that the requirement of full or partial security would impose undue hardship on plaintiffs and serious injustice would result.

(b) On termination of the derivative proceeding the court may:

(1) order the nonprofit corporation to pay the plaintiff's reasonable expenses (including counsel fees) incurred in the proceeding if it finds that the proceeding has resulted in a substantial benefit to the corporation;

(2) order the plaintiff to pay any defendant's reasonable expenses (including counsel fees) incurred in defending the proceeding if it finds that the proceeding was commenced or maintained without reasonable cause or for an improper purpose; or

(3) order a party to pay an opposing party's reasonable expenses (including counsel fees) incurred because of the filing of a pleading, motion, or other paper, if it finds that the pleading, motion, or other paper was not well grounded in fact, after reasonable inquiry, or warranted by existing law or a good faith argument for the extension, modification, or reversal of existing law and was

interposed for an improper purpose, such as to harass or cause unnecessary delay or needless increase in the cost of litigation.

(c) See Section 13.08 (applicability to foreign corporations).

Source Note: Subsection (a) is patterned in part after 15 PA. CONS. STAT. § 5782(c) (2008); see also CAL. CORP. CODE § 7710(d) (2008). Subsection (b) is patterned after Model Business Corporation Act, 3d Ed. (2002) § 7.46. Subsection (c) is new.

CROSS-REFERENCES

"Derivative proceeding" defined, see § 13.01.

OFFICIAL COMMENT

Section 13.07(b)(1) is intended to be a codification of existing case law. *See, e.g., Mills v. Electric Auto-Lite Co.*, 396 U.S. 375 (1970). It provides that the court may order the nonprofit corporation to pay the plaintiff's reasonable expenses (including counsel fees) if it finds that the proceeding has resulted in a substantial benefit to the corporation. The subsection requires that there be a "substantial" benefit to the corporation to prevent the plaintiff from proposing inconsequential damages in order to justify the payment of counsel fees. While the subsection does not specify the method for calculating attorneys' fees since there is a substantial body of court decisions delineating this issue, it does require that the expenses be reasonable, which would include taking into account the amount or character of the benefit to the corporation.

Section 13.07(b)(2) provides that on termination of a proceeding the court may require the plaintiff to pay the defendants' reasonable expenses, including attorney's fees, if it finds that the proceeding "was commenced or maintained without reasonable cause or for an improper purpose." The phrase "for an improper purpose" has been added to parallel Federal Rule of Civil Procedure 11 in order to prevent proceedings which may be brought to harass the nonprofit corporation or its officers or to divert assets to a purpose not consistent with the purposes of the nonprofit corporation. The test in this section is similar to but not identical with the test utilized in Section 13.31 of the Model Business Corporation Act, relating to dissenter's rights, where the standard for award of expenses and attorneys' fees is that dissenters "acted arbitrarily, vexatiously or not in good faith" in demanding a judicial appraisal of their shares. The situation of a derivative action involving a nonprofit corporation is sufficiently different from the dissenter's rights situation to justify a different and less onerous test for imposing costs on the plaintiff. The test of Section 13.07(b)(2) that the action was brought without reasonable cause or for an improper purpose is appropriate to deter strike suits, on the one hand, and on the other hand to protect plaintiffs whose suits have a reasonable foundation.

Section 13.07(b)(3) has been added to deal with other abuses in the conduct of derivative litigation which may be committed by the defendants and their counsel as well as by the plaintiffs and their counsel. This section follows generally the provisions of Federal Rule of Civil Procedure 11. Section 13.07(b)(3) will not be necessary in states which already have a counterpart to Rule 11.

§ 13.08. APPLICABILITY TO FOREIGN CORPORATIONS

In any derivative proceeding in the right of a foreign nonprofit corporation, the matters covered by this [chapter] shall be governed by the laws of the jurisdiction of incorporation of the foreign corporation except for Sections 13.04, 13.06, and 13.07.

Source Note: Patterned after Model Business Corporation Act, 3d Ed. (2002) § 7.47.

CROSS-REFERENCES

"Derivative proceeding" defined, see § 13.01.

Foreign corporations, generally, see §§ 15.01–15.32.

OFFICIAL COMMENT

Under generally prevailing practice, a court will look to the choice-of-law rules of the forum state to determine which law shall apply. If the issue is "procedural," the law of the forum state will apply; if the issuance is "substantive," relating to the internal affairs of the nonprofit corporation, the law of the state of incorporation will apply. *See, e.g., Hausman v. Buckley*, 299 F.2D 696, 700–06 (2d Cir. 1962); *Galef v. Alexander*, 615 F.2D 51 (2d Cir. 1980). *Compare* RESTATEMENT (SECOND) OF CONFLICT OF LAWS §§ 302, 303, 304, 306, 309 (1988) (the local law of the state of incorporation will be applied except in the unusual case where, with respect to the particular issue, some other state has a more significant relationship under the principles stated in Section 6 of the RESTATEMENT to the parties and the corporation or the transaction).

However, the distinction between what is procedural and what is substantive is not clear. *See, e.g., Cohen v. Beneficial Industrial Loan Corp.*, 337 U.S. 541, 555–57 (1949). For example, in *Susman v. Lincoln American Corp.*, 550 F. SUPP. 442, 446 n.6 (N.D. Ill. 1982), the court suggested that the standing requirement might be considered a federal procedural question under Federal Rule of Civil Procedure 23.1 and a matter of substantive law under the Delaware statute.

In view of the uncertainties created by these decisions, Section 13.08 sets forth a choice of law provision for foreign corporations. It provides, subject to three exceptions, that the matters covered by the subchapter shall be governed by the laws of the jurisdiction of incorporation of the foreign corporation. The three exceptions to the general rule are areas which are traditionally part of the forum's oversight of the litigation process: Section 13.04, dealing with the ability of the court to stay proceedings; Section 13.06, setting forth the procedure for settling a proceeding; and Section 13.07, providing for the assessment of reasonable expenses (including counsel fees) in certain situations.

§ 13.09. NOTICE TO ATTORNEY GENERAL

The plaintiff in a derivative proceeding must notify the attorney general within 10 days after commencing the proceeding if it involves a charitable corporation.

Source Note: Derived from Revised Model Nonprofit Corporation Act (1987) § 6.30(f).

CROSS-REFERENCES

"Charitable corporation" defined, see § 1.40.

"Derivative proceeding" defined, see § 13.01.

OFFICIAL COMMENT

Notice to the attorney general when a derivative proceeding involves a charitable corporation provides the attorney general with an opportunity to learn of and evaluate the dispute. The attorney general may, but does not have to, join in the action. See Section 1.70.

CHAPTER 14

Dissolution

Subchapter

A. Voluntary Dissolution
B. Administrative Dissolution
C. Judicial Dissolution
D. Miscellaneous

[Subchapter] A
VOLUNTARY DISSOLUTION

§ 14.01. DISSOLUTION BY INCORPORATORS OR DIRECTORS

A majority of the incorporators or directors of a nonprofit corporation that has not commenced activity, or of a membership corporation that has not admitted any members, may dissolve the corporation by delivering to the secretary of state for filing articles of dissolution that set forth:

(1) the name of the corporation;
(2) the date of its incorporation;
(3) either:
  (i) that the corporation has not commenced activity, or
  (ii) that the corporation is a membership corporation and has not admitted any members;
(4) that no debt of the corporation remains unpaid;
(5) that, except as provided in the articles of incorporation or bylaws, the net assets of the corporation remaining after winding up have been distributed to the members, if members were admitted; and
(6) that a majority of the incorporators or directors authorized the dissolution.

Source Note: Patterned after Model Business Corporation Act, 3d Ed. (2002) § 14.01. Subsection (a) is derived from Revised Model Nonprofit Corporation Act (1987) § 14.01(a).

CROSS-REFERENCES

Claims against dissolved corporation, see §§ 14.06 and 14.07.

"Deliver" defined, see § 1.40.

Dissolution by board of directors and members, see § 14.02.

Effect of dissolution, see § 14.05.

Effective date of dissolution, see § 14.03.

Filing and signature requirements, see § 1.20.

Filing fees, see § 1.22.

Incorporators, see § 2.01.

Initial directors, see § 2.05.

Revocation of dissolution, see § 14.04.

OFFICIAL COMMENT

Section 14.01 provides a simple method of voluntary dissolution for a nonprofit corporation that has not admitted any members or commenced activity. These provisions are alternative: a corporation may utilize Section 14.01 if it has not admitted members (even though it has commenced activity) or if it has admitted members but has not commenced activity. Dissolution may be accomplished in either of these situations simply by a majority vote of the incorporators or directors. (See Section 2.05 and its Official Comment for a discussion of the roles of "incorporators" or "initial directors" in the organization of a corporation.)

This simple method of dissolution is likely to be used by name-holding corporations or by corporations formed for the initiation of a new venture when the reasons for the initial creation of the corporation have been completely realized or will never come to fruition.

The form of articles of dissolution provided in Section 14.01 takes account of the fact that a nonprofit corporation may utilize this section even though it has received contributions from the admission of members or has incurred liabilities either from the commencement of activity without admitting members or from its organization; hence the articles must state that no debts remain unpaid, and that the net assets of the corporation remaining after winding up have been distributed to the members, if members have been admitted, subject to any provision of the articles of incorporation or bylaws restricting the distribution of assets.

The authority of the board of directors under this section may be vested by the articles of incorporation or bylaws in a designated body. See Section 8.12.

§ 14.02. APPROVAL OF DISSOLUTION

(a) The board of directors of a membership corporation may propose dissolution for submission to the members.

(b) For a proposal to dissolve to be adopted:

  (1) the board of directors must recommend dissolution to the members, unless the board of directors determines that because of conflict of interest or other special circumstances it should make no recommendation and communicates the basis for its determination to the members; and

  (2) the members entitled to vote must approve the proposal to dissolve as provided in subsection (e).

(c) The board of directors may condition its submission of the proposal for dissolution on any basis.

(d) The nonprofit corporation must give notice to each member, whether or not entitled to vote, of the proposed meeting of members. The notice must also state:

  (1) that the purpose, or one of the purposes, of the meeting is to consider dissolving the corporation; and

  (2) how the assets of the corporation will be distributed after all creditors have been paid, or how the distribution of assets will be determined.

(e) Unless the articles of incorporation, the bylaws, or the board of directors acting pursuant to subsection (c), requires a greater vote or a greater number of members to be present, the adoption of the proposal to dissolve by the members requires the approval of the members at a meeting at which a quorum exists, and, if any class of members is entitled to vote as a separate group on the proposal, the approval of each such separate voting group at a meeting at which a quorum of the voting group exists.

(f) If the nonprofit corporation does not have any members entitled to vote on its dissolution, a proposal to dissolve shall be deemed adopted by the corporation when it has been adopted by the board of directors.

(g) A charitable corporation must give the attorney general notice in the form of a record that it intends to dissolve before the time it delivers articles of dissolution to the secretary of state.

Source Note: Subsections (a)–(e) are patterned after Model Business Corporation Act, 3d Ed. (2002) § 14.02 and derived generally from Revised Model Nonprofit Corporation Act (1987) § 14.02. Subsection (f) is patterned after § 11.04(h). Subsection (g) is derived from Revised Model Nonprofit Corporation Act (1987) § 14.03(a).

CROSS-REFERENCES

Director standards of conduct, see § 8.30.

Dissolution by consent of members, see § 7.04.

Effect of dissolution, see § 14.05.

Notice generally, see § 1.41.

Notice of members' meeting, see § 7.05.

Quorum at members' meeting, see § 7.25.

Revocation of dissolution, see § 14.04.

Voting by voting group, see §§ 7.24 and 7.25.

Voting entitlement of members generally, see § 7.21.

"Voting group" defined, see § 1.40.

OFFICIAL COMMENT

Section 14.02(b) requires the board of directors, after approving a proposal to dissolve, to submit the proposal to the members entitled to vote thereon, if any, for their approval. When submitting the proposal the board of directors must make a recommendation to the members that the plan be approved, unless the board of directors makes a determination that because of conflicts of interest or other special circumstances it should make no recommendation. For example, the board of directors may make such a determination because the board is evenly divided as to the merits of the proposal but is able to agree that the members should be permitted to consider dissolution. If the board of directors makes such a determination, it must describe the conflict of interest or special circumstances, and communicate the basis for the determination, when submitting the proposal to dissolve to the members. The exception for conflicts of interest or other special circumstances is intended to be sparingly available. Generally, members should not be asked to act on a proposal for dissolution in the absence of a recommendation by the board of directors. The exception is not intended to relieve the board of directors of its duty to consider carefully the proposed dissolution and the interests of the corporation and its members.

Section 14.02(c) permits the board of directors to condition its submission of a proposal for dissolution on any basis. Among the conditions that a board might impose are that the proposal will not be deemed approved unless it is approved by a specified vote of the members, or by one or more specified classes of members, voting as a separate voting group, or by a specified percentage of disinterested members. The board of directors is not limited to conditions of these types.

Section 14.02(d) provides that if the proposal is required to be approved by the members, and if the approval is to be given at a meeting, the nonprofit corporation must give notice to each member, whether or not entitled to vote, of the meeting of members at which the proposal is to be submitted. Requirements concerning the timing and content of a notice of meeting are set out in Section 7.05. Section 14.02(d), however, does not require that notice be given to nonvoting members where the proposal is approved, without a meeting, by consent. The explanation of how the distribution of assets will be determined may be general in terms if the board will have the authority to make those determinations.

Section 14.02(e) provides that approval of a proposal for dissolution requires approval of the members at a meeting at which a quorum consisting of a majority of the votes entitled to be cast on the proposal exists. If a quorum is present, then under Sections 7.24 and 7.25 the proposal will be approved if more votes are cast in favor of the proposal than against it by the voting group or separate voting groups entitled to vote on the proposal.

The act does not mandate separate voting by voting groups in relation to dissolution proposals on the theory that, upon dissolution, the rights of all classes of members are fixed by the articles of incorporation or bylaws. Of course, group voting rights may be conferred by the articles or bylaws or by the board of directors, acting pursuant to subsection (c).

The authority of the board of directors under this section may be vested by the articles of incorporation or bylaws in a designated body. See Section 8.12.

§ 14.03. ARTICLES OF DISSOLUTION

(a) At any time after dissolution is authorized, the nonprofit corporation may dissolve by delivering to the secretary of state for filing articles of dissolution setting forth:
   (1) the name of the corporation;
   (2) the date dissolution was authorized; and
   (3) that the dissolution was approved in the manner required by this [act] and by the articles of incorporation and bylaws.

(b) A nonprofit corporation is dissolved upon the effective date of its articles of dissolution.

(c) For purposes of this [subchapter], "dissolved corporation" means a nonprofit corporation whose articles of dissolution have become effective and include a successor entity to which the remaining assets of the corporation are transferred subject to its liabilities for purposes of liquidation.

Source Note: Patterned after Model Business Corporation Act, 3d Ed. (2002) § 14.03. Subsections (a) and (b) are derived from Revised Model Nonprofit Corporation Act (1987) § 14.04.

CROSS-REFERENCES

"Deliver" defined, see § 1.40.

Dissolution by board of directors and members, see § 14.02.

Dissolution by consent of members, see § 7.04.

Effect of dissolution, see § 14.05.

Effective time and date of filing, see § 1.23.

Filing and signature requirements, see § 1.20.

Filing fees, see § 1.22.

Revocation of dissolution, see § 14.04.

Voting by voting group, see §§ 7.24 and 7.25.

"Voting group" defined, see § 1.40.

OFFICIAL COMMENT

The act of filing the articles of dissolution makes the decision to dissolve a matter of public record and establishes the time when the nonprofit corporation must begin the process of winding up and cease carrying on its activities except to the extent necessary for winding up. If dissolution was approved by the members, the articles of dissolution must state that dissolution was duly approved by the members in the manner required by the act and the articles of incorporation and bylaws of the corporation.

Under the act, articles of dissolution may be filed at the commencement of winding up or at any time thereafter. This is the only filing required for voluntary dissolution; no filing is required to mark the completion of winding up since the existence of the nonprofit corporation continues for certain purposes even after its activities are wound up and all of its assets have been distributed. No time limit for filing the articles is specified, and it may sometimes be desirable to postpone filing until winding up is far along or even complete.

A nonprofit corporation is dissolved on the date the articles of dissolution are effective. After this date the corporation is referred to as a "dissolved corporation," although its existence continues under Section 14.05 for purposes of winding up.

Section 14.03(c) defines "dissolved corporation" for purposes of Subchapter 14A to include successor entities to which assets are transferred subject to liabilities for purposes of liquidation. This provision covers the situation where a liquidating trust or other successor entity is used to complete the liquidation.

§ 14.04. REVOCATION OF DISSOLUTION

(a) A nonprofit corporation may revoke its dissolution within 120 days of its effective date.

(b) Revocation of dissolution must be authorized in the same manner as the dissolution was authorized unless that authorization permitted revocation by action of the board of directors alone, in which event the board of directors may revoke the dissolution without action by the members.

(c) After the revocation of dissolution is authorized, the nonprofit corporation may revoke the dissolution by delivering to the secretary of state for filing articles of revocation of dissolution, together with a copy of its articles of dissolution, that set forth:

  (1) the name of the corporation;

  (2) the effective date of the dissolution that was revoked;

  (3) the date that the revocation of dissolution was authorized;

  (4) that the revocation of dissolution was approved in the manner required by this [act] and by the articles of incorporation and bylaws.

(d) Revocation of dissolution is effective upon the effective date of the articles of revocation of dissolution.

(e) When the revocation of dissolution is effective, it relates back to and takes effect as of the effective date of the dissolution and the nonprofit corporation resumes carrying on its activities as if dissolution had never occurred.

Source Note: Patterned after Model Business Corporation Act, 3d Ed. (2002) § 14.04. Derived from Revised Model Nonprofit Corporation Act (1987) § 14.05.

CROSS-REFERENCES

Articles of dissolution, see § 14.03.

"Deliver" defined, see § 1.40.

Dissolution by:

board of directors and members, see § 14.02.
consent of members, see § 7.04.
incorporators or directors, see § 14.01.

Effective date of dissolution, see § 14.03.

Effective time and date of filing, see § 1.23.

Filing and signature requirements, see § 1.20.

Filing fees, see § 1.22.

OFFICIAL COMMENT

Voluntary dissolution may be revoked within 120 days of the effective date of the dissolution. Because of the importance and finality of dissolution, the decision to revoke dissolution generally requires member authorization (unless the dissolution was approved solely by the directors or incorporators under Section 14.01). Section 14.04(b), however, contemplates that the board of directors may revoke dissolution if it is granted that authority in advance by the members when approving the dissolution. Such authorization is often included in proposals to dissolve that are contingent upon the effectuation of another transaction, such as a sale of corporate assets not in the ordinary course.

Certain other action requiring member approval may be revoked by the board of directors without express member approval. (See Sections 11.04 and 12.02.) By contrast, dissolution under Section 14.04 may not be revoked by the board of directors without approval of the members.

Articles of revocation of dissolution must be filed to reflect the decision to resume the activities of the nonprofit corporation.

The information required in these articles parallels the information required in the original articles of dissolution.

The effect of articles of revocation of dissolution is to eliminate the requirement that the nonprofit corporation cease to conduct its activities except as part of the winding-up process and permit it to resume its activities without limitation and as if dissolution had never occurred.

The authority of the board of directors under this section may be vested by the articles of incorporation or bylaws in a designated body. See Section 8.12.

§ 14.05. EFFECT OF DISSOLUTION

(a) A dissolved nonprofit corporation continues its corporate existence but may not carry on any activities except those appropriate to wind up and liquidate its affairs, including:
   (1) collecting its assets;
   (2) disposing of its properties that will not be distributed in kind;
   (3) discharging or making provision for discharging its liabilities;
   (4) distributing its remaining property as required by law and its articles of incorporation and bylaws, and otherwise as approved when the dissolution was approved or among the members per capita; and
   (5) doing every other act necessary to wind up and liquidate its activities and affairs.

(b) Dissolution of a nonprofit corporation does not:
   (1) transfer title to the corporation's property;
   (2) subject its directors, members of a designated body, or officers to standards of conduct different from those prescribed in Chapter 8;
   (3) change quorum or voting requirements for its board of directors or members; change provisions for selection, resignation, or removal of its directors or officers or both; or change provisions for amending its bylaws;

(4) prevent commencement of a proceeding by or against the corporation in its corporate name;
(5) abate or suspend a proceeding pending by or against the corporation on the effective date of dissolution; or
(6) terminate the authority of the registered agent of the corporation.

(c) Property held in trust or otherwise dedicated to a charitable purpose may not be diverted from its purpose by the dissolution of a nonprofit corporation unless and until the corporation obtains an order of [*court*] [*the attorney general*] to the extent required by and pursuant to the law of this state on cy pres or otherwise dealing with the nondiversion of charitable assets.

(d) A person who is a member or otherwise affiliated with a charitable corporation may not receive a direct or indirect financial benefit in connection with the dissolution of the corporation unless the person is a charitable corporation or an unincorporated entity that has a charitable purpose. This subsection does not apply to the receipt of reasonable compensation for services rendered.

Source Note: Subsections (a) and (b) are patterned after Model Business Corporation Act, 3d Ed. (2002) § 14.05. Derived from Revised Model Nonprofit Corporation Act (1987) § 14.06.

CROSS-REFERENCES

Administrative dissolution, see §§ 14.20–14.23.

Claims against dissolved corporation, see §§ 14.06 and 14.07.

Deposit with state treasurer, see § 14.33.

Dissolution by:

board of directors and members, see § 14.02.
incorporators or directors, see § 14.01.

"Dissolved corporation" defined, see § 14.03.

Distribution, see § 6.40.

Effective date of dissolution, see § 14.03.

Judicial dissolution, see §§ 14.30–14.33.

"Proceeding" defined, see § 1.40.

Revocation of dissolution, see § 14.04.

Service of process on registered agent, see § 5.04.

OFFICIAL COMMENT

Section 14.05(a) provides that dissolution does not terminate the corporate existence but simply requires the nonprofit corporation thereafter to devote itself to winding up its affairs and liquidating its assets; after dissolution, the corporation may not carry on its activities except as may be appropriate for winding up.

The act uses the term "dissolution" in the specialized sense described above and not to describe the final step in the liquidation of the corporate activities. This is made clear by section 14.05(b), which provides that Chapter 14 dissolution does not have any of the characteristics of common law dissolution, which treated corporate dissolution as analogous to the death of a natural person and abated lawsuits, vested equitable title to corporate property in the members, imposed the fiduciary duty of trustees on directors who had custody of corporate assets, and revoked the authority of the registered agent. Section 14.05(b) expressly reverses all of these common law attributes of dissolution and makes clear that the rights, powers, and duties of members, the directors, members of a designated body, and the registered agent are not affected by dissolution and that suits by or against the corporation are not affected in any way.

§ 14.06. KNOWN CLAIMS AGAINST DISSOLVED CORPORATION

(a) A dissolved nonprofit corporation may dispose of the known claims against it by delivering notice to its known claimants of the dissolution at any time after its effective date.

(b) The notice must be in the form of a record and:

(1) describe information that must be included in a claim;
(2) provide a mailing address where a claim may be sent;
(3) state the deadline, which may not be fewer than 120 days from the effective date of the notice, by which the dissolved nonprofit corporation must receive the claim; and
(4) state that the claim will be barred if not received by the deadline.

(c) A claim against the dissolved nonprofit corporation is barred:
(1) if a claimant who was given notice under subsection (b) does not deliver the claim to the dissolved corporation by the deadline; or
(2) if a claimant whose claim was rejected by the dissolved corporation does not commence a proceeding to enforce the claim within 90 days from the effective date of the rejection notice.

(d) For purposes of this section, "claim" does not include a contingent liability or a claim based on an event occurring after the effective date of dissolution.

Source Note: Patterned after Model Business Corporation Act, 3d Ed. (2002) § 14.06. Substantially a reenactment of Revised Model Nonprofit Corporation Act (1987) § 14.07.

CROSS-REFERENCES

Administrative dissolution, see § 14.21.

"Deliver" defined, see § 1.40.

Dissolved corporation, see § 14.03.

Distributions, see §§ 6.40 and 8.33.

Effective date of dissolution, see § 14.03.

Judicial dissolution, see § 14.32.

Notice, see § 1.41.

"Proceeding" defined, see § 1.40.

Unknown claims, see § 14.07.

OFFICIAL COMMENT

Sections 14.06 and 14.07 provide a simplified system for handling known and unknown claims against a dissolved nonprofit corporation, including claims based on events that occur after the dissolution of the corporation. Section 14.06 deals solely with known claims while Section 14.07 deals with unknown or subsequently arising claims. A claim can be a "known" claim even if it is unliquidated; a claim that is contingent or has not yet matured or in certain cases has matured but has not been asserted is not a "known" claim (see Section 14.06(d)). For example, an unmatured liability under a guarantee or a potential default under a lease would not be a "known" claim.

Known claims are handled in Section 14.06 through a process of notice to claimants; the notice must contain the information described in Section 14.06(b). Section 14.06(c) then provides fixed deadlines by which claims are barred under various circumstances, as follows:

(1) If a claimant was given effective notice satisfying Section 14.06(b) but fails to file the claim by the deadline specified by the dissolved corporation, the claim is barred by Section 14.06(c)(1). See Section 1.41 as to the effectiveness of notice.

(2) If a claimant receives notice satisfying Section 14.06(b) and files the claim as required:

  (i) but the dissolved corporation rejects the claim, the claimant must commence a proceeding to enforce the claim within 90 days of the rejection or the claim is barred by Section 14.06(c)(2); or

  (ii) if the dissolved corporation does not act on the claim or fails to notify the claimant of the rejection, the claimant is not barred by Section 14.06(c) until the dissolved corporation notifies the claimant.

(3) If the dissolved corporation publishes notice under Section 14.07, a claimant who was not notified in a record is barred unless a proceeding is commenced to enforce the claim within three years after publication of the notice.

(4) If the dissolved corporation does not publish notice, a claimant who was not notified in a record is not barred by Section 14.06(c) from pursuing the claim.

These principles, it should be emphasized, do not lengthen statutes of limitation applicable under general state law. Thus, claims that are not barred under the foregoing rules—for example, if the corporation does not act on a claim—will nevertheless be subject to the general statute of limitations applicable to claims of that type.

Even though the directors are not trustees of the assets of a dissolved nonprofit corporation (see Section 14.05(b)(3)), they must discharge or make provision for discharging the corporation's liabilities before distributing its remaining assets. See Section 14.09.

The nonprofit corporation is free, of course, to negotiate with creditors or claimants and to compromise some or all of the corporation's debts or other claims against the corporation.

§ 14.07. OTHER CLAIMS AGAINST DISSOLVED CORPORATION

(a) A dissolved nonprofit corporation may publish notice of its dissolution and request that persons with claims against the dissolved corporation present them in accordance with the notice.

(b) The notice must:

(1) be published one time in a newspaper of general circulation in the county where the principal office of the dissolved nonprofit corporation (or, if none in this state, its registered office) is or was last located;

(2) describe the information that must be included in a claim and provide a mailing address where the claim must be sent; and

(3) state that a claim against the dissolved corporation will be barred unless a proceeding to enforce the claim is

commenced within three years after the publication of the notice.

(c) If the dissolved nonprofit corporation publishes a newspaper notice in accordance with subsection (b), the claim of each of the following claimants is barred unless the claimant commences a proceeding to enforce the claim against the dissolved corporation within three years after the publication date of the newspaper notice:

(1) a claimant who was not given notice under Section 14.06;

(2) a claimant whose claim was timely sent to the dissolved corporation but not acted on; or

(3) a claimant whose claim is contingent or based on an event occurring after the effective date of dissolution.

(d) A claim that is not barred by Section 14.06(b) or Section 14.07(c) may be enforced:

(1) against the dissolved nonprofit corporation, to the extent of its undistributed assets; or

(2) except as provided in Section 14.08(d), if the assets have been distributed in liquidation, against any person, other than a creditor of the dissolved corporation, to whom the corporation distributed its property to the extent of the distributee's pro rata share of the claim or the corporate assets distributed to the distributee in liquidation, whichever is less, but a distributee's total liability for all claims under this section may not exceed the total amount of assets distributed to the distributee.

Source Note: Patterned after Model Business Corporation Act, 3d Ed. (2002) § 14.07. Substantially a reenactment of Revised Model Nonprofit Corporation Act (1987) § 14.08, except that the limitations period has been reduced from five years to three years.

CROSS-REFERENCES

Administrative dissolution, see § 14.21.

"Claim" defined, see § 14.06.

"Deliver" defined, see § 1.40.

"Dissolved corporation" defined, see § 14.03.

Distributions, see §§ 6.40 and 8.33.

Effective date of dissolution, see § 14.03.

Judicial dissolution, see § 14.32.

Known claims, see § 14.06.

Notice, see § 1.41.

"Principal office":
- defined, see § 1.40.
- designated in annual report, see § 16.21.

"Proceeding" defined, see § 1.40.

Registered office:
- designated in annual report, see § 16.21.
- required, see §§ 2.02, 5.01, and 15.07.

OFFICIAL COMMENT

The prior version of the act did not recognize the serious problem created by possible claims that might arise long after the dissolution process was completed and the corporate assets distributed. The application of the act's provisions (and of the state dissolution statutes phrased in different terms) to this problem led to confusing and inconsistent results. The problems raised by these claims are intractable: on the one hand, the application of a mechanical limitation period to a claim for injury that occurs after the period has expired involves obvious injustice to the plaintiff. On the other hand, to permit these suits generally makes it impossible ever to complete the winding up of the nonprofit corporation, make suitable provision for creditors, and distribute the balance of the corporate assets.

The solution adopted in Section 14.07 is to continue the liability of a dissolved nonprofit corporation for subsequent claims for a period of three years after it publishes notice of dissolution. It is recognized that a three-year cutoff is itself arbitrary, but it is believed that the bulk of post-dissolution claims that can be estimated will arise during this period. This provision is therefore believed to be a reasonable compromise between the competing considerations of providing a remedy to injured plaintiffs and providing a basis for directors to estimate liabilities so that dissolved corporations may distribute remaining assets free of all claims and distributees may receive them secure in the knowledge that they may not be reclaimed. The period of three years for asserting claims is within the range of time periods adopted by state statutes.

Directors must generally discharge or make provision for discharging the nonprofit corporation's liabilities before distributing the remaining assets. See Section 14.09(a). Many claims covered by this section are of a type for which provision may be made by the purchase of insurance or by the setting aside of a portion of the assets, thereby permitting prompt distributions in liquidation. Claimants, of course, may always have recourse to the remaining assets of the dissolved corporation. See Section 14.07(d)(1). Further, where unbarred claims arise after distributions have been made in liquidation, Section 14.07(d)(2) authorizes recovery against the distributees receiving the earlier distributions. The recovery, however, is limited to the smaller of the distributees' pro rata share of the claim or the total amount of assets received as liquidating distributions from the corporation. The provision ensures that claimants seeking to recover distributions will try to recover from the entire class of distributees rather than concentrating only on the larger distributees and protects the limited liability of members. Members also may be liable to directors for recoupment under Section 8.33(b)(2).

§ 14.08. COURT PROCEEDINGS

(a) A dissolved nonprofit corporation that has published a notice under Section 14.07 may file an application with the [*name or describe*] court of the county where the dissolved corporation's principal office (or, if none in this state, its registered office) is located for a determination of the amount and form of security to be provided for payment of claims that are contingent or have not been made known to the dissolved corporation or that are based on an event occurring after the effective date of dissolution but that, based on the facts known to the dissolved corporation, are reasonably estimated to arise after the effective date of dissolution. Provision need not be made for any claim that is or is reasonably anticipated to be barred under Section 14.07(c).

(b) Within 10 days after the filing of the application, notice of the proceeding must be given by the dissolved nonprofit corporation to each claimant holding a contingent claim whose contingent claim is shown on the records of the dissolved corporation.

(c) The court may appoint a guardian ad litem to represent all claimants whose identities are unknown in any proceeding brought under this section. The reasonable fees and expenses of the guardian, including all reasonable expert witness fees, must be paid by the dissolved nonprofit corporation.

(d) Provision by the dissolved nonprofit corporation for security in the amount and the form ordered by the court under Section 14.08(a) satisfies the dissolved corporation's obligations with respect to claims that are contingent, have not been made known to the dissolved corporation, or are based on an event occurring after the effective date of dissolution, and such claims may not be enforced against a person who received assets in liquidation.

Source Note: Patterned after Model Business Corporation Act, 3d Ed. (2002) § 14.08.

CROSS-REFERENCES

"Dissolved corporation" defined, see § 14.03.

Notice, see § 1.41.

"Principal office":
- defined, see § 1.40.
- designated in annual report, see § 16.21.

"Proceeding" defined, see § 1.40.

Registered office:

designated in annual report, see § 16.21.

required, see §§ 2.02, 5.01, and 15.07.

OFFICIAL COMMENT

Section 14.08 adds a provision to the act allowing a dissolved nonprofit corporation to initiate a proceeding to establish the provision that should be made for unknown or contingent claims before a distribution in liquidation is made. Similar proceedings are authorized in several states to remove the risk of director and member liability for inadequate provision for claims.

Section 14.08(a) authorizes the proceeding and specifies that provision for unknown and contingent claims can only be for those claims that are estimated to arise after dissolution that are not expected to be barred by Section 14.07(d). The same analysis may be made by the board of directors under Section 14.09 if court proceedings are not used. As a result, estimates for unknown or contingent claims need only be made for those claims that the court determines are reasonably anticipated to be asserted within three years after dissolution. Such estimates might reasonably be based on the claims experience of the corporation prior to its dissolution.

If the dissolved nonprofit corporation elects to initiate a proceeding, it must give notice of the proceeding within 10 days after filing the court application to each holder of a contingent claim whose claim is shown on the records of the corporation. Notice to holders of guarantees made by the corporation typically would be required under this subsection.

Section 14.08(c) allows the court to appoint a guardian ad litem for unknown claimants, but does not make the appointment mandatory. Reasonable fees and expenses of the guardian ad litem are to be paid by the dissolved nonprofit corporation. Section 14.08 is designed to permit the court to adopt procedures appropriate to the circumstances.

If the proceeding is completed, Section 14.08(d) establishes that the dissolved nonprofit corporation is deemed to have satisfied its obligation to discharge or make provision for discharging its liabilities (see Section 14.05(a)(3)). With respect to claims that have not matured, directors are protected from liability by Section 14.09(b), and persons receiving distributions are protected from claims under Section 14.08(d).

If a court determines that the nonprofit corporation is dissolving for the primary purpose of avoiding anticipated claims of future tort claimants, it is expected that the court will use its general discretionary powers and deny the protections of Section 14.08 to the dissolved corporation.

§ 14.09. DIRECTOR DUTIES

(a) Directors shall cause the dissolved nonprofit corporation to discharge or make reasonable provision for the payment of claims and make distributions of assets after payment or provision for claims.

(b) Directors of a dissolved nonprofit corporation that has disposed of claims under Sections 14.06, 14.07, or 14.08 shall not be liable for breach of Section 14.09(a) with respect to claims against the dissolved corporation that are barred or satisfied under Sections 14.06, 14.07, or 14.08.

Source Note: Patterned after Model Business Corporation Act, 3d Ed. (2002) § 14.09.

CROSS-REFERENCES

"Claim" defined, see § 14.06.

Directors' liability for unlawful distributions, see § 8.33.

"Dissolved corporation" defined, see § 14.03.

Known claims, see § 14.06.

Other claims, see § 14.07.

Proceeding to determine security for contingent claims, see § 14.08.

OFFICIAL COMMENT

Section 14.09(a) establishes the duty of directors to discharge or make provision for claims and to make distributions of the remaining assets. The earlier version of Chapter 14 inferred the obligation from Section 14.05(3) and (4) concerning the powers of the nonprofit corporation to pay claims and make distributions upon dissolution. Liability of directors formerly was based on violations of Section 6.40 concerning distributions. Section 6.41(c) removed distributions in liquidation from the coverage of Section 6.40.

Section 14.09(b) provides that directors of a dissolved nonprofit corporation that complies with Section 14.06, 14.07, or 14.08 are not liable for breach of Section 14.09(a) with respect to claims that are disposed of under those sections. For example, directors need not make provision for claims of known creditors who are barred under Section 14.06 for failure to file a claim or commence a proceeding within the specified times, for contingent claimants whose estimated claims are barred by the three-year period after publication, pursuant to Section 14.07(c), or for claimants such as guarantors if provision for the claims has been approved by a court under Section 14.08(d).

Section 14.09(b) leaves unchanged the Section 8.33 provision that director liability is to the corporation. There are, however, cases that under various theories recognize liability directly to creditors for wrongful payments in liquidation. While there might be circumstances under which direct creditor claims are appropriate, the basic approach of Chapter 14 is that claims for breach of duty of directors for breach of Section 14.09(a) and claims for recoupment of amounts improperly distributed in liquidation should be mediated through the corporation.

If the articles of incorporation or bylaws vest some or all of the authority of the board of directors with respect to dissolution in a designated body, this section applies to the members of the designated body. See Section 8.12.

[Subchapter] B
ADMINISTRATIVE DISSOLUTION

§ 14.20. GROUNDS FOR ADMINISTRATIVE DISSOLUTION

The secretary of state may commence a proceeding under Section 14.21 to administratively dissolve a nonprofit corporation if:

(1) the corporation does not pay within 120 days after they are due any taxes or penalties imposed by this [act] or other law which are collected by the secretary of state;
(2) the corporation does not deliver its annual report to the secretary of state within 120 days after it is due;
(3) the corporation is without a registered agent or registered office in this state for 120 days or more;
(4) the corporation does not give notice to the secretary of state within 120 days that its registered agent or registered office has been changed, that its registered agent has resigned, or that its registered office has been discontinued; or
(5) the corporation's period of duration, if any, stated in its articles of incorporation expires.

Source Note: Patterned after Model Business Corporation Act, 3d Ed. (2002) § 14.20. Derived from Revised Model Nonprofit Corporation Act (1987) § 14.20, except that the period in paragraph (4) has been increased to 120 days.

CROSS-REFERENCES

Annual report, see § 16.22.

Appeal from administrative dissolution, see § 14.23.

"Deliver" defined, see § 1.40.

Duration of corporation, see § 3.02.

Judicial dissolution, see §§ 14.30–14.33.

Registered office and agent, see Ch. 5.

Reinstatement following administrative dissolution, see § 14.22.

Voluntary dissolution, see §§ 14.01 and 14.02.

OFFICIAL COMMENT

The experience in most states has been that administrative dissolution, or the threat thereof, is an effective enforcement mechanism for a variety of statutory obligations. A requirement of judicial dissolution would be inappropriate for many of these violations because of its cost and the diversion of limited legal resources, particularly since most violations reflect the abandonment of the corporation.

The advantages of administrative dissolution in these circumstances are compelling: it not only reduces the number of records maintained by the secretary of state, but also avoids further wasteful attempts to compel compliance by the abandoned nonprofit corporations and returns the corporate name promptly to the status of available names. Therefore, the act includes, in Sections 14.20 through 14.23, a model provision for the administrative dissolution of corporations in certain limited circumstances. These circumstances are set forth in Section 14.20 and closely parallel provisions found in most state statutes on this subject.

§ 14.21. PROCEDURE FOR ADMINISTRATIVE DISSOLUTION

(a) If the secretary of state determines that one or more grounds exist under Section 14.20 for dissolving a nonprofit corporation, the secretary of state shall serve the corporation with notice in the form of a record of that determination under Section 5.04.

(b) If the nonprofit corporation does not correct each ground for dissolution or demonstrate to the reasonable satisfaction of the secretary of state that each ground determined by the secretary of state does not exist within 60 days after service of the notice is perfected under Section 5.04, the secretary of state shall administratively dissolve the corporation by signing a certificate of dissolution that recites the ground or grounds for dissolution and its effective date. The secretary of state shall file the original of the certificate and serve a copy on the corporation under Section 5.04.

(c) The administrative dissolution of a nonprofit corporation does not terminate the authority of its registered agent.

(d) A person is not liable in contract, tort, or otherwise solely by reason of being a director, member of a designated body, officer, or member of a nonprofit corporation that was dissolved under this [subchapter], with respect to the activities or affairs of the corporation that have been continued, with or without knowledge of the dissolution.

Source Note: Subsections (a)–(c) are patterned after Model Business Corporation Act, 3d Ed. (2002) § 14.21 and derived from Revised Model Nonprofit Corporation Act (1987) § 14.21. Required notice to attorney general in the case of public benefit corporations is omitted. Subsection (d) is patterned after Colo. Rev. Stat. § 7-128-401(7) (2008).

CROSS-REFERENCES

Appeal from denial of reinstatement, see § 14.23.

Claims, see §§ 14.06 and 14.07.

Deposit with state treasurer, see § 14.33.

Effective date of service, see § 5.04.

Reinstatement following administrative dissolution, see § 14.22.

Winding up, see § 14.05.

OFFICIAL COMMENT

Many failures to comply with statutory requirements that may give rise to administrative dissolution under Section 14.20

occur because of oversight or inadvertence by responsible corporate officers of nonprofit corporations that are continuing their activities. Such failures are usually corrected promptly when brought to the corporation's attention. Sections 14.21(a) and (b) therefore provide a mandatory notice by the secretary of state to each corporation subject to administrative dissolution and a 60-day grace period following the notice before the certificate of administrative dissolution may be filed.

In most instances, the issue of whether the nonprofit corporation is subject to administrative dissolution will not be controverted. If a corporation is administratively dissolved, it may petition the secretary of state for reinstatement under Section 14.22 and, if this is denied, it may appeal to the courts under Section 14.23.

§ 14.22. REINSTATEMENT FOLLOWING ADMINISTRATIVE DISSOLUTION

(a) A nonprofit corporation administratively dissolved under Section 14.21 may apply to the secretary of state for reinstatement. The application must state:
   (1) the name of the corporation at the time of its administrative dissolution;
   (2) a new name of the corporation if its prior name is not available at the time of the filing of the application for reinstatement;
   (3) the effective date of its administrative dissolution; and
   (4) that the grounds for dissolution either did not exist or have been eliminated.

(b) If the secretary of state determines that the application contains the information required by subsection (a) and that the information is correct, the secretary of state shall cancel the certificate of dissolution and prepare a certificate of reinstatement that recites that determination and the effective date of reinstatement, file the original of the certificate, and serve a copy on the nonprofit corporation under Section 5.04.

(c) When the reinstatement is effective, it relates back to and takes effect as of the effective date of the administrative dissolution and the nonprofit corporation resumes carrying on its activities as if the administrative dissolution had never occurred.

Source Note: Patterned after Model Business Corporation Act, 3d Ed. (2002) § 14.22. Substantially a reenactment of Revised Model Nonprofit Corporation Act (1987) § 14.22.

CROSS-REFERENCES

Appeal from denial of reinstatement, see § 14.23.

Effective date of administrative dissolution, see § 14.21.

Filing fees, see § 1.22.

Filing requirements, see § 1.20.

Grounds for administrative dissolution, see § 14.20.

OFFICIAL COMMENT

This section may apply when a nonprofit corporation through inadvertence or a failure to maintain a registered agent fails to receive or respond to the predissolution notice of default required by Section 14.21. A corporation that is reinstated pursuant to this section resumes carrying on its business as before dissolution. There is no time limit on when a corporation may apply for reinstatement.

In order to be eligible for reinstatement, a nonprofit corporation must comply with all statutory requirements at the time it seeks reinstatement. It must establish, for example, that all taxes and fees have been paid. Because dissolution makes its name available for use by another person, a corporation may need to change its name when it files the application for reinstatement.

§ 14.23. APPEAL FROM DENIAL OF REINSTATEMENT

(a) If the secretary of state denies a nonprofit corporation's application for reinstatement following administrative dissolution, the secretary of state shall serve the corporation under Section 5.04 with a notice in the form of a record that explains the reason for denial.

(b) The nonprofit corporation may appeal the denial of reinstatement to the [*name or describe*] court within 90 days after service of the notice of denial is perfected. The corporation appeals by petitioning the court to set aside the dissolution and attaching to the petition copies of the secretary of state's certificate of dissolution, the corporation's application for reinstatement, and the secretary of state's notice of denial.

(c) The court may summarily order the secretary of state to reinstate the dissolved nonprofit corporation or may take other action the court considers appropriate.

(d) The court's final decision may be appealed as in other civil proceedings.

Source Note: Patterned after Model Business Corporation Act, 3d Ed. (2002) § 14.23. Substantially a reenactment of Revised Model Nonprofit Corporation Act (1987) § 14.23.

CROSS-REFERENCES

Effective date of service, see § 5.04.

Grounds for administrative dissolution, see § 14.20.

Notice, see § 1.41.

Reinstatement following administrative dissolution, see § 14.22.

OFFICIAL COMMENT

Section 14.23 provides for an appeal from a decision by the secretary of state denying a petition for reinstatement. The court with jurisdiction over an appeal should be specified, and states adopting this section of the act should specify who has the burden of proof on appeal and the standard for judicial review. See the Official Comment to Section 1.26.

[Subchapter] C
JUDICIAL DISSOLUTION

§ 14.30 GROUNDS FOR JUDICIAL DISSOLUTION

The [*name or describe court or courts*] may dissolve a nonprofit corporation:

(1) in a proceeding by the attorney general, if it is established that:
   (i) the corporation obtained its articles of incorporation through fraud; or
   (ii) the corporation has exceeded or abused, and is continuing to exceed or abuse, the authority conferred upon it by law;

(2) except as provided in the articles of incorporation or bylaws, in a proceeding by 50 members or members holding at least 5% of the voting power, whichever is less, or by a director or member of a designated body, if it is established that:
   (i) the directors or a designated body are deadlocked in the management of the corporate affairs, the members, if any, are unable to break the deadlock, and irreparable injury to the corporation or its mission is threatened or being suffered because of the deadlock;
   (ii) the directors or those in control of the corporation have acted, are acting, or will act in a manner that is illegal, oppressive, or fraudulent;
   (iii) the members are deadlocked in voting power and have failed, for a period that includes at least two consecutive annual meeting dates, to elect successors to directors whose terms have, or otherwise would have, expired;
   (iv) the corporate assets are being misapplied or wasted; or

(v) the corporation has insufficient assets to continue its activities and it is no longer able to assemble a quorum of directors or members;

(3) in a proceeding by a creditor, if it is established that:

(i) the creditor's claim has been reduced to judgment, the execution on the judgment returned unsatisfied, and the corporation is insolvent; or

(ii) the corporation has admitted in a record that the creditor's claim is due and owing and the corporation is insolvent; or

(4) in a proceeding by the corporation to have its voluntary dissolution continued under court supervision.

Source Note: Patterned after Model Business Corporation Act, 3d Ed. (2002) § 14.30. Derived from Revised Model Nonprofit Corporation Act (1987) § 14.30(a).

CROSS-REFERENCES

Administrative dissolution, see §§ 14.20–14.23.

Director action, see §§ 8.20–8.24.

Election of directors, see § 8.03.

Member voting, see §§ 7.24–7.26.

Revocation of articles of incorporation by state, see § 2.03.

Terms of directors, see §§ 8.05 and 8.06.

Ultra vires acts, see § 3.04.

Voluntary dissolution, see §§ 14.01–14.05.

OFFICIAL COMMENT

Section 14.30 provides grounds for the judicial dissolution of nonprofit corporations at the request of the state, a member, a creditor, a director, a member of a designated body, or a corporation that has commenced voluntary dissolution. This section states that a court "may" order dissolution if a ground for dissolution exists. Thus, there is discretion on the part of the court as to whether dissolution is appropriate even though grounds exist under the specific circumstances.

1. Involuntary Dissolution by State

Section 14.30(1) preserves long-standing and traditional provisions authorizing the state to seek to dissolve involuntarily a nonprofit corporation by judicial decree. While this power has been exercised only rarely in recent years, this right of the state involves a policing action that provides a means by which the state may ensure compliance with, and nonabuse of, the fundamentals of corporate existence. Section 14.30(1) limits the power of the state in this regard to grounds that are reasonably related to this objective.

The legality of proposed corporations or of proposed actions has sometimes been tested by the secretary of state's refusal to accept documents for filing. The role of the secretary of state in reviewing documents for filing has been restricted by the act (see Section 1.25 and its Official Comment). It is intended that suits under this subchapter will replace those actions.

2. Involuntary Dissolution by Members or Others

Section 14.31(2) provides for involuntary dissolution at the suit of a member, director, or member of a designated body under circumstances involving deadlock or significant abuse of power by controlling members or other persons.

A. DEADLOCK

Dissolution because of deadlock is available if the board of directors or a designated body is deadlocked, but only if (1) the members are unable to break the deadlock, and (2) "irreparable injury" to the corporation or its mission is being threatened or suffered. Dissolution because of deadlock at the board of directors or a designated body is not dependent on the lapse of time during which the deadlock continues.

Dissolution is also available because of deadlock at the members' level if the members are unable to elect directors over a two-year period. Dissolution under Section 14.30(2)(iii) is not dependent on irreparable injury or misconduct by the directors then in office; if injury or misconduct is present, a deadlocked member may proceed under another clause of Section 14.30(2).

B. ABUSE OF POWER

A member may sue for involuntary dissolution upon proof either that those in control of the nonprofit corporation are acting illegally, oppressively, or fraudulently (Section 14.30(2)(ii)) or that the corporate assets are being misapplied or wasted (Section 14.30(2)(iv)). The application of these grounds for dissolution to specific circumstances obviously involves judicial discretion in the application of a general standard to concrete circumstances. The court should be cautious in the application of these grounds so as to limit them to genuine abuse rather than instances of acceptable tactics in a power struggle for control of a corporation.

3. Dissolution by Creditors

Creditors may obtain involuntary dissolution only when the nonprofit corporation is insolvent and only in the limited circumstances set forth in Section 14.30(3). Typically, a proceeding under the federal Bankruptcy Act is an alternative in these situations.

4. Dissolution by Corporation

A nonprofit corporation that has commenced voluntary dissolution may petition a court to supervise its dissolution. Such an action may be appropriate to permit the orderly liquidation of the corporate assets and to protect the corporation from a multitude of creditors' suits or suits by dissatisfied members.

§ 14.31. PROCEDURE FOR JUDICIAL DISSOLUTION

(a) Venue for a proceeding by the attorney general to dissolve a nonprofit corporation lies in [*name the county or counties*]. Venue for a proceeding brought by any other party named in Section 14.30 lies in the county where a corporation's principal office (or, if none in this state, its registered office) is or was last located.

(b) It is not necessary to make directors or members parties to a proceeding to dissolve a nonprofit corporation unless relief is sought against them individually.

(c) A court in a proceeding brought to dissolve a nonprofit corporation may issue injunctions, appoint a receiver or custodian pendente lite with all powers and duties the court directs, take other action required to preserve the corporate assets wherever located, and carry on the activities of the corporation until a full hearing can be held.

Source Note: Patterned after Model Business Corporation Act, 3d Ed. (2002) § 14.31(a)–(c). Reenactment of Revised Model Nonprofit Corporation Act (1987) § 14.31(a)–(c).

CROSS-REFERENCES

Custodian, see § 14.32.

Grounds for judicial dissolution, see § 14.30.

"Principal office":
- defined, see § 1.40.
- designated in annual report, see § 16.21.

Receiver, see § 14.32.

Registered office:
- designated in annual report, see § 16.21.
- required, see §§ 2.02, 5.01, and 15.07.

OFFICIAL COMMENT

Section 14.31 designates the attorney general as the officer to bring suits for involuntary dissolution by the state. The county or counties where these suits must be commenced should be specified; it typically is either the state capital or the county in which the corporation's principal office is located. See the Official Comment to Section 1.26. Suits brought by other persons for judicial dissolution under Section 14.30 must be brought where the corporation's principal office is located or, if not located in this state, where its registered office is or was last located.

§ 14.32. RECEIVERSHIP OR CUSTODIANSHIP

(a) A court in a judicial proceeding brought to dissolve a nonprofit corporation may appoint one or more receivers to wind up and liquidate, or one or more custodians to manage, the affairs of the corporation. The court shall hold a hearing, after giving notice to all parties to the proceeding and any interested persons designated by the court, before appointing a receiver or custodian. The court appointing a receiver or custodian has exclusive jurisdiction over the corporation and all of its property wherever located.

(b) The court may require the receiver or custodian to post bond, with or without sureties, in an amount the court directs.

(c) The court shall describe the powers and duties of the receiver or custodian in its appointing order, which may be amended from time to time. Among other powers:

- (1) the receiver:
  - (i) may dispose of all or any part of the assets of the nonprofit corporation wherever located, at a public or private sale, if authorized by the court, and
  - (ii) may sue and defend in his or her own name as receiver of the corporation in all courts of this state;
- (2) the custodian may exercise all of the powers of the corporation, through or in place of its board of directors and any designated body, to the extent necessary to manage the affairs of the corporation consistent with its mission and in the best interests of its members, if any, and creditors.

(d) During a receivership, the court may redesignate the receiver a custodian, and during a custodianship may redesignate the custodian a receiver, if doing so is consistent with the mission of the nonprofit corporation and in the best interests of the corporation, its members, and creditors.

(e) The court from time to time during the receivership or custodianship may order compensation paid and expense disbursements or reimbursements made to the receiver or custodian and counsel from the assets of the nonprofit corporation or proceeds from the sale of the assets.

(f) This section does not apply to a nonprofit corporation that is a religious organization.

Source Note: Patterned after Model Business Corporation Act, 3d Ed. (2002) § 14.32. Subsections (a)–(e) are substantially a reenactment of Revised Model Nonprofit Corporation Act (1987) § 14.32. Subsection (f) is new.

CROSS-REFERENCES

Custodianship pendente lite, see § 14.31.

Notice, see § 1.41.

Receivership pendente lite, see § 14.31.

OFFICIAL COMMENT

In many states, general statutes or rules of court regulate the appointment of receivers or custodians and define their duties. Section 14.32 is designed to supplement these general provisions and grant the court power to take the steps it considers necessary to resolve the internal corporate problem or to effect liquidation of the nonprofit corporation in an efficient manner.

§ 14.33. DECREE OF DISSOLUTION

(a) If after a hearing the court determines that one or more grounds for judicial dissolution described in Section 14.30 exist, it may enter a decree dissolving the nonprofit corporation and specifying the effective date of the dissolution, and the clerk of the court shall deliver a certified copy of the decree to the secretary of state, who shall file it.

(b) After entering the decree of dissolution, the court shall direct the winding-up and liquidation of the nonprofit corporation's affairs in accordance with Section 14.05 and the notification of claimants in accordance with Sections 14.06 and 14.07.

Source Note: Patterned after Model Business Corporation Act, 3d Ed. (2002) § 14.33. Substantially a reenactment of Revised Model Nonprofit Corporation Act (1987) § 14.33.

CROSS-REFERENCES

Claims, see §§ 14.06 and 14.07.

Custodianship, see §§ 14.31 and 14.32.

"Deliver" defined, see § 1.40.

Deposit with state treasurer, see § 14.40.

Dissolution does not terminate authority of registered agent, see § 14.05.

Receivership, see §§ 14.31 and 14.32.

Secretary of state's filing duties, see § 1.25.

Winding-up, see § 14.05.

OFFICIAL COMMENT

A court decree ordering that a corporation be dissolved involuntarily has the same legal effect as articles of dissolution. Section 14.33 requires that the secretary of state receive and file a copy of the decree. Thereafter the corporation's activities and affairs are to be wound up as provided in Sections 14.05, 14.06, and 14.07.

[Subchapter] D
MISCELLANEOUS

§ 14.40 DEPOSIT WITH STATE TREASURER

Assets of a dissolved nonprofit corporation that should be transferred to a creditor, claimant, or member of the corporation who cannot be found or who is not competent to receive them shall be reduced to cash and deposited with the state treasurer or other appropriate state official for safekeeping. When the creditor, claimant, or member furnishes satisfactory proof of entitlement to the amount deposited, the state treasurer or other appropriate state official shall pay the amount held.

Source Note: Patterned after Model Business Corporation Act, 3d Ed. (2002) § 14.40. Derived from Revised Model Nonprofit Corporation Act (1987) § 14.40.

CROSS-REFERENCES

Administrative dissolution, see § 14.20.

Claims, see §§ 14.06 and 14.07.

Judicial dissolution, see § 14.30.

Voluntary dissolution, see § 14.05.

OFFICIAL COMMENT

Section 14.40 is a deposit provision, not an escheat provision. It does not provide for ultimate disposition of unclaimed funds. Rather, it permits a nonprofit corporation that has dissolved to pay over for safekeeping to the state treasurer (or other appropriate state official with statutory authority to receive such funds) funds belonging to a creditor, claimant, or member who cannot be found.

The handling and ultimate disposition of unclaimed funds by the state treasurer or other appropriate state official is to be determined by state law other than the act.

CHAPTER 15

Foreign Corporations

Subchapter

[Subchapter] A
CERTIFICATE OF AUTHORITY

§ 15.01. AUTHORITY TO CONDUCT ACTIVITIES REQUIRED

(a) A foreign nonprofit corporation may not conduct activities in this state until it obtains a certificate of authority from the secretary of state.

(b) The following activities, among others, do not constitute conducting activities within the meaning of subsection (a):

(1) maintaining, defending, or settling any proceeding;

(2) holding meetings of the board of directors, a designated body, members, or delegates or carrying on other activities concerning internal corporate affairs;

(3) maintaining bank accounts;

(4) maintaining offices or agencies for the transfer, exchange, and registration of memberships or securities or maintaining trustees or depositaries with respect to those memberships or securities;

(5) selling through independent contractors;

(6) soliciting or obtaining orders, whether by mail, electronically, or through employees or agents or otherwise,

if the orders require acceptance outside this state before they become contracts;

(7) creating or acquiring indebtedness, mortgages, and security interests in real or personal property;

(8) securing or collecting debts or enforcing mortgages and security interests in property securing the debts;

(9) owning, without more, real or personal property;

(10) conducting an isolated transaction that is completed within 30 days and that is not one in the course of repeated transactions of a like nature;

(11) soliciting or accepting contributions;

(12) conducting activities in interstate commerce.

(c) The list of activities in subsection (b) is not exhaustive.

Source Note: Patterned after Model Business Corporation Act, 3d Ed. (2002) § 15.01. Substantially a reenactment of Revised Model Nonprofit Corporation Act (1987) § 15.01.

CROSS-REFERENCES

Application of act to existing qualified foreign corporation, see § 17.02.

Certificate of authority, see § 15.03.

"Foreign corporation" defined, see § 1.40.

Penalty for conducting activities without authority, see § 15.02.

"Proceeding" defined, see § 1.40.

OFFICIAL COMMENT

A state may prescribe the terms and conditions upon which a foreign nonprofit corporation is permitted to conduct activities within the state, subject, of course, to the restrictions of the United States Constitution. Chapter 15 requires that a foreign corporation seeking to conduct activities within the state must (1) obtain a certificate of authority from the secretary of state, and (2) maintain a registered office and appoint a registered agent within the state.

Section 15.01(a) states the basic requirement that a foreign nonprofit corporation must obtain a certificate of authority before it conducts activities within the state. Section 15.05 describes the scope of the privilege obtained by a certificate of authority while Section 15.02 describes the consequences of conducting activities in the state without first obtaining the certificate of authority.

The act does not attempt to formulate an inclusive definition of what constitutes the conduct of activities. Rather, the concept is defined in a negative fashion by Section 15.01(b), which states that certain activities do not constitute the conduct of activities. In general terms, any conduct more regular, systematic, or extensive than that described in Section 15.01(b) constitutes the conduct of activities and requires the foreign nonprofit corporation to obtain a certificate of authority. Typical conduct requiring a certificate of authority includes maintaining an office to conduct local intrastate activities, selling personal property not in interstate commerce, entering into contracts relating to the local activities, and owning or using real estate for general corporate purposes. But the passive owning of real estate for investment purposes does not constitute conducting activities. See Section 15.01(b)(9).

The test of "conducting activities" defined in a negative way in Section 15.01(b) applies only to the question whether the foreign nonprofit corporation's contacts with the state are such that it must obtain a certificate of authority. It is not applicable to other questions such as whether the corporation is amenable to service of process under state "long-arm" statutes or liable for state or local taxes. A corporation that has obtained (or is required to obtain) a certificate of authority to conduct activities under Chapter 15 will generally be subject to suit and state taxation in the state, while a corporation that is subject to service of process or state taxation in a state will not necessarily be required to obtain a certificate of authority under Chapter 15.

The list of activities set forth in Section 15.01(b) is not exhaustive. See Section 15.01(c). The list excludes several different types of activities from the definition of "conducting activities," which are discussed below.

1. Engaging in Litigation

Section 15.01(b)(1) excludes "maintaining, defending, or settling any proceeding." The word "proceeding" is defined in Section 1.40 to include all civil, criminal, administrative, or investigative suits or actions. Thus, a foreign nonprofit corporation is not "conducting activities" solely because it resorts to the courts of the state to recover an indebtedness, enforce an obligation, recover possession of personal property, obtain the appointment of a receiver, intervene in a pending proceeding, bring a petition to compel arbitration, file an appeal bond, or pursue appellate remedies. Similarly, a foreign corporation is not required to obtain a certificate of authority merely because it files a complaint with a governmental agency or participates in an administrative proceeding within the state.

2. Internal Affairs of the Corporation

A foreign nonprofit corporation does not "conduct activities" within a state under Section 15.01 merely because some of its internal affairs occur within the state. Thus, a corporation may hold meetings of its board of directors, a designated body, members, or delegates within a state without first obtaining a certificate of authority (Section 15.01(b)(2)). It also may maintain offices or agencies within a state relating solely to the transfer, registration, or exchange of its memberships without obtaining a certificate of authority (Section 15.01(b)(4)). Other activities relating to the internal affairs of the corporation that do not constitute the conduct of activities under Section 15.01(b) include having officers or representatives of a corporation who reside within or are physically present in the state; while there, the officers or representatives may make executive decisions relating to the affairs of the corporation without imposing on the corporation the requirement that it obtain a certificate of authority in the state, so long as these activities are not so regular and systematic as to cause the residence to be viewed as a business office.

3. Maintaining Bank Accounts

A foreign nonprofit corporation may maintain a bank account with a bank within the state, make deposits, and write checks on the account without obtaining a certificate of authority (Section 15.01(b)(3)).

4. Interstate Transactions

A foreign nonprofit corporation is not "conducting activities" within the meaning of Section 15.01(a) if it is conducting activities in interstate commerce (Section 15.01(b)(10)) or soliciting or obtaining orders that must be accepted outside the state before they become contracts (Section 15.01(b)(6)). These limitations reflect the provisions of the United States Constitution that grant to the United States Congress exclusive power over interstate commerce, and preclude states from imposing restrictions or conditions upon this commerce. These sections should be construed in a manner consistent with judicial decisions under the United States Constitution. Under these decisions, a foreign corporation is not required to obtain a certificate of authority even though it sells goods within the state if they are shipped to the purchasers in interstate commerce. A corporation need not obtain a certificate of authority even if it also does work and performs acts within the state incidental to the interstate business, *e.g.*, if it takes or enforces a security interest incidental to these transactions. Nor is it required to obtain a certificate of authority merely because it sends traveling salesmen or solicitors into a state so long as contracts are not made within the state. Similarly, an office may be maintained by a corporation in a state without obtaining a certificate of authority if the office's functions relate solely to interstate commerce.

Purchases of goods may of course be in interstate commerce as readily as sales. Thus, the purchase of personal property by a foreign nonprofit corporation for shipment in interstate commerce out of the state does not require the corporation to obtain a certificate of authority.

5. Sales Through Independent Contractors

A foreign nonprofit corporation does not need to obtain a certificate of authority if it sells goods in the state through independent contractors (Section 15.01(b)(5)). These transactions are viewed as transactions by the independent contractors, not by the corporation itself even though the corporation sets some limits or ground rules for its contractors. If these controls are sufficiently pervasive, however, the corporation may be deemed to be selling for itself in intrastate commerce, and not through the independent contractors and therefore engaged in the conduct of activities in the state.

6. Creating, Acquiring, or Collecting Debts

The mere act of making a loan by a foreign nonprofit corporation that is not in the business of making loans does not constitute conducting activities in the state in which the loan is made. On the same theory a foreign corporation may obtain security for the repayment of a loan, and foreclose or enforce the lien or security interest to collect the loan, without being deemed to be conducting activities. See Section 15.01(b)(7) and (8). Similarly, a refunding or "rollover" of a loan or its adjustment or compromise does not involve the conduct of activities.

7. Isolated Transactions

The concept of "conducting activities" involves regular, repeated, and continuing business contacts of a local nature. A single agreement or isolated transaction within a state does not constitute the conduct of activities if there is no intention to repeat the transaction or engage in similar transactions. Since the question is entirely one of fact, Section 15.01(b)(10) has a partially objective test that a transaction completed within 30 days does not constitute "conducting activities" if it is not one in the course of "repeated transactions of a like nature." A continuing transaction that is not completed within 30 days will likely require obtaining a certificate of authority, whether or not it is one of a number of repeated transactions, but that issue is not addressed by the act. The 30-day provision is, in other words, a "safe harbor" for not requiring a certificate of authority.

8. Contributions

Although Section 15.01(b)(11) provides that soliciting or accepting contributions is not an activity that requires a foreign nonprofit corporation to obtain authority under this section to conduct activities in the state, those activities in many states require registration with the secretary of state or another official under laws regulating the solicitation of charitable contributions.

9. Other Transactions

Section 15.01(c) makes clear that the list of transactions in Section 15.01(b) is not exhaustive. Among the large number of other transactions which do not give rise to the requirement that a certificate of authority be obtained are the ownership of all the shares of stock in a corporation that is engaged in local business within the state or as a limited partner in a limited partnership engaged in local business, or taking ministerial actions such as filing financing statements or registering trademarks.

§ 15.02. CONSEQUENCES OF CONDUCTING ACTIVITIES WITHOUT AUTHORITY

(a) A foreign nonprofit corporation conducting activities in this state without a certificate of authority may not maintain a proceeding in any court in this state until it obtains a certificate of authority.

(b) The successor to a foreign nonprofit corporation that conducted activities in this state without a certificate of authority and the assignee of a cause of action arising out of those activities may not maintain a proceeding based on that cause of action in any court in this state until the foreign corporation or its successor obtains a certificate of authority.

(c) A court may stay a proceeding commenced by a foreign nonprofit corporation, its successor, or its assignee until it determines whether the foreign corporation or its successor requires a certificate of authority. If it so determines, the court may further stay the proceeding until the foreign corporation or its successor obtains the certificate.

(d) Notwithstanding subsections (a) and (b), the failure of a foreign corporation to obtain a certificate of authority does not impair the validity of its corporate acts or prevent it from defending any proceeding in this state.

Source Note: Patterned after Model Business Corporation Act, 3d Ed. (2002) § 15.02(a)–(c) and (e). Reenactment of Revised Model Nonprofit Corporation Act (1987) § 15.02(a)–(c) and (e). Prior subsection (d) providing for a civil penalty for noncompliance has been omitted.

CROSS-REFERENCES

Certificate of authority, see § 15.03.

Conducting activities, see § 15.01.

"Foreign corporation" defined, see § 1.40.

"Proceeding" defined, see § 1.40.

OFFICIAL COMMENT

The purpose of Section 15.02 is to induce foreign nonprofit corporations that are required to obtain a certificate of authority, but have not done so, to qualify promptly, without imposing harsh or erratic sanctions. The act rejects the provisions adopted in a few states that make unenforceable intrastate transactions by nonqualified corporations or that impose punitive sanctions or forfeitures on nonqualifying corporations. Often the failure to qualify is a result of inadvertence or bona fide disagreement as to the scope of the provisions of Section 15.01, which are necessarily imprecise; the imposition of harsh sanctions in these situations is inappropriate. Further, as a matter of state policy it is generally preferable to encourage qualification in case of doubt rather than to impose severe sanctions that may cause corporations to resist obtaining a certificate of authority in doubtful situations.

Section 15.02 closes the courts of the state to suits maintained by foreign nonprofit corporations that should have, but have not, obtained a certificate of authority. However, this sanction is not a punitive one: Section 15.02(e) states that the failure of the corporation to qualify does not affect the validity of corporate acts, including contracts. Thus, a contract made by a nonqualified corporation may be enforced by the corporation simply by obtaining a certificate. Further, Section 15.02(c) authorizes a court to stay a proceeding to determine whether a corporation should have qualified to conduct activities and, if it concludes that qualification is necessary, it may grant a further stay to permit the corporation to do so. Thus, the corporation will not be compelled to refile a suit if the corporation qualifies to conduct activities within a reasonable period. The purpose of these provisions is to encourage corporations to obtain certificates of authority and to eliminate the temptation to raise Section 15.02 defenses only after applicable statutes of limitation have run.

Section 15.02(e) does not prevent a foreign nonprofit corporation that has failed to obtain a certificate of authority from "defending any proceeding." The distinction between "maintaining" a proceeding under Section 15.02(a) and "defending any proceeding" under Section 15.02(e) is determined on the basis of whether affirmative relief is sought. A nonqualified corporation may interpose any defense or permissive or mandatory counterclaim to defeat a claimed recovery, but may not obtain an affirmative judgment or decree based on the counterclaim unless it has obtained a certificate of authority.

In addition to closing the courts of the state to a nonqualified foreign nonprofit corporation, some states impose a penalty equal to all fees and franchise taxes that the foreign corporation would have been liable for if it had qualified to conduct activities when it was first required to do so. This penalty is usually defined to equal the sum of fees and franchise taxes for each year or part thereof that the corporation conducted activities in the state without a certificate of authority. A similar provision has not been included in the act.

Section 15.02(b) prevents evasion of Section 15.02(a) by an assignment of a claim on which the foreign nonprofit corporation is barred from bringing suit under Section 15.02(a). If the successor has acquired all or substantially all of the assets of the foreign corporation, the successor may maintain suit after it has qualified. In the case of all other assignments, the foreign corporation itself must obtain a certificate of authority before the assignees may maintain suit on the claim. The phrase "all or substantially all" has the meaning set forth in the Official Comment to Section 12.01.

§ 15.03. APPLICATION FOR CERTIFICATE OF AUTHORITY

A foreign nonprofit corporation may apply for a certificate of authority to conduct activities in this state by delivering an application to the secretary of state for filing. The application must set forth:

(1) the name of the foreign corporation or, if its name is unavailable for use in this state, a corporate name that satisfies the requirements of Section 15.06;
(2) the name of the state or country under whose law it is incorporated;
(3) its date of incorporation and period of duration, if any;
(4) the street address of its principal office;
(5) the address of its registered office in this state and the name of its registered agent at that office; and
(6) the names and usual business addresses of its current directors and officers.

Source Note: Patterned after Model Business Corporation Act, 3d Ed. (2002) § 15.03(a). Reenactment of Revised Model Nonprofit Corporation Act (1987) § 15.03(a), except paragraphs (a)(7) and (8) which have been omitted.

CROSS-REFERENCES

Amended certificate of authority, see § 15.04.

Application of act to existing qualified foreign corporation, see § 17.02.

Certificate of existence, see § 1.28.

Corporate name, see § 15.06, Ch. 4.

Corporate purposes, see § 3.01.

"Deliver," see § 1.40.

Filing and signature requirements, see § 1.20.

Filing fees, see § 1.22.

Forms, see § 1.21.

"Principal office":
- defined, see § 1.40.
- designated in annual report, see § 16.21.

Registered office and agent, see §§ 2.02, 5.01, and 15.07.

Report to secretary of state, see § 16.21.

OFFICIAL COMMENT

1. Disclosure Requirements in General

Section 15.03 provides that a foreign nonprofit corporation seeking a certificate of authority to conduct activities in the state must file an application that contains the information set forth in this section. These disclosure requirements are supplemented by the requirements of other sections in this chapter—15.04, 15.06, and 15.07—which require amended or supplemental filings in certain circumstances, and by Section 16.21, which requires every qualified foreign corporation to file annual reports containing specified information. Generally, the act eliminates repetitious filings, so that information need be submitted to the secretary of state in only one document.

The purposes of these disclosure requirements are: (1) to ensure that citizens of the state have adequate information about foreign nonprofit corporations in their transactions with them; (2) to put foreign corporations in a status of equality with domestic corporations with respect to information required to be furnished; (3) to facilitate the subjection of foreign corporations to the jurisdiction of the state's courts, thereby removing any disadvantage citizens of the state may have when dealing with them; and (4) to provide readily accessible evidence of the existence of foreign corporations. Other statutes relating to franchise taxes and regulatory matters may require a qualified foreign corporation to provide additional information.

2. Application for a Certificate of Authority

The information required to be included in the application for a certificate of authority by Section 15.03 is the minimum needed to administer the filing requirements of the act. The application must also be accompanied by a certificate of existence and the filing fee required by Section 1.22. A corporation that qualifies to conduct activities in a state must comply with the requirements of other applicable statutes. See Section 15.05.

§ 15.04. AMENDED CERTIFICATE OF AUTHORITY

(a) A foreign nonprofit corporation authorized to conduct activities in this state must obtain an amended certificate of authority from the secretary of state if it changes:
   (1) its name;
   (2) the period of its duration; or
   (3) the state or country of its incorporation.

(b) The requirements of Section 15.03 for obtaining an original certificate of authority apply to obtaining an amended certificate under this section.

Source Note: Patterned after Model Business Corporation Act, 3d Ed. (2002) § 15.04. Reenactment of Revised Model Nonprofit Corporation Act (1987) § 15.04.

CROSS-REFERENCES

Annual report, see § 16.21.

Certificate of authority, see § 15.03.

Change of registered office or agent, see § 15.08.

Corporate name, see § 15.06, Ch. 4.

Duration, see § 3.02.

Filing fees, see § 1.22.

Filing requirements, see § 1.20.

Forms, see § 1.21.

Resignation of registered agent, see § 15.09.

OFFICIAL COMMENT

Section 15.04 requires a foreign nonprofit corporation to obtain an amended certificate of authority if it changes its corporate name, its duration, or the state or country of its incorporation. An amendment is not necessary to reflect changes in its principal office address or in its current officers or directors since that information is supplied in the annual report. In addition, Section 15.07 requires an immediate filing if the foreign corporation changes its registered office or registered agent within the state.

Other fundamental changes by a foreign nonprofit corporation do not require amendments to the certificate of authority. The secretary of state will be advised of most of these changes through the annual report. See Section 16.21. Thus, a person seeking to obtain current information about a foreign corporation should examine the annual reports of the corporation as well as the application for certificate of authority and amendments to it. This procedure of requiring most changes to be reported in the annual reports rather than as amendments to the certificate of authority should eliminate many unnecessary filings with the secretary of state without reducing the information available through the secretary of state's office.

§ 15.05. EFFECT OF CERTIFICATE OF AUTHORITY

(a) A certificate of authority authorizes the foreign nonprofit corporation to which it is issued to conduct activities in this state, subject to the right of the state to revoke the certificate as provided in this [act].

(b) A foreign nonprofit corporation with a valid certificate of authority has the same but no greater rights and has the same but no greater privileges as, and except as otherwise provided by this [act] is subject to the same duties, restrictions, penalties, and liabilities now or later imposed on, a domestic nonprofit corporation of like character.

(c) This [act] does not authorize this state to regulate the organization or internal affairs of a foreign nonprofit corporation authorized to conduct activities in this state.

Source Note: Patterned after Model Business Corporation Act, 3d Ed. (2002) § 15.05. Substantially a reenactment of Revised Model Nonprofit Corporation Act (1987) § 15.05.

CROSS-REFERENCES

Corporate powers, see § 3.02.

Corporate purposes, see § 3.01.

Revocation of certificate of authority, see §§ 15.30–15.32.

Withdrawal of foreign corporations, see § 15.20.

OFFICIAL COMMENT

A certificate of authority authorizes a foreign nonprofit corporation to conduct activities in the state subject to the right of the state to revoke the certificate. The privileges of this status are defined in Section 15.05(b): a qualified foreign corporation has the same (but no greater) privileges as a domestic corporation.

Section 15.05(b), by granting to qualified foreign nonprofit corporations all of the rights and privileges enjoyed by a domestic nonprofit corporation, avoids discrimination that might otherwise be subject to constitutional challenge. On the other hand, Section 15.05(b) also contains a restriction or limitation: a qualified foreign corporation is subject to the same restrictions as a domestic corporation, including the same duties, penalties, and liabilities. This latter aspect of Section 15.05(b) has declined in importance as states have eliminated unnecessary or outdated restrictions on domestic corporations and, as a consequence of Section 15.05(b), on qualified foreign corporations as well. In particular, Section 15.05(b) makes Section 3.01 (corporate purposes) applicable to a qualified foreign corporation, and grants substantially the same powers to it as are possessed by a domestic corporation.

Section 15.05(c) preserves the judicially developed doctrine that internal corporate affairs are governed by the state of incorporation even when the foreign nonprofit corporation's activities and assets are located primarily in other states.

Obtaining a certificate of authority under this subchapter is independent of compliance with a state's laws on the solicitation of charitable contributions and possibly attendant registration requirements.

§ 15.06. NAME OF FOREIGN CORPORATION

(a) If the name of a foreign nonprofit corporation does not satisfy the requirements of Section 4.01, the foreign corporation, to obtain or maintain a certificate of authority to conduct activities in this state, may use a fictitious name to conduct activities in this state if its real name is unavailable and it delivers to the secretary of state for filing a copy of the resolution of its board of directors, certified by its secretary, adopting the fictitious name.

(b) Except as authorized by subsections (c) and (d), the name (including a fictitious name) of a foreign nonprofit corporation must be distinguishable upon the records of the secretary of state from:

  (1) a name that is not available under Section 4.01; or

  (2) a name reserved or registered under Section 4.02 or 4.03 or other law of this state.

(c) A foreign nonprofit corporation may apply to the secretary of state for authorization to use in this state the name of another domestic or qualified foreign nonprofit corporation, domestic or qualified foreign business corporation, or domestic or qualified foreign filing entity that is not distinguishable upon the records of the secretary of state from the name applied for. The secretary of state shall authorize use of the name applied for if:

(1) the other corporation or entity consents to the use and submits an undertaking in the form of a record satisfactory to the secretary of state to change its name to a name that is distinguishable upon the records of the secretary of state from the name of the applying corporation; or

(2) the applicant delivers to the secretary of state a certified copy of a final judgment of a court of competent jurisdiction establishing the applicant's right to use the name applied for in this state.

(d) A foreign nonprofit corporation may use in this state the name (including the fictitious name) of another domestic or foreign nonprofit or business corporation or other entity that is used in this state if the other corporation or entity is incorporated, organized, or authorized to transact business or conduct activities in this state and the foreign corporation:

(1) has merged with the other corporation or entity;

(2) has been formed by reorganization of the other corporation or entity; or

(3) has acquired all or substantially all of the assets, including the name, of the other corporation or entity.

(e) If a foreign nonprofit corporation authorized to conduct activities in this state changes its name to one that does not satisfy the requirements of Section 4.01, it may not conduct activities in this state under the changed name until it adopts a name satisfying the requirements of Section 4.01 and obtains an amended certificate of authority under Section 15.04.

Source Note: Patterned after Model Business Corporation Act, 3d Ed. (2002) § 15.06. Substantially a reenactment of Revised Model Nonprofit Corporation Act (1987) § 15.06.

CROSS-REFERENCES

Amended certificate of authority, see § 15.04.

Corporate names generally, see Ch. 4.

"Deliver," see § 1.40.

Effective time and date of filing, see § 1.23.

Filing fees, see § 1.22.

Filing requirements, see § 1.23.

Registered name, see § 4.03.

Reserved name, see § 4.02.

OFFICIAL COMMENT

The purpose of Section 15.06, like that of Section 4.01 relating to the name of a domestic nonprofit corporation, is to ensure that names are distinguishable from one another upon the records of the secretary of state. Like Section 4.01, it does not impose upon the secretary of state the responsibility of deciding issues of unfair competition or commercial similarity of names.

A foreign nonprofit corporation applying for a certificate of authority must apply under its true name if that name qualifies under Section 15.06(a) or (c). If the true name is unavailable because it is indistinguishable upon the records of the secretary of state from a name already in use or reserved, the corporation may use a fictitious name (if available) under Section 15.06(a) simply by delivering to the secretary of state for filing, together with its application for a certificate of authority, a certified copy of a resolution of its board of directors authorizing the use of the fictitious name in the state. Finally, the otherwise unavailable name of a foreign corporation may be augmented by the name of the state of its incorporation so as to make it distinguishable upon the records of the secretary of state. For example, a Delaware corporation named "Utopian Products, Inc." which finds that a domestic corporation is using that name may qualify under the name "Utopian Products, Inc. (Delaware)."

A foreign nonprofit corporation that qualifies to conduct activities in the state may use an assumed name to the same extent as a domestic corporation. The name requirements of Section 15.06, including the fictitious name of a corporation whose real name is unavailable, are designed to ensure that each corporation qualified to conduct activities in this state has a unique official name. For a fuller description of the policies underlying Section 15.06, see the Official Comment to Section 4.01.

If a foreign nonprofit corporation changes its name it may (1) file an amended certificate of authority under its new name or, if the new name is not available, (2) continue to conduct activities under its former name as an assumed name, or (3) adopt a new assumed name, by filing a certified resolution of its board of directors authorizing it to do so.

§ 15.07. REGISTERED OFFICE AND REGISTERED AGENT OF FOREIGN CORPORATION

Each foreign nonprofit corporation authorized to conduct activities in this state must continuously maintain in this state:

(1) a registered office that may be the same as any of its places of business; and

(2) a registered agent, who may be:

- (i) an individual who resides in this state and whose business office is identical with the registered office;
- (ii) a domestic nonprofit or business corporation or unincorporated entity whose business office is identical with the registered office; or
- (iii) a foreign nonprofit or business corporation or unincorporated entity authorized to transact business or conduct activities in this state whose business office is identical with the registered office.

Source Note: Patterned after Model Business Corporation Act, 3d Ed. (2002) § 15.07. Substantially a reenactment of Revised Model Nonprofit Corporation Act (1987) § 15.07.

CROSS-REFERENCES

Changing registered office or agent, see § 15.08.

Registered office and agent generally, see Ch. 5.

Resignation of registered agent, see § 15.09.

Revocation of certificate of authority does not affect authority of registered agent, see § 15.31.

Revocation of certificate of authority for failure to appoint and maintain registered office and agent, see § 15.30.

Service on foreign corporation, see §§ 15.10, 15.20, 15.31.

OFFICIAL COMMENT

A foreign nonprofit corporation that obtains a certificate of authority in a state thereby agrees that it is amenable to suit in the state. Section 15.07 requires every such corporation continuously to maintain a registered office and registered agent within the state upon whom service of process may be made. As is the case with a domestic nonprofit corporation, the registered office may be, but need not be, a business office of the foreign corporation.

Section 15.07 is patterned after Section 5.01, relating to the registered office and registered agent of a domestic nonprofit corporation. For a fuller description of the policies underlying Section 15.07, see the Official Comment to Section 5.01.

§ 15.08. CHANGE OF REGISTERED OFFICE OR REGISTERED AGENT OF FOREIGN CORPORATION

(a) A foreign nonprofit corporation authorized to conduct activities in this state may change its registered office or registered agent by delivering to the secretary of state for filing a statement of change that sets forth:

(1) its name;

(2) the street address of its current registered office;

(3) if the current registered office is to be changed, the street address of its new registered office;

(4) the name of its current registered agent;

(5) if the current registered agent is to be changed, the name of its new registered agent and the new agent's written consent (either on the statement or attached to it) to the appointment; and

(6) that after the changes are made, the street addresses of its registered office and the business office of its registered agent will be identical.

(b) If a registered agent changes the street address of its business office, the agent may change the street address of the registered office of any foreign nonprofit corporation for which the person is the registered agent by delivering notice to the corporation in the form of a record of the change and signing and delivering to the secretary of state for filing a statement of change that complies with the requirements of subsection (a) and recites that the corporation has been notified of the change.

Source Note: Patterned after Model Business Corporation Act, 3d Ed. (2002) § 15.08. Substantially a reenactment of Revised Model Nonprofit Corporation Act (1987) § 15.08.

CROSS-REFERENCES

"Deliver" defined, see § 1.40.

Effective time and date of filing, see § 1.23.

Filing fees, see § 1.22.

Filing requirements, see § 1.20.

Notice, see § 1.41.

Resignation of registered agent, see § 15.09.

Revocation of certificate of authority for failure to file notice of change of registered office or agent, see § 15.30.

OFFICIAL COMMENT

A foreign nonprofit corporation that changes its registered agent or registered office, or both, must file a statement with the secretary of state containing the information set forth in Section 15.08(a). A registered agent, typically a corporation service company, that changes the street address of its business office (and thereby the street address of the registered office of all corporations for which it serves as registered agent) may notify the secretary of state by complying with Section 15.08(b) rather than with Section 15.08(a).

This section is patterned after Section 5.02, relating to changes of registered office or registered agent of a domestic nonprofit corporation. For a fuller description of the policies underlying Section 15.08, see the Official Comment to Section 5.02.

§ 15.09. RESIGNATION OF REGISTERED AGENT OF FOREIGN CORPORATION

(a) The registered agent of a foreign nonprofit corporation may resign as agent by signing and delivering to the secretary of state for filing a statement of resignation. The statement of resignation may include a statement that the registered office is also discontinued.

(b) After filing the statement, the secretary of state shall deliver a copy of the statement to the registered office if not discontinued. The secretary of state shall also deliver a copy to the foreign nonprofit corporation at its principal office address shown in its most recent annual report.

(c) The agency appointment is terminated, and the registered office discontinued if so provided, on the 31st day after the date on which the statement was filed.

Source Note: Patterned after Model Business Corporation Act, 3d Ed. (2002) § 15.09. Substantially a reenactment of Revised Model Nonprofit Corporation Act (1987) § 15.09.

CROSS-REFERENCES

Annual report, see § 16.21.

Change of registered agent, see § 15.08.

"Deliver," see § 1.40.

Filing fees, see § 1.22.

Filing requirements, see § 1.20.

"Principal office":
- defined, see § 1.40.
- designated in annual report, see § 16.21.

OFFICIAL COMMENT

Section 15.09 permits the registered agent of a foreign nonprofit corporation to resign by following the procedure set forth in the section, which is designed to maximize the probabilities that the corporation is advised of the resignation of the agent. This section is principally used by compensated registered agents who are corporation service companies and who desire to resign as registered agent as a result of nonpayment of fees. Section 15.09 is patterned after Section 5.03, relating to the resignation of a registered agent of a domestic corporation. For a fuller description of the policies underlying Section 15.09, see the Official Comment to Section 5.03.

§ 15.10. SERVICE ON FOREIGN CORPORATION

(a) The registered agent of a foreign corporation authorized to conduct activities in this state is the corporation's agent for service of process, notice, or demand required or permitted by law to be served on the foreign corporation.

(b) A foreign corporation may be served by registered or certified mail, return receipt requested, addressed to the secretary of the foreign corporation at its principal office shown in its application for a certificate of authority or in its most recent annual report if the foreign corporation:

(1) has no registered agent or its registered agent cannot with reasonable diligence be served;

(2) has withdrawn from conducting activities in this state under Section 15.20; or

(3) has had its certificate of authority revoked under Section 15.31.

(c) Service is perfected under subsection (b) at the earliest of:

(1) the date the foreign corporation receives the mail;

(2) the date shown on the return receipt, if signed on behalf of the foreign corporation; or

(3) five days after its deposit in the United States mail, as evidenced by the postmark, if mailed postpaid and correctly addressed.

(d) This section does not prescribe the only means, or necessarily the required means, of serving a foreign corporation.

Source Note: Patterned after Model Business Corporation Act, 3d Ed. (2002) § 15.10. Reenactment of Revised Model Nonprofit Corporation Act (1987) § 15.10.

CROSS-REFERENCES

Annual report, see § 16.21.

Application for certificate of authority, see § 15.03.

"Principal office":

defined, see § 1.40.

designated in annual report, see § 16.21.

Revocation of certificate of authority does not revoke authority of registered agent, see § 15.31.

Service of process fees, see § 1.22.

Service on foreign corporation with revoked certificate of authority, see § 15.31.

Service on withdrawn foreign corporation, see § 15.20.

OFFICIAL COMMENT

Service on the registered agent is the typical method of service of process on a qualified foreign nonprofit corporation. Section 15.10(a). But if the corporation does not have a registered agent, or if the agent cannot be found at the registered office, Section 15.10(b) authorizes service on the secretary of the corporation at its principal office as shown in its certificate of authority or most recent annual report. Service may be effected in the same way on a corporation which has withdrawn from the state or whose certificate of authority has been revoked. Section 15.10(c) establishes the date on which service is effective under Section 15.10(b), while Section 15.10(d) makes clear that the method of service provided by this section does not preclude the use of other means of effecting service of process. Service of process may also be effected, for example, under a "long-arm" statute or under other special statutes authorizing service in some other manner.

Section 15.10 is patterned after Section 5.04, relating to service of process on domestic nonprofit corporations. For a fuller description of the policies underlying Section 15.10, see the Official Comment to Section 5.04.

[Subchapter] B
WITHDRAWAL OR TRANSFER OF AUTHORITY

§ 15.20. WITHDRAWAL OF FOREIGN CORPORATION

(a) A foreign nonprofit corporation authorized to conduct activities in this state may apply for a certificate of withdrawal by delivering an application to the secretary of state for filing. The application must set forth:

(1) the name of the foreign corporation and the name of the state or country under whose law it is incorporated;

(2) that it is not conducting activities in this state and that it surrenders its authority to conduct activities in this state;

(3) that it revokes the authority of its registered agent to accept service on its behalf and appoints the secretary of state as its agent for service of process in any proceeding based on a cause of action arising during the time it was authorized to conduct activities in this state;

(4) a mailing address to which the secretary of state may mail a copy of any process served on him under paragraph (3).

(b) After the withdrawal of the foreign nonprofit corporation is effective, service of process on the secretary of state under this section with respect to activities of the foreign corporation in this state prior to withdrawal is service on the foreign corporation. Upon receipt of process, the secretary of state shall mail a copy of the process to the foreign corporation at the mailing address set forth under subsection (a)(4).

Source Note: Patterned after Model Business Corporation Act, 3d Ed. (2002) § 15.20. Derived from Revised Model Nonprofit Corporation Act (1987) § 15.20.

CROSS-REFERENCES

Conducting activities, see § 15.01.

"Deliver" defined, see § 1.40.

Effective time and date of filing, see § 1.23.

Filing fees, see § 1.22.

Filing requirements, see § 1.20.

Forms, see § 1.21.

Registered agent, see § 15.07.

Service of process fees, see § 1.22.

Service of process on foreign corporation, see § 15.10.

OFFICIAL COMMENT

A foreign nonprofit corporation that ceases to conduct activities within a state may withdraw from the state only by obtaining a certificate of withdrawal. The certificate of withdrawal is recognition by the state that the foreign nonprofit corporation has ceased to conduct activities in the state.

The application for certificate of withdrawal must appoint the secretary of state as the withdrawing corporation's agent for service of process in any proceeding based on a cause of action which arose during the time it was authorized to conduct activities in the state. The application must also set forth a mailing address to which the secretary of state may forward any process received, and the corporation must agree to notify the secretary of state of any change in that address. There is no time limit on the obligation to advise the secretary of state of changes of mailing address. To ensure that the appointment of the secretary of state is unqualified and meets the precise requirements of this section, the secretary of state may require that an application for certificate of withdrawal be on a prescribed form. See Section 1.21.

Service of process on the secretary of state pursuant to the statements in the application for certificate of withdrawal effects service on the corporation under Section 15.20(b). The secretary of state must then mail the process to the corporation at the mailing address specified in the application or in a subsequent communication to the secretary of state advising of a change in mailing address.

§ 15.21. AUTOMATIC WITHDRAWAL UPON CERTAIN CONVERSIONS

A foreign nonprofit corporation authorized to conduct activities in this state that converts to a domestic business corporation or any form of domestic filing entity shall be deemed to have withdrawn on the effective date of the conversion.

Source Note: Patterned after Model Business Corporation Act, 3d Ed. (2002) § 15.21.

CROSS-REFERENCES

"Domestic business corporation" defined, see § 1.40.

"Filing entity" defined, see § 1.40.

"Foreign nonprofit corporation" defined, see § 1.40.

OFFICIAL COMMENT

The procedures by which a foreign nonprofit corporation may convert to a domestic business corporation or a domestic filing entity are outside the scope of this act. The purpose of this section is simply to coordinate the foreign corporation provisions of this act with those other procedures.

States that authorize a foreign nonprofit corporation to convert to a domestic business corporation or a domestic filing entity may wish to include the rule of this section in the statute or statutes providing for those conversions and, in that event, this section may be omitted.

§ 15.22. WITHDRAWAL UPON CONVERSION TO A NONFILING ENTITY

(a) A foreign nonprofit corporation authorized to conduct activities in this state that converts to a domestic or foreign nonfiling entity must apply for a certificate of withdrawal by delivering an application to the secretary of state for filing. The application must set forth:

(1) the name of the foreign nonprofit corporation and the name of the state or country under whose law it was incorporated before the conversion;

(2) that it surrenders its authority to conduct activities in this state as a foreign nonprofit corporation;

(3) the type of unincorporated entity to which it has been converted and the jurisdiction whose laws govern its internal affairs;

(4) if it has been converted to a foreign unincorporated entity:

(i) that it revokes the authority of its registered agent to accept service on its behalf and appoints the secretary of state as its agent for service of process in any proceeding based on a cause of action arising during the time it was authorized to conduct activities in this state;

(ii) a mailing address to which the secretary of state may mail a copy of any process served on the secretary of state under paragraph (i); and

(iii) a commitment to notify the secretary of state in the future of any change in its mailing address.

(b) After the withdrawal under this section of a corporation that has converted to a foreign unincorporated entity is effective, service of process on the secretary of state is service on the foreign unincorporated entity. Upon receipt of process, the secretary of state must mail a copy of the process to the foreign unincorporated entity at the mailing address set forth under subsection (a)(4).

(c) After the withdrawal under this section of a corporation that has converted to a domestic unincorporated entity is effective, service of process must be made on the unincorporated entity in accordance with the regular procedures for service of process on the form of unincorporated entity to which the corporation was converted.

Source Note: Patterned after Model Business Corporation Act, 3d Ed. (2002) § 15.22.

CROSS-REFERENCES

"Domestic unincorporated entity" defined, see § 1.40.

Effective time and date of filing, see § 1.23.

"Foreign nonprofit corporation" defined, see § 1.40.

"Foreign unincorporated entity" defined, see § 1.40.

"Nonfiling entity" defined, see § 1.40.

"Unincorporated entity" defined, see § 1.40.

OFFICIAL COMMENT

The procedures by which a foreign nonprofit corporation may convert to a domestic or foreign nonfiling entity are outside the scope of this act.

In the case of a conversion of a foreign nonprofit corporation to a domestic business corporation or a domestic filing entity, a filing with the secretary of state will be necessary to effectuate the conversion, and thus it is possible for Section 15.21 to provide that the previous filing by the converting entity as a foreign nonprofit corporation will be cancelled automatically. In the case of a conversion that is the subject of this section, however, a filing with the secretary of state is not necessary to effectuate the conversion. Thus, absent the procedures in this section, there would be no document of public record indicating that the conversion has occurred and the converted entity would incorrectly continue to appear in the public records as a foreign nonprofit corporation.

§ 15.23. TRANSFER OF AUTHORITY

(a) A foreign nonprofit corporation authorized to conduct activities in this state that converts to a foreign business corporation or to any form of foreign unincorporated entity that is required to obtain a certificate of authority or make a similar type of filing with the secretary of state if it transacts business in this state must file with the secretary of state an application for transfer of authority executed by any officer or other duly authorized representative. The application must set forth:

(1) the name of the corporation;

(2) the type of entity to which it has been converted and the jurisdiction whose laws govern its internal affairs; and

(3) any other information that would be required in a filing under the laws of this state by an entity of the type the corporation has become seeking authority to transact business in this state.

(b) The application for transfer of authority shall be delivered to the secretary of state for filing and shall take effect at the effective time provided in Section 1.23.

(c) Upon the effectiveness of the application for transfer of authority, the authority of the corporation under this [chapter] to conduct activities in this state shall be transferred without interruption to the converted entity which shall thereafter hold such authority subject to the provisions of the laws of this state applicable to that type of entity.

Source Note: Patterned after Model Business Corporation Act, 3d Ed. (2002) § 15.23.

CROSS-REFERENCES

"Deliver" defined, see § 1.40.

Filing and signature requirements, see § 1.20.

Filing fees, see § 1.22.

"Foreign business corporation" defined, see § 1.40.

"Foreign nonprofit corporation" defined, see § 1.40.

"Foreign unincorporated entity" defined, see § 1.40.

"Unincorporated entity" defined, see § 1.40.

OFFICIAL COMMENT

The procedures by which a foreign nonprofit corporation may convert to a foreign business corporation or a foreign unincorporated entity required to register to transact business in this state are outside the scope of this act.

The purpose of this section is to clarify the status of the foreign entity in the public records of this state. A filing under this section has the twofold effect of canceling the authority of the foreign nonprofit corporation to conduct activities in this state while at the same time reregistering it as a foreign entity under the appropriate law of this state. If the foreign entity subsequently wishes to cancel its registration to transact business in this state, it may do so under the foreign entity provisions to which it has become subject as provided in Section 15.23(c).

[Subchapter] C
REVOCATION OF CERTIFICATE OF AUTHORITY

§ 15.30. GROUNDS FOR REVOCATION

The secretary of state may commence a proceeding under Section 15.31 to revoke the certificate of authority of a foreign nonprofit corporation authorized to conduct activities in this state if:

(1) the foreign corporation does not deliver its annual report to the secretary of state within 120 days after it is due;

(2) the foreign corporation does not pay within 120 days after they are due any taxes or penalties imposed by this [act] or other law;

(3) the foreign corporation is without a registered agent or registered office in this state for 120 days or more;

(4) the foreign corporation does not inform the secretary of state under Section 15.08 or 15.09 that its registered agent or registered office has changed, that its registered agent has resigned, or that its registered office has been discontinued within 120 days of the change, resignation, or discontinuance;

(5) an incorporator, director, member of a designated body, officer, or agent of the foreign corporation signed a document the person knew was false in any material respect with intent that the document be delivered to the secretary of state for filing; or

(6) the secretary of state receives a duly authenticated certificate from the secretary of state or other official having custody of corporate records in the state or country under whose law the foreign corporation is incorporated stating that it has been dissolved or did not survive a merger.

Source Note: Patterned after Model Business Corporation Act, 3d Ed. (2002) § 15.30. Substantially a reenactment of Revised Model Nonprofit Corporation Act (1987) § 15.30(a).

CROSS-REFERENCES

Annual report, see § 16.21.

Appeal from revocation, see § 15.32.

"Deliver," see § 1.40.

Delivery of false document to secretary of state, see § 1.29.

Procedure for revocation, see § 15.31.

Registered office and agent, see §§ 15.07 and 15.08.

OFFICIAL COMMENT

Section 15.30 authorizes the administrative revocation of the certificate of authority of a foreign nonprofit corporation on the grounds specified. Administrative revocation is effective only upon compliance with the procedure specified in Section 15.31. A foreign corporation that believes the administrative revocation is unwarranted may obtain judicial review of the secretary of state's determination pursuant to Section 15.32.

If a qualified foreign nonprofit corporation has dissolved or merged into another corporation, the secretary of state may proceed to revoke its certificate of authority to conduct activities solely on the basis of a certificate from the secretary of state or other official of the state of incorporation. Section 15.30(6). This subdivision provides a simple and inexpensive method to eliminate the names of corporations that are no longer in existence from the records of the secretary of state, thereby making the corporate names available for use by other entities.

Section 15.30 is patterned after Section 14.20, relating to the administrative dissolution of domestic corporations. See the Official Comment to Section 14.20 for a fuller description of the policies underlying Section 15.30.

§ 15.31. PROCEDURE FOR AND EFFECT OF REVOCATION

(a) The secretary of state, upon determining that one or more grounds exist under Section 15.30 for revocation of a certificate of authority, shall serve the foreign nonprofit corporation with notice of that determination under Section 15.10.

(b) If the foreign nonprofit corporation does not correct each ground for revocation or demonstrate to the reasonable satisfaction of the secretary of state that each ground determined by the secretary of state does not exist within 120 days after service of the notice is perfected under Section 15.10, the secretary of state may revoke the foreign nonprofit corporation's certificate of authority by signing a certificate of revocation that recites the ground or grounds for revocation and its effective date. The secretary of state shall file the original of the certificate and serve a copy on the foreign corporation under Section 15.10.

(c) The authority of a foreign nonprofit corporation to conduct activities in this state ceases on the date shown on the certificate revoking its certificate of authority.

(d) The secretary of state's revocation of a foreign nonprofit corporation's certificate of authority appoints the secretary of state the foreign corporation's agent for service of process in any proceeding based on a cause of action that arose during the time the foreign corporation was authorized to conduct activities in this state. Service of process on the secretary of state under this subsection is service on the foreign corporation. Upon receipt of process, the secretary of state shall mail a copy of the process to the secretary of the foreign corporation at its principal office shown in its most recent annual report or in any subsequent communication received from the corporation stating the current mailing address of its principal office, or, if none are on file, in its application for a certificate of authority.

(e) Revocation of a foreign nonprofit corporation's certificate of authority does not terminate the authority of the registered agent of the corporation.

Source Note: Patterned after Model Business Corporation Act, 3d Ed. (2002) § 15.31. Derived from Revised Model Nonprofit Corporation Act (1987) § 15.31(a) and (c)–(e).

CROSS-REFERENCES

Annual report, see § 16.21.

Appeal from revocation, see § 15.32.

Grounds for revocation, see § 15.30.

"Principal office":
  defined, see § 1.40.
  designated in annual report, see § 16.21.

Service on foreign corporation, see § 15.10.

OFFICIAL COMMENT

The procedure for revocation of a certificate of authority in Section 15.31 establishes a simple method of completing the revocation while at the same time ensuring that the foreign nonprofit corporation is advised of the contemplated action and has an opportunity to contest it in appropriate situations. In most situations, revocation by the secretary of state will not be contested.

After revocation, the secretary of state is appointed the foreign nonprofit corporation's agent for service of process; upon receipt of service, the secretary of state must forward the process to the foreign corporation's principal address, as shown in its last filing. Revocation, however, does not of itself terminate the authority of the foreign corporation's registered agent, so that process served on that agent by a third person who was unaware of the revocation may be effective.

Section 15.31 is patterned after Section 14.21, relating to the administrative dissolution of a domestic corporation. See the Official Comment to Section 14.21 for a fuller statement of the policies underlying Section 15.31.

§ 15.32. APPEAL FROM REVOCATION

(a) A foreign nonprofit corporation may appeal the secretary of state's revocation of its certificate of authority to the [*name or describe*] court within 90 days after service of the certificate of revocation is perfected under Section 15.10. The foreign corporation appeals by petitioning the court to set aside the revocation and attaching to the petition copies of its certificate of authority and the secretary of state's certificate of revocation.

(b) The court may summarily order the secretary of state to reinstate the certificate of authority or may take any other action the court considers appropriate.

(c) The court's final decision may be appealed as in other civil proceedings.

Source Note: Patterned after Model Business Corporation Act, 3d Ed. (2002) § 15.32. Reenactment of Revised Model Nonprofit Corporation Act (1987) § 15.32.

CROSS-REFERENCES

Effective date of service, see § 15.10.

Grounds for revocation, see § 15.30.

Procedure for revocation, see § 15.31.

OFFICIAL COMMENT

A foreign nonprofit corporation whose certificate of authority is revoked may obtain judicial review of the revocation decision. In the review proceeding the court may summarily order the secretary of state to reinstate the corporation or take other action it deems appropriate.

The court with jurisdiction over an appeal should be specified; it is typically either a court in the state capital or a court in the county in which the corporation's principal office is located. Moreover, states adopting this section of the act should specify who has the burden of proof on appeal and the standard for judicial review. See the Official Comment to Section 1.26.

CHAPTER 16

Records and Reports

[Subchapter] A
RECORDS

§ 16.01. CORPORATE RECORDS

(a) A nonprofit corporation must keep as permanent records minutes of all meetings of its members, board of directors, and any designated body, a record of all actions taken by the members, board of directors, or members of a designated body without a meeting, and a record of all actions taken by a committee of the board of directors or a designated body on behalf of the corporation.

(b) A nonprofit corporation must maintain appropriate accounting records.

(c) A membership corporation or its agent must maintain a record of its members, in a form that permits preparation of a list of the names and addresses of all members, in alphabetical order by class, showing the number of votes each member is entitled to cast.

(d) A nonprofit corporation must maintain its records in written form or in any other form of a record.

(e) A nonprofit corporation must keep a copy of the following records at its principal office:

  (1) its articles of incorporation or restated articles of incorporation and all amendments to them currently in effect;

  (2) its bylaws or restated bylaws and all amendments to them currently in effect;

  (3) the minutes and records described in subsection (a) for the past three years;

(4) all communications in the form of a record to members generally within the past three years, including the financial statements furnished for the past three years under Section 16.20;

(5) a list of the names and business addresses of its current directors and officers; and

(6) its most recent annual report delivered to the secretary of state under Section 16.21.

Source Note: Patterned after Model Business Corporation Act, 3d Ed. (2002) § 16.01. Derived from Revised Model Nonprofit Corporation Act (1987) § 16.01.

CROSS-REFERENCES

Action by members without meeting, see § 7.04.

Board of directors' meeting, see § 8.20.

Committees of board of directors, see § 8.25.

"Deliver" defined, see § 1.40.

Directors' action without meeting, see § 8.21.

Inspection of corporate records, see §§ 16.02 and 16.04.

Meetings of members, see §§ 7.01–7.03.

Officers, see § 8.40.

"Principal office":
  defined, see § 1.40.
  designated in annual report, see § 16.21.

Reports of corporation, see §§ 16.20–16.21.

Restatement of articles of incorporation, see § 10.07.

OFFICIAL COMMENT

Section 16.01 describes in general terms the records every nonprofit corporation must keep or maintain, the form in which they may be maintained, and, to a limited extent, where the records must be kept.

1. *Minutes and Related Documents*

Section 16.01(a) requires a nonprofit corporation to "keep" as permanent records the minutes of meetings of its members, board of directors, and any designated body, and a record of actions taken by consent by those groups without a meeting. In addition, each corporation must "keep" a record of all actions taken by a committee of the board of directors or a designated body; this includes, for example, action taken by an executive committee between meetings of the board and final action of a special litigation committee authorized to act on behalf of the board.

Section 16.01(a) does not require a record of actions taken by a committee when the committee is not acting in place of the board of directors or a designated body, *e.g.*, when the committee is discussing policy and formulating recommendations for action by the board of directors. Also, it does not require either minutes or a record of committee deliberations under any circumstances. Committee meetings are preserved as forums for open and frank discussion and discussion of sensitive corporate data without fear of recordation or disclosure.

Section 16.01 also does not address the amount of detail that should appear in the minutes of meetings—the content of minutes is largely fixed by tradition and no inference about their content should be drawn from the section's treatment of the records of committee deliberation and action.

The minutes of a designated body required to be kept under Section 16.01(a) are for meetings when the designated body is meeting with respect to the affairs of the nonprofit corporation. What practices must be followed by the designated body when meeting in a situation not related to the nonprofit corporation will be determined by other law or practice.

2. *Member Lists and Accounting Records*

Sections 16.01(b) and (c) require the nonprofit corporation to "maintain" appropriate accounting and member records.

The word "maintain" is used to denote current records only and does not require the corporation to keep data or information of merely historical interest on hand as permanent records; the periods for which these records, data, or information should be kept is not addressed by the act.

Section 16.01(b) relates to accounting records. The word "appropriate" is used to indicate that the nature of the financial records to be kept is dependent to some extent on the nature of the nonprofit corporation's activities; the phrase "adequate records" is used in some state statutes to convey essentially the same meaning. "Appropriate" records are generally records that permit the preparation of" financial statements which fairly present the financial position and transactions of the corporation. In some very small corporations operating on a cash basis, however, "appropriate" accounting records may consist only of a check register, vouchers, and receipts.

Section 16.01(c) requires the nonprofit corporation to maintain such records of its members as will permit it to compile a list of members when required.

3. *Form of Records*

Section 16.01(d) generally authorizes nonprofit corporations to retain records in the form of a record. The basic requirement is that the method chosen must be capable of retrieval in perceivable form. See the definition of "record" in Section 1.40. In addition, in the case of the record of members, the method must permit the development of an alphabetical list of members of record as required by Section 16.01(c).

4. *Keeping Records at Principal Office*

Section 16.01(e) requires certain basic records to be kept at the principal office of the nonprofit corporation, including minutes of member meetings for the preceding three years and records of member action taken without a meeting during the same period. This requirement is imposed because these records must be available for inspection by any member at that office.

See Section 16.02(a). The "principal office" of the corporation is defined in Section 1.40 to be the location of the executive offices of the corporation and its address must be set forth by the corporation in its annual report required by Section 16.21. The act does not generally specify where records other than those described in Section 16.01(e) must be kept. They may be kept in one or more offices within or without the state; indeed, in the case of records kept in nonwritten form, it may be impossible to determine "where" they are located.

§ 16.02. INSPECTION OF RECORDS BY MEMBERS

(a) A member of a nonprofit corporation is entitled to inspect and copy, during regular business hours at the corporation's principal office, any of the records of the corporation described in Section 16.01(e) if the member delivers to the corporation a signed notice in the form of a record at least five business days before the date on which the member wishes to inspect and copy.

(b) A member of a nonprofit corporation is entitled to inspect and copy, during regular business hours at a reasonable location specified by the corporation, any of the following records of the corporation if the member meets the requirements of subsection (c) and delivers to the corporation a signed notice in the form of a record at least five business days before the date on which the member wishes to inspect and copy:

(1) excerpts from any records required to be maintained under Section 16.01(a), to the extent not subject to inspection under Section 16.02(a);

(2) accounting records of the corporation; and

(3) subject to Section 16.07, the membership list.

(c) A member may inspect and copy the records described in subsection (b) only if:

(1) the member's demand is made in good faith and for a proper purpose;

(2) the member describes with reasonable particularity the purpose and the records the member desires to inspect; and

(3) the records are directly connected with this purpose.

(d) The right of inspection granted by this section may be abolished or limited by a nonprofit corporation's articles of incorporation or bylaws.

(e) This section does not affect:

(1) the right of a member to inspect records under Section 7.20 or, if the member is in litigation with the corporation, to the same extent as any other litigant; or

(2) the power of a court, independently of this [act], to compel the production of corporate records for examination.

Source Note: Patterned after Model Business Corporation Act, 3d Ed. (2002) § 16.02. Derived from Revised Model Nonprofit Corporation Act (1987) § 16.02.

CROSS-REFERENCES

Board of directors' meeting, see § 8.20.

Committees of board of directors, see § 8.25.

Corporate records required, see § 16.01.

Court-ordered inspection, see § 16.04.

"Deliver" defined, see § 1.40.

Directors' action without meeting, see § 8.21.

Effective date of notice, see § 1.41.

Notice, see § 1.41.

"Principal office":
- defined, see § 1.40.
- designated in annual report, see § 16.21.

OFFICIAL COMMENT

1. Section 16.02(a)

Section 16.02(a) provides that every member is entitled to examine upon demand at the principal office of the nonprofit corporation all documents described in Section 16.01(e). These documents all deal with the member's interest as such in the corporation. While some of these documents may also be a matter of public record in the office of the secretary of state, a member should not be compelled to go to a public office that may be physically distant to examine the basic documents relating to the corporation.

2. Section 16.02(b)

Section 16.02(b) grants a member who meets the requirements of Section 16.02(c) the right to inspect three classes of corporate records:

(1) Excerpts from minutes required to be maintained under Section 16.01(a) (to the extent they do not fall within Section 16.02(a)). The corporation is required to make available only relevant excerpts of minutes and need not make available minutes of entire meetings merely because a portion of the minutes is directly connected with the member's purpose.

(2) The accounting records of the corporation. The act does not attempt to define what accounting records must be kept. See the Official Comment to Section 16.01.

(3) The list of members, subject to Section 16.07. If a member makes a demand in good faith and with a proper purpose under Section 16.02(c), the member is entitled to inspect the membership list under Section 16.02(b) without regard to the nature or class of membership. This right is independent of the right to inspect a membership list immediately before a meeting under Section 7.20. See Section 16.02(e).

3. Section 16.02(c)

Section 16.02(c) permits inspection of the records described in Section 16.02(b) by a member only if demand is made in good faith and for a "proper purpose." A "proper purpose" means a purpose that is reasonably relevant to the demanding member's interest as a member. Some statutes do not use the phrase "proper purpose"; the act continues to use it because it is traditional and well-understood language defining the scope of the member's right of inspection and its use ensures that the very substantial case law that has developed under it will continue to be applicable.

As a practical matter, a member who alleges a purpose in general terms, such as to communicate with fellow members, or to determine whether improper transactions have occurred, has been held to allege a "proper purpose." Section 16.02(c) thus attempts to require more meaningful statements of purpose, if feasible, by requiring that a member designate "with reasonable particularity" the purpose and the records sought to be inspected; the records demanded must also be "directly connected" with that purpose. If disputed by the corporation, the "connection" of the records to the member's purpose may be determined by a court's in camera examination of the records.

4. ***Section 16.02(d) and (e)***

Section 16.02(d) states that the inspection rights granted by this chapter are inherent rights of members and may not be abolished or limited by the articles of incorporation or bylaws. No inference of any kind should be drawn from this subsection as to whether other, unrelated sections of the act may be modified by provisions in the articles of incorporation or bylaws.

Section 16.02(e) provides that the right of inspection granted by Section 16.02 is an independent right of inspection that is not a substitute for or in derogation of rights of inspection that may exist (1) under Section 7.20, to inspect the membership list following the establishment of a record date for a meeting; (2) as part of a right of discovery that exists in connection with litigation; and (3) as a "common law" right of inspection, if any is found to exist by a court, to examine corporate records. Section 16.02(e) simply preserves whatever independent right of inspection exists under these sources and does not create or recognize any rights, either expressly or by implication.

§ 16.03. SCOPE OF INSPECTION RIGHT

(a) A member's agent or attorney has the same inspection and copying rights as the member represented.

(b) The right to copy records under Section 16.02 includes, if reasonable, the right to receive copies. Copies may be provided through an electronic transmission if available and so requested by the member.

(c) The nonprofit corporation may comply at its expense with a member's demand to inspect the record of members under Section 16.02(b)(3) by providing the member with a list of members that was compiled no earlier than the date of the member's demand.

(d) The nonprofit corporation may impose a reasonable charge, covering the costs of labor and material, for copies of any documents provided to the member. The charge may not exceed the estimated cost of production, reproduction, or transmission of the records.

Source Note: Patterned after Model Business Corporation Act, 3d Ed. (2002) § 16.03. Derived from Revised Model Nonprofit Corporation Act (1987) § 16.03.

CROSS-REFERENCES

Corporate records, see § 16.01.

Court-ordered inspection, see § 16.04.

Inspection right generally, see § 16.02.

Membership list inspection, see § 7.20.

OFFICIAL COMMENT

The right of inspection set forth in Section 16.02 includes the general right to copy the documents inspected. Section 16.03 follows precedent established under earlier statutes and extends the right of inspection to an agent or attorney of a member as well as the member. The right to copy means more than a right to copy by longhand and extends to the right to receive copies made by copying machines or through an electronic transmission with the cost of reproduction and transmission being paid by the member. The requirement of availability with respect to electronic transmissions is intended to ensure that the nonprofit corporation can provide the document electronically and that an undue burden is not placed on the corporation to provide copies through an electronic transmission or other similar means.

Section 16.03(c) is designed to give the nonprofit corporation the option of providing a reasonably current list of its members instead of granting the right of inspection; a "reasonably current" list is defined in Section 16.03(c) as one compiled no earlier than the date of the written demand, which under Section 16.02(b) must provide at least five days' notice.

Many nonprofit corporations make available to members without charge some or all of the basic documents described in Section 16.01(e). Section 16.03(d) authorizes the corporation to charge a reasonable fee based on reproduction costs (including labor and materials) for providing a copy of any document. The phrase "estimated cost of production, reproduction or transmission of the records" in Section 16.03(d) refers to the cost of assembling information and data to meet a demand as well as the cost of reproducing and transmitting documents that are already in existence.

Section 7.20 creates a right of members to inspect a list of members in advance of and at a meeting that is independent of the rights of members to inspect corporate records under Chapter 16.

§ 16.04. COURT-ORDERED INSPECTION

(a) If a nonprofit corporation does not allow a member who complies with Section 16.02(a) to inspect and copy any records required by that subsection to be available for inspection, the [*name or describe court*] of the county where the corporation's principal office (or, if none in this state, its registered office) is located may summarily order inspection and copying of the records demanded at the corporation's expense upon application of the member.

(b) If a nonprofit corporation does not within a reasonable time allow a member to inspect and copy any other record, the member who complies with Sections 16.02(b) and (c) may apply to the [*name or describe court*] in the county where the corporation's principal office (or, if none in this state, its registered office) is located for an order to permit inspection and copying of the records demanded. The court shall dispose of an application under this subsection on an expedited basis.

(c) If the court orders inspection and copying of the records demanded, it shall also order the nonprofit corporation to pay the member's costs (including reasonable counsel fees) incurred to obtain the order unless the corporation proves that it refused inspection in good faith because it had a reasonable basis for doubt about the right of the member to inspect the records demanded.

(d) If the court orders inspection and copying of the records demanded, it may impose reasonable restrictions on the use or distribution of the records by the demanding member.

Source Note: Patterned after Model Business Corporation Act, 3d Ed. (2002) § 16.04. Reenactment of Revised Model Nonprofit Corporation Act (1987) § 16.04.

CROSS-REFERENCES

Corporate records, see § 16.01.

"Principal office":

- defined, see § 1.40.
- designated in annual report, see § 16.21.

Registered office:

- designated in annual report, see § 16.21.
- required, see §§ 2.02, 5.01, and 15.07.

Service on corporation, see § 5.04.

Voluntary inspection, see § 16.02.

OFFICIAL COMMENT

Section 16.04 provides a judicial remedy if a nonprofit corporation refuses to grant the right of inspection provided by Section 16.02.

If the right of inspection under Section 16.02(a) is invoked and the nonprofit corporation refuses to grant inspection, the member may seek a summary order compelling inspection. A summary order is appropriate since the right of inspection under this subsection is either automatic or subject only to a determination that the person is in fact a member of the corporation. By contrast, if inspection is demanded under Section 16.02(b), the member's good faith and purpose may be in issue; in this situation Section 16.04(b) directs the court to handle the proceeding "on an expedited basis." The purpose of this phrase is to discourage dilatory tactics to avoid or delay inspection without requiring the court to resolve these issues on a summary basis. This language does not mandate any specific procedure by which these issues are to be resolved.

If a court enters a summary order directing inspection under Section 16.02(a), the cost of reproducing the records, if any, is placed on the nonprofit corporation. Section 16.04 does not address who should bear the cost of reproducing other records ordered by the court; this is a matter for the courts to decide in light of the policy of the act that costs of reproduction are generally the responsibility of the requesting member and should be assessed against the member.

The principal sanction against unreasonable delay or refusal to grant inspection is provided by Section 16.04(c), which imposes on the nonprofit corporation the plaintiff's costs, including attorneys' fees, unless the corporation can establish that it acted reasonably. The corporation may avoid these costs by showing that the corporation refused inspection in good faith because it had a reasonable basis for doubt about the right of the member to inspect the records demanded. This normally will involve reasonable doubt whether the member had the necessary good faith and proper purpose or whether the records demanded are directly connected to the member's purpose. The phrase "in good faith because it had a reasonable basis for doubt" establishes a partially objective standard, in that the corporation must be able to point to some objective basis for its doubt that the member was acting in good faith or had a purpose that was proper. For example, a corporation may point to earlier conduct of the member involving improper use of information obtained from the corporation in the past as indicating that reasonable doubt existed as to his present purpose. A corporation may not avoid the imposition of costs under this section merely by showing it had no information one way or the other about the issues in controversy.

§ 16.05. INSPECTION OF RECORDS BY DIRECTORS

(a) A director of a nonprofit corporation is entitled to inspect and copy the books, records, and documents of the corporation at any reasonable time to the extent reasonably related to the performance of the director's duties as a director, including duties as a member of a committee, but not for any other purpose or in any manner that would violate any duty to the corporation or law other than this [act].

(b) The [*name or describe the court*] of the county where the nonprofit corporation's principal office (or if none in this state, its registered office) is located may order inspection and copying of the books, records, and documents at the corporation's expense, upon application of a director who has been refused such inspection rights, unless the corporation establishes that the director is not entitled to such inspection rights. The court shall dispose of an application under this subsection on an expedited basis.

(c) If an order is issued, the court may include provisions protecting the nonprofit corporation from undue burden or expense, and prohibiting the director from using information obtained upon exercise of the inspection rights in a manner that would violate a duty to the corporation, and may also order the corporation to reimburse the director for the director's costs (including reasonable counsel fees) incurred in connection with the application.

Source Note: Patterned after Model Business Corporation Act, 3d Ed. (2002) § 16.05.

CROSS-REFERENCES

Corporate records, see § 16.01.

Court-ordered inspection, see § 16.04.

Director standards of conduct, see § 8.30.

Duties of board of directors, see § 8.01.

OFFICIAL COMMENT

The purpose of Section 16.05(a) is to confirm the principle that a director always is entitled to inspect books, records, and documents to the extent reasonably related to the performance of the director's oversight or decisional duties so long as the requested inspection is not for an improper purpose and the director's use of the information obtained would not violate any duty to the nonprofit corporation. The statute attempts to reconcile and balance competing principles articulated in the common law which suggest that a director has a nearly "absolute" right to information subject only to limitation if it can be shown that the director has an improper motive or intent in asking for the information or would violate law by receiving the information. In addition, the statutory provision sets forth a remedy for the director in circumstances where the corporation improperly denies the right of inspection.

Under subsection (a), a director typically would be entitled to review books, records, and documents relating to matters such as (i) compliance by a nonprofit corporation with applicable law, (ii) adequacy of the corporation's system of internal controls to provide accurate and timely financial statements and disclosure documents, or (iii) the proper operation, maintenance, and protection of the corporation's assets. In addition, a director would be entitled to review records and documents to the extent required to consider and make decisions with respect to matters placed before the board. Inspection by a director may be limited, however, by applicable privacy laws.

Subsection (b) provides a director with the right to seek on an expedited basis a court order permitting inspection and copying of the books, records, and documents of the nonprofit corporation, at the corporation's expense. There is a presumption that significant latitude and discretion should be granted to the director, and the corporation has the burden of establishing that a director is not entitled to inspection of the documents requested. Circumstances where the director's inspection rights might be denied include requests that (i) are not reasonably related to performance of a director's duties (*e.g.*, seeking a specified confidential document not necessary for the performance of a director's duties), (ii) impose an unreasonable burden and expense on the corporation (*e.g.*, compliance with the request would be duplicative of information already provided or would be unreasonably expensive and time-consuming), (iii) violate the director's duty to the corporation (*e.g.*, the director could reasonably be expected to use or exploit confidential information in personal or third-party transactions), or (iv) violate any applicable law (*e.g.*, the director does not have the necessary governmental security clearance to see the requested classified information).

Section 16.05 does not directly deal with the ability of a director to inspect records of a subsidiary of which he or she is not also a director. A director's ability to inspect records of a subsidiary generally should be exercised through the parent's right or power and subsection (a) does not independently provide that right or power to a director of the parent. In the case of wholly owned subsidiaries, a director's ability to inspect should approximate his or her rights with respect to the parent. In the case of a partially owned subsidiary, the ability of the director to inspect is likely to be influenced by the level of ownership of the parent (this ability can be expected to be greater for a subsidiary which is part of a consolidated group than for a minority-owned subsidiary). In any case, the inspection by a director of the parent will be subject to the parent's fiduciary obligation to the subsidiary's other members.

Subsection (c) provides that the court may place limitations on the use of information obtained by the director and may include in its order other provisions protecting the nonprofit corporation from undue burden or expense. Further, the court may order the corporation to reimburse the director for costs (including reasonable counsel fees) incurred in connection with the application. The amount of any reimbursement is left in the court's discretion, since it must consider the reasonableness of the expenses incurred, as well as the fact that a director may be only partially successful in the application.

The rights granted by this section are also available to members of a designated body. See Section 8.12.

§ 16.06. EXCEPTION TO NOTICE REQUIREMENTS

(a) Whenever notice would otherwise be required to be given under any provision of this [act] to a member, the notice need not be given if notice of two consecutive annual meetings, and all notices of meetings during the period between such two consecutive annual meetings, have been returned undeliverable or could not be delivered.

(b) If a member delivers to the nonprofit corporation a notice setting forth the member's then-current address, the requirement that notice be given to that member is reinstated.

Source Note: Patterned after Model Business Corporation Act, 3d Ed. (2002) § 16.06.

CROSS-REFERENCES

Annual meeting, see § 7.01.

Notice, see § 1.41.

OFFICIAL COMMENT

Section 16.06 balances the requirement that the nonprofit corporation deliver notice to members regarding meetings and the practical need to allow corporations to cease providing notices where notices are being returned undelivered and it is clear that the member no longer is located at the address previously provided to the corporation. Absent such a provision, the corporation technically may be required to continue to attempt to deliver a notice to the member in order to satisfy a statutory requirement regarding notices to members or otherwise risk questions concerning the validity of the meeting for which the notice is required.

Section 16.06 provides that notice is not required to be given to a member if a notice of two consecutive annual meetings, and all notices required during the period between the meetings, are returned undeliverable. In this instance, notice is not required, and any meeting that is held will have the same force and effect as if notice had been given. The notice for a particular member is reinstated if a notice setting forth the member's then-current address is delivered to the nonprofit corporation.

Based upon these provisions, the nonprofit corporation generally will be required to continue to provide the notice unless undeliverable items are returned over a period that could not be less than twelve months and could extend for up to twenty-four months. For instance, if the first undeliverable communication were delivered to a member six months before the next notice of an annual meeting is required, the corporation would have to wait until the annual meeting notice proves to be undeliverable to commence the nondelivery period, and then would have to wait until the next annual meeting notice after that also proves to be undeliverable before suspending the notification requirement. This amounts to a nondelivery period of eighteen months which could extend to two years under the right circumstances. It is believed that this accomplishes the proper balance between protecting the rights of members and eliminating unnecessary notices.

§ 16.07. LIMITATIONS ON USE OF MEMBERSHIP LIST

(a) Without consent of the board of directors, a membership list or any part thereof may not be obtained or used by any person for any purpose unrelated to a member's interest as a member. Without limiting the generality of the foregoing, without the consent of the board a membership list or any part thereof may not be:

(1) used to solicit money or property unless the money or property will be used solely to solicit the votes of the members in an election to be held by the nonprofit corporation;
(2) used for any commercial purpose; or
(3) sold to or purchased by any person.

(b) Instead of making a membership list available for inspection and copying under this [subchapter], a nonprofit corporation may elect to proceed under the procedures set forth in Section 7.20(f).

Source Note: Reenactment of Revised Model Nonprofit Corporation Act (1987) § 16.05.

CROSS-REFERENCES

Court-ordered inspection, see § 16.04.

Inspection rights, see § 16.02.

"Member" defined, see § 1.40.

Required corporate records, see § 16.01.

Voting lists, see § 7.20.

OFFICIAL COMMENT

A nonprofit corporation's membership list is a valuable asset. In many cases, the membership list may represent a list of contributors. Section 16.07 sets forth the basic premise that a membership list may not be obtained or used by any person for any purpose unrelated to a member's interest as a member. It then provides that a membership list may not be used for any of the following three purposes without the board's consent:

(1) The solicitation of money or property unless the money or property will be used solely to solicit the votes of members in an election held by the corporation. A membership list therefore cannot be used by members who in good faith believe the organization has strayed from its purposes and want to solicit the members to contribute to a competitive organization that is carrying out the true purposes of the corporation

whose membership list is sought. Nor can members use a membership list to solicit contributions for a noncompetitive organization, even if the noncompetitive organization has laudable purposes.

(2) Any commercial purpose. Commercial organizations frequently desire to use membership lists of nonprofit organizations to contact members. That use is only allowed if approved by the board of directors of the nonprofit corporation.

(3) The sale to or purchase by any person. Members of a nonprofit organization do not have the right to sell a membership list to any person. Nor may a person seeking a membership list purchase it except from the corporation with the approval of the board of directors.

A corporation must have some factual basis for believing that the member seeking the membership list will violate the provisions of Section 16.07 to deny inspection rights pursuant to Section 16.07. If a corporation has a legitimate doubt as to the purposes for which a member seeks a membership list, the matter can be heard by a court pursuant to Section 16.04. The court should closely scrutinize the transaction to determine whether a member has a legitimate purpose or whether the corporation was simply using Section 16.07 as a ruse to prevent and frustrate a member's rights. See the Official Comment to Section 16.04 for the circumstances in which a court may order the corporation to pay attorney fees and costs.

[Subchapter] B
REPORTS

§ 16.20. FINANCIAL STATEMENTS FOR MEMBERS

(a) Except as provided in the articles of incorporation or bylaws of a nonprofit corporation engaged in religious activity, upon a demand in the form of a record from a member, a corporation must furnish that member with its latest annual financial statements, which may be consolidated or combined statements of the corporation and one or more of its subsidiaries, as appropriate, that include a balance sheet as of the end of the fiscal year and a statement of operations for the year. If financial statements are prepared for the corporation on the basis of generally accepted accounting principles, the annual financial statements must also be prepared on that basis.

(b) If the annual financial statements are reported upon by a certified public accountant, the accountant's report must accompany them. If not, the statements must be accompanied by a statement of the president or the person responsible for the nonprofit corporation's accounting records:

 (1) stating the reasonable belief of the president or other person as to whether the statements were prepared on the basis of generally accepted accounting principles and, if not, describing the basis of preparation; and

 (2) describing any respects in which the statements were not prepared on a basis of accounting consistent with the statements prepared for the preceding year.

Source Note: Patterned after Model Business Corporation Act, 3d Ed. (2002) § 16.20(a) and (b). Derived from Revised Model Nonprofit Corporation Act (1987) § 16.20.

CROSS-REFERENCES

Inspection of records, see § 16.02.

OFFICIAL COMMENT

Section 16.20 requires every nonprofit corporation to prepare and submit to its members annual financial statements consisting of a balance sheet as of the end of the fiscal year and a statement of operations for the year. Consolidated statements of the corporation and any subsidiary, or subsidiaries, or combined statements for corporations under common control, may be used. Section 16.20 does not require financial statements to be prepared on the basis of generally accepted accounting principles ("GAAP"). Many small nonprofit corporations have never prepared financial statements on the basis of GAAP. "Cash basis" financial statements (often used in preparing the tax returns of small corporations) do not comply with GAAP. Even small corporations that keep accrual basis records frequently do not make the adjustments that may be required to present their financial statements on a GAAP basis. In light of these considerations, it would be too burdensome on some small corporations to require GAAP statements. Accordingly, internally or externally prepared financial statements prepared on the basis of other accounting practices and principles that are reasonable in the circumstances will suffice for these types of corporations. If a corporation does prepare financial statements on a GAAP basis for any purpose for the particular year, however, it must send those statements to the members as provided in the last sentence of Section 16.20(a).

Section 16.20(b) requires an accompanying report or statement in one of two forms: (1) if the financial statements have been reported upon by a public accountant, that report must be furnished; or (2) in other cases, a statement of the president or the person responsible for the corporation's accounting records must be furnished (i) stating the person's reasonable belief as to whether the financial statements were prepared on the basis of generally accepted accounting principles, and, if not, describing the basis on which they were prepared, and (ii) describing any respects in which the financial statements were not prepared on a basis of accounting consistent with those prepared for the previous year.

In requiring a statement by the president or person responsible for the corporation's financial affairs, the drafters of this section recognized that in many cases this person will not be a professionally trained accountant and should not be held to the standard required of a professional. To emphasize this difference, Section 16.20 requires a "statement" (rather than a "report" or "certificate") and calls for the person to express a "reasonable belief" (rather than "opinion") about whether or not the statements are prepared on the basis of GAAP or, if not, to describe the basis of presentation and any inconsistencies in the basis of the presentation as compared with the previous year. The person is not required to describe any inconsistencies between the basis of presentation and GAAP. For example, the description might state, with respect to a cash basis statement of receipts and disbursements, that the statement was prepared on that basis and that it presents the cash receipts and disbursements of the entity for the period but does not purport to present the results of operations on the accrual basis of accounting.

This section does not prescribe a set period of time in which the financial statements must be delivered to the members. Failure to comply with the requirements of Section 16.20 does not adversely affect the existence or good standing of the nonprofit corporation. Rather, failure to comply gives an aggrieved member the right to compel compliance or to obtain damages, if they can be established, under general principles of law.

§ 16.21. ANNUAL REPORT FOR SECRETARY OF STATE

(a) Each domestic nonprofit corporation, and each foreign nonprofit corporation authorized to conduct activities in this state, must deliver to the secretary of state for filing an annual report that sets forth:

(1) the name of the corporation and the state or country under whose law it is incorporated;
(2) the address of its registered office and the name of its registered agent at that office in this state;
(3) the address of its principal office; and
(4) the names and business addresses of its directors and principal officers.

(b) Information in the annual report must be current as of the date the annual report is signed on behalf of the nonprofit corporation.

(c) The first annual report must be delivered to the secretary of state between January 1 and April 1 of the year following the calendar year in which a domestic nonprofit corporation was incorporated or a foreign nonprofit corporation applied for a certificate of authority under [Chapter] 15. Subsequent annual reports must be delivered to the secretary of state between January 1 and April 1 of the following calendar years.

(d) If an annual report does not contain the information required by this section, the secretary of state may deliver a notice in the form of a record to the reporting domestic or foreign nonprofit corporation and return the report to it for correction. If the report is corrected to contain the information required by this section and delivered to the secretary of state within 30 days after the effective date of notice, it is deemed to be timely filed.

(e) See Sections 14.20(2) (grounds for administrative dissolution) and 15.30(1) (grounds for revocation).

Source Note: Patterned after Model Business Corporation Act, 3d Ed. (2002) § 16.21. Derived from Revised Model Nonprofit Corporation Act (1987) § 16.22.

CROSS-REFERENCES

Annual report form prescribed by secretary of state, see § 1.21.

"Deliver" defined, see § 1.40.

Effective time and date of filing, see § 1.23.

Filing and signature requirements, see § 1.20.

Filing fees, see § 1.22.

Involuntary dissolution for failure to file annual report, see § 14.20.

Notice, see § 1.41.

Officers, see § 8.40.

"Principal office" defined, see § 1.40.

Registered agent, see §§ 5.01 and 15.07.

Registered office, see §§ 2.02, 5.01, and 15.07.

Revocation of certificate of authority for failure to file annual report, see § 15.30.

OFFICIAL COMMENT

The annual report that each nonprofit corporation must submit to the secretary of state is a limited information document for use by the secretary of state, members of the general public, and members. The purpose of the annual report is to show the location of the principal office of the corporation, the names and business addresses of its directors and principal officers, and the general nature of the corporation's activities. It permits members of the general public to ascertain the identity of the corporation and communicate directly with it. It also establishes the alternative to the registered office for service of process and related matters. The "principal office" of the corporation is defined as the location of its executive office in Section 1.40.

The reference to "principal officers" in Section 16.21(a)(4) is intended to simplify reporting requirements of nonprofit corporations with very large numbers of employees who have some managerial responsibility and who, for business reasons, are designated as officers. The "principal officers" of a corporation include at least the chair of the board of directors, the chief executive officer, and the officers performing the traditional functions performed by the corporate secretary and treasurer, no matter what their designation.

The annual report is required of both domestic nonprofit corporations and foreign nonprofit corporations qualified to conduct activities in the state. The failure to file the annual report, like the failure to satisfy other mandatory requirements of the act, is a ground for administrative dissolution or revocation of the certificate of authority to conduct activities.

CHAPTER 17

Transition Provisions

INTRODUCTORY COMMENT TO CHAPTER 17

Most states, when enacting this act, should establish a single effective date for the new statute and all nonprofit corporations should become subject to the new act on that date. See Sections 17.01, 17.02, and 17.07.

Some of the provisions of the revised act may differ in significant respects from earlier laws. When this occurs, it may be appropriate for the state to "grandfather" existing nonprofit corporations, provide an opt-in election for them, or provide delayed effective dates for certain provisions, or certain types of provisions, to give existing domestic corporations adequate time to revise controlling corporate documents to take into account the provisions of the new act. The provisions that are most likely to give rise to transitional problems are discussed below.

1. Changes in Voting Requirements

All state statutes require that certain important transactions be approved by a specified fraction of the members. This fraction varies from state to state. Most states require a majority of all the members, but some states require a 2/3 or larger vote. Few states have yet adopted the lower vote required in the revised act of a majority of the votes cast at a meeting at which a quorum is present. In states with higher voting requirements, it may be necessary to "grandfather" existing corporations and provide an opt-in election for them.

2. *Cumulative Voting*

Under the revised act, cumulative voting by the members in the election of directors is not available. Because many states provide for cumulative voting, Section 17.03(c) provides a special transitional rule that preserves existing cumulative voting rights.

3. *Obsolete Provisions in Articles of Incorporation*

Under the revised act, corporations automatically have unlimited purpose clauses (Section 3.01) and perpetual duration (Section 3.02). Under many state statutes, these privileges are available only if specifically provided in the articles of incorporation. These special provisions will become unnecessary once the corporation becomes subject to the act. While they should cause no direct harm, it would generally be desirable to eliminate them in order to avoid possible negative inferences as to the scope of the purpose or duration of the corporation. See the Official Comment to Section 3.01. These inferences are probably more likely to be drawn from purpose clauses than from duration clauses.

4. *Classification of Corporations*

The prior act classified nonprofit corporations into three categories: public benefit corporations, mutual benefit corporations, and religious corporations. The articles of incorporation were required to include a statement as to which of the three types the corporation was. That classification scheme has been eliminated from the revised act, and a statement in the articles of incorporation as to which of those types the corporation is will have no meaning under the revised act. When they have the occasion to do so, existing corporations may remove such a statement from their articles.

In place of the former classification scheme, the revised act includes certain provisions dealing with charitable corporations. Those provisions are automatically applicable to corporations that meet the definition of a charitable corporation, and thus a transitional rule in this regard is not necessary.

5. Conclusion

Because it is impossible to anticipate precisely what changes adoption of the revised act will make in the rules applicable to nonprofit corporations of particular jurisdictions, it is not feasible to draft a model provision to cover all transitional problems. Generally, however, the only transitional provisions required should be extended grace periods for certain provisions becoming applicable to existing domestic corporations, and upon expiration of these grace periods, all domestic and foreign corporations should become subject to all provisions of the revised act.

§ 17.01. APPLICATION TO EXISTING DOMESTIC CORPORATIONS

This [act] applies to all domestic nonprofit corporations in existence on its effective date that were incorporated under any general statute of this state providing for incorporation of nonprofit corporations if power to amend or repeal the statute under which the corporation was incorporated was reserved.

Source Note: Patterned after Model Business Corporation Act, 3d Ed. (2002) § 17.01. Substantially a reenactment of Revised Model Nonprofit Corporation Act (1987) § 17.01.

OFFICIAL COMMENT

The fundamental principle underlying Section 17.01 is that the revised act should ultimately be made fully applicable to all existing business corporations as well as to all new nonprofit corporations formed after the effective date of the new statute. It is undesirable to "grandfather" existing corporations under earlier statutes since that results in the permanent coexistence of two different and overlapping systems of corporation law, with resulting confusion. This is particularly true of the revised act, which builds directly on the experience of many years with existing corporation statutes and contains few major substantive changes.

Section 17.01 applies this basic principle in its broadest sense by making the revised act applicable as of its "effective date" (prescribed in Section 17.07) to all domestic nonprofit corporations formed under general statutes for nonprofit corporations.

Section 17.01 applies the revised act to all corporations to which that application is constitutionally permissible. In view of the universal adoption of "reservation of power" clauses in all states for more than a century, there are very few active nonprofit corporations to which this act will not be applicable under this section.

§ 17.02. APPLICATION TO QUALIFIED FOREIGN CORPORATIONS

A foreign nonprofit corporation authorized to transact business in this state on the effective date of this [act] is subject to this [act] but is not required to obtain a new certificate of authority to transact business under this [act].

Source Note: Patterned after Model Business Corporation Act, 3d Ed. (2002) § 17.02. Substantially a reenactment of Revised Model Nonprofit Corporation Act (1987) § 17.02.

OFFICIAL COMMENT

Section 17.02 makes the revised act applicable on its effective date to all foreign nonprofit corporations that are qualified to transact business in the state on that date. But these corporations need not refile and obtain new certificates of authority under the act. While Chapter 15 of the revised act may change the rules applicable to foreign corporations in some states, these changes are not of a type that require a transition period. It is therefore recommended that only a single effective date be provided for the application of the act to foreign corporations and that delayed effective dates for specific provisions in this regard are unnecessary.

§ 17.03. SAVING PROVISIONS

(a) Except as provided in subsection (b), the repeal of a statute by this [act] does not affect:
   (1) the operation of the statute or any action taken under it before its repeal;
   (2) any ratification, right, remedy, privilege, obligation, or liability acquired, accrued, or incurred under the statute before its repeal;

(3) any violation of the statute, or any penalty, forfeiture, or punishment incurred because of the violation, before its repeal;

(4) any proceeding, reorganization, or dissolution commenced under the statute before its repeal, and the proceeding, reorganization, or dissolution may be completed in accordance with the statute as if it had not been repealed.

(b) If a penalty or punishment imposed for violation of a statute repealed by this [act] is reduced by this [act], the penalty or punishment if not already imposed shall be imposed in accordance with this [act].

(c) Members of a nonprofit corporation who were entitled to cumulate their votes for the election of directors on [*the date of enactment of this act*] shall continue to be entitled to cumulate their votes for the election of directors until otherwise provided in the articles of incorporation or bylaws of the corporation.

(d) This [act] modifies, limits, or supersedes the federal Electronic Signatures in Global and National Commerce Act, 15 U.S.C. § 7001 et seq., but this [act] does not modify, limit, or supersede Section 101(c) of that act or authorize electronic delivery of any of the notices described in Section 103(b) of that act.

Source Note: Subsections (a) and (b) are patterned after Model Business Corporation Act, 3d Ed. (2002) § 17.03 and are substantially a reenactment of Revised Model Nonprofit Corporation Act (1987) § 17.03. Subsection (d) is patterned after Uniform Limited Partnership Act (2001) § 1203 and Uniform Limited Liability Company Act (2006) § 1102, and is required by § 102(a)(2) of the Electronic Signatures in Global and National Commerce Act, 15 U.S.C. § 7002(a)(2)(B).

OFFICIAL COMMENT

Section 17.03(a) and (b) are similar to Section 16 of the Uniform Statute and Rule Construction Act, which was promulgated by the National Conference of Commissioners on Uniform State Laws in 1995.

Section 17.03(d) is patterned after Uniform Limited Partnership Act (2001) § 1203, and Uniform Limited Liability Company Act (2006) § 1102, and is required by § 102(a)(2) of the Electronic Signatures in Global and National Commerce Act, 15 U.S.C. § 7002(a)(2)(B).

§ 17.04. SEVERABILITY

If any provision of this [act] or its application to any person or circumstance is held invalid by a court of competent jurisdiction, the invalidity does not affect other provisions or applications of the [act] that can be given effect without the invalid provision or application, and to this end the provisions of the [act] are severable.

Source Note: Patterned after Model Business Corporation Act, 3d Ed. (2002) § 17.04. Substantially a reenactment of Revised Model Nonprofit Corporation Act (1987) § 17.04.

§ 17.05. CONSISTENCY OF APPLICATION

In applying and construing this [act], consideration must be given to the need to promote consistency of the law with respect to its subject matter among states that enact it.

Source Note: Patterned after Model Entity Transactions Act § 601 (2007).

§ 17.06. REPEAL

The following laws and parts of laws are repealed: [*to be inserted by enacting state*].

Source Note: Patterned after Model Business Corporation Act, 3d Ed. (2002) § 17.05. Substantially a reenactment of Revised Model Nonprofit Corporation Act (1987) § 17.05.

OFFICIAL COMMENT

The act is intended to be a complete substitute for earlier statutes of general applicability to nonprofit corporations and it is contemplated that all these statutes should normally be repealed when the revised act is enacted. A few states in the past have retained portions of earlier statutes while enacting integrated codifications of nonprofit corporation law. This practice is generally undesirable since it tends to cause unnecessary confusion in determining the applicable law as well as creating possible internal statutory conflicts.

§ 17.07. EFFECTIVE DATE

This [act] takes effect ____________________.

Source Note: Patterned after Model Business Corporation Act, 3d Ed. (2002) § 17.06. Substantially a reenactment of Revised Model Nonprofit Corporation Act (1987) § 17.06.

OFFICIAL COMMENT

The transition provisions of the revised act contemplate that a single effective date will be provided for the entire act. As indicated in the Introductory Comment to this chapter, however, some states may wish to make special provisions, including delayed effective dates, for particular sections.

Table of Cases

Index

B

D

E

F

G

H

I

J

M

N

O

Q

R

S

T

V

W